Fine, But Hardly Dandy
Book 2

an exposé in true to life narrative

By
Cleon E. Spencer

To our friends
Bob & Myra
From Cleon & Ada Spencer

Airleaf Publishing
airleaf.com

ISBN: 1-59453-939-1

Dedication

To all the nice people of this great country, and that means most of them. The others are much discussed in this book.

Introduction

This book is an exposé about fine, clean cut, often highly intelligent, well charactered, cultured, down to earth people and the discrimination widely practiced against them. These people are often exceptional in one or more ways, not necessarily academically, though that may be, and they have the potential to make a wonderful contribution to life. Some academics have a problem with this, as if academically is the only way to be exceptional. Indeed, it is one of the most noble. But there are other ways. For example, a well known publication tells us of shy people: "Shyness in its milder forms is associated with traits such as greater empathy, more acute perceptiveness, canny intuition, and beneficent sensitivity. All qualities that are nothing to be shy about." (U.S. News & World Report, Inc., June 21, 1999, P.57, New York, N.Y.) This is just one instance among many where a person can be exceptional in a manner that numerous academics are not, and it should be an accepted fact by them and others.

However, a considerable portion of the general population, in high places and low, for various reasons which are stated and illustrated by case stories in the book, discriminate against these fine exceptional people in ways that often amount to gross mental abuse. The practice, though widely exercised, has seldom been recognized for what it is: severe, often intentional damaging of human personhood and character, or attempts at such. This is a story of mental cruelty; of a long overlooked social problem and its effects on government, industry, commerce, education, and including, by no means least, many branches of the Christian church. It is also a story of often victorious living on the part of the victims, despite the abuse they have to, sometimes continuously, deal with.

Use is herein made of the vehicle of a fictional support group of fine people in a fictional setting, who are willing to share their problems of discrimination against them because of the kind of people they are. The book describes at length the actions of the abusers and the effects of it on the victims and on society as a whole. The many and varied, both subtle and not so subtle, twists and turns the mind-games and other actions of the abusers take are described in detail.

The subject matter of this writing is intentionally extensive and detailed in order to verify that the experiences of the afflicted characters are not isolated incidents in their lives, but rather an almost continuous and stress laden way of life that such people have to live. It is par for the course for fine people most everywhere, but more predominately so in some areas than in others.

The book is not meant to be simply quick and easy reading for entertainment. It purposely contains much detail, is meant to be informative, and seeks to fully expound, for the serious minded and concerned reader, a harmful social problem.

The author makes no claim to academic excellence; much less to what he sees as the over-sophistication of psychological theory. On the contrary, considering his background as a constantly assailed fine person he regards himself to be very fortunate indeed to have attained even one university level degree. Again, his prime purpose is to expose a serious problem in society. Cliches, colloquialisms, and slang are at times used because the writer believes they best describe some of the idiosyncrasies of the abusive people he is writing about and the satire of them in the everyday language of the people. Incidently, many of these lower levels of speech are now beginning to appear in the latest dictionaries.

The book is written from the Christian perspective of the writer, in true to life narrative based on experiences and observations in several fields of life over a period of almost a lifetime. Places and people have been disguised for the usual reasons. Simple Latin names have been used for locations. Names of the fictitious characters of the book have been chosen for their meaning and coincide with their general character make-up. This was, more or less, a matter of convenience in finding suitable names, though it adds authenticity to the characters and the story. Some of the true to life stories have also been placed in either a fictional or a disguised setting.

The writer has no desire to harm any persons or organizations by this writing; only to bring to public awareness the gross abusiveness to fine, clean-cut, well charactered, often smart and exceptional people, by a very significant portion of society in all walks of life; to emphasize the magnitude and seriousness of the problem; to create awareness of how society generally is short-changed by this strange phenomenon. In addition to establishing improved awareness to help curtail the problem, the writer also has a desire that ways be found to curb it legally, through litigation when necessary. Intentional infliction of emotional distress is illegal. So far, however, this law has generally been applied only to spousal and child abuse.

The fact is the victims of these abusive people presently have little or no way to protect themselves. It is hoped that public awareness, and where necessary and possible, a legal perspective on the matter, will expose the problem for what it is, a destruction, or attempt at such, of career, character, and personhood.

This book can be of interest to people in many occupations in life. Business, industry, government and education certainly can benefit from the understanding of how their organizations can be deeply affected by the abusers and, as a result, have their better employees, customers or students damaged, stymied, or driven away. Hopefully too, the church will be motivated to take a much needed look within itself. Society generally, needs to be more aware of the problem.

Some traces and reflections of a previouly written book, *Fine, But Hardly Dandy - Book I,* will be found in this writing. Hopefully readers will be moved to read it as well. In the meantime this *Fine, But Hardly Dandy - Book II* covers what the writer believes to be the aspects of the problems that are the more damaging, and hopefully of serious interest to the North American scene.

The author.

CHAPTER I

Collin Seldon and his wife Vita, with a spring in their usual rapid stride, and filled with joyous enthusiasm, once again walked up the city sidewalk, and took a right angled turn plus a few steps more to the glass doors of the Arts building of Quilibet University. As he often liked to do, Collin glanced upward at the impressive glass front of the several storied structure.

"Something majestic about its appearance," he remarked to Vita.

"Quite a contrast to some of the traditional architecture and stone art work of some of the older buildings of the city," she responded.

"Yea, but there is something about contemporary architecture that catches the eye with awesomeness."

"I know what you mean."

Collin liked coming here, and yet there was always that adverse factor that would put a damper on it if he would let it to any great extent. He would talk about that factor with his friend Owen Winslow when they meet here in the foyer of this building, in about twenty minutes, he figured as he looked at his watch. He had arrived a little early.

His wife departed for the library via an enclosed connecting passageway from the foyer to the separate library building next door, where she would await his return from the meeting. He then proceeded to the far end of the foyer to sit on one of the benches to await Owen's arrival. They had met there many times during last semester.

Vita's presence with him was mainly to accompany Collin in the socializing that usually took place at a nearby coffee shop after each meeting, but also to be with him on the long drive home after a sometimes very mind occupying meeting. Collin and Vita always shared one another's burdens in a very compatible way.

As Collin proceeded down the spacious foyer, there were numerous people, students and staff, going here and there, criss-crossing the floor. Many were heading towards the elevators to go to classrooms on other floors. Some took the stairways, and some the passageway to the library, and of course some were on the way out the main doors, finished for the day.

Collin walked through the crowded foyer to near its end and, as planned, sat on a bench near the elevators where he would meet his friend and collegue, Owen Winslow. He was amused at the variety of reactions he received as he passed by the people in this one single space of earth. Most of them were preoccupied with their business of the evening and didn't even notice Collin, or anyone much for that matter. Collin appreciated that. He preferred to be inconspicious. But that wasn't always possible for a person like Collin Seldon, not nearly always.

Some people in the foyer that evening looked at him and smiled, for which Collin was grateful and returned it. Others looked at him, and then as if in fright, looked quickly away. Collin knew that their problem with him was either shyness, or a sense of inferiority that had been triggered simply by Collin's presence. Such people may or may not be a problem to him if he were to have any reason for interaction with them.

Still others looked at him with an instant sneer, or with some sort of negative facial expression such as a pushing up of the lower lip in contempt. The most emphatic of all were those who after spotting him, turned their head upward and away to the side with their nose high in the air—'with their nose out of joint' as the familiar jest goes about such people. 'I'm better than you,' they were saying in effect.

Collin knew their problem with him. Among other things they hated him. He avoided such people as much as possible, for such hatred is often turned into either open or subtle hostile action towards people like Collin. In all probability such people would pose a serious problem to him if he had social, academic or business interaction with them. In some areas of North America, this problem is advanced to a destructive science, bringing destruction to innocent victims like Collin if they are not wise to its perpetrators.

Collin smiled to himself. Here he was in a university, taking a course in psychology, and yet even here little or nothing is formally known about this destructive problem and its drastic effects on society as a whole. Government, industry, commerce, education, the church, yes even this very university, all are damaged by this problem which can become vicious abuse, and yet it has never been publicly aired. In fact it is this very problem and the exploration of it in a support group that brought Collin here this evening. Owen Winslow is the facilitator of the support group.

And what is it about a person like Collin Seldon and the other members of the support group that brought on these symptoms this evening - these mild symptoms of a far greater problem. *O vanity of vanities, if the world only knew,* he mused, *but society in general doesn't know its full extent.*

Collin, although approaching retirement age, still had a youthful and healthy appearance as he had over the years of his adult life. There were some signs of aging—his light brown hair thinning at the top and greying at the sides; his bright complexioned face just beginning to show wrinkles in its past middle age fullness; his once atheletic body now showing to be somewhat overweight. Collin was just beginning to show his years, but he looked, and was, a healthy person still.

Moreover, although Collin was older by years than the other members of the support group in which he is participating here at the university, he had this in common with them, that even now in his aging, as in his youth and young manhood, he stood out among others. He had an air of distinction about him, a clean cut and assuring appearance. Furthermore, his appearance was a reflection of the high quality character, integrity, and wisdom oriented intelligence within. He was the kind of person that good people looked to and smiled at with respect and affection and trust. But not nearly all of the people of this world are good.

Among the several people who had shown negative symptoms towards Collin in the foyer that evening were those who actively work against, and block the way of people like Collin and the other members of the support group as they pursue life in the work-a-day world. Fine, smart, clean-cut distinctive looking, well charactered people are the prey and game of these wayward ones. Obviously there are other fine characteristics besides appearance, that bring out the hostility of these assailants, but appearance is the one that first stirs their hatred. *O vanity of vanities,* mused Collin some more.

As Collin now sat on a bench, he reflected back over his last semester interaction with the support group *of fine,* i.e. clean cut, healthy and wholesome looking, well charactered, distinctive looking people of integrity and often high intelligence; not perfect by any means, but down to earth nice people. It consisted of five men and two women, plus a semi-retired psychiatrist who was overseer of the project that Owen Winslow had uniquely brought together with the sanction of the Student Guidance Department.

Collin and Owen first met in a psychology classroom at the beginning of the previous semester. Collin was at that time invited by Owen to participate in the support group he had formed. The group members were all younger, in their twenties and thirties, and all struggling with a common problem. Collin could help the younger members, Owen had determined, and rightly so, because Collin was much older than the others and had already been through much of the mill of life. By the grace of God he had survived it intact—something that many of his kind are not fortunate enough to accomplish. His longer experience in understanding and coping with the problem would be helpful. Dr. Eldren was present to keep the group under professional oversight.

The support group met each Wednesday evening, 7:00 p.m. in Room 405 of the Arts building, a room set aside by Quilibet University for seminars, group meetings and occasional gatherings.

Throughout last semester's meetings, each member of the support group told significant portions of his or her life's story. There were instances of sibling rivalry gone awry—without proper discipline, and even supported by biased parents. But the group members were able to establish that this was not their main problem. Experiences with biased teachers in elementary and high school were also related. And although these experiences had a profound effect in some cases, their damages were still not the most formidable to overcome.

The group was able to establish that their main and most difficult problems come not from childhood, as psychology usually zeros in on, but from the society in which they later as adults tried to establish themselves. Collin tagged it as their *bridgehead in life.*

For some this bridgehead took place in their late teens or early twenties. For others it was in their thirties, or even later if they attempted to establish further bridgeheads as they changed their occupations. The problems encountered with a particular type of difficult people became the focus of the support group, and much light was shed upon it by the almost life-long experiences of Collin Seldon.

This particular type of wayward and difficult people are the proud and envious ones. A dictionary gives two meanings for pride:

1. An undue sense of one's own superiority; arrogance; conceit.
2. A proper sense of personal dignity and worth. (Standard Desk Dictionary, P.524. Funk and Wagnalls Publishing Co., Inc.,1969).

The type of proud ones who give trouble to fine people are more akin to the type of those described in the first dictionary meaning, but not exactly. Rather, they are people of a wayward, undiciplined, sometimes empty pride; pride that is kept intact no matter what or how; pride that is protected and defended under all circumstances, whether warranted or not and often by untruths and/or foul means. People of such undisciplined pride, and the envy that almost certainly ensues from it, are trouble makers for fine, distinctive people.

Envy is described by the biblical scholar, William Barclay, as "the most warped and twisted of human emotions." (The Rev. William Barclay, *The Daily Study Bible,* The Letter to the Romans, P.28. The Saint Andrew Press, Edinburgh, 1966). Again Barclay writes, "Envy is literally the evil eye that looks on the success and happiness of another in such a way that it would cast an evil spell upon it if it could." (The Rev. William Barclay, *The Daily Study Bible,* The Gospel of Mark. P.178. The Saint Andrew Press. Edinburgh, 1966.)

The undisciplined pride and the envy, and prejudiced hatred and hostility that in turn ensues from it, are the main characteristics of those who make trouble for fine people. It works this way: The trouble makers are ruled by undiciplined pride, and are smug as they are. When a fine person comes along, their undisciplined pride and smugness is disturbed into envy. They are like a balloon, all puffed up. When a fine, high caliber person comes along and just by his presence unintentionally pricks the balloon, they are deflated, and more often than not burst into hostility.

Actually there is one of two things they could do about their predicament if they understood it. First, they could rise up to do better for themselves, learning what they can from others, including fine people, on their way, which most of them don't do. Or, secondly, they could decide to remain as they are, putting beneath them the fine person whom they see as doing them wrong by upsetting them. Most of them follow this devious course of behavior. Hence their belittling comes into action.

At a previous support group meeting, Collin tagged those of the latter category simply as *belittlers.* Also, in the previous semester, the fine people of the support group and others like them in society, for matters of convenience in discussion, were referred to *as fine* people, or sometimes people like *us.*

The term belittlers seems such a harmless little word. But as it was explored by the group it can at times be a monster. It robs society of some of its most promising and potentially exceptional people. In many geographical areas it also establishes these often crude and inferior people, these belittlers, as the predominant influence in their society, thereby keeping it on an inferior level. The group members came to the concensus that dealing with such troublesome belittlers as these has been their most difficult experiences in life.

These experiences took Dr. Eldren outside the sphere of his professional training as a psychiatrist, to a world he had formally learned little or nothing of. But being the good natured and mature kind of person he was, he kept an open mind on it continually. When the group members saw that he wasn't going to label them with abnormal psychological terms, they felt free to open up and tell of their experiences objectively. Some of these experiences were shocking to say the least, and therefore took a great deal of mental and emotional stamina on the part of the group members to recall the painful experiences of their lives.

Collin had been able to analyze the events for them objectively in the light of his own experiences and observations over several decades of his adult life. These younger students would not now have to re-invent the wheel, as the cliché so accurately puts it, in order to find their way through the treachous paths in life that would surely come their way because of the fine people they are. Their increased knowledge and understanding of circumstances peculiar to their lives would enable them to better cope.

As he sat on the bench, Collin reflected back over the experiences of the support group members. Being much older than they he was therefore able, as he heard their stories and told his own, to shed much light on the problems they had all experienced with belittlers. As were the other group members, Collin too was highly intelligent in a wise and fair-minded sort of way. This together with his experiences gave him meaningful and objective insight into the problems, and he could offer practical, common sense explanations that would aid in coping as much as that is possible with a problem largely unrecognized by the better side of society.

This wisdom oriented intelligence, together with his high quality integrity, was an asset to Collin, but also a liability as Collin had previously demonstrated to the group. When belittlers get to know that a fine looking, well charactered person is also wisely intelligent and possessed of integrity, they turn on him all the more. Belittlers in the academic field especially are perturbed by these characteristics and react with unfriendliness to say the least.

Collin continued to reflect on the matter: then of course, in the business world, there are belittlers aplenty also. When they see a fine person, they see dollar signs. They almost invariably think that a person like us must be rich, and must have had special opportunities and privileges in order to be as we are.

In many cases, it is a matter of culture rather than economics. For example, if many of our more shabby belittlers would stop spending money excessively on smoking, drinking and so-called junk food, and spend more on healthy foods, their countenance would be much improved. Moreover, they would still be money in. With it they could buy sensible, yet inexpensive clothes with some style and color, instead of baggy T-shirts and trousers which they wear till they are falling off them. Then with personal body cleanliness and tidyness, they too could have a good public physical image. If they don't want to do that, it is their decision, but they have no right to come down on those of us who do, and only some of them do come down on us. Actually there is no need. Collin thought deeply and sincerely to himself: *I have never yet met a functional person, no matter how homely, who couldn't look pleasantly presentable in public if they had the desire to do so.*

Strangely though, only a minority of our belittlers come from the shabby side of society, he continued to reflect. Most of them by far, come from well dressed, financially secure middle, and upper middle class society; people who may have much more materially than we have; people who have much going for them, but are ruled by undisciplined pride and the ensueing envy, hatred, and hostility. They cover this waywardness by making the excuse for themselves that we are priviliged and therefore should be despised. It is an attitude many of them have inherited from the past, and even though they themselves may be big shots now, to use the term they like to use on us, they still practice this malady. That too is a cultural problem. So in business they will bleed every last dollar they can from us, and when they can and get away with it, will treat us shabbily in return both in the products they give and in their personal attitude towards us. Yes, fine people have to beware, or we will end up financially broke in no time at all.

All of this had been borne out by the life stories of the support group participants. By Collin telling his story after he had heard the stories of all the others, he had been able to shed much light on the reasons and tactics of the whole gruesome phenomena.

Collin's story was one of not only childhood sibling rivalry gone awry, not only of belittling outside the home environment in the tender adolescent years, but much more emphatically of vicious belittling in adult life out in society as he tried to make a place for himself and his family.

His problems were compounded when he went to psychiatrists for consultation. They couldn't even conceive of his problem and labeled him as almost hopelessly paranoid. Thank heavens, in later consultations, his problem was seen to be fatigue from having to work under too much stress in adult life, caused by difficult people. He was relieved to be freed from the paranoia label.

A more mentally cruel story than Collin's has seldom evolved in a free society. But in the semester just beginning he would tell an even more cruel story that has evolved in *the free* society of *Terraprima,* a part of that North American land to the south of the lands of *Secundaterra* and *Lower Secundaterra* where Collin's story had taken place.

The lands Secundaterra and Lower Secundaterra, or second lands, the authors Latin names for a portion of eastern North America are made up of an area approximately two thousand miles from the east to the west of it, and with a population of about fifteen million. Terraprima, or first land, a portion of the land south of the border of the Secundaterras is smaller geographically, but more densely populated.

Quilibet (a Latin name meaning any) *University,* is based on the writers experience with a support group at a university in the core of one of Secundaterra's major cities. The metropolitan area of the city had a population in the seven figure category, and therefore offered a wide social experience in a varied society.

Collin still refers to the land south of the border as Terraprima, even though he presently sees it in many ways as Terraprima fallen. His story still to come, of a friend who went to live in Terraprima, will illustrate his view on that.

Some members of the group had wondered at the end of the last semester whether or not they might be able to fare better in the Terraprima society. Collin promised to tell them this semester the story of a fine friend who had gone there believing that might be so. Then they could make up their own minds. It was this story Collin was here to begin this evening, if it was still okay with Dr. Eldren the psychiatrist, and Owen Winslow facilitator of the group on behalf of the Student Guidance Department of Quilibet University. Collin was strongly hoping that with Dr. Eldren's help, he could somehow find a way to bring this grave social problem, which robs society of many of its most promising people, out into full view. As it is now many belittlers operate quite openly because they know nothing will be done about it. For the most part, only the perpetrators and the victims are aware it is going on.

Besides Collin's story there had been first that of Leo Aidan, a fine looking, well charactered intelligent young man from a well cultured family. His father is a highly respected judge in the area in which they live. Leo had been picked on - discriminated against - as a 'big shot's' son, a motivation belittlers like to use on the surface. But as his story unfolded Collin was able to discern and point out that Leo's two brothers were not similiarly abused to any extent. It would take Leo a long time, with the help of Collin and the support group, to realize and openly and objectively acknowledge, without fear of seeming vain and conceited, that he was picked on, not because of whose son he was, but because of who he himself was. He was simply a fine looking, well charactered, smart person who stood out distinctively among other people. Being such a person as that, he is fair and constant game for envious belittlers. As Leo told his story we could see how belittlers affected his whole life, including his present efforts in furthering his education.

Then there was Donna Coyne, a fine smart young lady with an air of gracious modesty about her. She and Leo, since meeting at the support group, had become personal friends and were dating.

They would make a fine modest and distincitive couple together, and it looks like that may become permanently so, thought Collin. He knew, however, that life will not be at all easy for two such lovely people together. Belittlers will see to that. One great plus for them is they will be able to understand each others plight and therefore cope with it more effectively.

There is the other lady of the group, Gilda Emerson. Collin reflected on how she stood in sharp contrast to Donna Coyne, yet both were ladies indeed in their own right. Unlike Donna, Gilda was not modest in her distinctiveness. She was quite naturally sophisticated and confident with some good academic accomplishments to support it, and yet totally unpretentious. She dressed well, but would stand out among others no matter what she wore. Her lovely complexion and total appearance would assure that. But obviously she was a woman of high quality taste and decorum. Both of these women and Leo Aidan, all three, had the good fortune of having solid and supportive parents.

Gilda's story shows another classic example of neither sibling rivalry nor the bias of parents having any bearing on her problems in adult life. Both of these aspects were absent from her childhood. One thing was lacking. The parents of all three knew little or nothing about what such lovely daughters and a fine son had to put up with from the numerous belittlers out in the world in which as young adults they had to make their way. Collin for years had longed to do something about such lack of knowledge. Perhaps now he might have the opportunity through this support group to do so.

Brett Culver also told his life's story to the group; how he might have been a medical doctor instead of a young businessman with a degree in Business Administration and well on his way to success in his own already extensive business.

This is a classic example of how a very capable young person who, because of belittlers in adult life, couldn't get what he first set out for, but made the very best of what he could get.

He was a quiet unassuming type. People generally would not associate such a modest and seemingly reserved person with such business accomplishments. Brett is a mild mannered, strong charactered gentleman; an above board straight shooter, honest and trustworthy. Though still young, in his early thirties, Brett's hair was thinning back from the temples on either side. Rather than detracting from, it served to augment his distinctive appearance. He is another fine person in both appearance, character and intellect. He came from well meaning and helpful parents who did have some knowledge and experience in dealing with difficult people. Brett also has to deal with belittlers in everyday life. He has a fine, compatable wife, which fact doubles his trouble with belittlers, but also gives him an understanding partner to share the burden and to cope all the better.

Next to cross Collin's mind was Owen Winslow. Owen had achieved more academically than any of the others, and has held some responsible teaching positions as well as being a minister of the Church. Yet even he in his quest for a career had to forfeit a desired degree in literature, and who knows, perhaps a distinguished career in the same, for a degree in history which he made very good use of. Belittlers got in his way of course and caused that change. Owen, as well as being fine looking, is also big in size, tall and of medium build, which makes him stand out all the more in public.

His troubles began, however, in childhood, with sibling rivalry not only undisciplined, but actually aided by a wayward thinking father. Regardless, Owen has done well in life thus far, and continues on the upward swing. To Collin's mind this is a classic example of a person being able, by the grace of God and the help of friends, including a well meaning but naive mother, to overcome childhood damages. Owen would have done even better were it not for belittlers present in his adult life. He is a high profile and confident person. This matches Gilda Emerson's high caliber qualities, and since meeting at the support group they have begun dating. *They will be good support for each other,* thought Collin.

Albin Anders had also told his story to the support group. Albin is the younger member, not long out of his teens. He has a good father but a difficult, belittling mother. She did damage to him in his childhood. He herocially strived to overcome, only to be put down time and again in adulthood by belittlers outside the family. This to Collin is yet another classic though different example of the adverse effects of belittlers at work in adult life and how his childhood problems could have been overcome were it not for belittlers at work on him as he sought to establish himself in adult life. His father was good to him but had little knowledge and understanding of Albin's basic problem. Hence he was virtually on his own until he was brought into the support group. Albin too is a fine looking, fine charactered, intelligent person, but sadly lacking in self esteem and therefore very shy. He has never had the freedom to blossom and grow into his own person. Physically, like the other group members, he stands out among people. Being so young and so inexperienced in life the odds at present are not in his favor. Collin knew from experience what that was like. He resolved to do his utmost to help Albin get ahead against almost formidable odds.

Collin had told his more lengthy story last, and used it, among other things, to show the extent to which belittling, often intentional, can go to ruin lives, especially young lives; and in accordance with his purpose, he also used it to shed helpful light on the lives of the other support group members.

Collin stirred from his reflection as he saw Owen Winslow coming across the foyer and stood to meet him.

"Nice to see you again," said Collin.

"Likewise," replied Owen, cheerfully. "Are you ready to tell us the story of your friend who went to live in Terraprima?"

"Yes if it's still okay with Dr. Eldren, if he is still in empathy with people like *us.*"

"Oh, no problem there."

"And the Student Guidance Department?".

"Oh, no problem there. They have left us pretty much on our own."

The two walked to the elevator chatting about the helpfulness and hopes of this venture of theirs, and proceeded to Room 405 to begin the second semester of the support group.

They entered the room but were a little early and only Dr. Eldren was present. The three exchanged greetings and friendly small talk, passing the time until the others arrived. Dr. Eldren stood tall, well built and distinguished as usual. His near white hair and his now noticably pale face portrayed him as a man in his retirement years, and perhaps still working too much, or, with a health or nutrition problem.

The other group members arrived, Brett Culver as usual being the last to come in. His business life was sometimes more than he could keep up with. This is often characteristic of having one's own growing business. It is quite contrary to what many people, especialy belittlers, think about the privileged and easy life of owning and managing one's own prospering business.

The members pulled up chairs and sat around in a circle as usual. By now they knew each other well, and also their procedure at such meetings. They looked to Dr. Eldren to set things in motion.

"Collin," he began, "you have agreed to tell us the story of your friend who went to Terraprima to live. I personally am interested in hearing it because I believe we are isolating a peculiar fact of life as opposed to simply dealing with difficult people as a whole."

"Yes, Doctor Eldren, that's it and I am ready to tell the story if it is still the desire of the group."

"I'm all ears!" exclaimed Leo Aidan in his sometimes boisterous manner, setting a relaxed atmosphere over the gathering.

"I really do want to hear it," said Owen Winslow. "It will help me decide which direction to go in life."

The other group members expressed a desire to hear the story.

Collin began his presentation, "before I get into the story itself, there are some preliminaries that I think will help prepare you for it.

Recalling the stories of belittling in Secundaterra and Lower Secundaterra, we noted that belittling here is done mainly by individual envious people. Occasionally one or two or three may team up against you, or, a single belittler may gain the support of others, including some innocent people.

"In Terraprima, however, the belittling may become *a conspiracy of sorts* as I call it. That is groups of people that are close knit together, like in the church, may turn on a person like us."

"In the church!" exclaimed Leo Aidan in amazement.

"Yes, in the church," Collin repeated.

"Oh, oh," was Owen's brief response, as his thoughts of perhaps one day having a career in the church there took a downturn.

Collin continued, "you need to know that in some parts of Terraprima, including in some of its churches, belittlers treat people like us, either openly or subtly, as though we had no right to function fully, or in some cases even partially, in society. Why? Because in so doing we make them feel deflated, which is their problem, not ours. We unintentionally prick the balloon of their undisciplined pride. Their envy and hostility are aroused. They seek to drive us away or destroy us. It is so common in Terraprima that people in high places and low help one another do the dirty deed. It never having been brought out openly in public, makes it one of North America's most guarded and frequently practiced fallacies.

"It is a highly developed and craftily specialized way of life among, I would guesstimate, about a third of the population. It was especially practiced in the denomination of the church in Terraprima to which my friend went; practiced among both clergy and laity in high places and low, and much of it in between. They are not only belittlers in the sense that we have already explored. They are cunning and crafty con-artists and 'mind-game players' as well."

The support group members sat speechless and wide-eyed. Collin continued, "let me familiarize you with some of the tricks and mind-games they play; just enough now to give you some idea of what my friend and his wife were up against. As I go through the different phases of the story I will point out more of both the subtlities and also blatant openness belittlers use in putting down people like us; subtly when they are cautious of being smoked out into the open, blatantly open when they know they can get away with it.

"Belittlers actually do feel inferior to people like us and are very sensative about it—over sensative in fact. But they will never admit to that fact. They seek instead to make us feel inferior to them and over sensative about it. So one of their chief mind-games is to go negative on everything you say or do and try to make you feel and look inferior to them. At the same time, in a phony and authortative, yet seemingly friendly manner they will, by hint and innuendo, try to make you believe you should be heading in life and character, the way they are pointing out to you.

"It will be an inferior way to theirs. For example," interjected Collin, "I once had the experience of a belittler trying to pressure me into buying the same make of car as he had just bought, only I was to have a cheaper model of that same make, with less options. I had to be copying after him, but kept below him.

"In the instance of a car such action even though absurd could be possible. But with a lot of things, such as the way you do your work, it is impossible to copy at a lower caliber than the overbearing belittler. It would warp ones personhood and wear one out trying to do so. Obviously the belittler's insinuated demands cannot be met, so his envy is aroused all the more and hostility sets in.

"If you are not wise to them they will then lead you down the garden path to trouble and/or destruction. If when you do allow the belittlers to steer you wrong, their accomplices are ready to jump on you, critize you and put you down for the wrong way you have headed.

"It becomes a conspiracy of sorts as I have previously called it, in which a whole cluster of belittlers are involved. They may even have one person, usually someone in an insignificant position, or a young person, man or woman, plant downward ideas in your head verbally and quite clearly. Then the others, again by hint and innuendo, try to steer or press you in that direction. If the verbal planting were to be brought out into the open by you, a reaction would come from them such as: 'Oh well, that person doesn't count for much, or, Oh well, he's only young, don't let it bother you; you're just too sensative.' Or, in the case of a female accomplice, 'Oh well, she's only a young girl,' or, 'that's a woman's point of view.' Strangely enough, even belittlers who believe in equality for women, still use this latter ploy in their trickery. By these ploys they seek to trivialize the whole matter and tell you that you are too sensative about such things.

"If a fine, smart person makes any worthwhile accomplishment or does a job well, the belittlers will either pretend they didn't notice, or trivialize it as though it is nothing, or find some way to disagree with it. Quite often, when they can, they will make the opportunity for you to do something they know you can do well disappear by taking it out of the program or cancelling an event. Usually, in conversation with a cluster of people you will be ignored by them, even walked away from.

"Confront a belittler with what he is trying to do to you, and he will very innocent-like tell you that such a motive never entered his mind. He will then imply that you, poor type of person that you are, need help, and he is only trying to help you. Confront a belittler with some particular incident in which he has wronged you and very often he will be able to come up with an alibi, an excuse, a different story, flimsy and shabby as it often is.

"Then, of course there are the belittlers who like to needle you and make you angry with one or more of several intentions; namely, to send you away in anger and feeling deflated to which they will say you can't take it, you're soft and over-sensative; to make you quit on a job or project, to which they will say you don't stay at anything very long; and their ultimate is they like to damage your fine character, destroy your self-confidence, and wear you down, so that you will be afraid to ever try again.

"When belittlers find out you have exceptional thinking ability they turn on you all the more. They try desperately to overtax your mind and wear you out. They themselves have the ability, sometimes exceptionally so, to attain and retain knowledge. But they may have little ability to think for themselves. It would be strenuously difficult for them to do so. Assuming we also are the same they try to give us plenty to think about. When, because of our exceptional ability to think, it doesn't wear us out, they get all the more envious and hostile. I will illustrate this further along in the story.

Another game they play is: by implication and innuendo they try to impress upon you that they are of the opinion you don't really have much ability at all, and that you think too much of yourself—that you are conceited. So they put on the facade that they are doing a wonderful thing, even a Christian service, by bringing you down. So down, down, down they try to wear you—blocking, stymying, ruining everything you try to do, all under the guise of keeping you from thinking too much of yourself. The real reason they are doing it is because they see you as a cut above them and they are envious of you. They know right well what harm they are doing to you and why.

When you express a different opinion than they, or when they perceive you may be doing something better than they can or that they never thought of doing, or when you tell them something they didn't already know, they brand you as arrogant.

Of course, if you already have low self esteem from being treated that way when you were young, then this present assailing will, if you let it, destroy your self-esteem all the more. That is one of the belittler's main pruposes.

"They will dare, and indeed try to tantilize you into openly accusing them of the various things they are trying to do to you. If you were to do so you would be labeled with words according to the education and position in life of the respective belittlers—words such as 'nuts', 'mad', 'crazy', 'paranoid.' That being so, we generally have to bear our burden in silence and without recourse.

"A favorite weapon at the local church when the minister makes a suggestion, is for the belittlers present to each take a very different stand from each other and from the minister and start a heated discussion about it. They do this to shatter the proposal to bits, then brush it aside and go on with something of their own devising and usually more trivial or routine. This way the minister cannot accomplish anything.

"But I will hold off telling you more of the tactics and mind-games of the church till next week, when we get into that gruesome phase of the story. Tonight I will tell you the first phase of the story: how belittlers in the Immigration Department of Terraprima quite openly and brazenly, no mind-games used for cover up, abused my friends as they sought to go through the immigration process after being told they could do so in a quite satisfactory manner. Later also, I will tell of belittlers at work in business and industry in Terraprima, and show what a detrimental effect they have on the same.

"You will no doubt be surprised that belittlers can do what they do and get away with it, often unnoticed. One of the foremost reasons is that North Americans generally are not very cognizant of the various ways people are motivated to do what they do. They may say of an action or attitude, it is right or wrong, good or bad. However, to discern whether it is rightly or wrongly motivated; whether, for example, it was done with good reasoning and good intentions, or done out of a wayward emotion such as envy, is generally out of the common orbit of most people.

"I think you will understand all the foregoing more fully as I tell the story."

CHAPTER II

Collin began his presentation on the Lawtons in Terraprima. "My fine, distinctive friends, Durwin Lawton and Canda his wife of more than thirty years were fine people too; both exceptional people in many ways even after years of belittling. To protect their privacy and personal interests, the names I am using for them, Durwin and Canda Lawton, are fictitious. However, they are very real people, and the story I am about to tell of their experiences in Terraprima (another fictitious name as you already know) is not fictitious but true and factual. They were both in their early fifties when this story began more than a decade ago. As I tell the story, I will emphasize the pride and envy motivation of the belittlers—why they do what they do.

"The several states that make up the area I call Terraprima are, as you will see, largely under the influence and dominance of belittlers. Durwin went to Terraprima as a minister of the church, and Canda his wife to work at various levels of office work in industry and commerce. Each of them found both occupations to be overladen with belittlers. In time I will tell you of their experiences in each of these fields of work. For now I will tell you of their experiences together with the government office of immigration through which process they had to go in order to take up permanent residency.

"As I said, Durwin was a minister, but it was not only in the church the Lawtons had trouble with wayward people. Quite near the beginning of their story you will see that an area of government civil service was practically overrun by belittlers.

"Altogether, you will be able to see the terrible damage that belittlers, both in high places and low, do to their country. They actually cripple, and in some cases eliminate the vast contribution that potentially exceptional people could make to it.

"So let me begin," said Collin, "by telling you of the grotesque experiences Durwin and Canda Lawton had with one unit of the Immigration Department located in Terraprima.

"Before they had decided to move to the area, they had heard stories of weird behavior of members of this government department. They were to soon find out that it was even worse than they had heard. The ignorance and outright open abuse with which they were treated was unfit for any human beings in a country of the quality Terraprima is purported to be. Having heard of this strange behavior, the Lawtons took every precaution to avoid problems with them. However, their fine personal makeup was such that trouble was unavoidable. Fine people get picked on aplenty.

"The Lawtons, while still living in Secundaterra, were on another of their frequent visits to one of the states of Terraprima when they learned that it would be possible for Durwin to be appointed to a church somewhere in the area. They went immediately to the Immigration Office in the state they were visiting and made known their desire to move to Terraprima where Durwin would be appointed minister of a church. They were treated in a mannerly fashion in this office and given the necessary papers and instructions. Within a few days, while still visiting in the state, the Lawtons got all the papers in order, each had a medical, and then returned to the immigration office with everything ready.

"After examining all the papers, the immigration officer responded: 'All your papers and medical records are in good order except that you still give a Secundaterra address as your place of residence.'

"'Yes,' replied Durwin, 'we haven't moved to Terraprima yet, we are just visiting now.'

"'Well,' she said, 'you have to move down first and then apply. You can do that as a minister of the church.'

"Durwin and Canda and their Terraprima friends who were with them were delighted to hear that, but wanted to make sure the officer was right. They questioned her. 'Are you sure we can actually move to Terraprima and then take care of immigration matters after our move?'

"'Yes,' she replied. Then added assuredly, 'I am certain of that, but if it will make you feel better I will consult my supervisor on it. I'll be back in a minute or two.' She took all the papers and disappeared through a door behind her. Shortly she returned. 'Yes, my supervisor agrees that it is quite in order for you to come into this country as a clergyperson and submit these papers immediately after you have taken up residence here.'

"The Lawtons and their friends were overjoyed. The way was open for Canda and Durwin to fulfill a long-held desire and move to the land of opportunity for all."

Collin interjected, "You will see in time just what opportunity there was, or rather was not in this land, for fine people like the Lawtons."

He then continued with the story. "Upon returning to Secundaterra the Lawtons made plans to move. Durwin resigned from his church there, and also turned down a good offer for a move to another congregation in Secundaterra. Soon he was notified as to the name and location of his church-to-be in Terraprima. The location, however, could possibly pose one problem - maybe. It was in a state other than the one in which he had contacted the Immigration Office. They may now have to apply to a different Immigration Office - the office in the state to which Durwin had received the church appointment. This gave them some concern. On the other hand, they thought the rules must be the same in every office of the country. Still, they would check it out. It wasn't something to be taken lightly or to take a chance on. If the Lawtons moved out of their present location with all their possessions in a rented truck, they had to be sure they had some place to go, and not end up out in the street, homeless. It could take as much as several months to find another church in Secundaterra.

"With this concern in mind, Durwin and Canda drove one day to the nearest border crossing, and asked to see the supervisor in charge there. The supervisor was a very congenial man who listened to their plans and concerns with interest. 'Sit down in the waiting room for half an hour or so,' he invited them. 'I know there are some special provisions for clergy, but it's so seldom we have to refer to it. I'll read up on it in the rule book while you wait.'

"He went across to the other side of the large room and into his glassed-in private office in the corner. Taking a big book about four inches thick off the shelf he sat down to read. After twenty minutes or so he came back across the larger room again. 'Yep,' he said with a smile, 'you can do it that way, just as the woman in the other office told you.'

"'So,' asked Durwin, 'if I come here to this border crossing driving a rented truck load of my belongings, and my wife behind me driving our car, we will be able to enter Terraprima, no problem?"

"'That's right,' responded the supervisor. 'According to the book there should be no problem. Tell you what,' he continued, 'I'll write down for you the days of the week and hours I'm on duty. Can you arrange to cross the border on a day and within the hours I'm on duty?'

"'Yes I can,' said Durwin delightedly. So they arranged that the Lawtons would cross the border on a Tuesday morning in approximately a month's time. The Lawton's were assured by this very cooperative officer that if everything was in order after the usual inspection, there would be no problem in crossing the border with all their possessions. He also told them that within ten days of the arrival at their destination they would be required to put in their applications for residency at the office in the state in which they took up residence.

"The Lawtons came away from the border crossing much more assured, but not totally. There was one more assurance Durwin would seek. He had two telephone numbers for twenty four hour seven days a week information regarding immigration procedures. One number was for the office in the state he had already dealt with on his visit, the other for the office in the state which he would now have to deal with.

"One evening he called the first number. After some delay due to the line being very busy, he connected with a woman who seemed quite conversant with immigration procedures. Durwin carefully outlined all the circumstances of his pending move. Knowing there were questions about mental illness on the papers later to be submitted, he was very careful to mention that he once had what was termed at the time, some brief nervous breakdowns. 'Would that pose a problem for me?' he asked.

"'How long ago since you have had the last breakdown?' she asked.

"'Approximately ten years,' replied Durwin.

"'That will not make any difference after all that time. You will have no problem with it.' she assured him.

"In actual fact it is debatable whether Durwin Lawton ever had a nervous breakdown. He had experienced some trouble to be sure. The psychiatrists whom he had first consulted termed it a mental illness caused by childhood problems. The psychiatrists who attended him in his later bouts termed it as excessive exhaustion brought on by too much stress with difficult people. His treatment for it in the latter cases was rest and sleep with the use of medication for a brief period." Collin paused, then smiled, "Sounds familiar to some members of this group, eh!"

"Very familiar," said Gilda Emerson, and the others agreed.

"But," continued Collin, "Durwin didn't want to enter into a debate about it on the phone at that time. Rather, to be sure, he went for the worst scenario, a nervous breakdown, received a satisfactory reply and thought that would be the end of that. He had no reason to think otherwise.

"Durwin then phoned the second number, for the city where he now would have to report. This time a man came on the line. Durwin explained to him the plans and circumstances of his pending move, including the information about his supposed nervous breakdowns, and that the last one was approximately ten years ago."

"'No problem,' said the man in his obviously jolly, perhaps flamboyant manner. 'Just get in your truck and come on down. Then report to the office here within ten days as you were previously told.'

"Durwin was almost convinced that everything was okay for his move. Still other peoples stories of difficulties with immigration in Terraprima came to his mind. He would try for one more assurance, he decided, by calling the same number on the week-end when likely there would be different persons on shift to give information. On the weekend Durwin phoned again, and a man answered the call. Not recognizing the voice, Durwin again outlined his plans and circumstances.

"The voice on the phone responded, 'What you again?' he said cheerfully, 'come on down man. I told you earlier in the week you will have no problem. We are nice people down here, and we like you people of Secundaterra, you are just like us. Come on down and be at home.'

"This information officer had spoken in such a friendly reassuring way that all doubt left Durwin's mind. He would not question the matter further. After thanking the person most warmly, Durwin came away from the phone feeling sure all would be well. He and Canda were delighted. They felt assured.

"There was one more assurance they were pleased with also. Some of Durwin's colleagues in ministry who perhaps knew, from stories of others, more about the pitfalls of such a venture than did Durwin, took steps to protect his future in case he wanted or had to return to Secundaterra. They had his name placed in the record as on leave of absence from his present denomination, rather than removed and transferred to another denomination. Durwin was very grateful for this. Later, it would give him badly needed security as you will understand later in the story.

"There was opposition to this leave of absence status by belittlers of the Secundaterra church, but they weren't in control and were overruled, to Durwin's advantage. Later, however, when staff was changed, it left Durwin out on a risky limb in Terraprima, as I shall explain more fully later on in the story.

"Most people wished Durwin well on his new venture. One well meaning colleague, however, made a statement that Durwin didn't understand at the time. Later, it would have much meaning for him. The colleague said to Durwin, 'We don't have any ministers from here go down to that denomination of Terraprima anymore. We have several who have gone there to other denominations and done well. I wish you well in your venture though,' he said, shaking his head gently.

"On the pre-planned Tuesday morning the Lawtons set out, Durwin driving their large size rented truck, and Canda following behind in their car, having had the truck loaded by experienced movers the previous day. After going through immigration and customs at the border under the friendly, respectful and efficient facilitation of the supervisor, the Lawtons drove uneventfully along the highway to a new yet very different life than ever they had expected.

"Durwin had previously notified the people at his new church in Terraprima that he and Canda were aiming at arriving at the church at approximately six p.m. They came close to that, arriving at six-thirty p.m. There was a welcome reception for them for which they were a little late. The half hour delay was caused by a final gas-up and truck check which could have been eliminated had they known they were only twenty miles from their destination instead of the sixty they thought they still had to go.

"Perhaps an experienced bus driver who was very familiar with both the route and his vehicle could time it more closely. The Lawtons were familiar with the route, except for the last end of it, but had never driven it in a large truck before, which required extra gas stops, oil checks, etcetera. Even though they arrived within half an hour of their estimate, one of the church members had been complaining about the lateness and undermining the enthusiasm of others. This complainer would later turn out to be a chief belittler and troublemaker.

On arrival from another country with the truck, et al, and although a half hour late the attention of the twenty or so people present became focused on the new pastor and his wife. This was quite a natural thing, yet it was to the dismay of the complaining woman, who until now it seems had been the main focus of the group. In future, the Lawtons would see similar reactions to this on occasion. The cause of it was usually that when someone had done perhaps an exceptional job of some sort for the church, that person then felt qualified to be the main leader and decision maker in all things pertaining to the administering of the many and varied functions of the whole congregation. But expertise in one area of service, as good as it may be, and as much acclaim as they may receive for it, does not give a person licence to be overbearing in all that goes on in a church. In time, rivalry for first place would set in - a rivalry in which neither Durwin nor Canda would intentionally participate. Overall though, the reception was a warm and joyful one.

"Within a few days the Lawtons, after receiving directions from a church member, set out in their car for the immigration office they were required to contact. The office was in the big city. They had driven in there a few times before, so it would pose no problem for them. They found the right building, paid the very expensive city parking rate, entered the building and proceeded to the required floor. It was early morning, around eight o'clock when they arrived, yet the line was already hundreds of people long. They were directed to get into the line and in turn would be taken care of by one of several officers at the long counter.

"It was after ten o'clock when they began to get anywhere near the counter. The lines between the cords going up and down the room moved slowly, but usually steadily. Ten employees worked the counter, each having an opening in the countertop metal rod barrier. In the background were two other women, who appeared to be supervisors floating around each to one-half of the area, overseeing the work of the others.

"As Durwin and Canda came down the line between the cords to near the lower end of the room, with still another up and down to go, the supervisor of that lower end caught site of them in the line. She quite noticeably bristled and looked harshly at the Lawtons for the longest time.

"'Oh, Oh,' whispered Canda to Durwin, in as unnoticably a way as possible. 'I think we are over dressed for here, or something. We may have trouble. Did you see the way that woman glared at us?'

"'Yes,' replied Collin, 'I couldn't help but notice. Perhaps we will end up in the area of the other supervisor.

"'Hope so, Durwin, but she looks vicious,' said Canda.

"'We have our preliminary papers from the border crossing, and it's just a matter of getting them processed,' Durwin tried to sound reassuring. 'She may not like us, but we should get through okay.'

"'Hope you're right,' said Canda with a sigh.

"As the Lawtons slowly followed the line around the turn and up and down the rows once more, this woman, as she moved around her territory, continued glaring at them with increased intensity the nearer they came to being waited on. Coming down the final aisle was the worst, for then because of her location and theirs she could look straight at them. As she did she began to strut around with an air of authority all the more, occasionally slapping papers here and there, placing them down hard on the counter in a very perturbed looking manner.

"This supervisor was a very hefty, hard boiled looking woman, between fifty and sixty they guessed, with an upswept peroxide blonde hairdo and a very sour face. She was obviously down on the Lawtons for their appearance, for she had as yet no other criteria for which to take such a dislike to them. As awkward and overdone as her own hairdo, make-up and gawdy clothes were, she was very obviously concerned about her own appearance. Not having the taste it takes, however, she was plainly resenting the Lawtons who were dressed in a relatively modest manner, yet tastefully, and quite unintentionally stood out in the crowd there as they did most any place."

Pausing in the story telling, Collin remarked, "This is an obvious and severe case of balloon puncturing."

The group members laughed aloud, and Owen remarked, "Just by their appearance and presence, the Lawtons unintentionally punctured that supervisor's balloon of undiciplined pride."

"Yeh," added Donna Coyne," and I'll bet she got plenty angry. I know what that's like."

"She did get very angry, as we shall see," responded Collin as he continued the story.

"Durwin and Canda had been standing in line now for nearly three hours. Finally it was their turn. They were called from the end of the line to the wicket at the very end of the counter by the young woman working there. This woman was probably in her late twenties—a different generation and therefore not a pal of the sour looking supervisor who was supervising that same area of the counter. The supervisor was presently busy overseeing a transaction at another wicket. The Lawtons explained their case to the young officer at the counter and presented to her the papers they had received at the border crossing. She was very pleasant and efficient, examined the papers carefully and handed them back to Durwin. 'From here,' she said, 'you have to go up to the twelfth floor. I will give you the room number and the name of the man you are to see.' She wrote the room number and name on a slip of paper. As she tore it off the pad to give to Durwin the supervisor came roaring down. 'What's this,' she growled as she snatched the slip of paper out of her hand. Then she turned to Durwin 'Where are you from?'

"'From Secundaterra,' said Durwin.

"You have no business to be in this country, and I'd suggest you get back out of it,' she snarled.

"As she began to say something else, the near mortified counter person shouted above her, to the Lawtons, 'go and see Mr. so and so in room number such and such.'

"The Lawton's got the message and after thanking the young woman walked away as the supervisor continued to sputter. It was a case of open and unabashed hostility by a belittler. No subtleties were necessary in this office. She knew she could openly do as she pleased and get away with it.

"Durwin and Canda went to the twelfth floor, found the room and the person they were to see. He, being a very cordial and helpful man, examined their papers received at the border crossing, approved their temporary immigration into the country for one year, and gave them another paper granting them permission to work.

"'From here,' he instructed, 'you should go back down to the counter you just left and pick up a set of papers each, number such and such for permanent residency and come back another day with them prepared for submission to the same counter. You have a year in which to obtain your permanent residency.'

"'Do we have to stand in line all over again today' asked Durwin, 'it took us nearly three hours there this morning?'

"'No, not this time, but the next,' replied the man. 'For today I will give you a signed slip which will enable you to go directly to the counter, and hand in the slip. The counter person will give you the papers.' He then smiled at the Lawtons. 'Good luck,' he said to them, 'I wish you well.' They were encouraged greatly.

"As they rode down the elevator, Durwin and Canda decided they would go to the same counter woman they previously had. She was positioned at the end of the counter, and easily accessible to them without their breaking through the lines of people. And besides, this young woman had been very pleasant and now already familiar with their case. The supervisor wouldn't be able to do them much harm they reasoned, because they had already been admitted to the country.

"As another customer left the young woman's wicket, the Lawtons approached and handed her the slip from the man upstairs to whom she had sent them. She bent down beneath her counter momentarily, came up with the necessary papers, and began to give a brief commentary on them as she passed them one by one to Durwin. There were several papers.

"As Durwin held some of the papers in his hand, and the young woman held some in her hand, still commenting on them, the supervisor came roaring over again.

"'What are you back here for now?' she snapped showing much hostility on her face.

"The young woman protested, 'they have come to pick up such and such sets of papers.'

"Durwin chimed in sternly. 'Look Lady, Mr. so and so has approved our temporary admission to this country, and told us to pick up these papers here.'

"The supervisor snatched the remaining papers out of the young woman's hand, throwing them out across the counter as she snarled, 'take your papers and see where they'll get you.' Most of the papers fell to the floor at Durwin's feet. While he stooped down to pick them up, Canda attempted to gather the few papers remaining on the counter. The angry supervisor snatched them out of Canda's hands and threw them down to the floor where Durwin was stooping to pick up the others. Some of them fell over his head. Durwin patiently gathered them all together. Then he and Canda, ignoring the supervisor, thanked the young woman for her helpfulness. She looked at them kindly, tilting her head sideways in affection, then immediately called the next person in line.

"The Lawtons walked away in near shock. 'Is this what it means to be an immigrant in the land of opportunity?' Canda remarked to Durwin.

"'We have to come back to the same counter with these completed papers,' responded Durwin. 'We are in for a hard time, I do believe.'

Making an interlude in the story, Collin said to the support group, "Incidentally, some years later, when Durwin told this actual experience to a Christian person in a responsible position, that person said that such a thing could only happen in a communist or third world country. He wouldn't believe the story."

"I guess that Christian person had never read in newspapers or heard on television how employees of another North American government department were ruining peoples lives. News of it was widespread in the media.

"To quote one of them:

"Nationwide, IRS abuses are the product of a badly dysfunctional agency, a seemingly totalitarian financial regime where bullying personalities can find a place to exercise unbridled power over peoples lives. As tearful witnesses testified to the Senate, that power wielded arbitrarily, has destroyed businesses and broken up families. In other cases, taxpayers have been unjustly imprisoned—even driven to suicide." *(NEWSWEEK,* 251 West 57th St, New York, NY 10019, Page 34, October 13,1997)

The cover of that same issue of the magazine read: "Inside the IRS, Lawless, Abusive, and Out of Control."

"That system was eventually fool-proofed somewhat so that the employees couldn't do such things to people. However, what motivated them to do it in the first place was their wayward characters; seeking power and control over people even to the point of destroying them.

"Then there are the stories on various media about government prosecuting attorneys concealing evidence from defense attorneys so as to secure a conviction in the interests of promoting their own career; and sending innocent victims to prison for life to do it.

"All it takes to have such things happening in any democratic country is a sizable number of its people of such wayward character as living for self alone. In such a life, they use self as the measuring stick by which to measure what is allowed and what is not allowed, what should be and should not be, what is good and what is not good. They let no higher being, God or human, guide their standards. If someone else is a cut above them, then to them that is wrong, and that someone has to be put down or destroyed. Such selfish, self-centered mind-sets as that cause numerous and diverse problems in society. The Lawtons' experience with immigration is only one manifestation of many similar and related problems.

"The woman supervisor in the Immigration Department, in her treatment of the Lawtons wouldn't even let herself be guided by the laws of the government she worked for. The Lawtons pricked her pride. So being governed first and foremost by self, she decided that since the Lawtons were too much for her and therefore upset her wayward undisciplined pride, which in turn stirred her envy, hatred and hostility, they had, according to her, to leave the country. She did not use the laws of her country as the criteria for admitting or dismissing the Lawtons, but rather, her own self-centeredness. Self was the ruling criteria for her."

Adding further, Collin said, "Christians are not meant to be like the ostrich with its head buried in the sand not knowing what is going on around it. Christians are supposed to be tuned in to what is going on in the world, and working to make it better. Durwin told some other of his experiences to the same Christian person. He did not believe these either. However, the experiences of Durwin Lawton I am relating to you are true and factual, as hard as they may be to believe.

"Furthermore, one of the main defenses of belittlers is to deny that such a thing would be done by them or in their country. When they are riled up enough, power and control belittlers do some brazenly ridiculous things that most people wouldn't believe if they heard it. They have already outwardly established their own public image, as phony as it may be, and dare their victims to openly accuse them of what they have done to you. Then they will flatly deny it and accuse you of doing wrong things to them by accusing them falsely.

"So wake up Mr. *Christian.* Either you really are like an ostrich with your head in the sand, or, you are supporting the evil of belittlers by trying to cover up their dirty work. Either way you are wrong.

Returning to the story, Collin remarked to the support group, "You will notice I mentioned that the hard-boiled supervisor was older, and the woman at the wicket younger. This is not meant to indicate that belittlers are older people and younger people are not belittlers. That is not so. There are many belittlers among both old and young. This case does indicate, as the story will bear out, that there was a whole segment of belittlers approximately the same age throughout this vast office complex. Obviously they have been working together for years, and you will later see how they work together as, 'a conspiracy of sorts' as I call it, to put fine people down.

"When the Lawtons went home that day, they almost immediately went over the papers and list of requirements, which they found to be identical to those they had prepared on their visit to Terraprima approximately two months earlier. A complete medical report including X-ray not more than three months old was required for each of them. The Lawtons had this on hand on the required forms from their initial contact with immigration. They decided to fill out the remaining new papers, puting the present date and address on them, and go back into the city next morning. They aimed at being there seven o'clock to be in line early for the seven thirty office opening.

"Arriving at the planned time, they found the lines to be already hundreds of people long. They would have to stand in line a long time, which they did. At the end of this line they would be issued tickets which would give them entrance to a large waiting room on another floor, where the procedure was that as they presented their tickets upon arrival, their names would be recorded in a book. Then they would be called for an interview as it became their turn according to the order in which the names were listed.

"So the Lawtons stood in line for their tickets for nearly four hours. Tickets were generally issued until eleven a.m. which allowed enough people through to keep the department to which the people would go from there, busy for the remainder of the day. It was twenty minutes before eleven when the Lawtons reached the ticket wicket and asked for their tickets. As the aimiable young counter man tore the tickets off the roll, the same hostile supervisor came barging in still another time. She snatched the tickets from the man's hand before he had time to pass them on to the Lawtons. 'There are no more tickets to be issued today,' she snarled angrily. 'We have reached our quota for today.' The young man looked at her aghast, then at his watch, then at her again.

"'It's almost eleven o'clock,' she growled in extreme hostility. 'We have given out enough tickets for today. There is no more today,' she said firmly in a near tantrum. The man put up his hand slightly in a gesture of resignation. The Lawtons walked away empty handed after nearly four hours in line.

"Out in the hallway of the building, Durwin asked a security officer what time in the morning did the line start to form. 'Oh,' he replied, 'there are a few here at five thirty, and it starts to get heavy by six a.m. sometimes.'

"The Lawtons decided they would be there next morning at five thirty, which they were. There were a few people in line even at that time, but they were near the beginning of the line. This allowed them to approach the wicket for their tickets shortly after eight. They approached with much apprehension. The same supervisor was there, and she had spotted them in the line very early. Strangely enough, however, she did not continue with her glaring at them this time. In fact as she walked around she noticably kept turning her back on them, which the Lawtons appreciated. Under great tension they finally approached the wicket and were very politely given tickets. The supervisor did not come near.

"The Lawtons thanked the man and left the area. 'Thank heavens there was no clash with the supervisor this morning,' remarked Canda with relief.

"'It seems we are rid of her,' said Durwin, 'maybe we are well on our way now.'

"'Don't count on it.' cautioned Canda.

"At the time Canda's attitude seemed to Durwin to be a negative one considering the progress they had just made. Time would show that Canda's caution was more than warranted. They were in for years of wrangling and abuse with this Immigration Department as it became more and more clear that belittlers were in control there, were well entrenched and were a law unto themselves.

"The Lawtons went directly to the other room located on another floor. Almost immediately and without incident they were able to present their tickets, have their names recorded, and then choose a seat from the hundred or more that filled the room. The seats were less than quarter filled when the Lawtons arrived there. Over the next three hours or so the room would fill up, the morning influx being faster than the processing. By eleven a.m. the influx would cease and by mid-afternoon everyone would be taken care of. That was how the system worked.

"There was a notice on the wall stating that once persons had presented their tickets and had their names recorded, they should not leave the room. If their names were called and they were not there to respond, they would lose their appointment for that day. There were wash rooms nearby to which one could go provided there was another to stay and hear the name called. There was another sign stating there was to be no food or drinks in the room. There was a water fountain in the hallway, which could be used by one while the other listened for the name.

"The Lawtons sat there from shortly after eight in the morning until after three in the afternoon. The room filled to capacity by eleven in the morning and became near empty by mid-afternoon. People were called in approximately the same order as they had been registered—all except the Lawtons, that is.

"By noon they began to suspect that something was wrong. The number of people in the room was thinning out. The Lawtons should have been through by now. Canda said to Durwin, 'the battle axe downstairs is getting her way after all.'

"'I believe you are right,' said Durwin, 'she was unconcerned about us downstairs this morning because she has fouled our procedure up here.'

"I'll go to the counter and make inquiry,' volunteered Canda.

"'Good luck,' said Durwin, with a hopeful smile.

"Canda approached a woman at the counter with her usual friendly smile and pleasant manner, explained that they had been in the room since shortly after eight and now it was afternoon. 'Shouldn't we be called in for our interview soon?' she asked.

"'We-l-l,' said the woman in a smooth, cold manner, we are very busy here you know.'

"'Yes, I can see that,' replied Canda, 'it's no trouble to tell, but we have been here since shortly after eight. It's now afternoon. Many people who came after we did are through and gone.'

"'Oh, well', she said, as she kept a calm, even more cold composure, there may be something special about your case. We'll call you when we're ready.'

"Canda returned and sat with Durwin. They noticed they were being watched when one of them went to the wash room or the water fountain. They felt sure that if two of them were to go out together their names would have been called, and they would have missed their appointment for the day. They were careful not to do this. Between Canda's first inquiry and three o'clock they made two other inquiries.

Each time they were put off with a cold and casual, 'we'll call you when we are ready for you.'

"'By three fifteen the room was all but empty; only a handfull of people left. Durwin and Canda decided to go to the counter together and be firm. They approached the same woman they had talked to earlier. Durwin spoke firmly, 'We have sat here all day. We haven't eaten since four o'clock this morning. It is near closing time. Don't you think its time we had our interview?'

"She replied in a drawl as though unconcerned about the long arduous day, I'll go and see if you can be seen now.' She went through a door behind the counter and was gone for about ten minutes. Upon return she drawled coldly again, 'You can't be seen today. You'll have to leave your papers with me, and you'll be called in for an interview sometime within the next three months.'

"The Lawtons protested.

"'That's the word from the supervisor of the section,' she said with a coldness that seemed devoid of any human feeling.

"'Can we speak to the supervisor?' they asked.

"'The supervisor has no time to see anyone else today. You had better give me your papers. That is her instructions,' came the firm reply.

"They handed her the new set of papers, making sure to keep the papers that admitted them for a year. Then they left the office."

Collin paused in the story, "So you see the 'conspiracy of sorts' I mentioned earlier, was taking formation here in this government office. It isn't that they sit down and plan together how to get you. It's birds of a feather working together. They just pass the word along. And since they all have been playing the same game at times over the years, and know it well, they automatically join in putting you down.

"Durwin and Canda had been observing all morning the people and procedures in the room, as they also had done in the line up in the previous room downstairs. There were people from every part of the world, so it seemed; people of all colors and languages; people dressed in the varied clothes of many lands. There were very few white Caucasians there, maybe a half dozen or so out of all the hundreds the Lawtons had seen in both large rooms that day, and that few in number were shabby in dress and personal decorum. But everyone there were all being treated courteously and with patience, even though many of them spoke little English, and had trouble understanding papers and instructions. Nearly everything was done for them by the staff. Most of the staff were white. All of the staff the Lawtons had direct contact with, by coincidence were white. No racial discrimination was involved. There were other reasons for the cold treatment the Lawtons were receiving; reasons of undisciplined pride, envy, and hatred for fine caliber people.

"The group members should note that the cold treatment began before any of the staff there knew anything at all about the Lawtons; not even their names or where they were from. The obnoxious supervisor downstairs eventually did in the conversation learn where they were from and later their names would be available to her from the register book upstairs. But that was all that was known about them in the whole office building. Not even the man who issued the one year papers had information on them yet, other than name, address and occupation. Not until after the papers the Lawtons eventually handed in that day were read by the immigration people, would they know anything about Durwin's previous supposed illness, or have any basis at all for turning them away. No basis, that is, except prejudice brought on by the Lawtons' fine appearance.

"The rough treatment was indeed solely on the basis of their appearance. They were fine looking people, far above the caliber that were passing through that office; far above the caliber that were in charge of that office. There were some nice, good people working there; mostly of a younger generation, the young woman who first saved the situation for them, the friendly man to whom she sent them, the ticket man who did the best he could. But in contrast, there was the hostile supervisor downstairs, and the supervisor behind the scenes upstairs and her out front woman at the upstairs counter. It did seem already that the office was dominated by a generation of belittlers. It would be fully verified as time went by."

Gilda Emerson of the support group interrupted Collin's story of the Lawtons experience with Terraprima Immigration. "What would have happened if the Lawtons had protested more vigorously? Could they have been more demanding and broken their way through the barriers?"

"Not likely," replied Collin, "it has been my experience with belittlers that they twist everything around and blame it on the other person. When it becomes necessary, belittlers quite openly deny that they did anything wrong to the belittled. They would support each other in such denial, and their victims wouldn't stand a chance. I will give you examples of this later. The Lawtons probably would have been blamed for causing a scene in a government office for no reason and labled as undesirable aliens. The belittler's mind-set is to continually probe to get some concrete complaint against the person they are putting down."

"I agree," said Brett Culver, "and it has been my experience that belittlers put you down in subtle and not so subtle ways, often without thought of the very serious end results of what they are doing. But you had better be careful how you defend yourself against them. They will be very quick to say, 'listen to what he or she is saying about me,' or, 'look what they are doing to me, and I didn't do a thing to deserve it.'"

"I've experienced that lots of times," said Donna Coyne, "there are numerous times when you can only be silent and take it."

"We are really up against it, aren't we?" added Owen Winslow. "Looks like avoidance is our best defense."

"Not always but quite often," said Collin, "especially where the belittlers are in total control." Then looking to young Albin Anders, "Albin, take my word, never go to a college or university, or work in a place where belittling is the domineering factor. There are some belittlers everywhere, and you learn to dodge and/or cope with them, but in a place where they are in control, it is better to move out as soon as possible. The risk is high that sooner or later they will do you in. Either that or you have to be practically super - human, and careful almost to perfection, to avoid them getting the better of you."

Albin raised his eyes a little and chuckled at himself. "I guess I have a long way to go before I can handle all that by myself, don't I?"

"Keep in touch with us and we'll help you through until you are older and more experienced," Collin assured him. "Now I wish to tell you what happened to the Lawtons next."

"It is most interesting," commented Dr. Eldren.

Collin felt encouraged and continued, "The Lawtons waited at home for notification of their interview. Three months passed and yet there was no sign of it. They debated many times whether to take the initative and get the process rolling again, or wait it out. After about two weeks past the three month period a letter arrived from the department.

"'We may get our interview after all', said Durwin to Canda as he opened the letter with them both very anxious to read it. The letter was a shock. They were now informed by this letter that some time soon they would receive another letter informing them when and where they were to appear in an immigration court. At that time they would be instructed as to how and when they were to leave the country. There was no mention of an interview. The letter bore the signature of the Director of Immigration for the Area in which the office was located. It could not be discerned whether the signature was an original done with a pen and black ink, or a rubber stamp signature.

"Durwin carefully composed a return letter to the director. In this letter he outlined in detail the procedures and precautions he had taken in preparation for his move to Terraprima; the inquiry at the other office while on his visit, the inquiry at the border, the inquiries by telephone, and his prompt reporting to the area office after arrival. He also detailed the responses he had received in each instance. Furthermore he informed them that he still had the phone bills on hand to prove he had made the calls, and that his temporary admittance to the country was good for a year and only a little more than three months had passed so far.

"The Lawtons never received a reply from that letter. Neither did they recieve any notice to appear in court. In fact there was no further response during that first year. When the one year period of their temporary admission was nearing its end, Durwin and Canda wrote again to the immigration office reminding them of the pending expiration date and expressed the desire to bring the matter to a conclusion. There was no answer until long past the end of the first year and their temporary admission had expired. In the meantime they had decided to stay on, as they had tried everything possible, and could take no responsibility for the lapse of their temporary admission.

"It seems some immigration officials were making it a stand-off between them and the Lawtons. So the Lawtons decided to take them up on it and stay in the country until they were officially notified to leave, or granted the permanent residence status they had applied for. The Lawtons never were notified in writing to leave the country. In the light of all the circumstances of their entry into it, there was no case against them to do so.

"In hind-sight they felt they would have done better to not have replied to the letter that informed them of the pending court hearing. Had they remained silent and let the matter go to court, they most likely would have received a fair hearing and been admitted permanently to the country. In their letter, however, they had tipped their hand and shown they had a winning case. They were now of the opinion that this was why they heard no more about court. They had an air-tight case, so to speak.

"When another letter finally did come, several weeks after the year had passed, it raised a problem that Durwin knew would come sooner or later. Belittlers always find some area in a person's life on which they can pounce. They were now zeroing in on the fact that Durwin had had some sort of nervous breakdowns in his past. That these were of short duration and had happened many years ago was now being overlooked. Durwin, trying always to be honest and above board, had mentioned this in his application, feeling at the time that it would be handled in a modern, up-to-date way, without stigma and in the light of the latest knowledge on the subject. In reality it would be handled very crudely as a weapon for belittling.

"This latest letter requested that Durwin submit a recent psychiatric examination to the department. This posed no problem. He already had a good one from a renowned psychiatrist in Secundaterra. He would now seek one from a psychiatrist in Terraprima.

"Upon inquiry, a friend told Durwin of a psychiatrist who did some work for the church in Terraprima. He was located in a very favorable part of a high caliber town, with well appointed offices located on the second floor over some fashionable boutiques, where he was accustomed to dealing with well-to-do people. Durwin felt okay about it.

"In an interview with this psychiatrist things went very amicably and favorably. The doctor inquired into Durwin's past illness and causes, and also into his present outlook and activities. He then told Durwin he would have an appraisal in the mail to him in a day or two. It was a very favorable report that arrived.

"The doctor stated in his appraisal that Durwin's present performance in all areas of life was exceptional, that he had never had a mental illness and that his past problems were due to problems in life. Durwin also requested and received a letter of reference from the C.E.O. of the area church. In this letter, Durwin's ministry was described as 'excellent'. I ask you to note," said Collin to the group members, "that in the psychiatrists letter, Durwin's 'performance is superior.' In the C.E.O.'s letter, his ministry is 'excellent'. We will be referring to these letters in another context later.

"Durwin sent these letters of reference to the department together with the report of the psychiatrist in Secundaterra which was also very favorable. There was no further action from the department for nearly another year and even then it had to be prodded by the Lawtons.

"Through social contacts, Durwin had made acquaintance with a prominent lawyer in the area of his church. After he had become acquainted well enough with this lawyer, he spoke to him one day about his immigration problem and about the inaction of the department on his case. The man didn't understand the full depth of the problem. Few people would. So Durwin made no effort to discuss personalities, but merely that his application wasn't being processed on schedule. The lawyer remarked that government offices are like that sometimes, and suggested he work through the office of the local congressman to get faster action. He made an appointment for Durwin.

"Durwin went for the appointment, but it turned out to be an appointment with the congressman's secretary. Durwin asked if he could see the congressman personally and was informed he was presently in the capitol and that his help to constituents was generally handled through his secretary.

"Durwin outlined to her the delay in the processing of his application, discussed with her the supposed nervous breakdown problem that had arisen, and gave her copies of the psychiatric appraisals of both psychiatrists. Her opinion was there shouldn't be any problem. She added that 'some people, when they hear the word mental or psychiatric or nervous breakdown do think in terms of something drastic and dangerous. But one has only to look at these appraisals, and to talk with you to know different than that. She added, 'and you are from Secundaterra. There certainly shouldn't be any problem with that.' Durwin informed her that they had never yet interviewed him to get to know what he was like. She couldn't understand that, now going on the second year and not interviewed.

"'We will get it moving right away,' she said.

"Several more months passed, but the Lawtons received no word either from the department or the congressman's office. Durwin went to the congressman's office and reported the inaction again."

"'I don't understand that,' the secretary said, 'I will speak to the congressman about it when he is in town again. It won't be for another month or so, as he is out of the country.'

Collin paused in the story telling. Then he asked the group members, "Do you notice how so many people, including a congressman's staff, don't understand such things as you and I and people like us have to put up with?"

"They don't have the foggiest idea of what is going on for people like us," answered Donna Coyne.

"Mostly, only we and the belittlers who do those things to us, know about it, and they cover themselves well don't they?" added Owen Winslow.

"Yes Owen, they cover themselves well. A few good people are wise to them, people who have been stung and survived. They know the dirty mind-games and all. A few others know it from observing it in action against other people, but they don't always realize the intensity of it. Many people don't know it is even going on at all.

"Another two months passed. The Lawtons then each received a large packet from the department together with a letter of instruction. They were informed that their previous medical reports and applications were now outdated. They were to fill out the enclosed forms, have new medicals, including X-rays, and report to the immigration office, room such and such on the date and time given. Examination of the packets revealed that they were of similar content to the ones they had received on their first trip to the office. They now had to start from scratch and do the whole thing over again, the time and expense of it all being duplicated.

"Upon closer examination it was revealed that one form was missing from Durwin's set of forms. Canda's set was complete. The missing form for Durwin was a medical history form, a very necessary one, for sure. The belittlers miss no opportunity in their manipualtions. The medical history form was essential if Durwin was to continue to be open and fair about his mental health.

"Rather than go to the same office and possibly a hostile confrontation with the original hostile supervisor, Durwin decided to drive to another city and pick up a form at the immigration center located there. He decided to arrive there shortly before closing time when the lines would be fizzled out for the day. When he got there, he discovered that this center had a booth separate from all the other offices. It was staffed by one white woman. The booth was for information and forms, so the sign over it read. There were only two people in line ahead of him. This is the easiest yet, he thought. He was wrong!

"Durwin stood behind the two women already in line, one a middle aged woman just asking for directions to another part of the building. Next in line was a disarrayed young woman, perhaps around twenty years old, of an ethnic race from another country. She was completely disheveled in dress and personal decorum. Her clothes looked dirty and her hair uncombed. She neither spoke nor understood English very well. This description is not intended to categorize or discriminate against the people of any race. I am simply describing this young woman objectively.

"The conversation could not be heard by Durwin in detail, but the white woman operating the information booth, took considerable time to get forms for the girl, go over them with her and explain the whole process to her with great patience, repeating herself often to compensate for the customer's lack of understanding, due to the language difficulty and perhaps the intelligence factor as well.

"Durwin thought it was very nice of the woman in the booth to be so pleasant and empathetic to a young person obviously in need of care. He didn't mind waiting the ten or fifteen minutes it took for such a deed of kindness. *There are some human beings in this department,* he mused to himself, *hope she is half as pleasant to me.*

"When the time came, Durwin stepped up to the booth. Before he had time to speak, the woman snapped at him hostilely, 'What do you want,' she said with an emphasis on the 'you' that indicated contempt. Here again is a case of Durwin, a fine person, being turned on by a belittler on the basis of his appearance. He would learn in time that it is uncommon in some circles of Terraprima for a person like him to make the grade at all in life. In fact, it is so uncommon in these circles, that the hostility by belittlers is brazenly open and public.

"Durwin calmly told her he just needed a form, number such and such.

"'We don't hand out that form here,' she snapped again. 'You can get it when you go for an interview.'

"'But', protested Durwin, 'I need to have the form ready when I go for the interview.'

"'You can get no such form here,' she came back angrily, then looked past Durwin to call the next person in the line that had now formed behind him.

"Durwin, the only white person in the line, stepped aside. He knew he would get no satisfaction here. As he walked around the corner away from the booth, he paused and looked back. The woman, with smiles and friendliness was now greeting the next man in line, again a disheveled person of ethnic race from another continent. Standing tall and proud and beaming, this government worker really thought she was doing her job in a wonderful manner, when in reality all she was doing was subverting her country to less than mediocrity.

"Durwin went home, wrote a letter to the Forms Division of the department asking for the form to be mailed to him. He received it by return mail. When it was sight unseen there was no problem.

"The Lawtons reported at the appointed time of two in the afternoon with their new forms and medicals ready. When they arrived, they were relieved to see it was a smaller office they had to report to this time; no long line-ups or tickets necessary. There were only a few people seated and waiting in this office. Interviews were taking place at desks spaced out and separated by room dividers. But although there was no line up in this room, for the Lawtons there would still be delay. Long after the others were all processed, they still sat there waiting. Finally someone came and told them to come and sit at one of the interviewing desks. She led them over, seated them and left.

"They sat there for another half hour before another woman arrived on the scene and sat behind the desk. She was an older woman, near retirement age they discerned, tall and of average weight for her height, looking unfriendly and hard-boiled and puffing continuously on a long cigarette.

"'What brings you people here today?' she growled sternly, as a swirl of smoke enveloped the Lawtons.

"'We received a letter to be here with our new applications and medicals,' replied Durwin firmly.

"She blinked, and grunted contemptuously, 'Ugh', as she reached for the envelopes, then separated Durwin's packet from Canda's. Upon opening Durwin's packet, she quite obviously looked for one part only, the medical history form. To her obvious surprise it was there. She took a quick look at it, then at Durwin accusingly, 'A question on this paper asks if you have ever had a mental illness and you answer no.'

"'Right,' said Durwin, pulling a paper out of his pocket, 'and I have here a copy of my psychiatric appraisal stating that I never had a mental illness, but problems in life caused my breakdowns.'

"'A copy is not acceptable to this office,' she growled with yet a little more hostility, 'we require an original.'

"Durwin spoke with yet more firmness, 'You already have the original here in this office. I sent it to you in a letter when you previously requested it.'

"She blinked again, but then came back forcefully. 'You cannot be admitted to this country,' her cold growling voice asserted.

"'Why not?' asked Durwin strongly now tired of pussy-footing.

"She declined to answer.

"'Why not?' repeated Durwin strongly.

"'Because it is illegal,' she quivered as she tried to keep up her hard-boiled appearance.

"'Why is it illegal?" demanded Durwin.

"'Because it is. It's against the law,' she snapped as she turned her attention to the papers to divert her focus from Durwin at whom she could no longer look, for shame. She did not look at the papers for long, being in no emotional condition to do so. Then trying to compose herself again she said as firmly as she could muster, 'You'll be hearing from us soon. That's all for today.' She took the papers and left the room. The interview had been very short—about three minutes. There was no one else in sight. The Lawtons had no choice but to leave empty handed."

Leo Aidan interrupted the story, "Durwin almost broke through to her that time when she quivered, didn't he Collin?"

"Almost, Leo, at least that's one plausable analysis, or perhaps he just shook her hollow pride. Then again it may be that he did get through to her. But if she had given in, then how would she face her colleagues in the back office?"

"I see what you mean," said Leo.

Collin continued, "there was such a delay in her coming out for the interview that there well could have been a get-together behind the scenes to decide who would take on the Lawtons today and get rid of them. She may have volunteered, or she may have been pushed into it. She had to go back and face the gang. It is a case of birds of a feather acting together against the Lawtons whom they perceived to be a common enemy—an enemy because they prick their pride and stir their envy.

"Again, it is a 'conspiracy of sorts,' as I call it. They have to turn their hatred on such a supposed enemy to preserve themselves, so they think in their 'most warped and twisted of human emotions'. (The Daily Study Bible. The Letter to the Romans, William Barclay, P.28. The Saint Andrew Press, Edinburgh, 1966). It's the way their mind-set has been since their younger, formative years."

"Paranoid," quipped Leo Aidan.

"Yes, truly paranoid," affirmed Collin. "They really felt the Lawtons were doing them harm. In reality, the Lawtons were just being themselves, and this hurt these proud envious ones, so they supposed the Lawtons to be enemies really doing them harm; very paranoid indeed.

"Another possible explanation of her behavior is that since she was a bully, and since a bully is a coward, she began to cower when the chips came down on her. The bully started to whimper when Durwin got firm with her, and it looked like she might be cornered."

"Should he have pushed a little harder at that point?" asked Leo inquisitively.

"I don't think so," replied Collin. "If he had pressed her hard enough to break fully through the facade and make her cower too much for her comfort she would probably have bolted from the room to report how she was being mistreated by the applicant. Durwin would most certainly be blamed for a scene. This could have resulted in a total loss of their chances of staying in the country. Belittlers never take the blame, it's always the belittled whom they see to be in the wrong. When someone breaks through the facade of belittlers too fully they are devastated. Then they will do most anything to protect it. Besides, there wasn't any opportunity to push it further. She simply picked up the packages of papers, said 'that's all for today,' and left the room, leaving the Lawtons sitting there with no one else in sight.

"How defiant of a congressman's office they were!" remarked Owen.

"Yes indeed," answered Collin, "and they knew they could get away with it. I have heard of several such cases. They have been doing it for years and getting away with it. The Lawton's never heard from that area immigration office again.

"They waited several months, then Durwin reported to the congressman's secretary again. She acted in a manner of resignation, saying, 'I don't understand it and I don't know what else we can do.' Here again it is notable that many people in high places even in government have no idea or concept of the existence and destructiveness of belittlers. Durwin didn't go there again.

"Here were the Lawtons, high quality candidates for immigration; healthy physically in all respects; psychologically mature, Durwin's mental health clear for ten years, a near six figure bank account, guaranteed permanent employment, covered by health and disability insurance, covered by good pension plans, and with quality references from very credible sources. These people would be a credit to any country, but in Terraprima, the land of opportunity for all, they were being treated less than human by one of its government departments.

"The Lawtons now retained the services of an immigration lawyer who had been recommended to them as one who had helped other ministers. This lawyer, a very capable and aimable man, tried time and again to get some action from this office of the immigration department, but none was forthcoming. They gave no response whatsoever."

Gilda Emerson broke into the conversation, "they defied the congressman and his office, now they ignore a lawyer!"

"A law unto themselves!" added Leo.

"Indeed," said Collin, "they behaved as though they were autonomous—a power unto themselves, answerable to no one.

"There are other stories circulating about the treatment certain people from various countries receive from this department. Many of these stories are of people from Secundaterra, which country has tried officially over the decades to be a good friend to Terraprima, and continues to do so. Yet some of its fine people who wish to move to Terraprima are often on the one hand allowed to enter the country, but on the other are shunned by the immigration department when they get there. Some of them, fine people as they are, have had it implied to them that they are criminals, breaking the law by trying to stay in Terraprima. This is what was happening to the Lawtons.

"In casual conversation with a police chief in Terraprima one day, Durwin and Canda told him of their immigration problem. 'My dear people,' he said, 'you came from the wrong country. We have people pouring into this country illegally, with nothing except the clothes on their backs and not much of that. I picked up three of them in this town the other day, phoned the Immigration Department about it and they answered, 'Well what do you want us to do?'

"'Don't they have to be deported?' asked the police chief.

"'No,' came the reply. 'We have no means here to handle that. Eventually they will be legalized.'

"The police chief then reiterated to the Lawtons, 'You people are from the wrong country, you are just too good a caliber of people to be admitted to this country anymore.'

"He was near right. Although it wasn't altogether the country they came from, but rather the kind of people they were from that country —too good for the many envious immigration people."

Collin continued to the group, "Statistics show that more people now leave Terraprima to live in Secundaterra, whereas it used to be the other way around. No wonder, with this kind of treatment in store for them.

"However, even with such odds against them, Durwin and Canda decided they would continue to ride out the storm to see where it would lead. Another year or more passed with no further word on their immigration status.

"In the meantime, the Lawtons were missing out on a lot of opportunities to solidify their life in Terraprima. For example their bank, by whom they were personally well regarded, was offering some good group insurance and investment plans by which they could invest for retirement. They had to turn them down because they may have to leave the country anytime. Long term investments had to be by-passed.

"For years now they had been preparing the means whereby they would own their own home upon retirement after living in a church-owned house during their working years. The prices of real estate around the area of Terraprima where they were living began to rise. Before it had risen too far, the Lawtons could easily have made a downpayment on a house, rented it, and eventually have a house for their retirement in the area they had planned. But again they had to pass it up because of the impermanence of their circumstances.

"So you see, the Lawtons were being severely damaged. It wasn't a matter of them being over-sensative to little hurts as some try to imply. The remainder of their lifetime would be drastically affected. When belittlers and their supporting psychiatrists try to make you believe you are a super sensative pansy, don't let them do it to you. If they had to put up with a quarter as much they would fold like wilted flowers or break like match sticks. I have often heard them whimper like small children over far less."

Leo broke in, "Belittlers appear to be proud and powerful when they have you down and think they are getting away with it. But I know how they are when they are tripped up in their weird and dirty game and fearful of being brought to light on it. I also have heard them whimper like babies! We folks too sensative? Not on your life! They are, but for different reasons than we are accused of."

The other group members all agreed with Leo. Dr. Eldren gave a grin of satisfaction at the way things were going in the group.

"Did the Lawtons ever get their immigration approved?" asked Albin Anders.

"Yes they did," answered Collin, "so we do win at times, Albin, but often at great cost. I'm a firm believer that people like us can always make the grade, damaged and scarred though we may be, but nevertheless winners at least to some degree. If only we could put half the energy and effort we are forced to put into survival, into creative living for the benefit of ourselves and others, we would be out on top where exceptional people should be. Alas, we are destined to be short-changed by foul means not of our own making."

"You'll have to tell us tonight how the Lawtons got their papers," said Albin exuberantly.

"I will right now," said Collin and continued with the story. "After four years of excessive negative behavior by belittlers in the church, the Lawtons were moved to another congregation. I will tell you much more about this when I tell you of the Lawtons' experiences with the church in general. Suffice it to say for now this congregation was in another state and within the jurisdiction of another immigration office, the office to which the Lawtons had gone in the first place when on their visit to Terraprima if you will remember.

"They decided to approach this office through their immigration lawyer who, although he had been unable to get a response from the first office, had higher hopes for this office. He was well known in immigration circles in this area, and therefore likely to get a courteous response and a fair hearing. This they did, and although the process was long and drawn out, another year in fact, it brought results.

"This immigration office was much more congenial, generally. There were some belittlers there, as there are nearly everywhere, but they were not in control of this office. They did not dominate the general atmosphere there. This together with the presence of a lawyer who was well known in the immigration circles of that area, kept the belittlers at bay.

"The lawyer requested that the Lawton's records be transferred to this area immigration office with which they were now dealing. He also arranged for the Lawtons to be interviewed by an immigration officer. He would be there with them and make a new approach.

"The interview was with a very friendly and helpful mature woman. It was obvious from the start that she was being positive toward the Lawtons and their case. However, she had the sad task of informing them that their previous records submitted to the other office could not be found. The records were lost. The Lawtons would now have to do all new papers, have new medicals, more X-rays and all, and bear the expense of it once more. The woman gave them the new sets of papers, and instructed them to submit them through their lawyer for processing. After the processing, they would be granted a final interview after which the process would be completed within a short time. So the Lawtons did the whole process once more, this time much more hopefully.

"After their submission of the new papers, this office came back with a request for a more recently dated and original copy of the psychiatric appraisal. Durwin had submitted a photo copy he had preserved from the original appraisal that went to the first office. Photo copies were not acceptable, and furthermore a recently dated paper was required.

"Durwin made an appointment with the same church related psychiatrist who had appraised him so well before by describing his performance as 'superior in all areas of living.' The psychiatrist again interviewed Durwin exhaustively, but this time not in the friendly, helpful tones of the first interview. This second interview was of a cold, stern nature, even bordering on hostility at times, and mixed with a seeming impatient concern at other times.

"First, of course, he asked Durwin why the need for another appraisal. Durwin explained to him that he was now living in a different state and applying through a different immigration office. Remember now," said Collin to the group, "this is after approximately four years of trying through the other office.

"The doctor spoke in mixed tones of perturbance and seeming, seeming that is, concern. Further he spoke very curtly and loudly, 'you have been trying for several years now to get these papers, and obviously without success. What's wrong with living in your own country? Why are you so adamant about staying in this country? Are you going to stay here till they wear you down?'

"'Not so,' replied Durwin calmly, 'I'm going to wear them down!'

"The psychiatrist was taken aback just a little. 'You have moved,' he still growled, but not quite as harshly. 'How many members are there in your new parish?' Durwin told him the figure that was in the church statistics record.

"'And how many members are in your previous church?" Durwin gave him the number. It was a little less than for his new church.

"'Where is this new church located?' he asked. Durwin told him. The psychiatrist pondered for a moment, then very demandingly, 'And what went wrong in your previous church that they placed you away out there?' he growled.

"Durwin replied calmly, 'I did my work faithfully and well. I gave them a good ministry. I guess it wasn't what they wanted."

Brett Culver interrupted the story, "If only Durwin could have simply said that the place was dominated by belittlers, how simple it could have been!"

"Right," said Collin, with a sigh, "and as I said earlier I will be telling you much about belittlers at work in the church at later meetings. But the way we use the term belittler is not yet used in psychological language in the same manner. However, that does not mean that some psychologists and psychiatrists do not play the belittling game. The fact remains though that it cannot be talked about because it is not a part of the professional language. To talk about it is to risk being labeled a nut, or a paranoid."

Collin continued the story, "The psychiatrist grilled Durwin again, 'Why did they put you away out there? What did you do wrong in your previous church?' he asked in a very demanding way.

"Again, Durwin couldn't give the doctor the complete reason why he had been moved from his previous parish to his present one. Psychology simply doesn't record the gross behavior of belittlers that we in this group know and speak of; their envy, hatred and tactics. Durwin simply and calmly replied, 'they told me that is all they had for me.'

"The psychiatrist seemed baffled by Durwin's ready answers. He growled again. 'Do you take medication for depression?'

"'No,' replied Durwin as calmly as ever, 'I don't need it.' The psychiatrist looked hard at him. Durwin continued, 'One night my wife and I watched an hour long TV program on depression. It doesn't fit me at all. I'm functioning just fine as I am.'

"The psychiatrist was taken aback some more, and in somewhat subdued tones asked pointedly, 'and you insist on trying to stay in this country?'

"'Yes,' said Durwin, without a ruffle, 'and I am at last making progress with it.' Then in an effort to explain his new circumstances, he said, 'in the previous immigration office they seemed to be doing all they could to prevent my acceptance into the country, but now…'

"The psychiatrist interrupted abruptly, 'What,' he snapped, as though questioning the soundness of Durwin's statement and attitude.

"Durwin knew what the psychiatrist had in mind. He was probing for paranoia. 'You didn't let me finish,' said Durwin still calmly, 'in the other office they seemed to be doing all they could to prevent my acceptance. In this office I am now dealing with, they are doing all they can to have me approved.'

"'I see,' said the psychiatrist, 'an altogether different atmosphere!'

"'Yes, altogether different,' replied Durwin pointedly.

Collin commented, "I would here ask you to note one of the ironies of the conversation. At one point the psychiatrist impatiently asked Durwin 'Are you going to stay here till they wear you down?' He was thereby admitting that "they" ', some people that is, were trying to wear Durwin down. Now, a little later in the conversation, he was trying to trip Durwin up in the paranoia trap that belittlers so often use to either defend themselves on their actions of belittling or to belittle some more."

Collin then continued with Durwin's story. "After a moment of silence, and in a mild tone of grudging resignation, the psychiatrist spoke again, 'Well, you have a larger parish this time. The membership is higher and that speaks well for you. I still think my first appraisal of you was accurate. I'll have a similar one drawn up and mailed to you within a few days.'"

Collin instructed the group members, "I will ask you to keep this second episode with the psychiatrist in mind for future reference in conjunction with other experiences of the Lawtons. But to sum it up for now, in this second interview this church-related psychiatrist revealed the vicious mind-game that has been played in this denomination of the church in Terraprima for generations. He knew the game, and he tried to play along with it, but he couldn't subdue Durwin with it, so then he protected himself from being revealed, so he thought.

"I will elaborate on that further, but let me add first that Durwin still didn't see through the game at the time of this second psychiatric interview. Rather, with this and other experiences he was later able to reflect back on the second interview with this psychiatrist. It helped him piece together the mind-game that was being played on him by the church at large.

"The second church, out of the way, unprogressive and almost totally unsuited to Durwin's ministry and present interests, was supposed to have depressed Durwin. Had he been a person of hollow undisciplined pride like his assailants it might well have. If the psychiatrist could have gotten him to admit to depression and to taking medication for it, or, given him medication for it, Durwin probably would have lost his opportunity to stay in the country. If Durwin, when pressed so hard, had admitted to any wrong doing in his first church, the psychiatrist would have an excuse to discredit him.

"When the psychiatrist couldn't pin down Durwin on these things he covered himself and the church by conceding that Durwin had received a larger parish this time. Durwin would later learn that this is another ploy of the area church. When they want to demote a person they put him in a worse situation than he had before, but there is always one or two items about the overall situation that can be said to be better. It is the 'better but worse' tactic as I call it, that is craftily played by the wider church, and has been for decades, and of which I will give you more examples later in the story.

"Because it is so important to other parts of the total story, I will review this incident again. In the interview, the church related psychiatrist was probing to use the whole circumstance to discredit Durwin. Being placed now in a remote and incompatable church, Durwin was supposed to be depressed over it. Also if a confession could have been wrung out of him for doing something wrong which brought about his placement to this church, then the two of it together would have given the psychiatrist ample reason to turn Durwin down for immigration. When the doctor couldn't make it stick he covered for himself and the church by casually saying, 'well you were given a larger parish anyway.' It's the better-but-worse tactic being utilized.

"At the time of the interview, however, Durwin left the psychiatrist's office and went home feeling assured of a favorable conclusion to his and Canda's immigration problem. He had to phone the psychiatrist's office twice before the appraisal was finally mailed out to him. However, I am happy to tell you that the Lawtons were now approaching a successful completion of their immigration problem."

"Hurrah," shouted Leo, "you're going to tell us they made it."

"Did they really?" asked Brett, hopefully.

"Yes, they did," said Collin assuredly. "The psychiatrist gave another good appraisal, though reluctantly I believe. Everything else was in good order.

"One other incident occurred which Durwin didn't like, but went along with. One day the lawyer's secretary, not the lawyer himself, but the secretary, phoned Durwin informing him that he needed to sign a declaration that at one time he had had a mental illness. Durwin protested that the psychiatric reports stated he did not have a mental illness. The secretary said that made no difference. If he wished to get his permanent residence status, he would have to sign this paper. Durwin stated that he would think, if anything, to sign such a paper might prevent him from getting his papers rather than help him. The secretary said that was not the case, and that if he signed the declaration he was virtually assured of getting his permanent resident status.

"Durwin thought it through at the moment and decided this may be the way of the belittlers in the department protecting themselves from being sued, or the like. Durwin had no thought of sueing anyone on this matter. He knew that few judges, and less jury members, would be wise enough to the devious tactics of belittlers against people like he and Canda, for him to get an honest to goodness fair trial on any matters pertaining to his treatment by the immigration department. He went to the lawyer's office and signed the paper.

"Soon the Lawtons were called into the immigration office for a final interview which went very amicably. There was the usual fingerprinting and photography. They were told they would in all likelihood receive their approval within three months. They were even told that their previous files, reported lost, had now been found.

"The approval did come through as anticipated. They were then hopeful of picking up the remnants of their lives and starting to live fully permanently. Numerous opportunities had passed them by while they had to live in many respects on a temporary basis because of the immigration problem, even though they did their church work as on a permanent basis. *Things will go better for us now, and we will make up for lost time,* so they thought. It was not to be. There was more trouble ahead for the Lawtons."

A dead silence came over the group. They were visibly saddened.

"It's too much to tell you tonight, or on any one night," said Collin. "I'd suggest we wait until next week to continue. Then I will begin to tell you of the Lawton's experiences as fine people with both of their local churches, their interaction with other ministers, and with the church hierarchy of the area, and much more. It will make what I've told you about their immigration experiences seem trifling in comparison."

The group members were in near disbelief.

"Still more trouble ahead for the Lawtons! How much can two people take?" asked Donna, with tears in her eyes.

Leo came to her rescue, with some success, "Let nothing surprise you when it comes to the meeting of belittlers and fine, smart people, Donna. As Collin, in first semester, has already pointed out to us by quoting the Christian scholar, William Barclay, envy is the 'most warped and twisted of human emotions.'" (Ibid).

"I know," said Donna, "but it hurts to think that two people could be treated so viciously."

Leo smoothed her hand as it rested on the arm of her chair.

After a brief silence, Albin evolving from his shyness a little more, as he had been doing all along, suggested it might be the right time to gather at the coffee shop for some lighter moments. The others agreed. Feelings could be better explored after the whole story is told. A sense of the ample presence of empathy was enough for now. Dr. Eldren departed from the group for the evening. The remainder of them headed for the Corner Coffee Shop just down the street as they had done many times before for a period of lighter fellowship.

CHAPTER III

During the week between support group sessions, Collin Seldon pondered the topic of his next presentation, the experiences of his close friends Durwin and Canda Lawton in the church in Terraprima. Durwin had been damaged by belittlers in his youthful years, in a somewhat similar manner as Albin Anders has. We need not go into details of that. The group members will know from last semester how it happens.

As Durwin grew older, guided by a deep religious faith, and with enormous and heroic courage, perserverance, and an increasing self-discovered knowledge of belittlers, overcame his damages to the point where no situation or circumstance was too much for him to take on. However, no person, no matter how strong, or at what age, remains undamaged when in a severely adverse environment for too long—about two years ordinarily, but much longer for some.

Durwin, during his several years as a minister of churches in Terraprima, would have the struggle of his life to not only hold on to his hard earned pesonality gains, but to preserve his very life and livlihood. He went to Terraprima as a top-notch person, as I already have verified, and will do so further. After many cruel, oppressive years he managed to come out of it, although with many scars, still a topnotch person. This is more than most people could do. Durwin, damaged severely in his youth, a courageous overcomer in his late teens and early adulthood, would now have the struggle of his life not to have all his gains in life - his personhood, and he with it, destroyed by a 'Christian' church. A more mentally cruel story has seldom been told.

The support group came into session shortly after seven o'clock, having waited a few minutes for the arrival of Brett Culver who, as often happened, was a little late arriving. This was to be the meeting at which they would hear from Collin the story of one who was not a participant in the group. When the members had settled down after the usual exchange of greetings and chitchat, Dr. Eldren gave the go ahead, and Collin began his presentation.

"Over the next few sessions I will tell you the story of my close colleague and friend, Durwin Lawton and his wife Canda, as they ministered in Terraprima. Last week I told you of their arduous experiences with the Immigration Department. Now I will concentrate on their experiences in the church. There is a lot of detail to include in order to illustrate the magnitude of the problem. Also, I think we are indeed familiar enough with the subject and with one another by now to include relevant analysis along the way. Would that be satisfactory with you, Dr. Eldren?"

"Yes it would," replied Dr. Eldren obligingly. "Include in your presentations whatever detail and analysis is needed to support your aim and purpose. However, it may help in various ways if we complete the stories before the end of this semester."

Dr. Eldren was very interested and concerned, but it seemed he wanted the process to move as quickly as possible for some reason.

"Thanks, I'll do my best to finish during this semester," replied Collin, and then began right away. "First I will tell you something of the background of these two fine people, Durwin and Canda Lawton.

"Durwin Lawton had been a minister in mainline protestant churches for many years. He was a fine, clean cut, well cultured person of distinguished character and appearance that made him stand out among others. With many favorable characteristics about him, in both physical profile and personality, he was the type of person that, under normal circumstances the majority of people take a very sure liking to. A true friend to all who accepted his friendship, showing no intentional unkindness toward anyone; sincere, honest and hard working in all spheres of his ministry, Durwin was the type of minister any sane and sound Christian congregation would love to have.

"But Durwin had some other positive charactertistics as well. As a part of his air of refinement he was easy speaking, kind, meek, sparing in words, scrupulously honest and fair with all people. Such characteristics are often interpreted by some people, belittlers in particular, as weaknesses. Some would at times infer that he was a 'whimp,' and try unsuccessfully to make it stick. Durwin was no weakling. When necessary, he could be very firm and strong, standing his ground, although easily able to acknowledge error, or if warranted to change his mind and agree with people offering a different opinion.

Durwin was able to utilize anger too, when injustice needed confrontation of that kind, although he seldom resorted to it.

"He was a good all around steward of money and of other possessions, whether his own or the church's. He had confidence in himself yet was able to resort to self-examination to improve himself. Although he had good appearance under most any circumstance, he also felt it his duty to be always well groomed as a minister of the church and as a person - one of God's people. Durwin didn't take life for granted. He worked at it to keep that life on a high plane, believing that it is God's calling to do so. One main characteristic of his ministry was to help others to continually lift their lives to an ever higher plane. He humbly strived personally to be an example in this regard.

"It was for all of these reasons and more that many people liked and loved Durwin Lawton. It was for these same reasons that proud, envious belittlers hated him and sought continually to bring him down.

"Reviewing a little, I will emphasize that this in turn was the reason why Durwin, like many others including the members of our support group, always have to be very careful of what we ever say about belittlers to psychiatrists or psychologists or others of that field. Some of them would say he was paranoid; others that he was oversensitive to little things, and running or hiding, or overconcerned when there was nothing much to be concerned about.

"As indicated in our earlier discussions, we have heard psychiatrists say, 'Oh, I have had something like that happen to me occasionally, but I just shrug it off as the other person's ignorance and go on my way. Why let it bother you?' The fact is that as far as his own circumstances are concerned, such a psychiatrist may be quite right. He may only very occasionally experience such a problem. For you and I it is a way of life. We have it continuously. For those who only occasionally have to put up with it, it may be very easily shrugged off, although I have heard of people being very seriously, if sometimes only temporarily, affected by this occasional experience with belittlers.

"How then are we who have it continuously to fare when it affects our lives so perpetually and drastically, and there are so few who understand—practically no one to turn to for help without being inadvertently or otherwise put down further by the would be helpers, by being told we are oversensitive, or worse, we are paranoid. We have some support, not much but some, and not from psychology, as they generally are not yet on to it professionally.

"I have previously mentioned the Biblical scholar William Barclay. He writes of living at peace with all people, and quotes the Apostle Paul's qualification to do that as 'if it be possible, as far as you can.' *(The Daily Study Bible,* William Barclay, Romans 12:18, page 181, Barclay translation), or 'If possible, so far as it depends on you.' (Romans 12:18, R.S.V.), or 'If it is possible, so far as it depends on you.' (Romans 12:18, New R.S.V.). Barclay then goes on to say, 'Paul knew very well that it is easier for some to live at peace than it is for others. He knew that one person can be compelled to control as much temper in an hour as another person in a lifetime. We would do well to remember that goodness is a great deal easier for some people than it is for others.'(The Daily Study Bible, William Barclay, The Letter To The Romans, Page 184).

"Barclay also states, concerning the same topic, "Christianity is not an easy-going tolerance which will accept anything and shut its eyes to everything. There may come a time some battle has to be fought, and when that time comes the Christian will not shirk it.' *(The Daily Study Bible,* William Barclay, The Letter To The Romans, Page 184).

"Fine, smart people of the present era are continually in conflict with the gross evil of belittlers and are not meant simply to tolerate and appease just to be at peace with evil people. The world has long since learned that appeasement doesn't work when dealing with such people. Battles have to be fought. Occasionally anger is the only language evil belittlers understand, especially when they think they are getting away with their evil. However, uncontrolled anger is not an answer to the problem. So fine people have to learn, as much as lies in them and as much as is possible under the circumstances, to resort to other attitudes and defenses. Nevertheless, because he is assailed more by evil belittlers, the fine person is compelled all the more to control his anger, and defend himself by other means.

"Furthermore it is much more difficult for belittled fine people to be at peace with evil belittlers when the battle Barclay refers to is continuous. Tolerance and appeasement is not a Christian response to it.

It depends on us to be at peace with other peaceful people. But it does not depend on us to be at peace with evil people. It depends on them—if they will cease their evil. The Christian cannot rightly be at peace with evil. We can apply this to our circumstances.

"Barclay is here stating for us, in effect, that some people have a whole lot more trouble with difficult people than do others. It is therefore, as the Bible indicates, not as possible for them to live at peace with all people.

"So," said Collin, "I have no trouble disagreeing with psychiatry on this issue. As I said some people have only an occasional brush with belittlers, and may well be able to shrug it off. On the other hand, as I said earlier, I have known of some people who at times were hurt and their lives damaged quite severely, sometimes only temporarily by this occasional experience. But people like us have to put up with it continuously as a matter of course in life. If we should need help we are hard pressed because we will be told we are oversensitive, or worse, we won't be believed at all. Needless to say, I place more confidence in Barclay's statement than in the approach of most psychiatrists. The usual psychiatric approach works along with the belittlers to put us down all the more.

"During Durwin's first two years of ministry in Terraprima, a high church official described his ministry as 'excellent.' Another official in high places described his performance in all areas of life as 'superior.' Yet in two more years we see Durwin demoted to a much lesser ministry with a large decrease in remuneration, and looked upon and treated as a third class or less minister of an obscure, out of the way, unprogressive congregation without potential for the kind of ministry Durwin felt called to pursue.

"I can substantiate and compare this case with two other cases, spread years apart, to show that this problem has been around for a long, long time - for decades at least. It is handled today in the same way it was many years ago with no change in its evaluation or its handling by the church.

"The first of these happenings occurred approximately seventy five years ago, and with another similar incident about forty years ago. Both victims 'escaped' and went on to success in other areas of life. I know of others, and there are probably many, who have had similar experiences. I will tell you briefly of these two cases later, after I have told you a more complete story of Durwin Lawton. Then you will better understand all three stories.

"Just a word or two about Durwin's wife, Canda, before I go on," continued Collin. "Canda was made up of similar characteristics as Durwin to a large extent; she too was a warm, open, friendly type of person; an honest to goodness, down to earth friend to all who accepted her friendship.

"Durwin and Canda were a well matched pair who got along well throughout their many years of marriage. Their major difference was that Durwin was a more reserved person to a degree, at least moreso than Canda. Durwin had been very shy and lacking in self-esteem in his younger years and teens. But he conquered it adequately in his twenties. After thirty, as I indicated before, there was no place or people that Durwin would hesitate to go or take his place with in private or public. However, he preferred to remain himself, naturally low-keyed, rather than be the exuberant type; one would say he was calm, cool and collected under most circumstances.

"Canda, on the other hand was very extroverted and outgoing, the leading conversationist in a group, often the initiator of new and challenging ideas and projects, the spirited venturer with usually sound ideas. Durwin on the other hand, was more cautious and had always been the epitome of diplomacy and tact, skillfully endeavoring to go about things in a manner that would not offend or disturb. You may have often heard it said, as I have, that every reserved or quiet person needs an extrovert as a partner, and vice versa. Durwin and Canda complimented each other near perfectly in that manner. Most people appreciated that about them, but not all.

"I wish to emphasize again, they were both very highly intelligent, and the majority of people appreciated that, but not all, as you shall see. They were both fine people and well rounded personalities. And I would add to that, because the majority of people liked them for all that they were, one would think the world was at their doorstep. But not so, as you members of this group can well surmise because of your own experiences in life."

Collin knew his friend Durwin Lawton quite well, had a full knowledge of his ministry and keen insight into its problems and what it did for and to, mostly to, Durwin. With the group members listening very attentively he continued with another significant preliminary to the story of Durwin and Canda Lawton as Durwin was a pastor in Terraprima.

"During his several years as a minister in both Secundaterra and Lower Secundaterra, Durwin had more than his share of troubles with belittlers in the church and elsewhere, as you in this group can well imagine. We need not go into the details of these ministries and difficulties here because I wish to get on with the story of his ministry in Terraprima. Just one more thought before I do.

"The Lawtons had travelled much in Terraprima over the years. They had come to know the land and its people somewhat, although visiting a place is not the same as living in it, as they were to later find out. When you visit a place, people show their best side for you. When you live there you get drawn into the nitty-gritty of life and see its other side.

"During the sixties and seventies, when its society was in a turmoil, Durwin and Canda still visited Terraprima often. Many of their colleagues and acquaintances in both Secundaterra and Lower Secundaterra derided them heavily for their favoritism of Terraprima, and said it was on the way to self-destruction.

"In the Secundaterras at that time, and even on into the eighties, both government and church derided Terraprima and established policies that would prevent Terraprima culture from overwhelming the Secundaterras, thus allowing them to develop their own distinct cultures. It was extremely unpopular for anyone to speak favorably of Terraprima. Yet Durwin and Canda did so. They insisted that, in time, Terraprima would pull itself together again and become the promising land it had always been.

"The friendly people allowed them their opinion whether they agreed with it or not. The belittlers used it as a means to degrade them. 'How shameful, how stupid, how utterly wrong,' they would say, 'to stand up for a nation so deeply enmeshed in chaos and corruption, decline and decay!' Durwin and Canda always stood their ground and insisted that Terraprima was basically a good land and would eventually wend its way to a higher plateau. It would once again have life on a higher plane than ever before.

"Some years later, there were indications on the horizon that the Lawton's predictions of the renewal of Terraprima were evident. It was around that time Durwin secured a position as minister of a church in that land, as I mentioned last week in conjunction with their immigration problem. Before he entered into negotiations for it, he discussed it with a friend in Terraprima who somewhat understood Durwin's predicament with belittlers. Durwin inquired of his friend and was given the opinion that in no way would officials place him in a situation where a fine person like him would be mentally mutilated for what he was. The friend felt sure they would place him where he would be among people of his type. The friend's opinion was influenced by the fact that his area of the church was under sound leadership at the time.

"In addition to this, Durwin was very careful in his interviews and negotiations for the position, being careful at his age at the time to insure that he would have continuing membership in a pension plan, guarantee of employment, and access to disability benefits as did the long-time ministers of the denomination. He was offered a good salary, not quite as much as he had been making in Secundaterra, but adequate to enable his pension in Terraprima to be built up to a satisfactory level.

"He was also told at the time that he would be given standing in the denomination that guaranteed him employment until retirement. He would not have moved there were it otherwise. To risk being out of a job when he was too old to get anything else worthwhile, or, to jeopardize his pension at that age would not have been acceptable to Durwin. He was pleased with the good deal he was offered and accepted it. It would give him an opportunity to live in the land where individual initative, ingenuity, and hard work would be welcomed, so he thought. He was in for the shock of his life a little later on.

"The church to which Durwin went in Terraprima was located in a small suburban city. The church buildings were of white clap-board siding with a tall white steeple rising high over a large segment of the city. The city itself was built on a very flat plain that was filled with older type houses, also mainly of clean white paint appearance. The adequate lots around these homes were well studded with large trees, oak and maple, and beautiful shrubery. The newer parts of the city, further from the center, had more modern type houses of many different colors, but equally nice in appearance.

"The church was set back a hundred feet or so from the street, as was the minister's residence beside it. Both church buildings were notably in need of paint. The grounds around the church were not impressive. It was obvious they had been well planted at one time, as there were trees and shrubs in the right places, but they were not well kept. The shrubs were growing wild. The lawn had bare spots and looked badly in need of nutrition all over. The church-owned heavily treed vacant lot beside the church had grown wild, with no pruning, or clearing of underbrush. The church property on the whole was not by any means one of the nicer places of the community as Durwin thought it should be.

"Durwin decided at the start that he would try to do something about that as soon as possible. It would be one item of his infrastructure for church growth—to have the church buildings and grounds first class instead of among the shabbiest in the community. He could visualize a renewed church exterior standing tall over the already beautiful community, making it an imposing and impressive delight to the eye. He would try to bring it about. It needn't take much money to do so. The Lawtons were always very thrifty and innovative in ways that would get things accomplished with a minimum amount of spending.

"The church interior was a practical type of building for its purpose. It had a medium sized sanctuary—medium size in comparison to the general size of churches in the area, a fellowship hall, several classrooms, and a good size office. It was noticable that the sanctuary interior had very good appearance, having had work done on it recently. Durwin was to learn that there was an interior decorator in the congregation who had headed up some work on it. She had done an excellent job. There were other improvements that could be made, but for the time being it was quite satisfactory. The remainder of the church rooms, although not worked on in recent years, were in good enough condition.

"The interior of the minister's residence had had considerable repairs and cleaning done just prior to the Lawtons' arrival. They were grateful for that as it didn't always happen that way. Ministers' residences are often in sad disarray upon the arrival of a new minister.

"The congregation was made up of people of all ages and varied occupations in life. The lay-administrative body of the congregation was a mixture of men and women of the middle class and mostly middle age. Durwin's early calculated observation was that if the lay -administration of this church was co-operative and helpful there could be some growth ahead for the congregation. As Durwin saw it, it would take time to lay the infra structure for growth. If things went well for considerable time and belittlers didn't arise and take control it could be done, Durwin believed. A church never flourishes when belittlers are in control—never, not even when there are only some unchecked belittlers in key positions.

"A few weeks after their arrival in Terraprima, the Lawtons mailed change of address cards to friends and acquaintances in various parts of Secundaterra and Lower Secundaterra. Durwin soon received a letter from a friend in Secundaterra telling him he had made a grave mistake in going to the church in Terraprima. 'They will put a person like you down hard,' this friend wrote. 'You are in for a hard time. If you stay they will eventually ruin your life. Seeing you are already there, you should plan to stay only a short time, a year at most, and then return to some part of Secundaterra where you are known and will be treated better.' The writer of this letter went on to tell of the experinece of another fine person many years earlier who went to the church in Terraprima, but 'escaped' their wrath before much damage was done to him and his family. This person had returned to Secundaterra and a successful life.

"Durwin considered the letter seriously, and weighed the evidence in the light of his as yet brief experience in Terraprima. Nothing much had happened to him so far. *Perhaps only in certain areas of the country -would it be like as described in the letter, or, perhaps things have changed by now,* he reasoned. He and Canda decided to stay, for now at least, and to live and do their church work and prepare for the future as though they would be staying permanently as much as their circumstances, made tentative by the immigration problem, would allow.

"About eight months later, other friends visited Durwin and Canda in their new home in Terraprima. They brought with them a similar message, 'You may be in for a hard time with this denomination in Terraprima. It has happened before. Beware, it may happen to you. This church has a problem.'

"Durwin and Canda again weighed the matter. They were now several months into ministry there. Some belittlers had appeared on the horizon all right. There had been one especially peculiar incident which, even with all the Lawtons' experience, was new to them. I will describe it. Before Durwin had taken up his ministry in this church, a few of its members had left for other churches. Two or three months after Durwin arrived, one of these members came back one Sunday for worship. Durwin had an excellent worship service that Sunday. He had been there several Sundays now, long enough for most people to take a liking to his worship and pastoral care, so Durwin could tell his ministry was taking hold well.

"During the fellowship time that followed the service, Durwin approached this returned visitor to chat with him. Durwin was a person who could easily put another at ease, when the other person was responsive that is. This man was very up tight and Durwin could not thaw him out. He held his head high as though aloof. He was curt in his response to Durwin's attempts at conversation. Finally, the visitor, in cold, formal tones asked, 'Why don't you come and visit my place of work tomorrow? I will take you on a tour of the school in which I work.'

"'Fine,' replied Durwin, 'I would be very pleased to do so.'

"A time was set for the visit and tour next day, and Durwin was briefed on which office he should go to meet the school executive. Durwin was there on time next day. After a brief and blunt 'good morning,' the executive took Durwin's top coat, hung it up, and immediately said, 'Follow me.' Durwin thought it very strange, no introductory conversation, no remarks or comment on the school or on the tour that was to take place. *Well,* thought Durwin, *perhaps we 'll sit down for a chat after the tour.*

"So Durwin walked along with the man on the tour. His steps were long and fast for an indoor tour. *Perhaps his time is limited this morning,* thought Durwin. As they walked rather swiftly throughout the building the man explained this and that about it, its equipment, its services and curriculum, always in cold unfriendly tones. It was a large school, well equipped, with a large staff and student body. Durwin was impressed with that, but not with the conductor of the tour. Still Durwin tried to be friendly. However, when they arrived back at the office from which the tour had begun, Durwin was no sooner inside the door when he was curtly handed his coat again, with still no conversation except, 'Good-day, I hope you liked our school.'

"'It's a great school,' remarked Durwin with a smile, as he reached to shake hands with his tour guide. As the man shook hands, he grunted arrogantly and sarcastically at Durwin and turned away. Durwin just turned in the opposite direction and walked out of the building to the parking lot alone. He thought, at the time, that it was one of the most ignorant behaviors he had ever witnessed. Later, much later, he would learn that it is a ploy used in Terraprima by proud and envious belittlers to put others beneath them, at least in their own warped mind's eye."

"An absolute ignoramus," blurted Leo Aidan.

Gilda Emerson shook her head in disgust. "It's easy to see what it is all about. He became envious of Durwin at church, most likely of both Durwin as a person, and of his worship service, so he had to show Durwin he had better in his big school. He had an education, but no proper culture."

"A childish social illiterate," remarked Leo disgustedly.

"And he was an executive well up in the education field?" questioned Owen Winslow.

"Yes," said Collin.

Owen responded aghastly, "no doubt he has helped to educate many students, some good students too, but how many fine, well cultured, promising and would-be exceptional students has he damaged and/or ruined? Heaven help Terraprima!"

Collin continued, "As we get further into the story we will understand this incident more fully. Sufficient for me to say now that that man did not return to attending Durwin's church. Much later it would be implied that some families did not return because Durwin's ministry was not good enough. The reality is, Durwin and his ministry were too good for them.

"In addition to the incident just described, there were some minor signs of envy and belittling, but overall it was to date just a little worse than some congregations in the Secundaterras. As for the denomination at large, there were some peculiarities looming on the horizon there as well which seemed strange indeed. But given time, Durwin and Canda felt, they would better understand these peculiarities and find a way to cope with them. They both had analytical minds. They felt they would be able to cope. Besides, there were so many nice people around, the kind of people that had always caused them to stand up for Terraprima. Surely, with the majority of people so friendly, respectful, and appreciative of friendship, Durwin and Canda would get along well. Once again they decided to stay, and to live and plan their church work as though they were staying permanently. Durwin and Canda at this point in their lives could handle sporadic belittlers well. They felt sufficiently secure.

"Nevertheless, the letter and the visit from friends both bringing warnings to the Lawtons, caused them to reflect on still another incident. When they were making arrangements to leave the church at Secundaterra to go to Terraprima, a senior colleague remarked somberly to Durwin, 'We don't have any ministers from here go down to that denomination anymore. We have several who have gone down there to other denominations and done well, but not to that one,' he reemphasized as he shook his head gently, 'I wish you well.'"

"Some time later Durwin and Canda were to learn of yet another case, years earlier, where a minister coming from the church of Secundaterra was very badly used. I briefly mentioned his case before. He was a fine person, well cultured, and educated in two of the highest caliber seminaries of his time. His wife was equally a fine well cultured, well educated person. They were both gifted in many ways. The best appointments he could get from this church were the pits, where he and his wife didn't even have a fit place to live. This dedicated, well adjusted couple, since they were still young, and with plenty of time to start over, 'escaped' to another denomination with a different system of placement for ministers. In this denomination he did extremely well throughout his long ministry. Among other attainments he was responsible for the building of a very large mega-church complex from zero beginnings, of which he remained the senior minister for several years.

"I wish to add that this is not necessarily to say that one system of placement of ministers is better than another. I do not wish to get into that here. I will simply say it often depends on the character of the people operating the system, and what often long standing prides, prejudices and false concepts they are ruled by.

"From the very beginning of their arrival at their congregation in Terraprima, the Lawton's could not help but notice that generally the members were going all out to be friendly to them. Durwin had already heard that there had been a difficult relationship there with the previous minister. So he assumed they were determined that their relationship with him would be better. He and Canda responded with friendliness, kindness, and cooperation.

"Soon the life on a higher plane that Durwin and Canda always strived to promote began to rub off and take effect on many. For example, now when there was a fellowship meal served at church for any occasion, the tables were more daintly set, whereas near the beginning of their arrival they were rather slovenly placed. Worship was conducted in a semi-formal manner which allowed for inspiration that comes with an air of dignity, which in turn promotes the awesomeness of God's presence. Throughout the service, and particularly in the sermon, Durwin concentrated more on meaningful content than on highly animated and exciteable action. Most people liked his worship services and were spiritually moved by them. No later than his second Sunday there did he get an enormous response to them by parishoners.

"It became notable how people settled down in the pews when sermon time came. Again for example, one scholarly type woman, on Durwin's first Sunday there, scrutinized Durwin throughout the whole service. On the second Sunday clutching hymn book in hand, she did so again until about quarter ways into the sermon. Suddenly she relaxed, quickly placed the hymn book on the pew beside her, folded her arms loosely, settled down in the pew more comfortably, and with a smile that showed her pleasure, became totally absorbed in the sermon and the remainder of the service. After only two or three Sundays more of Durwin's ministry there, by far the majority of the congregation responded in a similarly positive manner. It remained so for approximately two years.

"As I mentioned before, during that time Durwin had occasion to request a letter of reference from the chief administrative officer of the church of the area. In the letter, this officer described Durwin's ministry as 'excellent'. At the same time, another letter from an official in high places who often acted on behalf of the church described his performance in all aspects of life as 'superior.' Still another official of the church at large with a position of responsibility remarked to a friend who passed it on to Durwin, 'whatever Durwin is doing in that church, tell him to keep on doing it.' The response to Durwin's ministry was excellent."

Collin paused as the group members listened intently for more. Then he broke the silence with a question, "How then, with a ministry like that did Durwin end up as he did, demoted and in future relegated to small country churches with little potential and a much smaller salary, and eventually so battered and maligned he had to find a way out of that area altogether?"

Leo, who had been listening with joy to the story of Durwin's brief success and who was now deflated at the obvious outcome, blurted out with his characteristic emotion, "I'll tell you how it happened, as if you don't already know,' he said angrily, 'the envious rotten belittlers went to work on him, and few if any of the others were wise to them."

"Right," said Collin. "In fact they started working on him not far from the beginning in a mild sort of way. In time it intensified, and then, when the belittlers could stand excellence no longer, they toppled him. And as you say, few others of the congregation were wise to them, so there was no understanding type of help for Durwin and Canda."

Gilda spoke, "I suppose the administration of the church area, with its bias, as it calls it, towards the so called 'little guy,' and their 'down with the so called big shots', dealt the final belittling blow to Durwin on behalf of the local church?"

"Yes, Gilda, it did," replied Collin.

"Inadvertently or otherwise, I suppose, "said Gilda.

"Inadvertently 'and' otherwise, I would say," added Collin, emphasizing the 'and'. "But you can make up your own minds about that yourselves as you hear Durwin's story."

Owen looked on in grim silence as a cloud of doubt enveloped his hope for his future. *Would he, or -would he not ever find a future where his gifted spirit would be free from the shackles of belittlers, he thought in his literary mind; a freedom that -would allow him to give to the world to his fullest extent the abundance it has to offer; freedom to receive what the world has in store for a person who gives his best—dignity, respect, acceptance, things like that; things that are a far cry from the oppression, rivalry and mental cruelty of belittlers.*

Collin read Owen's face. "Don't be too discouraged yet, Owen," he said. "You are young, and Terraprima is big. You have ample time to find your way. Durwin was older, and time ran out on him. It won't be a bed of roses for you, but you will learn from this group how to better your chances. Be optomistic, Owen. You have done well so far, haven't you?"

"Yes, I have," Owen said, as he perked up a little. "Sure, I have done well in spite of all the belittlers. And the cautious optimism that sometimes settles in on me will eventually replace my grave doubts and will in time serve me well. It won't be a shock to me now when I don't find that bed of roses."

"Good," said Collin as he smiled in return.

He continued, "Without further delay I will relate to you some of the devious trickery of the belittlers in the local church. At first the tactics were passive in nature, but later as Durwin made progress, passivity was replaced by hostility. The devious tactics of belittlers are numerous, so as I tell you the basics of the story of Durwin and Canda, I will include enough of them to give you a picture of the kind of life they were subjected to.

"As I mentioned earlier, the people of Durwin's congregation, having had difficulty with previous ministers, now had the desire to treat this one well and to get along with him. They had the desire, but not the character within them to do so. As the saying goes, 'they just didn't have it in them', as you will see.

"One of these, who held high office in the local church, said to Durwin on several occasions, in an overly nice manner, 'You are to be our leader now. We will be directed by you.' Durwin was pleased to hear that. So many churches want the minister to be the good little puppet on their string, so this was a pleasant beginning. Regardless though, Durwin knew enough to move slowly on any changes he wished to bring about. On another day, this same person in conversation with Durwin said, 'We want you to take a day off each week, why don't you take Mondays as your day off?'

"There were two reasons why Durwin was hesitant about taking Monday as his day off. The first he wasn't ready to discuss yet. It was because in time his wife would be taking a secular job, working Monday through Friday, and he would want to have Saturday free with her. Some congregations have an aversion to minister's wives working. Durwin would prepare the congregation for this in due time.

"The second reason Durwin had for not taking Monday as his day off was sufficient to discuss at the present time. He said to the person concerned, 'I would rather take my time to decide about my day off. As far as Mondays go, this church has practically all its meetings scheduled for Monday evenings. There may not be any reason to change that. Just give me a little time on it and I'll decide.'

"The man's face dropped. Obviously he hadn't given any previous thought to the fact that in that church Monday evenings were prime time for regularly scheduled church meetings of various committees. He turned and walked away without saying another word and never approached Durwin on that topic again. Durwin thought that strange.

"A little later a Bible study group was begun. The same man and his wife, together with many others, mostly from the local church administration were in the group which Durwin was leading. It was in this group, at the very first meeting, that the trouble, begun with the day off incident, began now to manifest itself for what it really was.

"The Bible study group met weekly. Each participant had a copy of a well known Bible study guide in which a particular book of the Bible was broken down into sections. Each section had a series of questions to which the participants could answer according as they understood a passage of scripture as it had been read by a member of the group. Durwin felt, and rightly so I would say, that his role in the group would be to intersperse the comments of the members with views presented by various biblical scholars and Bible commentaries on the scripture at hand. In this manner, participants wouldn't be limited to their own thoughts on a matter, but would have the expertise of the scholars to enrich and nurture their own views.

"The Bible commentaries used for this purpose would be writings easily understandable by the average lay person. In fact some of them were written expressly for lay people. Also Durwin's presentation of them would be easily understandable as were all his sermons.

"So a passage of Scripture was read and the discussion on it began. Durwin remained silent until the participants had ample time to express their views which in general were good and worthy. Then Durwin mentioned how one world renowned biblical scholar, calling him by name said such and such of that passage. The participant who had been so upset by the Monday as day off discussion came on angrily and restated what he had previously said of the passage, cutting Durwin down to silence. The man's wife looked at her husband in a hurt manner, calling him by name in a tone meant to bring him to discipline. He stuck to his position, repeated his statement on the passage again, perturbedly, to assert his statement. His wife was visibly upset and shaken.

"Durwin responded softly and as tactfully as possible. 'We will find, as we do Bible study, that there are different interpretations for many Bible passages, and what makes Bible study so interesting is that we can discuss these various interpretations and come to our own conclusions about them. That is what protestant Christian theology refers to as having the freedom to work out one's own salvation in Jesus Christ. One person may interpret a saying or incident concerning Jesus one way, and another person may interpret it another way. Both have the freedom to do that.

"A derogatory snort came from another man across the room. 'Ugh,' he snorted loudly in contempt as he glared at Durwin. The man who started it all also sat glaring with piercing eyes at Durwin. Durwin glanced around the room quickly and noticed that several other men and women were doing the same thing.

"The first man's wife was near tears. I'll read the next passage of Scripture,' she volunteered in an effort to save the situation. So she read, and then referred to the first question in the guide to initate discussion. But no discussion came. Durwin waited and waited, trying his best to avoid a repetition of the previous scene. They all remained silent.

"Durwin reasoned that perhaps, perhaps I say, since this is a difficult passage, it may be safe for him to speak. He put forward the views of two different scholars on the Scripture passage. The others made no comment on the topic at all. Apparently, since it was a difficult passage they were not willing to venture an opinion on it. So Durwin made a contrast and comparison between the views of the two Biblical scholars he had quoted.

"After that, Durwin decided to take a different approach. He would present the views of the biblical scholars on the topic at hand before the participants presented any of their views. Perhaps, he thought again, they felt inferior to the biblical scholars in comparsion to their own views, even though, in Durwins opinion they did present worthy views. And by presenting the views of the biblical scholars first, they then need not present any personal views that they would feel sensative about in comparison to the scholars.

"So Durwin tried this. Immediately after the reading of the Scripture passage, he began to present the views of the scholars and the commentaries. As he did so, he was twice angrily cut down with different views by the man who had started the trouble in the first place. Durwin knew now, that the problem did not lie in how the presentations were made. The man who started the trouble, as well as several others in the group had a problem with Durwin. He was too good for them. They couldn't stand him to have or express any opinions that were different from theirs. From then on, by inference they branded him as a know-it-all-smart-aleck.

"The name 'smart aleck' has connotations of such things as conceit, offensive assertion of oneself, cockiness. Durwin was anything but. He was a humble, self examining type of person, intelligent, but well charactered; smart, but not smart aleck. He very cautiously and sparingly used his intellect in dealing with others. The defamation of Durwin Lawton, and his highly intelligent wife Canda, had begun. It had begun in, of all places, a Bible study group.

"This Bible study group went on for several months, similar as I have described it; continuously tense, hostile and frigid. A recess for the Christmas season finally broke it up. It did not come back together after the holiday season. Of course, Durwin would be blamed for that.

"There you have a picture of the kind of people Durwin was dealing with and these were all well to do middle class people, well educated to varying degrees."

"How childish," said Gilda, "spoiled brats."

"Babies," quipped Leo.

"Hollow pride," commented Donna.

"Sick," said Albin, "and extremely over-sensative."

"They certainly didn't know how to respond to a higher intelligence or authority than their own, did they?" remarked Brett.

"Not in the least," responded Collin, "neither to the expertise of their trained minister, nor to the sound and widely accepted knowledge of the biblical scholars and their commentaries.

"A very notable aspect of this is their complete lack of knowledge and ability on how to interact with someone they perceived to be smarter or superior in some way to themselves. Of course that is somewhat of a problem for lots of people. As for these belittlers they were completely at a loss on the matter. It would be so simple for people like you and I."

"It's their problem, isn't it?" remarked Leo, "their shortcoming."

"Yes," responded Collin, "it is the mind-set they grew in, and their minds haven't budged on it since childhood. They learned, or more accurately, automatically took on from their parents, peers and a large portion of society, the distasteful characteristic of hating and being prejudiced against what is commonly referred to in their language as 'big shots' and 'smart alecks.' They are just that way automatically since childhood. They give no thought to the fact that they, in this era of education and opportunity for all people, are better off than many of the types of people they had learned to scorn when they were children and which they still scorn now.

"Again, it is worth noting," continued Collin, "that most of the people they label big shots and smart alecks are people whom you and I see as successful people. True, there are many seemingly successful, yet arrogant and otherwise questionable characters out there whom we would not endorse. But these people are not the ones the belittlers go after. Its the better quality people they like to bring down."

Brett quipped, "especially if they have been successful in business."

"Why in business?" asked Albin.

"That's easy, Albin," answered Brett, "belittlers like to bring down anyone in any occupation if they perceive them to be superior in certain ways. But my opinion is they come down harder on fine people who are successful in business. You will hear them say or imply that making money is wrong. Again, it is my opinion many of them say that because they haven't been successful at making money themselves, and they envy those who have. So they label us as bad guys, crooks, etc. but you should see how they go after money when the opportunity arises."

After Brett paused momentarily, he added, "of course the belittlers usually think the only reason a person is in business is to make money; greedy after money. That's a widespread notion in the church. What they don't entertain in their minds is that although we have to make money to stay in business, often our primary incentive is building and creating something that makes life worthwhile for ourselves and others.

"The minister or teacher aims high in their academic training to qualify them to go up the ladder of success in their chosen field. If they are successful the result is a higher position with a higher salary. You can't tell me they don't appreciate the higher salary. So it is with the business man. If he has good qualifications and well developed incentive he will build his business up to the highest his ability will allow. Sure this will earn more money for him. And he will appreciate it, just as the minister and teacher does. The principle is the same. In practice, the business man is likely to make more money than the minister or teacher, but that is no reason for envy and hatred. Each has freely chosen his own field.

"Besides, the good business man is not likely to hoard his profits. Chances are he will reinvest them and continue to build for the good of all. In my opinion, business people like that deserve high respect. But they reap the scorn of belittlers perhaps moreso than do the dubious greedy ones of the business world. There are ministers and teachers to whom I wouldn't want to send my family, as we have heard previously in this group. Likewise there are good and bad business people."

Collin replied positively to Brett's business perspective. "I agree with you one hundred percent, Brett. There is a lot of envy that lumps good business people like yourself in with the shabby and questionable business people, or even turns on the good business people, leaving the questionable ones alone. To me, business and money are gifts of God to be properly used by us. When so used they are a blessing to God's people. They can only be properly used by well charactered well meaning people. At a later session I will be discussing belittlers at work in the business and commerce of Terraprima, so I'm glad you mentioned it now. It is a good preview of some of what is yet to come. Keep the topic in mind for later."

"Thanks," said Brett, "I may have taken the group off track here. Let us get back to Durwin. Imagine that, he had to put up with abuse in the Bible study group for several months.

Owen added, "I can imagine the tension it produced for him. It must have been nerve racking."

"It would have been nerve racking for most people" replied Collin, "but not for Durwin. He had been dealing with belittlers all his life and could cope well with them. Yet, even though it didn't rack his nerves, it was extremely stressful. It got so that he didn't know when to speak and when not to speak. Either way it didn't please them.

"Tension there was aplenty," continued Collin, "it was now obvious to Durwin that this congregation was dominated by belittlers. Such churches never prosper nor get ahead. Durwin knew what he was up against, but his reputation with the larger church of the area was already established, with his ministry described as excellent and superior. Good reports were getting out from the congregation generally. So with that kind of back up, Durwin resolved to try to change the mind-set of the administration of his local church. Easier said than done! Their proud position would in time be observed in essence as, 'we are perfect as we are. Just give us the right minister and our church will floruish.'"

Collin went on with the story. "A second incident that set the stage of belittling in this congregation occurred simultaneously with the Bible study event. Even though the interior of the ministers residence had been put in top condition before the Lawtons' arrival, there had been no smoke detectors installed in it. It was a simple oversight, easy to happen, easy to remedy. Durwin and Canda both had experience with fires in their lifetime and knew what could happen. One of their main concerns was that the bedroom windows were high above the ground which in the event of fire would make escape through the windows hazardous even though they had a rope ladder type of contraption for that purpose. Early warning would allow for possible escape through the doors. They wanted smoke detectors installed. So at a meeting of the appropiate committee, Durwin asked that two smoke detectors be installed in the minister's residence at a cost of twelve dollars each, with volunteer installation by Durwin or by anyone else who wished to install them. It was a logical request, yet mouths dropped when it was made. The chairman of the committee sputtered out excuses, 'Well we have to consider our budget and be thrifty; I don't see any problem with that residence to cause a fire; there hasn't been a fire there yet; we have an excellent fire brigade in the area; you can have a rope ladder to exit through the windows.' Their undisciplined pride was ruling far, far above their reasoning.

"Durwin responded very gently so as not to ruffle that hollow pride any further, 'But we already have a rope ladder. We are just asking for earlier warning; two smoke detectors at a cost of twelve dollars each. I will install them myself.

"The chairman raised his voice in rebuttal, 'I will install the smoke detectors,' he said, as his chest came up and his pride took over. 'I am a member of a fire company. I can buy them at a discount,' he snapped as he asserted himself.

"A few days later this person arrived at the residence with the smoke detectors and screw driver. Durwin and Canda had already chosen the places to install them. They suggested it to the man. He became outwardly perturbed. 'No,' he snapped, 'I will place them here and here,' and immediately began to install one where the smoke on its way to the master bedroom would go up the ceiling fan opening before it reached the detector. Canda was quick to stand her ground. 'Look here, it's my life that's in the balance in this house and that smoke detector is going right where I say. Now leave it here and we will install it ourselves.' Durwin backed her up. But since it appears to many that a minister is not supposed to get angry, or even speak firmly, he did so less emphatically than did Canda. That was a maneuver Durwin and Canda had long ago learned in the ministry. They couldn't blame a minister for what his wife did or said. So Canda performed the task of firm assertion. Durwin reaffirmed her simply by saying calmly, while looking him straight in the face, 'we know what will make us feel safe.'

"There was no real relenting in the man's mind. In hostility he snapped, 'okay, I'll install them where you say. You can have your way.' He said it as though Durwin and Canda were people who wanted their own way all the time. He installed the smoke detectors near but not exactly where they suggested. He did the work hastily, and without finding a place where the screws would go into something solid. Consequently, before long one of them fell from the ceiling, and Durwin and Canda had to reinstall it themselves and patch needless holes in the ceiling.

"One of the damaging results of this incident was that almost the total administration of the church took up the position that the Lawtons were demanding type spendthrifts who would have to be watched carefully. This impeded Durwin's ministry among them greatly thereafter. The Lawton's, both of them, had always been thrifty over how church money was spent, just as they were over their own. The defamation of the Lawtons' characters was continuing."

Brett spoke in tones revealing his difficulty in fathoming such a personality. "You say, Collin, that this man was a member of a fire company?"

"Yes that is so," reaffirmed Collin.

"Then," said Brett, "he would certainly know the value of smoke detectors, wouldn't he?"

"Yes," said Collin again.

"Well," said Brett, "the man's pride was beyond all his reasoning powers. First he tried to deny the need for smoke detectors. Then he tried to install them in ineffective places. He was playing around with the Lawtons' lives. Then as important as it was he installed them carelessly so that the Lawton's had to do the job over. That kind of pride surely is ill founded, isn't it?"

"Grossly, I would say," replied Collin with a smile of approval for Brett's observations. "Grossly and more."

"And there is more," came in Gilda. "That man couldn't bring himself to admit a little oversight like smoke detectors, a minor thing really. His silly pride was in the way all right, so much so that life or death didn't matter. Moreover, the Lawtons' characters were damaged and their ministry impeded by the labels of 'demanding and spendthrifts'. They put the Lawtons down, or tried to, in order to gain a sense of superiority over them; a sense of superiority based not on performance or the like, but on pride alone, hollow, empty, undisciplined pride, based on nothing except the putting of someone else beneath them to make themselves feel good."

"That's it," replied Collin, "that's the way these people operate. They gain their false sense of superiority by belittling others around them whom they perceive to be a cut above them. They can't accept that they are not the most superior ones even though they may be very good. They make themselves feel superior in their own minds by finding reasons, valid or otherwise, to bring down the better people like the Lawtons. They cannot admit, even to themselves, that they are bringing them down because of their envy of them and because of their damaged pride. So they search for derogatory reasons to bring them down.

"In this case, the Lawtons were labeled spendthrifts in order to give the belittlers an excuse and to cover up the real reason for their bringing them down. If they can't find any excuses, they invent them, or twist some of the good characteristics of people like the Lawtons into bad characteristics. Also nobody is perfect, so they pick little holes in their victim's weaker areas. But worse still, they take every outstandingly good point about a person and twist it into something derogatory as I shall illustrate later. The better the person is, the more they will victimize him."

Collin looked at Gilda as he continued, "There is even more here than silly wounded pride, Gilda. Pride that has to put down and/or destroy another person is also riddled with envy and often results in hostility in various ways and to varying degrees."

Collin then looked around at the group. "I am going to quote two scholars to you now," he said with a grin. "I hope it is safe to do so in this group!"

"Careful," quipped Leo, "we may get perturbed." Collin smiled, "I'll take my chances with you people," then continued, "the renowned biblical scholar, William Barclay, in his Bible commentary, says of envy:

> 'There is a good and a bad envy. There is the envy which reveals to a man his own weakness and inadequacy, and which makes him eager to copy and to rise to some greater example. And there is the envy which is essentially a grudging thing. It looks at a fine person, and is not so much moved to aspire to that fineness, as to resent that the other person is fine. It is the most warped and twisted of human emotions.' *(The Daily Study Bible,* William Barclay - THE LETTER TO THE ROMANS. Page 28).

Collin then commented, "as we go on with our stories, we will see how the resentment to a fine person, mentioned by Barclay, issues in hostility, strife and rivalry. Barclay defined strife this way:

> 'The meaning is the contention which is born of envy, ambition, the desire for prestige, and place, and office and prominence. It comes from the heart in which there is jealousy. If a [person] man is cleansed of jealousy he has gone far to being cleansed of all that arouses contention and strife.' (Ibid).

Collin paused briefly, and spoke again, "Barclay adds this terrific sentence that needs to be drilled into the mind of every belittler:

> 'It is a God given gift to be able to take as much pleasure in the successes of others as in one's own.' (Ibid).

Collin added emphatically, "Therein lies the big problem of belittlers. They scorn rather than take pleasure in the successes of others; more especially the successes of fine people of whom they are envious. I'll just repeat that again:

> 'It is a God given gift to be able to take as much pleasure in the successes of others as in one's own.' (Ibid).

Collin continued. "Barclay makes another interesting comment which I quoted earlier and which needs emphasis because it is so adaptable to our cause. He is commenting on the Apostle Paul's exhortation to 'live at peace with all [people].' But, says Barclay, Paul points out that there are two biblical qualifications for living at peace with all people, (a) 'if it be possible,' and (b) 'as far as you can.' Barclay then adds,

> 'Paul knew very well that it is easier for some to live at peace than it is for others. He knew that one [person] can be compelled to control as much temper in an hour as another [person] in a lifetime. *(The Daily Study Bible,* William Barclay, THE LETTER TO THE ROMANS, page 184).

Collin added his own comments, "We can apply this passage or rule to the circumstances of people like you and I in our interaction with belittlers. We have to at times, and quite often, put up with more from belittlers with their undisciplined pride, envy, jealousy and strife, in an hour than some people do in a lifetime. With others, it may well indeed be a very occasional occurence. With us it becomes a way of life, almost continuous, always annoying, stressful and cruel.

"So let no psychiatrist, therapist, clergy person, supervisor, or other person tell you that you are just oversensitive to the little annoyances of life. The people who tell you that may very well have only little annoyances in their life, or they may have had only one or two larger annoyances throughout their lifetime, which they survived with limited hurt, and which they were eventually able to put behind them and go on to live peaceful lives. They will lightly tell you to do the same.

"Then again, the matter is often passed off as 'personality clash'—two opposing characters who cannot come to terms. That explanation is lacking in that it is the belittler, one person, who causes the trouble. And again, some envious belittlers themselves when confronted about the abuse they inflict on others, while trivializing the whole matter in doing so, will pass it off as just 'mean spirited.' In their pride they cannot bear to admit they are envious of someone else, because that would be an admission that the someone else is gifted better than they in some ways. Rather than admit to that they shrug it off lightly as just a little mean spirited, as though there wasn't much to it, and the recipient of it is too sensitive. In actuality, what is passed off as a little mean spirited is often brutal, and career, health and life damaging.

"The fact is, to paraphrase Barclay, we of our type have to put up with more envy in an hour than do some people in a lifetime. Personally, I have never known a time in my adult life when I wasn't dodging a person or persons who were trying to bring me down, with often a substantial number of people getting a kick out of them doing so. Many others in their naivete and unawareness just don't even see what is going on. It is a way of life for persons like you and I. It becomes a continuous and heavy burden to carry, particularly in our younger years. And like our friend and colleague Alban has illustrated since this group began, we sometimes snap under the cruel and oppressive load and are then labelled weaklings. This in turn plays into the hands of the belittlers and puts us down further. For me personally, the friendship of nice people who understand, even though often silently, helps tremendously to make the burden of the almost constant behavior of belittlers bearable and possible to cope with.

"But," said Collin, "we can discuss all that further later on if you wish. Now I wish to quote another scholar, Lance Webb and his book on the traditional sins of the church and of Christian theology. Webb sees envy as a by-product of pride, or what I prefer to tag misplaced or undisciplined pride.

> 'Each of the other six sins in a very definite way is a child of pride. Envy is self-love unable to permit anyone to excel or rise above one's own superiority, with resulting hate, jealousy, intolerance, prejudice, slander, gossip, and use of sarcasm or more violent means of leveling others to one's own height.' (Lance Webb: *CONQUERING THE SEVEN DEADLY SINS.* Page 41. Abingdon Press, 1955).

"This is a good definition," remarked Collin, "except that envious belittlers not only want to level us to their own height, they want to level us below their own height. They are often power and control people as well. It is not power and control for the sake and furtherance of the church, but rather an egotistical desire to satisfy something lacking in their own self-centered mind-set. They don't usually come across to us as people of power, but their sought after control over matters gives them a sense of being up there with the better natured, truly influencial people. Hence I feel right in referring to them as power and control freaks. When envy is present with this desire for power it makes them feel a need to feel superior to others around them, especially to fine, smart people. They cannot look up to us. They cannot be on the same level with us. They can only look down. They want to be on top. They feel they can only do so by putting down those whom they perceive to be above them. Their sick and twisted motto is, 'if I can't get them down, then I can't be up.' They have to put us below themselves so they can look down on us. They do this by some or all the means and more listed by Webb—'hate, jealousy, intolerance, prejudice, slander, gossip, and use of sarcasm or more violent means.' The devious deeds by which they put these weapons to work will be further illustrated in my presentation. "Webb reiterates and expands on his definition of envy:

> 'It includes those sins such as hate, intolerance, jealousy and prejudice, which are the result of my self-love seeking to keep an exalted place among my fellows and therefore unable to bear excellence or superiority on the

> part of others. The sin of envy also is seen to include the sins which result from my attempt to lower those who have risen above me to my own level; namely, slander, gossip, and sarcasm - the tools I use to get even.' (Lance Webb: *CONQUERING THE SEVEN DEADLY SINS.* P.58 Abingdon Press 1955.)

"I wish to add though," said Collin, "that the belittlers are often much more subtle than Webb states. They are crafty enough to avoid open slander, gossip and sarcasm. They often play the psychological mind-game and imply it. Some belittlers will even be outwardly nice to you while attempting through deception to lead you to destruction. Beware of the person who, while seeming to be nice to you outwardly—nice smiles, cheerful greetings, and all that—is attempting to lead you in questionable directions, perhaps by inuendo only. They are expert con artists at times. These are mind- games belittlers play—childish, to be sure, on their part—but it becomes a destructive weapon to victims who may not have sufficient awareness of it to discern what is happening to them.

"They mutilate the character and sometimes the mental health of their victims by derogatory hint and innuendo, or even by glance or other silent expression, all of which can be craftly covered when necessary, since they have stated nothing openly. If what they are doing is ever held up to them they can readily cover up and say they never said a word. Sometimes they imply that that person is never satisfied with what I try to do for him. I was just trying to be a friend. If they are openly accused of trickery, they can easily say, 'you took it all wrong,' or, 'you are imagining things,' or worse still, 'you are nuts -paranoid.'

"Furthermore, a belittler is never bothered by others suspecting him of this devious trickery. He thinks it is the smart way to be. To honest, open people it is deceitful and repulsive. But the belittler, as long as he is able to, in his own mind, rationalize and justify himself, he feels his constant ego trip, and consequently his hollow, undisciplined pride, are intact."

Collin commented further, "Webb has given us reasons why belittlers treat us the way they do; out of envy they have to whittle us down. Also, you can see why, the better the person is in the eyes of the envious ones, the more that person has to put up with the ravages of their envy."

Continuing, Collin said, "one more very worthy point of Webbs is, I believe, relevant to this story and should be taken note of. Webb states:

> 'Intellectual pride is the most difficult of all pride to displace.' (Lance Webb. *CONQUERING THE SEVEN DEADLY SINS,* page 48, Abingdon Press 1955).

"I am of the opinion," said Collin, "that this intellectual pride to which Webb refers is most prevalent in academic circles; among people whose chief pride and ego stems from the fact that they have a measure of attainment in the academic sphere. I will therefore refer to it as academic pride. I would emphasize first and foremost, and very readily that academically is not the only way to be an exceptional person, although many academics with a false sense of pride would have you think so. The world has known many exceptional people who either never had an opportunity, or, didn't have much interest in pursuing academics to its fullest. This is not to downplay the value of education. I think you will perceive for yourself as I continue, that I realize fully the place of quality education in life.

"Having said that, let me say, the truly educated person is humbled by genuine academic attainment, realizing how much he doesn't yet know and how much more there is to discover. The proud belittler has to have a feeling of superiority to go with his academic attainments, and often he has to put less educated people, or even more highly educated well charactered people, beneath him in order to, in his own mind, retain his sense of superiority.

"An amusing anecdote that has been passed around for years is 'a person, through his education and position in life, either grows or swells, one or the other.' The truly educated person, with his mind humbled and therefore open to a vast world of continuing knowledge, will grow to further spheres of personal development and attainments. The proud, egotistical belittler will continue to swell in hollow, undisciplined pride and a false sense of superiority. He will hold on to this sense of superiority not by further maturing growth, but by belittling and/or getting rid of any persons around him whom he perceives to be a threat to that sense of superiority.

"Actually, there is another difference between types of well educated people. There are those who, as they read, hear and absorb, also think through things for themselves, and formulate their own conclusions on the topics at hand. These people may or may not get top grades. If they do, they have a wonderful combination of learning, thinking through, assimilating, and truly taking to oneself the ingredients present for personal growth.

"In contrast to this, there is the other type; those who read, listen, absorb, and retain all the knowledge imparted to them. They have perhaps excellent absorption and retention abilities. Consequently, they get high grades, some very high, perhaps even higher than many in the aforementioned group. However, they develop little or no thinking ability along the way, only the retention of facts. A colloquial saying sums it up: 'They couldn't think their way out of a wet paper bag!'

"Belittlers in this category are the worst kind. They envy others, paricularly those with less formal education than they, who have the ability to think through old problems and resolve them, or come up with new ideas. The belittlers have learned mainly by rote and memory retention. When they can look up the solution to a problem in a book, they shine. To come up with an original solution or idea is for the most part beyond them. Therefore, out of undisciplined pride and envy, many of them become the most vicious of those who practice belittling."

"I am of the opinion," said Collin, "that academic pride accounts for the major portion of Durwin Lawton's belittlement coming from many but not all of the teachers in his congregation and many of the other ministers he tried to work with in the greater church. These are the people educated to do the educating. When their undisciplined pride and false sense of superiority is in the way, fine, smart people in particular are at risk when either intentionally or unintentionally we teach them something they didn't know before about the church and its functioning. They believe that they are all right as they are, and have built up a great deal of undisciplined pride on that belief. Later I will illustrate some of their reactions towards exceptional people like the Lawtons who unintentionally upset that pride by performing a very effective ministry that didn't fit the preconceived and familiar ideas of the belittlers' own choosing.

"Belittlers, both in the local church and the wider church have their field day with exceptional ministers, or members, whom they want out of the way. This destructive vice is more skillfully developed in the church denomination in which Durwin Lawton was involved in Terraprima, than anywhere else I have ever heard of or experienced. This will be further illustrated in the continuing story of Durwin Lawton and his wife Canda. I wish to add also, that such mind-games are frequently utilized by belittling teachers in schools, where young students are at their mercy; also it is a widespread disease in industry and business, where in many cases owners and/or management do not know what is going wrong with their business. These things will also be illustrated as my story of the Lawtons in Terraprima continues.

"Webb further states:

> 'Even among sincere religious persons who want to "help others" and "do a great deal of good," this prideful self picture insists: 'The good must be done through me. I must be the center of attention.' (Ibid. P. 41)

"Durwin was eventually handicapped almost completely by members of the administration of his congregation who would not allow any progress unless they could take credit for it; hence the strife and rivalry continuously. This is not to say that people should not feel good about helping others or doing church work. Durwin always, and without fail, encouraged others to do things their own way in church activities, provided it was within the bounds of church polity. It had always been the policy of Durwin to encourage the laity to use their own creativity in church activities and administration. The problem Durwin had was when the belittlers blocked him at every turn from doing his ministry his way and using his creativity. If the church was going to improve and grow, it had to be by their hand, and not Durwin's, not any part of it."

"There is one other book I would bring to your attention before we go on with the sad story of the Lawtons. That book is simply the Dictionary. As you no doubt already know, the dictionary has two different meanings for the word pride:

'1. An undue sense of one's own superiority; arrogance, conceit.
2. A proper sense of personal dignity and worth.' *(Funk & Wagnalls Standard Desk Dictionary.* New York, 1975).

"'Pride' and 'proud' are very commonly used words today, especially in Terraprima where it is quite acceptable and the thing to do, to say one is proud of oneself or of someone or something else. To take pride in something worthwhile is considered good decorum. This corresponds with the meaning, 'A proper sense of personal dignity and worth.' That is good. But people who keep up an undisciplined, false, or empty pride by belittling others are establishing that 'undue sense of one's own superiority.' A person cannot be superior to another if he has to put that other person down in order to feel superior. That would be false, empty, improperly developed pride.

"Now this false, empty, or undisciplined pride, as I will refer to it in future story telling, is wayward pride, established upon 'an undue sense of one's own superiority.' It is conceited and often arrogant, as is stated in the first dictionary meaning I quoted. Being proud this way is a false, undisciplined, hollow pride, and it is easily pricked.

"Belittlers, as much as pride is a part of their life, are not willing to share in the pride of another, especially when they perceive that other person to be a cut above them. Going further afield, they are not willing to recognize that other peoples and other countries have their reasons to feel proud, and that we should at times acknowledge that some of their accomplishments may be greater than ours. Belittlers are wanting, not just sometimes, not even most of the time, but always, to be first and out front, which is not so and cannot be. They are not willing to let others have the credit that is due them, but wanting it all for oneself or one's own country. People like these, although a minority, are the ones who have caused people, even in the well developed and generally friendly parts of the world to cry out to Americans,'Yankee go home, Yankee go home, we don't like you.' It doesn't have to be that way. It can easily be corrected by omitting the belittling and giving credit where credit is due.

"Of course there are the less friendly and usually less developed countries that have a more harsh envy and hatred for the United States that cannot be corrected in such a peaceful manner. It is of a different strain, intermingled with much evil and ignorance and/or a different philosophy of life, and often a grave disregard for civilization as most of the world knows it. This kind of envy and hatred responds only to strict curtailment and strong discipline.

"But as for the first mentioned kind, belittlers in the media have been among the foremost of those who cause this reaction in various parts of the world. For example, they do a write up on another land. The first mistake they make is they compare it to the better parts of America; or worse still, compare a rural part of it to a very large and progressive city in which they themselves perhaps live, instead of seeing that land for what it is in itself. From there they concentrate on the down side of that land, barely or not at all mentioning its better side. Their pride and envy won't allow them to mention anything in it that may be better than anything in the United States of America.

"I have seen write ups, with pictures, of other lands which would give you the impression that there is absolutely nothing good at all about that country. But having either lived or visited extensively in that land we can know differently. To take one case in point, there was an article with pictures of a remote land with many problems indeed. The article concentrated on the land's remoteness and the problems of its main city. What the article failed to acknowledge in any way was that most of the people of that city had a standard of living as good as the average in the United States. No credit was given for this.

"Of course, the United States has its better side, its world leading side, no doubt about it. But some other lands have their better side too; sometimes a leading side if ever so small. Some belittling Terraprima media people cannot acknowledge this in their articles. It is as if someone were with pen and camera, to tour one of the poorer areas of the United States, add a few pictures of the less desirable parts of some major city; then in another not very geographically knowledgable country, publish the article saying this is the United States of America.

"Belittling media who try to promote their own country as superior by belittling other countries, succeed in doing so only in their own mind and in the eyes of some of their own people. In the eyes of the people they write about they diminish it. Belittlers in the media, and belittling tourists as well, are a disgrace to, and do disgrace their own country when they cannot, because of undisciplined pride, acknowledge the things about other countries that may be as good or better than their own. They bring on the 'Yankee go home' syndrome. The media needs to give credit where credit is due. People of other lands also need to have 'a proper sense of personal dignity and worth.' (Ibid).

"Belittlers in many walks of life are the dominant force and influence in some parts of the United States. The part I speak of as Terraprima is one of the parts in which they are a powerful and controlling factor.

"People who practice belittling behave as though they are quite justified in doing so. Occasionally, when their true colors are showing through, you may hear them mutter, 'O well I have my pride to keep up.' So they feel quite justified in putting others down. The trouble with that is that when carried out on a sufficiently large scale, as it often is, it robs other people of their right to feel properly proud of themselves, with 'a proper', not a false, but 'a proper sense of personal dignity and worth.'

"There are some proud ones who do not belittle, but only pout when their pride is hurt by the attainments of others. These may readily admit that their pride has been pricked. These people may not be harmful, but nevertheless it goes to show the great need for people to learn to accept and co-exist in a friendly, peaceful manner with people they perceive to be a cut above themselves in one or more ways.

"I have often wished," said Collin, "that linguists would take such a word as pride, trace it back to its origins in our own or some other language, and find two separate, usable words for the two different meanings; to invent or re-invent a new name for at least one of the meanings. In that manner, each of these two human characteristics could have its own distinct name.

"Christian scholars have almost accomplished a similar feat by dividing the English word 'love' into the Greek words 'eras', 'philia' and 'agape,' three very different aspects of love, with agape being the most noble of them all to Christians. However, the word agape is not adaptable enough to the English language, nor appealing enough to the average person to be commonly used."

Collin added, "While we are focused on the dictionary, let us look very briefly at what the dictionary says about the word 'envy.' The meaning given for envy is:

> '1. A feeling of resentment or discontent over another's superior attainments, endowments or possessions.' *(Funk & Wagnalls Standard Desk Dictionary,* New York 1975, P.213).

"Once again then we are told it is a wayward characteristic, or as Barclay says, 'the most warped and twisted of human emotions,' aimed at superior people.

"To touch on Christian theology for a moment, one would think that Christians would be very conscious and wary of being envious, for it was out of envy that Jesus was crucified. As I have said before, Matthew in his Gospel (27:18 RSV) writes, 'For he (Pilate) knew that it was out of envy that they had delivered him (Jesus) up.' "Some modern socialist would be theologians, and social activists warped by the bias commonly found in a segment of the church of these times, claim Jesus was crucified because he radically upset the established political and economic establishment of his time. Traditional theology of the centuries tells us, and I believe accurately, that Jesus put forward no political or economic systems. "Of course, most of the world, myself most certainly included, believes that democratic systems work better than other systems. Nevertheless, any democratic system can only be as good as the people running it and living in it. Jesus' main goal was to make it possible for people to be better people. That, in turn, would make the system work better. He showed them how and gave them the spirit to be better people.

"Matthew writes in his Gospel (Matthew 27:18 RSV) that, Pilate 'knew that it was out of envy' that Jesus was delivered to be crucified. If Matthew didn't agree with Pilate on that, he would not have written it the way he did. He might have said Pilate 'thought' that it was out of envy. But no, Matthew writes, Pilate 'knew' indicating that Matthew himself agreed with Pilate on that particular matter. Neither would Mark in his Gospel (15:10 RSV) have written likewise if he didn't believe it to be so."

"This explanation may seem oversimplified amid all the theological speculation there is about the matter. But it is still the basic reason for Jesus crucifixion, and the only reason that is explicit in the Bible. Furthermore, it wasn't simply a matter of Jewish people being down on Jesus. It was the envious religious leaders of that time who were down on Him, just as some religious leaders of present time Terraprima, Christian though they claim, are down on fine, exceptional people of today.

After a pause, Collin then concluded that topic by adding, "Since this is not a Bible study or theology class, I don't think I need to pursue this particular issue further. I hope I have made my point to this group."

"You have for me," responded Gilda, "Christians should indeed have an aversion to envy. No need for more detail as far as I am concerned."

The others agreed. Dr. Eldren smiled and nodded approval.

Collin looked at his watch, then spoke again. "This session has been heavy going with quotations and definitions, as well as the behavior of belittlers. I think this would be a good time to end it for this evening if that is okay, Dr. Eldren?"

"About right for me," replied Dr. Eldren, and he soon left for other work.

The group members agreed to proceed to the Corner Coffee Shop after connecting with Vita Seldon on the way.

CHAPTER IV

The following week the support group came together again, eager to hear more about the mind-game playing belittlers of Terraprima. Collin resumed the story immediately after the usual good evening courtesies.

"This evening" he began, "we will have more incidents pertaining to the life of the Lawtons in their congregation in Terraprima; the continued belittling of the ministry described as excellent and superior that Durwin was giving them regardless, and as he did, the attempts at belittling becoming more openly offensive, as opposed to that of a hitherto more passive belittling.

"I mentioned previously that the church landscaping hadn't been well cared for, and that it was a part of Durwin's general plan for the church to improve it. He asked for a Saturday morning work bee to do so. Several people turned up for it. Durwin and Canda were very much accustomed to such work. They brought along some tools among which was a full size bow or buck saw to use for cutting off the large lower limbs of big trees in the vacant lot.

"One of the men, using the saw, began to cut off a limb about two to three inches in diameter. He had to reach up to that limb with the saw. Consequently he sawed into it from its side rather than its top. About two thirds of the way through, the weight of the limb caused it to snap at the saw mark, but only partly. The result was the saw blade was critically jammed in the cut. Durwin saw the predicament and the possibility of the saw blade being broken.

"It became obvious as the man twisted frantically to free the blade, that he was not used to this kind of work. Durwin rushed to his aid. 'Hold it,' said Durwin calmly and helpfully, 'you have to push that limb back up into its original place before you can get the saw out without breaking the blade. The man's face immediately grew somber with the corners of his mouth dropping noticably as though Durwin had done him some grave injustice.

"One would think I had shot his very dear mother, thought Durwin as he saw the man's face so disdraught. Then he quickly said to the man in as relaxed a manner as he could under the tension, 'well I guess I

know these things because I grew up with lots of forest around me. It was a part of our growing up to learn the techniques of things like this such as they are.'

"The man's countenance did not change an iota. Durwin immediately added, 'I guess you can teach me lots of things you learned in the environment in which you grew up.'

"Still there was no change in the man's face. Durwin grabbed a rake, pushed up the limb which in turn freed the saw blade. The man pulled the saw down, handed it to Durwin and walked away, far too proud and oversensitive to handle such a situation rationally. He never worked with the saw or near Durwin for the remainder of the day.

"But there was a lot of good work done that day. Durwin and Canda did much of it, because as I said, they were accustomed to that kind of work. Some people appreciated it. However, the mood of the man who tried to work with the saw spread through a portion of the work team. It would be hard to get them back again to continue and finish that particular job of tidying the landscape. In fact it would prove impossible with some of them. Later, much later, Durwin and Canda would continue the job themselves, much to their own detriment. I will tell you the details later. For now I wish to point out how sensitive was the pride of these people."

"Hollow, undisciplined pride again," remarked Donna Coyne. "Hollow, but with a stubborn enough crust not to let anything new enter into their minds."

"Childish enough not to let anyone be superior even in such a little way as cutting a limb off a tree," added Gilda Emerson.

"And to think," said Albin Anders, "that a psychiatrist tried to tell me I was too sensitive to the slights of other people. What about the sensitivity of these people?"

"Right you are, Albin," said Collin. "You remember that in future if someone tries to make you believe you are too sensitive to a few slights from belittlers. The slights are many, and often so subtle they can hardly be described. They are even sometimes hard to decipher from things that well meaning people say and do to you. These subtle slights are delivered by people so sensitive that the least little thing will trigger off their pride and envy and all the harm they can inflict because of it."

"Well taken," said Albin confidently.

"But be sure, Albin," Collin cautioned, "to learn and practice discerning the well meant remarks and overtures of good people from the often subtle, sly, underhanded belittlements of those who mean to bring you down. We all make mistakes in this. It isn't always easy. But a true friend will make allowances for mistakes of that kind, especially after you have yourself recognized it."

"Thanks Collin," said Albin appreciatively, "that's very helpful."

"You're very welcome, Albin, and now let's get on with the story," said Collin. "One day Durwin received a telephone call from the chairperson of the board of a large not-for-profit community organization that did some of their work with the cooperation of the churches. This chairperson asked Durwin if he would serve as a member of the board of directors of the organization. Durwin was still feeling new to the situation and wanted to please his church board to whatever degree possible without losing his own personhood. So he told the man he would talk it over with the appropriate committee of his church.

"When he next met with the committee whose duty it was to assist the minister to plan his work and priorities, he brought the matter before them. They stalled and avoided a decision on it. They said they would think it over and let him know at the next meeting. At the next meeting they told him they had decided he shouldn't accept the position. There might be a conflict of interest with the church."

Gilda interrupted the story. "So they made their decision between meetings and away from Durwin's presence did they?"

"Yes, they did," replied Collin, "and Durwin wasn't ready to quarrel with them or put them in their place yet. So he dropped the matter and informed the chairperson of the organization that he wouldn't be accepting the position."

"Too bad," said Gilda, "I think he should have gone ahead."

"Well," said Brett Culver, "I think he shouldn't have even consulted the committee on it."

"I know how you can feel that way folks," responded Collin, "but a minister's life and work is supposed to be supported and helped by committees and boards. Durwin thought at the time they would support him on it. It would have been a good thing for the church to have its minister serving in the community. In hind-sight he later realized he should have gone ahead with it without asking. But take note that before a year was up, several of the church committee members were serving on the board of that same organization."

"Ha, Ha," said Leo, laughingly, "no conflict of interest with the church now."

"Not a bit," said Collin disgustedly, "but to them it now meant they had outsmarted Durwin and were superior to him again. However, before long another organization not connected with the church, the area chapter of the Red Cross contacted Durwin to sit on one of its boards which met weekly for a luncheon, followed by the work of reviewing hundreds of applications for assistance to needy people sent in from several counties. This committee was especially busy during the colder months. Without discussing it with his church committee Durwin served on this Red Cross committee for more than a year and a half. He served it well and regularly without any absence and was asked to continue. He left it only when he needed the time to pursue a demanding continuing education course that would help people with a different need and further the work of his local church. I will elaborate on that shortly."

Continuing with the story, Collin led the group into another incident. "Durwin could see that at least for the present he could make no more headway with the beautification of the church exterior property. He would approach the matter again at a later date. In the meantime he turned to another aspect of preparing the infra-structure for church growth. This also would be one of the more secondary preparations, as was the tidying of the land.

"As it was, the local church newsletter and the Sunday worship bulletin were third rate productions; scrappy looking to say the least. These could be greatly improved with the use of a photo copier and the tasteful and creative use of clip art. In addition, from his exceptionally large collection of books and various church resources, Durwin was accustomed to utilizing litanies and other items of worship and also keeping files of ideas from these resources. Durwin was one to spend a great deal of his own money on worthwhile church resources. He was a firm believer in the business slogan, 'you have to spend money to make money,' so he had long ago adapted this slogan to church work. He didn't see church as a business, but the same basic rule that applied for any undertaking would also apply to the church. That is, if you want to get good results which in the church would be spiritual results, you have to put good things into it: self, money, et al, with sacrifice when necessary. Consequently, Durwin didn't spare anything in that direction when it was for a worthy cause. Of course he had excellent discernment as to what was good and not so good in that regard. Anyway, Durwin badly needed a photocopier to help keep up his high caliber worship.

"Furthermore, the church at large in its interaction with the local congregations was becoming more and more geared to the local congregation having a photo copier. This was before computers were commonly used in churches. There were numerous items that could be photo copied and distributed to the church board and committee members and at times to the whole congregation. Communication of various sorts could be greatly improved with the use of a photo copier. Presently Durwin was treking to the shops to use commercial copiers for various purposes, again using his own money, which he didn't mind doing. But it was inconvenient time wise and so on, as you can imagine.

"At a meeting of the local church board, Durwin spoke of the opportunity to buy a photo copier from an assortment of models rebuilt by the manufacturer and with a full warranty for a year, at an affordable price. The church finances were in good condition at the time, as a result of Durwin's good quality ministry. As he began to explain why a copier was needed, he was cut down briskly by several members. They glanced around subtly at one another. 'We have no plans to buy a photo copier,' said one leading member curtly. 'We see no need for a photo copier,' said the next one firmly. Durwin tried to explain the need. 'We have no money to spend on a photocopier,' said the next person, cutting Durwin off from speaking, and brushing the whole matter aside by bringing up discussion about another topic altogether.

"There had been no debate as to the needs or pros and cons of a photo copier. It was as though their minds were previously made up. Yet there had been no previous mention of buying a photo copier.

Durwin could only assume at the time, that since they had already made up their minds that he was a spendthrift, they would never entertain any idea of allowing Durwin to spend 'their' money. This assumption would be further adjusted in Durwin's mind later on when he became more familiar with the full force of the many devious tactics of belittlers in Terraprima. He would then realize that they didn't intend to let him accomplish anything in their church, period, money involved or not.

"Durwin and Canda pondered many times how they might break through the crust these people had built around themselves; a crust of undisciplined pride which they were determined to protect no matter what, even when it short-changed their church. The Lawtons decided to temporarily put aside any ideas for significant change of any kind in the church. They would move more slowly in that regard—move more gradually, giving the board and committee members more time to adjust and adapt to change. They would try to socialize with these people, hoping to eventually break through and befriend them.

"Before long, an opportunity arose. There was to be a special event at a school, in which many of the congregation's children were participating. Durwin and Canda showed an interest in attending. The woman who had done the good, though incomplete job of decorating the church sanctuary interior had been showing some signs of initative in her own way lately. 'If you would like to go to the event,' she said half-heartedly and passively, 'I will get some tickets for you when we get ours."

"'Good,' said Durwin. 'we'd love to go.'

"The Lawtons were later informed that the tickets had been obtained. They were to meet the woman at the auditorium door at a set time. She would have the tickets with her, and since she knew the seat number arrangements would be able to show them to their seats. The Lawtons thought they were getting somewhere at last. They arrived on time. The woman was there, together with a group of parents from the inner church circle. The Lawtons were immediately taken to their two seats located in the center of a block of seats. They sat down expecting the group to sit down as well. But then the whole group of a dozen or so moved en masse across the aisle and sat together in the center of another block of seats, but on the other side of the auditorium. A small number of people unfamiliar to the Lawtons did come and sit here and there in the vicinity of them, but the Lawtons were isolated from their church members, and not due to lack of seating space in either of the blocks of seats.

"Over in the other block of seats, far removed from the Lawtons, the woman who had purchased the tickets sat in the center of the group of, as I said, a dozen or so. There she made herself the center of attention with her loud and showy mannerism. It became obvious to the Lawtons why she didn't want them sitting with the group. She was in competition with the minister and his wife for first place in the congregation.

"Over a period of time this woman with a problem did build up a following for herself, mainly by putting the minister and his wife down by complaining about them and their work. In order to build herself up to first place she created discontent over the minister. Her fellow belittlers, of course, fell right in with her as did a few others. They pursued with vigor their long-standing, wayward policy of 'give us the right preacher and *we* will build up this church.' They weren't looking for a minister who by his preaching, pastoral care and leadership of laity combined would build up the church. The attitude was, 'just give us the right minister, and we will build up the church.' It cannot work that way. It simply cannot be done. For one thing, over the years, the 'right' minister had never come. The fact is, the right minister for such a church as that does not exist and never has.

"The majority of this, as well as any other congregation, want the minister to be the focal point of ministry, and not by making himself or herself the center of attention either. He is to do it by drawing people's attention past himself to God. The majority of people of this congregation believed Durwin was doing just that. The belittlers were in rivalry with it. If this church was to be built up, they wanted the credit for doing so."

"Durwin had a person with a real problem personality there didn't he?" remarked Owen.

"Yes," replied Collin, "and with her ignorance, snobbery and belittling, she would later cause him much trouble. And she wasn't alone. As we discussed earlier in the sessions, birds of a feather flock together. They were in a minority but in this denomination of Terraprima they would get their way. Needless to say, the denomination was in decline in this area, numerically as well as in quality.

"As time went on, the Lawtons made every attempt to socialize with these people in events in and outside of church. But always they were kept on the periphery of this ingrown little society in which most of the church administration had encrusted itself. The Lawtons showed themselves to be quite capable socially in other spheres, as we shall see. But they could make no headway with it in this sick, misdirected church. And it wasn't the whole congregation that was sick. Neither was it the entire administration. It was those in control of its administration. Power and control was their way of life. It boosted their pride, which in turn was protected by their envious strife and rivalry. When this scenario was, in their minds, interfered with, by good well meaning people like the Lawtons, it turned to rivalry and enmity.

"The Lawtons continued trying to participate in the social activities of the church, but were always involuntarily placed on the periphery of everything by the near social illiteracy and ignorance of these people. At least, that is how the Lawtons saw it then. In time they would learn there was more to it. Meanwhile they decided to make yet another different thrust. They would participate in activities outside the congregation, as much as time would allow, in order to preserve their own sociability and their reputation as sociable people. This could also be good for the church, for the Lawtons would make good friends and acquaintances in the area, which in turn could make friends for the church, giving it a positive image in the community. Such an image had been, from the beginning, a part of Durwin's planned infra-structure for growth—to make his church a first rate organization in the community, creating the concept of a church on the move.

"The belittlers wouldn't see it that way. Their mind-set wasn't capable of such a view. In time it would be evident they would see the minister as wasting his time and their money. They would see it that way because that's the way they wanted to picture it for themselves and others for their devious purposes of belittling Durwin and also brainwashing him into thinking he was not giving a satisfactory ministry.

"Later in the story, I will concentrate on Canda's part more fully. For the present, let us look more closely at Durwin's ministry. It was now obvious that he wasn't going to have much cooperation from most of the church officers. So, at least for the present, he put aside any hope of that. The congregation at large was unaware of the ill treatment Durwin and Canda were getting from the board members. So his reputation as a good minister was still intact in the public eye. It was from the congregation at large that Durwin was getting the name of an excellent minister, superior in quality. Concerning his personal ministry, Durwin's two main thrusts had always been, first, meaningful and inspiring worship services, and secondly, expert pastoral care. In his previous pastorates he had established excellent ministries in these fields. Regardless of the lack of cooperation on the part of the church administration he would continue to concentrate on these.

"Durwin's worship services were already well appreciated by the majority of the congregation. He had already established a satisfactory and well received visitation program to peoples' homes where needed and wanted, and to hospitals and nursing homes. It was difficult to visit many private homes where both husband and wife were out to work, and where the weekends were busy with family chores and church. As usual, he left these people to visiting when there was an invitation to do so. There were some such invitations, but none from the belittlers. He would only be in their homes when a church gathering of some sort was held there. That seemed to satisfy everyone for the present. Later, when there was a concerted effort to put Durwin down and get rid of him he would be accused by them of never visiting them in their homes, and the proverbial 'the minister doesn't do enough visitng.' The fact is that Durwin, in his ministry of the past and the present, had always done far more visiting than most ministers do.

"Durwin had received considerable high caliber training in pastoral care at seminary some years earlier. He now decided to update by enrolling in a two year part time course in psychology, pastoral care and short term counseling. Included in this course, as a necessity to understanding others, was a course in self awareness and self improvement. Durwin had always been open to things like that. As I said before, he was a moderately self-examining type of person. So each Monday, Durwin was off to the big city for a full day of school. At least for a time, it turned out to be a bright spot in a life that otherwise was becoming gradually more difficult.

"Durwin would now get further expert training for his pastoral duties. This was an area of his personal ministry he would concentrate on. Another church in the area was concentrating on its mission to the poor and underprivileged. It was conveniently located for that. Still another church in the area concentrated on programs for families of middle class people. This church was also conveniently located for its chosen ministry. Durwin had no desire to imitate these churches per se. They were doing effective work. His own church was doing a little of each; that is, helping the poor, and ministering to the middle class, but these other churches each were specializing in one of these areas.

"Durwin's idea was to have his area of specialization in the field of pastoral care to people within and without the congregation; a place where people could come for consultation, perhaps short term counseling, and if necessary be referred to expert longer term counseling with a pastoral therapist or secular counselor as requested. He knew he could expect no cooperation from the church administration. But this he could do on his own. He knew he could do it well. Perhaps, he dared to hope, he could save his personal ministry in this church and prosper the congregation as well."

Collin, changing the emphasis temporarily, continued, "you may have noticed that to date Durwin's troubles with the belittlers of his congregation's administration were mainly that the belittlers were for the most part backing away from him with pouting and disgruntlement. There was only a little offensive action here and there on their part. As you listen you may be inclined to think that they were merely afraid of Durwin because of their feelings of inferiority and the uneasiness it brought them. And under that circumstance Durwin would be free to go ahead with his own personal ministry of preaching and pastoral care. Well, I ask you to keep that thought in mind and let's see what happens when Durwin launches out with his program. We shall see that belittlers in the Terraprima church, when desperate to hold on to their undisciplined pride and the sense of power and control it gives them, will go to deep unchristian depths to preserve it. When the chips look down to them, passivity changes to offensive hostility.

"I would ask you to bring to mind again the person who had directed the re-decoration of the interior of the church sanctuary, and also had obtained the tickets for Durwin and Canda to attend the school event. Now she was showing leadership in church events generally, and making an increased effort to do things more efficiently and on a higher plain. For example, where food was involved, tables were now set more daintly. More planning was going into women's activities. Even though she was working quite independently of the minister she was taking more initative around the church. Durwin noticed this and appreciated it.

"After some consideration, he thought that perhaps he could get through to her over a period of time, and without interferring with her zeal and initative he could steer her into being a compatable officer of the church. When a new chairperson of the board was needed, she was, in Durwin's opinion, the most effective prospect. There really wasn't a non-belittler willing to take it on. They were mistakenly feeling inferior to the proud and belittling power and control people. Durwin recommended her and she was elected to the office. *Perhaps, thought Durwin, where the belittlers on the board won't cooperate with me, they may cooperate with her, and we will get improvement in some things at least.* In future, I will refer to this woman simply as the chairperson.

"It became obvious that it was a big step for the new chairperson. She was nervous and awkward at her first meetings. Durwin gave her pointers and coaching about conducting meetings and about her duties as chairperson. This he did unobtrusively through brief conversations, often just a word or two here and there, and in ways unnoticed by others. She learned from it and soon was doing the basic task well, but in time showed even less desire to align her work in cooperation with the minister's plans for the church. To use an analogy, she became more like an immature and overly prideful adolescent who was rebelling and becoming more independent than was good for her or her family. In this case the family was the local church. Later, she would actually turn on Durwin.

"As I mentioned a few minutes ago, Durwin was now attending school one day each week. He was receiving training in pastoral care and short term counseling, and was involved in a peer group where personal problems of life and ministry were meant to be explored. The two facets were planned to compliment each other in this program. On another night I will review in more detail Durwin's experiences in continuing education in this and other schools. It is sufficient to say now that for the most part and especially early on, Durwin was mostly well received and as far as he knows, highly regarded by most people in this school. He did well there and it launched him on his pastoral care program for his church. By coincidence, some very complex, even dangerous cases came his way. Durwin handled them very well in cooperation with local agencies, and was commended for his sound expertise.

"Previously, we have seen how Durwin's plans were blocked by the non-cooperation of the power block of belittlers in the church administration. As Durwin now succeeded on his own in his pastoral care program, we will see the offensive and hostile side of envy and jealousy of belittlers at work. First I think I should outline to you sketches of some of the cases Durwin handled, and I am sure you will readily agree he was very capable and of strong character without undue fear. As I said, these will be sketches or outlines only.

"There was a case involving a very troubled family, the Sheriffs department, a highly skilled county wide social agency, and a collection of guns with an alleged threat to use them. Durwin was drawn into the case by some of the family members. He conducted interviews where tact and diplomacy were of utmost importance to defuse a potential disaster. He acted as liaison when there could be no other communication. He played a major role in bringing about the safety of the innocent parties, and the prevention of the disturbed party from perhaps pursuing a criminal act.

"Another case Durwin was called into by the police. It involved a family and their dubious friends. Due to Durwin's intervention, two innocent victims of the group separated from the others and established themselves in another residence in a different environment and new life.

Some of the others were dealt with by the law after their dubious deeds had made headlines in the local newspapers.

"Yet another case came about through a mysterious phone call to Durwin from a person he had never heard of before. A hesitant and obviously aged woman's voice on the phone told Durwin, 'I used to be a member of your denomination, now I need your help. An address was forthcoming. During his training, Durwin had been cautioned about the possible dangers of responding to strange phone calls and going to strange addresses. For example, such a call could be from a mentally deranged person, armed and dangerous.

"Durwin verified the address in the phone book and left a note on the kitchen table telling his wife where he was going, in case anything went wrong. He then proceeded to the house. It was a large old house out in a country field, set behind a wall of hedges and trees. There were several doors to the house. Durwin knocked on the first side door he came to. He heard a shout, so looked in a nearby window where he saw an elderly man sitting in a chair and waving and shouting for him to come in by the back door around the corner. Durwin entered cautiously, but it turned out to be safe.

"A very elderly couple lived there. Their daytime housekeeper was presently out shopping for them. The elderly woman told Durwin her problem. The husband pointed out discrepencies in her story. Further talking with them, and a contact with relatives, who in turn involved the family doctor, brought the problem to a head. The doctor perscribed a mild anti-psychotic medication for the woman. However, the very elderly husband and his very elderly wife, because of their ages and health conditions, each had to spend most of their time sitting in a chair. The chairs were very comfortable, but they were in separate adjoining rooms where each could watch their preferred television programs. They were out of sight of each other. Also, with the wife's impaired hearing, she was for the most part out of hearing range. When the housekeeper would be discussing the household business with the more alert husband, she could neither see, nor hear very well, and felt left out of the decision making of her own household.

"At Durwin's suggestion, the relatively small part of the large house now being used was rearranged so as to encourage better vision, communication and socializing between the husband, the wife, and the housekeeper. Under this arrangement, the wife came to feel in charge of her own household again. All parties readily agreed to the arrangement. A follow-up visit by Durwin revealed that the problem was now under control.

"Durwin also handled an increasing number of miscellaneous cases from within and without his congregation—people with an assortment of personal problems. Those who came to him were very satisfied with the results."

"So now you are going to tell us that Durwin was on his way to success, are you Collin?" asked Donna with a wry smile.

"Not on your life," quipped Leo. "Belittlers can find ways to mess up even that. Right, Collin?"

"Right," answered Collin. "Durwin communicated to his church members the work he was doing as best he could without breaking confidentialities. And, of course, they knew he was studying. Now their true colors began to show. They weren't just afraid of him due to inferior feelings. They were envious of him, and instead of showing fear of him they became offensively hostile and competitive. Some of them set themselves up in their minds as pseudo-psychologists, suddenly coming up with bogus psychological solutions for everybodies' problems including Durwin's. He was going to school to learn such things, but their implication was they already knew all about it, and Durwin couldn't outdo them on that either. Such was their implied attitude, and they belittled him on every point they could pertaining to it; trivializing and making light of it and inferring that his going to school was a waste of his time and the church's money; implying they were paying him too large a salary. Now the offensive attempted brainwashing of Durwin Lawton had furiously begun."

"Brainwashing!" exclaimed Owen.

"Yes, brainwashing," emphasized Collin. "They trivialized and downplayed all that Durwin did. From here on, no matter what Durwin did, or how well he did it, they continuously implied that it was not good enough for them. They continuously supported their implications by making it as difficult as possible for Durwin to do anything. If anything was to be done, they would do it, and imply that they had to do it because Durwin couldn't. They had to brainwash Durwin into thinking he wasn't up to their standards—that he wasn't good enough for them."

"Did the brainwashing work," asked Owen, now aghast at this new development.

"Not at all," replied Collin. "They made absolute jack-asses of themselves trying to outdo Durwin. He could see through it without even trying hard. Of course it was annoying in that it blocked his own ministry. Progress became almost nil in the congregation. When Durwin did manage to accomplish something, they inferred, as their warped minds work, that he was only doing it to try to outdo them, and no way were they going to let him do that, or even think that he could possibly outdo them."

"But, said Owen in amazement, "that's the mind-set belittlers think in. They are the ones who push down others and try to outdo them. Here they are implying Durwin was doing just that to them."

"Remember what Barclay said," replied Collin, "envy is 'the most warped and twisted of human emotions.' Many of the things belittlers do are just to keep ahead of others, especially when they feel their undisciplined pride is threatened. So when someone else does something, they see that person as having a similar mind-set, and doing things for the purpose of putting them down and getting ahead of them. Projection, it is called in psychology."

"But we are doing no such thing," added Brett, "we are merely doing our work to the best of our ability."

"And," said Gilda, "if that 'best of our ability,' is perceived by them to be better than theirs, they shun us, or turn on us."

"You have it right," said Collin, "that is envy at work."

Collin went on with the story, "There are some other incidents that show the willingness and high quality of Durwin's ministry, and the extremely distorted reception of that ministry by the local chruch administration.

"There was a nursing home in that part of the county where some of the clergy of the area conducted worship services each Sunday, each on a monthly basis. The administration of Durwin's church expressed the opinion that their minister should be among those conducting services at the home. They weren't very diplomatic about the way they approached the matter. The chairperson in particular took the approach that it was her idea, that it was a worthy project, as indeed it was, but that she had to push Durwin into it. The fact is it was something Durwin would gladly do anyway. He had extensive training and experience in pastoral care of the elderly and had had exceptional results and response.

"Durwin went to the home and arranged a Sunday afternoon of each month when he would be the one to conduct worship. There was no problem in arranging this as the home was having a difficult time finding enough willing clergy to fill each Sunday. So Durwin began his Sunday afternoon worship at the home the same Sunday of each month. Canda always went along with Durwin to play the piano when the regular pianist wasn't there, and/or to lead in the singing, and to help with the patients generally. One or two others would go along most Sundays to help wheel the patients to the auditorium, help them find the hymns in the hymn books and generally care for them, with at least one nursing home staff member present. When others from the church could not go, Durwin and Canda went alone.

"Durwin had a natural gift of relating very well to the elderly and the sick, both in personal contact, and in his sermons, prayers and mannerism. They loved his worship services and looked forward to his coming each month. Canda's gift of relating well to them greatly complimented his ministry.

"After this had been going on and going well for a couple of years, the chairperson decided to come along and help out one Sunday afternoon, perhaps even to take some credit for it, as she was prone to often do. Durwin gladly made her welcome and showed her the routine of wheeling patients from the rooms and hallways to the auditorium. It wasn't long before her color began to pale and her face took on a feeble countenance. Twisted, and drooling mouths severly damaged by strokes, obviously weren't in her league. Drooping heads that could no longer be lifted up straight had little appeal to pride in accomplishment; neither did the many other deformities of the aged, wracked and disabled by disease.

"The chairperson didn't take to it. Neither did the patients take to her. But she could see how they took to Durwin and Canda, and what a compassionate and effective service they were rendering to these people.

She made no comment about it. After the service, Durwin expressed the desire that she would come back each Sunday when it was their church's turn for service. 'Oh, I don't know,' she said sickly. She never returned.

"Durwin and Canda continued this service to the home for as long as they were there, either with or without help from the congregation, but always with the warm welcome and appreciation of the staff and patients."

Leo asked, "Did the congregation ever express appreciation to Durwin and Canda for what they were doing there?"

"Not once," replied Collin. "They just considered it a part of Durwin's duty to earn the money they were paying him. Besides, they just didn't have the social graces within them to do such a thing as express appreciation."

Gilda spoke, "I know the church usually reaches out into the community with its services, but I would say Durwin and Canda in doing this were showing a willingness to go beyond what many ministers would consider to be the call of duty. Or at least they would have priorities, and this, they could say, was not one of them. The chairperson opted not to come back. Could not Durwin have done the same?"

Collin replied, "Most ministers would have that option and be free to exercise it. Durwin knew some that did because, like the chairperson, they couldn't take it. Apart from the fact that Durwin did not want to opt out, it would have caused him to be labeled uncaring or something like that if he had. Durwin, being the kind of person he was, his belittlers would never let him get away with it. He would be labeled for life had he chosen to discontinue this service.

"There is another revealing story," Collin continued. "There was a house in town that looked not too bad on the outside. Inside, the people lived in almost unbelievable squalor and utter stench, not for want of money, but because of the long standing character and life style of the inhabitants.

"For reasons of sentimentality about the church's caring for people of peculiar circumstances, the local church administration always included this home in the ministers special caring list. There was really no special spiritual need here, any more than a regular visit as it would be for any other home of the congregation. Besides, it was more than many ministers could or would take. However, to keep the peace, Durwin quietly devised a way to cope with the situation. To visit this home he would dress in all washable clothes, as opposed to clothes that needed dry cleaning. He would clean up his old canvas garden shoes and wear them. He would make his visit, and then return to his own home reeking with an offensive odor that would make many people sick. He would walk directly to the clothes washer, take off all his clothes, including canvas shoes, put them in the washer and set it going. With his hair and skin still smelling potently, he would then go straightway to the shower and clean himself up."

"Many ministers would balk at that and turn it down," remarked Owen.

"You are right," replied Collin, "but people like Durwin would never get away with it. He would be labeled an uncaring snob or the like by belittlers.

"There is another interesting story which shows Durwin's obliging manner. A very aged member of the congregation, due to an accident, had to give up her household, even though she was still alert and keen in mind. She went into a nursing home far away to be near relatives. From there she was moved to another nursing home even further away. Her elderly friends in the congregation lost contact with her, as did Durwin her minister.

"At their request, Durwin informed the friends that he would try to locate her. He drove considerable distance across the state to the first home she had entered, and where he had visited her once. There the staff cooperated by looking up records where they found a forwarding address for mail, and a phone number. It was the address and phone number of a relative. Durwin contacted this relative and obtained the name and location of the second nursing home. He then went the extra distance to visit her. She was very glad to see him and to know that her friends wanted contact with her. Durwin then announced in church her wherabouts and address. Several people took up correspondence with her and spoke appreciation to Durwin for finding her for them.

"Much, much later, at a meeting of the local church administrtion, a very trying person asked if Durwin had visited this aged person lately. He replied that he hadn't, that she was now located a long distance away, and that he wouldn't be going that way very often. It was far outside the sphere of regular visitation. There was silence and obvious glares from member to member of the administration. Durwin knew he had struck a sour note. He said nothing more. A little later, however, when he could find sufficient time to spare, he did take several hours to drive and visit the woman once more. As ever, she was glad to see him, but before the conversation went very far, she pointedly asked him a question, 'Is the local church short of money Durwin.?'

"Durwin, looking surprised, said, 'No, we are meeting our requirements, why do you ask?'

"'Well,' she said, in a kindly manner, 'you don't have to come all this way to visit me. There are ministers in here every day of the week. Our spiritual needs are well taken care of. Besides that, my relatives' minister pays personal attention to my needs. I really appreciate your visits, and it was certainly nice to receive letters from my friends, but it's more than I expect, and more than is necessary for you to travel all that distance again.'

"Durwin assured her he wasn't visiting her for money, but only to satisfy the interests of some people in the church.

"'I know you,' she said, 'and you're not the kind of person to be around looking for money. I really and truly appreciate you putting me in touch with my friends, but please don't feel you have to visit me at all that distance.'

"Durwin thanked her for her consideration, visited with her awhile longer, prayed with her and said good-bye. She thanked him frankly and sincerely for his visits and told him again that she did not expect him to continue coming. He responded by telling her he would visit her only once a year. However, he left and never saw her again. Before the year was up he heard of her demise from friends who had been in correspondence with her. Relatives had contacted some of them in response to their mail."

Again Leo asked, "Was there any appreciation shown to Durwin by the administration for all his troubles?"

Collin shook his head gently. "You should know by now, Leo, that belittlers never show appreciation to people like Durwin and you and I. They forever look for ways to discredit us. They haven't got what it takes within them to do otherwise."

Leo put on a wry smile. "I'm glad I'm not a minister in Terraprima!"

"Be thankful you didn't make that mistake, Leo," returned Collin. "People like Durwin, and we in this group are not the kind to survive in the ministry of the church in Terraprima, at least not in the denomination Durwin was in. It wouldn't be easy elsewhere, but certainly not in Terraprima.

"I will tell you of yet another example of the skillfulness of Durwin's ministry," said Collin. "As most ministers do, Durwin occasionally had a request for help, financial or otherwise, from local people or transients. Late one evening he received a call from a transient who requested help with overnight accomodation, breakfast, and a bus ticket to take him the remaining two hundred or so miles to his destination. After questioning him on his identity and circumstances, Durwin directed him to a motel on the highway just outide of town where there was a standing pre-arrangement with the management. The motel would put him up at Durwin's request and Durwin would pay for it the next day. He told the transient he would be there the next morning with some money for his bus ticket and breakfast. He then phoned the motel to let them know they would have a guest on his account.

"The next morning, about eight thirty or so, Durwin received a phone call from the man. 'My bus will be leaving in two hours, and I'd like to have breakfast if I can. Can you come up now?'

'I'll be there in a few minutes,' replied Durwin, 'first tell me what you are wearing?'

"The man described his clothes to Durwin.

"'Okay,' said Durwin, "stand in front of the motel office so I will know you.'

"Durwin took no chances with strangers. Without fear or trembling, he used calculated caution. Driving into the motel parking lot he saw the man standing in front of the office window. *That's right where I want him,* he thought to himself. Then parking considerable distance from him he got out of his car quickly and walked over to where the man was standing. He didn't want the stranger coming up to his car, taking it by some method of force, gun or otherwise, and perhaps taking Durwin hostage with it. It has been known to happen.

"The man explained to him that the bus ticket would be twelve dollars, and the motel clerk had told him the area bus stop is two miles up the highway at a restaurant where he could also get his breakfast. 'Can you give me a ride up there,' he asked.

"'How do I know you haven't got some sort of a weapon on you?' asked Durwin, briskly.

"'Oh no - no sir, I haven't,' came the quick reply.

"'Okay, lets see,' said Durwin, 'open your parka zipper and then frisk yourself, all pockets, around your waist and up and down your legs.'

"The man did so cooperatively.

"'Looks okay,' said Durwin, then as an extra precaution, 'but we'll have to make it fast. Before I came up I phoned the police and told them I was coming up here to meet a stranger. If I'm not back on time, they'll be up here looking for me. Jump aboard.'

"Durwin drove a little hurriedly up the highway to the restaurant. He took the man inside, and in order to prevent money being spent on booze or drugs, paid for his breakfast in advance rather than give him the money. When he found that the bus ticket had to be purchased on the bus, he parted from that rule by giving the man sixteen dollars to pay for his twelve dollar bus ticket, plus a little extra to buy lunch, then drove away, leaving the transient on his own.

"Durwin felt that in this case the man was on the level with regard to his need. In some cases this wasn't so, he knew, yet he felt he had developed very good discernment about such matters. When in doubt he often gave the benefit of the doubt. The thought of turning down a stranded person by error in judgement didn't sit well with him. Only seldom had he to his knowledge been taken. He had confidence that he was handling this part of his ministry safely and well.

"Let me tell you of one more event in Durwin's ministry that shows how well he could cope with all the varied circumstances of his ministry, even its dangers, and be highly regarded for it by those to whom he ministered," Collin continued.

"A woman of Durwin's congregation, just past middle age was in a very bad accident. Her body—many bones and internal and external parts included, was badly crushed. In a state of near unconsciousness she was transferred to a renowned hospital in a very old and difficult part of the big city. This hospital after decades of service, was still highly regarded for its exceptional work. But over the years, the part of the city in which it was located had become a risky, crime ridden area, very risky for a person like Durwin. His very appearance of a well to do person would make him a target for mugging, and robbing, and also for the further extremes that sometimes come with these crimes.

"Durwin was aware of the dangers. In fact, at a clergy gathering shortly after the accident, another seasoned clergy person had stated that he considered hospital visiting in that area from outside it to be beyond the call of duty. He would leave that to the chaplains or clergy of that area who knew it well. However, Durwin and Canda had already found their way in there, and now Durwin was visiting there frequently by himself when Canda was at her place of employment."

Said Collin with emphasis, "I wish you to note a particular incident in this story which shows there are belittlers in all occupations in life, and they cannot be trusted. On a Sunday afternoon, Durwin and Canda, making their first visit to this hospital had followed a map, and found it without problem, visited the patient and then set out to return home. They ran into difficulty, however, finding their way out of the city to the highway that would easily take them home. The problem arose when many one way streets and not straight or parallel ones at that, threw them off course.

"They saw a policeman on the sidewalk nearby so stopped and asked him directions to the freeway. The policeman smiled at first. But as he bent over to peer in the open window his smile turned quickly to a frown. Durwin and Canda, still relatively new to Terraprima didn't understand the quick change in that facial expression. In retrospect they would later realize their fine, clean cut appearance brought on the policeman's hostility. He was a belittler. He hesitated and pondered for a moment, then gave them directions; a series of turns that to the

Lawtons didn't seem to be in the right general direction. However, they thought they might be 'twisted around,' as the saying goes, and decided to follow the directions given them. To their dismay it took them much deeper into the core of this dangerous area of the city. They knew they had been misled by a belittling policeman.

"It is not plausable that a seasoned looking policeman wouldn't know that he was sending them into the not far away crime-ridden core of one of the well known boroughs of the big city.

"The Lawtons parked briefly in a place where there were lots of people around, and studied their map. They figured that from where they now were, they had best get on a nearby main city thoroughfare that would take them to a safer area of the big city, with which they were familiar. From there they could get to another expressway with which they were also familiar and which would take them home. In the Sunday evening traffic it took them three hours to get home. Had they recieved the right directions they could have done so in less than an hour.

"When at home again, the Lawtons studied a more detailed map, and during the weeks ahead, while Canda was at work, Durwin continued to visit the hospital. They soon came to know that from the place where they had asked the policeman for directions, all that was necessary was to proceed to the traffic light ahead, take a left turn, and then at the next street a right and this would have taken them onto the freeway that would take them home. I ask you to remember this incident of the belittler policeman as I will refer to it again later.

"To continue, Durwin visited that hospital regularly over the next two months, very early learning the area quite well. For safety reasons he visited during peak visiting hours when there would be more people around than usual. Utilizing the several storied parking garage, he carefully parked with open access to the elevators and stairs. This was done, not in fear and trembling, but with calculated caution. Durwin was quite pleased with this event in his pastoral care ministry. The satisfaction of being an effective helper in time of dire need far outweighed the risks involved.

"In time the accident victim's condition grew worse. Several of her family members came from various parts of the continent. Durwin and

Canda had them into their home at times for meals and supportive fellowship. When the patient died, the family members invited Durwin to near the other side of the continent, expenses paid, to officiate at her funeral. All of this, supported in many ways by Canda, was Durwin's ministry at its best—pastoral care, in which he excelled, to the appreciative satisfaction of those to whom he ministered.

"There is a relevant incident in Durwin's travel as he returned home from this funeral. The airplane arrived at the airport about ten o'clock at night. Rather than have someone come the hour or more drive to pick him up, Durwin decided to take a bus which had a regular stop at a hotel in the town in which he lived.

"Durwin stood in line to have his suitcase put into the luggage compartment in the undercarriage of the bus before boarding. As his turn came up, he motioned to hand his suitcase to the bus driver to put it aboard. The bus driver brazenly reached past Durwin to the next person in line, took that person's luggage, put it in the compartment, then reached past Durwin again to the next person, and on down the line. When Durwin realized what was happening, he put his luggage into the compartment himself, pushing it in sufficiently to assure it was there to stay. In addition, Durwin stood there until the compartment was about to be closed before proceeding to board the bus and to a seat. The bus driver came on board. Walking through the bus checking the tickets, he treated Durwin noticeably cooler than the other passengers.

"At the hotel, all the passengers unloaded from the bus for either local destinations or to transfer to another bus for further travel. The passengers picked up their luggage as the driver took it out of the luggage compartment. As he came to Durwin's suitcase, he at first pushed it to one side. Then after there was more room made he kept pushing it further into the compartment as he took out other luggage items. When Durwin figured out what was happening, he stepped directly in front of the bus driver, stooped down and went half the length of his body into the compartment, pulled out his suitcase, then stood firmly and directly in front of the bus driver, looking him straight in the face. The driver cowered and his face went rubbery. Then he got spiteful, pushed his way around Durwin, and stooped down to take the remaining few pieces of luggage out of the luggage compartment.

"That belittling bus driver was an Afro-American black man, by appearance in his forties; old enough to remember how his own people had been discriminated against for the kind of people they were. Durwin stood and stared at him. His face went rubbery with shame again as he boarded the empty bus to drive it away. Durwin has often wondered what some of the driver's liberated elders, still stinging from the days of gross discrimination against them, would think of the foul deeds of the belittling bus driver that night."

Collin paused momentarily, then did a brief summary, "I have related to you examples of the numerous events that helped make up the totality of Durwin's very busy and varied ministry to date. Normal people had much affection for him because of it. Belittlers hated him for it. The more he did and the better he did it, the more it pricked their undisciplined pride, and the more it stirred their envy and jealousy and hatred. And the more that happened, the more they felt compelled to discredit him."

"He was too good for them," spoke Leo again, this time more seriously and subdued, almost awestruck.

"Yes," said Collin in the same tone, "yes, it was more than they could stand."

After a brief, aghast silence in the group, Collin said, "I will relate to you an incident that confirms the high caliber of the sociability of Durwin and Canda. Durwin took some vacation time, and during a weekend, he and Canda participated in a secular event sponsored mainly by Christian people from several denominations. Of the two large bus loads that went there were no others present from Durwin's church. Shortly after the event, the Lawtons received a letter from a high ranking clergy person of a denomination other then their own. This letter thanked them for participating, and commended them for the high quality and geniality of their social involvement.

"I would add," said Collin, "this is not to say that other denominations do not have belittlers. They are everywhere to varying degrees. However, there were none present at this event, or at least none in a positon to affect the Lawtons' involvement. The point is Durwin and Canda were very socially capable people when circumstances allowed."

Collin continued, "As Durwin's personal ministry, mainly his worship services and pastoral care, were in full swing with continued improvement, relations with the belittlers grew worse and worse. The chairperson, as we call her, now aligning herself with the belittlers all the more, became very snooty to both Durwin and his wife Canda. At meetings she would subtly cut Durwin down, then turn to a friend and in a very unmmannerly little session they would whisper to one another and chuckle while everyone else waited; then return her attention to the meeting. At women's gatherings and at choir rehearsal she would often try to cut Canda down, always trying to make Canda wrong in everything she did or said. But Canda was quicker of mind and stronger in character, and therefore well able to put her in her place, always in a firm but friendly manner which left her no real reason to degrade Canda. For all that, the Lawtons would later have to take insinuations from other belittlers concerning what harm they were supposed to be doing to the chairperson. All they were actually doing was defending themselves from her, and that in a very diplomatic way and always with good decorum.

"However, the chairperson had full support of the belittlers, all of whom supported her in her by now well contrived and rapidly blossoming rivalry for leadership and popularity in the congregation. From now on there would be a popularity contest instituted by the chairperson between herself and the Lawtons. The other belittlers supported her in this. The Lawtons refused to be drawn into the rivalry with her. They just went on doing their work as much as circumstances would allow. That, to the chairperson and her supporting belittlers, in their warped minds, was rivalry. Durwin had been instrumental in having her appointed to the position and showing her how to handle it, and now she would use it against him. Durwin knew what they didn't know; that once a congregation begins to put its minister down, especially for no good reason, they put the congregation down with him. If they would build up their minister in a sound and healthy manner, they would build up their congregation with him. These people were bent on bringing him down. If they were successful, the congregation would go down as well, and certainly they would blame Durwin for the congregation's downfall.

"The majority of the congregation still liked Durwin and Canda. How long that would last remained to be seen. Little by little, bit by bit, one by one, the belittlers would turn others negative on the Lawtons, or at least try hard to do so. Durwin, while refusing to be drawn into the popularity contest, decided to go on the offensive to try and get some things done that would enhance the congregation's outlook among themselves and to the community. He chose a number of projects, and started with the one that looked least likely to cause trouble.

"Durwin asked for a meeting of the appropriate committee for the task. At the meeting he informed them that Canda, who was noted for her green thumb, and three other persons were willing to form a church beautification committee to beautify the church grounds. You may remember it had fallen through before by such a mundane thing as a saw blade caught in the limb of a tree. Some of the committee approved verbally, one after the other. However, remember also that open rivalry had now set into the church. The head of the committee saw the support of the members. He responded slowly, 'Yes, we can use a beautification committee, but I think the chairperson should head it up. She did such a beautiful job on decorating the sanctuary.' "Durwin responded, 'There is little similarity between the two tasks.'

"'Oh, but,' said the head of the committee, 'the chairperson has an eye for nice things.'

"So the chairperson was made head of the beautification committee. Canda knew that under that circumstance it was impossible for her to be involved, so she stepped down from the committee and left it to the chairperson. The committee was never formed and brought together. At a later board meeting someone asked how the beautification committee was coming along. Durwin waited for the longest time, but neither the chairperson nor her supporter who had named her to head it, spoke up. Then Durwin said, 'I guess it has fallen through.' The chairperson turned to her whispering friend. They whispered and chuckled, then the chairperson, as she turned back to the meeting, remarked laughingly, somewhat under her breath, 'ha, ha he can't do it.'

"From there on there was a noticable inference that Durwin was not a capable minister. The attempted intentional destruction of the personhood of Durwin Lawton was well underway. Later circumstances would indicate that it had the support of the area church hierarchy, as I will later illustrate. Durwin was a marked man.

"At a later meeting of the Christian Education Committee, Durwin expressed the desire to have the Sunday School curriculum changed to that published by the church's own denomination. The same person who messed up the formation of the beautifation committee now protested, 'We are busy people. The material we now use is well prepared for us. Our denomination's material takes too much preparation.'

"Durwin saw much the same thumbs down looming again. He quickly intervened. He knew the Sunday School superintendent wasn't a belittler. She wasn't wise to belittlers either. Many people are not. But she wasn't a belittler, herself. So in answer to the man protesting, Durwin firmly said, "Our denomination's curriculum is quite satisfactorily prepared. Your objection was valid several years ago, but the problem has long been corrected. Our curriculum is not only well prepared for presentation, but it teaches our children what our church at large wants to teach them. The man tried to intervene again and to crowd out Durwin with his loud voice. Durwin kept right on. 'Tell you what I'll do, I'll take the superintendent to the church bookstore where she can review the curriculum. She is a well trained and experienced teacher. If she approves of the material, then we use it. Okay everyone?"

"The superintendent agreed to the plan. An affirmative reply came from most of the others, who now had no reason to disagree.

"The man said, 'Well okay, it makes no difference to me. For my class I will continue to use my own material that I buy at another book store.' He looked defeated for once. The denominational curriculum was soon utilized for all classes except the one taught by the belittling protester.

"Another incident brought yet another change. Durwin invited a person from outside the congregation to sing solo and also with the choir for a special occasion. As a rehearsal took place, and as Durwin watched from a pew, he noticed the chairperson, who was also a choir member, pouting, turning up her lip to the other members, and trying to stir up shunning of the guest soloist. Durwin moved forward a few pews and looked at her in a questioning manner. She settled down and pouted some more for a while, then sang along with the choir. After rehearsal Durwin went forward, thanked the guest for coming, then suggested to the chairperson that she also sing a solo sometime. Durwin made several sincere attempts to bring this about, but she never did respond. From now on, however, a strange new twist entered in. According to the belittlers it was now Durwin who was down on the chairperson and not the chairperson down on Durwin. They were making Durwin out to be the bad guy.

"At another board meeting Durwin expressed a desire to put into action a planned approach to greeting visitors on their first time to that church. The goal was to interest them in coming again and eventually becoming members. Without hearing Durwin's plan the man who destroyed the beautificaion committee quickly flew into action. He had a lot of supporters on the board, including the chairperson, so Durwin didn't stand a chance.

"The man, loud and showy as usual, flew into first place so to speak. 'Yes,' he said, 'at one time we used to have a visitors packet. We should have one now.' He reamed off all the things they would put into it. The list included all the things they had in it some years previous. Obviously there was to be no change. Durwin let him spout on. It wasn't worth a quarrel. They ended up with a visitors packet far too large. It emphasized more than anything else the congregation's now precarious financial position, which of course was caused by lack of support for the minister by the several belittlers.

"The packet also contained a statement of purpose that had been used in this congregation for a long time, and which Durwin would have replaced with one emphasizing nurture and growth in faith and in Christian character. The Apostle Paul's exhortation in his letter to the Ephesians (4:12-13 RSV) would be the basis of this growth: 'to equip the saints for the work of ministry, for building up the body of Christ, until we all attain to the unity of the faith and of the knowledge of the Son of God, to mature manhood (and womanhood) to the measure of the stature of the fulness of Christ.' From Durwin's observation and opinion such nurture was also badly needed throughout much of the denomination in the whole geographical area.

"At that meeting Durwin made reference to emphasizing growth in the faith, but was quickly crowded out as though what he said was of no significance. The matter was trivialized. At a later gathering the man who so rudely interrupted him made light of the concept of further Christian growth. 'How could I do that?' he asked, then continued that he was already helping with teaching Sunday School, helping with outreach to the poor, and serving on three committees and boards. He had no time for further growth. He had already reached his limit he stated proudly and defiantly to Durwin. It seemed to Durwin that the man had no proper concept of what Christian growth was. What Durwin did not realize at the time is that belittlers have a ploy of that kind they sometimes utilize. They seek to put weird ideas into a victim's mind, and they think if they can get enough of them in there their victim will be mentally ill, or nuts, as some of them would call it. So much for their concept of mental illness! Either way the man was off track.

"Conditions were long past the point where Durwin could debate with them about Christian growth or any other serious matter. Their prejudice was firmly entrenched and they would just put him down and crowd him out of any conversation.

"Yet Durwin knew in his heart that the long absence of emphasis on Christian character in the mainline protestant church has greatly diminished that church's influence in society. The results are low cultural standards in various aspects of society including any church where wayward protestants, lacking in Christian character, are present in abundance. One of the main reasons for the decline in numbers and influence of mainline protestantism is the lack of emphasis on personal faith and Christian character. The field is wide open to belittlers, their power trips, and their lack of concern for other people's welfare, except where it gives them an ego trip.

"In addition Durwin would have hand picked three or so suitably charactered and cultured people to befriend visitors and newcomers on their first visit. He now refrained from this because he knew the same man would mess that up too. Overall, when the man's own grandoise plan was formulated, they had an incomplete plan suitable for a large church with dozens of visitors each Sunday. For example he and his supporters had name tags made for each member of the congregation, and tags marked 'visitors' so they could distinguish members from visitors. All that for a church in which everyone knew everyone, and where there was only an occasional visitor who could be spotted immediately by most people in the congregation. Instead of doing some original analysis and thinking about their own circumstance, they just copied a plan from larger churches in areas where visitors are plentiful every Sunday. It was neither useful nor necessary for Durwin's church. But this man and his supporters had kept ahead of Durwin again in their childish rivalry for popularity and first place.

"Speaking of visitors, it was only seldom that any came to this church in its present state. This was mainly a townsfolk church. But when a visitor did come occasionally, it would have been well to be prepared. Only in this manner would the congregation gain new members at the present time. Let me tell you of two occasions when high caliber people came to the church service for the first time. The first visitor was an industrial professional man who had just moved into the area. He was looking around for a church for he, and his family when they would later arrive. After the service, far too many of the 'wrong' people swarmed overanxiously around him. Durwin's plan would have been to have three select people befriend him. When he finally broke away from the crowd he came to Durwin at the door and shook hands warmly with him. 'I enjoyed your service,' he said, as he tipped his head affectionately towards Durwin, 'it was very good.'

"'Thank you,' I hope we'll see you again,' said Durwin.

"'A-ah, we will see,' he replied hesitantly, as he looked back at those who had surrounded him, pulling his mouth to one side in rejection of them. 'We'll see,' he said again, 'but God's blessing on you.' He left and they didn't see him again.

"On another Sunday, another business man visited. He too was new to the area. The result was much the same. He shook hands with Durwin and expressed sincere appreciation for the service. He looked back at the remaining members who had greeted him earlier, shook his head slightly and said, 'I don't think so, but good luck to you.'

"It was about this time that Durwin wrote the Chief Executive Officer asking for a change in pastorate. Durwin had been there nearly three years, and it was clear his ministry with this congregation wasn't going to work out. In Secundaterra when things were not working out for a minister in one church he generally moved to a situation more compatable to his type of ministry. Durwin didn't know that wasn't the policy of this denomination in Terraprima, if indeed there was any real policy at all. There seemed to be because some of the acquaintances Durwin had made in ministry, knowing what kind of a church he had, sometimes said to him, 'such and such a church would be a good place for you.' It was always nice, high caliber churches they mentioned. He would later learn that this was the opinion of only some well wishing friends who knew what he was presently up against.

"Durwin received no reply to his written request. Later, at a gathering of the larger church, he approached the C.E.O. personally about the matter. He was told abruptly to take the matter to his supervisor whom he said was the person to take care of such things, and who was quite capable of the job. As Durwin was told this, he was brushed aside by the C.E.O. He knew now he would have no support from the top. How much he would have from the middle was not yet clear. In time however, he would know their cruel deeds as well.

"Indeed, in time, at the risk of his reputation, health and personhood, Durwin would learn more of the mind-game and how it was played to maim and destroy. In Terraprima it would be played out not merely by individuals as in the Secundaterras. In Terraprima the cruel mind-game would be played out by a conspiracy of sorts, consisting of many people on various levels of life. I will show it to you as we wend our way through the story.

"Keep in mind as we proceed, that their motivation in always disagreeing with Durwin was to protect their undisciplined pride, to continually feel superior, and to make Durwin feel inferior.

"Most people, when called upon to make a decision on a matter, make it in such a way that it is good for the church or the business, as the case may be. When a person of hollow or undisciplined pride makes a decision, the welfare of the church or business is secondary. The decision, first and foremost, has to be good for the personal pride of the dubious decision maker. This means that the decision also has to belittle anyone perceived to be a threat to that proud person's need to feel superior.

"You may notice I have called it a mind-game, and that is what it is. It becomes, in deed, a barbaric game, in essence not altogether unlike that of the gladiators of ancient Rome. The victim is captive, has little recourse, and very few ways out. Often he can only temporarily dodge and maneuver until the victors, cheered on by a large portion of society and ignored by the remaining portion, one after another, wear him down, or attempt to, to the degree where he is rendered useless, and quite easily extinguishable. When the belittling mind-game players think they are winning they treat it like a sport, taking delight in their victories. When their game is thwarted they scurry like cowards and pout like the spoiled brats they are. Then they get busy with the mind-game of covering up, which is usually riddled with deceit.

"As members of this group know, this game is played in all segments of society. However, the belittlers of the church area involved in this story I am telling, due to its close-knit ties and effective grapevine, play the game more masterfully than any other segment of society. As I just indicated, when the church belittlers feel they are being victorious over their victim, they are on an elated power trip for themselves. When they are losing, they get whimpy and spiteful, and in time, after deceitful cover-up, are often more vicious and tricky.

"The devious manipulations and mind-games of belittlers are many and varied. However, some games are used more often than others, and are worth noting here because some time or other you may be having them used on you.

"Con-artists as they often are, while being friendly, even palsy walsy with you, they try first of all to gain control of your mind and make it deteriorate below the level of theirs; even to destroy it as a properly functioning entity. They usually begin by trying to make you feel inferior to them. Then by implication, they offer to lead you in what they want you to think is a superior direction, often a direction quite contrary to the one you are and want to be in, and perhaps have been headed in all your life. They offer a direction not suited to you at all. You would not only be a misfit there, but most likely a failure there. That's just the way they would want it. Of course the failure would be blamed on you. They would take the attitude that they gave you a chance, or, they tried to make something out of you, and you just couldn't make a go of it. Or, they would later imply that you wanted to do it, so they let you, knowing that it wasn't good for you.

"They pretend they take no notice of any worthwhile, and moreso any exceptional pieces of work you may accomplish. They imply by their attitude there is nothing to it. On the other hand, you make an error, or a mis-calculation, and they will, again by implication, try to make you feel small. One way or another you are trivialized.

"Express original opinions on something, and they find it easy to disagree. Quote an author on something and they will find fault with the author. Hold out some favorite public figure of yours and they will quickly criticize some aspect of that person's work. This is designed to make you out to be wrong so often, that you will be discouraged from venturing an opinion on anything. They do all this with an air of superiority towards you to make you feel small compared to them.

"When there is a number of them intentionally arrayed against you, and I am not paranoid in saying so, they may attempt to confound you drastically in an almost indiscernable manner; almost that is. For example, on a given topic in which you are involved under their tutelage, one person will agree with some things you have done or said and disagree with other things. The next one will agree with some of the things the other person disagreed with, and disagree with some of the things the other person agreed with. So it goes, when you get several people involved in such a mind-game you are in a no-win situation.

"They will give you little or no fair chance to defend yourself, so you have to walk away from them, and, they hope, walk away in despair. At other times, when there are several people of authority involved, one acts as though he doesn't know what the other knows or was told, or how that other has reacted to a given situation. So they are all reacting to that situation in a different manner. And so it goes again, when you get a number of people involved in this manner, it can become quite confounding. You have to either walk away from it or argue with them all. If they can, they will turn the argument into a quarrel. Quarrelling with a number of them together makes for a big fiasco, for which you get the blame, and get branded as hard to please and hard to get along with.

"Belittlers teach you nothing, tell you nothing. They imply and make you guess, and love to imply by head shaking and the like, that you have guessed wrong, that you are just not smart enough to catch on.

"The motive of envious belittlers is to confound you at every turn, to render you useless; to destroy you as a viable person. When you beat them to a game, they again by implication wipe it all out as though it never happened, or imply that you took it all wrong, you misunderstood them and what they were trying to do for you. You just don't catch on. Also belitters cover themselves well with people or groups that may be supportive of you. They see that their side of the story gets to your would-be supporters, and in time whittle their number down. Of course a good number of these supporters can see through the game, and continue with their often silent support."

Collin changed the emphasis, "And now Dr. Eldren and my other fine friends, I wish to suggest we adjourn for the evening and continue next week."

"It's about right timing for my next appointment," said Dr. Eldren.

The group members decided again they would congregate at the Corner Coffee Shop, except for Brett who, together with his wife who was at home, had business to prepare for early next morning. There was no easy and privileged life, past or present, for fine and exceptional Brett Culver. This is quite opposite to what belittlers often like to imply in order to have it as an excuse for putting down such well-to-do people.

CHAPTER V

The week seemed to pass quickly for Collin whose mind was so engrossed in this alarming story. It seemed no time at all before he was back in Room 405 with the other support group members and Dr. Eldren.

With the members seated around in their circle, Collin took up the story again. "The belittling of Durwin continued mercilessly. The persons doing it really behaved as though they were doing a wonderful Christian thing by tearing down this smart-aleck. They would show him who was the smarter. They were full of undisciplined hollow pride and envy. Durwin didn't have this pride in him, but he did have confidence in himself. It was this confidence they had to destroy. They played the mind-game to make Durwin think he was no good, so that he would feel and behave as though he was inferior to them. That way they could hold on to their false sense of superiority and their power and control over their church - their private little kingdom.

"The man who fouled up the beautification committee and the preparation for visitors continued to lead the onslaught for a further period. At a fellowship period after a business meeting he took the spotlight and came out with a question which from Durwin's point of view was very absurd. 'Durwin,' he said, 'supposing you were to have a funeral, how would you feel then?'

"To Durwin this was absurd indeed. It was known that he had been a minister for years and therefore had officiated at many funerals. From the tone in which it came, Durwin sensed that the question was asked in a derogatory way, perhaps to try to find some weakness in Durwin, so he thought at the time. Collin then paused and looked to Dr. Eldren. "Dr. Eldren, I know it is risky to say such a thing in the presence of a psychiatrist, but Durwin was a seasoned person well able to tell when a remark is made in good faith or bad."

"I see your point and it is well taken," said Dr. Eldren with a friendly smile.

Collin continued, "Durwin thought at the time that this man was hoping to establish that Durwin couldn't handle a funeral."

"Durwin calmly answered, 'Funerals are something a minister gets seasoned to and I am well seasoned in that respect. In the churches I served before I came here there were many older people. I had an average of fifteen funerals a year. I realize that's not a large number compared to some churches, but it was on average more than one a month, which means that death was nearly always before me. I have had some funerals since I have been in this church—including funerals for non-members, for which a funeral director calls and asks me to take occasionally. That too is a regular occurence for most ministers.'

"The man simply responded, 'Oh,' and went on to talk about something else entirely different.

"Over a further period of time, Durwin would experience from various belittlers a similar type of questioning about funerals and some other aspects of his work that, according to other people and also his own feelings about them, he did very well. Eventually he came to the conclusion, and rightly so I believe, that it was either a ploy of the belittlers to undermine him about his ability to handle, in this case, funerals in a stable manner; that it was a means of implanting weak ideas in Durwin's mind about the matter, a ploy I have referred to before and may do so again. Or, it may have been an attempt to trivialize and belittle that which Durwin did well, just to insult and infuriate him into defending himself on them. This, in their minds, would give them room to say he was boasting about his work. Then they would have punched a major flaw in his character. And it could have been both of these ploys. If it wasn't that, then it was a most absurd question for a highly educated man to ask of a minister of many years who had already conducted numerous funerals.

"Another possible ruse intended by this absurd question could be that loud and showy belittlers are usually of the impression, and try in various ways to make it stick, that people like Durwin, because they are soft spoken and easy going, are also delicate and whimpish. Nothing could be further from the truth. Durwin was a strong person. On the other hand I have known among loud and showy belittlers, for example one who was afraid to donate blood because the sight of blood and the process of extracting it made him very sick; another couldn't go to visit a dying person. He just couldn't face it. Another one practically folded at a funeral. Durwin Lawton, soft spoken and easy going, could take all such things as these, murder cases included, in his stride. He took them as a matter of course for his occupation and seriously responded to them under God's guidance and grace.

"On another occasion a church group, including Durwin, was going to meet at a place other than the church. The same man was giving directions to Durwin in the presence of others. He explained how to get to the building on such and such a street. Durwin said calmly, 'Yes, okay, I'll meet you there.' The man repeated the directions again and asked, 'Are you sure you can find it?'

"'Yes,' replied Durwin, 'I have been down that street before. I haven't seen that particular building because I never had any reason to look for it, but you have given me the number, so I'll find it, no problem.'

"'Well, I hope so,' replied the man as though he was doubtful. "The fact is," said Collin to the group, "they were not only trying to convince Durwin, but also trying to create throughout the church the false impression that Durwin was not only inferior to them, but that he was downright inept. Another fact is that even before they came to Terraprima to live, Durwin and Canda could find their way around numerous states of Terraprima without even a map. Throughout these states they even had favorite tourist, recreation, eating and shopping places which they had frequented on their many previous trips to Terraprima. Before and since they had been living here, they had frequently driven into and found their way very well around some of the largest cities on the continent without any problem. The belittlers wanted Durwin himself and others to believe otherwise.

"Also, from here on, Durwin would take frequent inuendos, both locally and in the wider area of the church, that he was an inept car driver. Actually, one of Durwin's very noticable qualities was his exceptional ability with driving. He could wheel a car around with little effort in the fastest and most crowded cities, on super highways and on winding, isolated country roads, in safety and with ease.

"To the envy of many, Durwin was also exceptionally good at long distance driving, having lots of stamina, but also knowing how to enjoy the trips. Many people are not good at, and do not enjoy long distance driving. Belittlers who do not, behave as though there is something wrong with those who do. They cannot acknowledge it as an exceptional ability. So throughout his lifetime, and moreso in Terraprima, Durwin had to take much flak on this.

"Durwin had numerous adverse experiences when he would be driving other people in his car with him. He would drive with ease and high capability, as he did when he was driving alone or with Canda. On many occasions, persons driving with him would frown or pout because of their envy of his ease of driving, and some would even make innuendos that his driving was poor. On occasion when Durwin would be riding in their car, they would practically crack their neck—actually endanger themselves trying to drive with the same ease that Durwin did. They should have been content to drive in their own usual style. That would be right for them. Likewise Durwin should have been free to drive in his own usual style and remain free from envious gestures or slights of any kind. He took the freedom to drive as he pleased within the law, but he often had to take slights with it. Durwin had no problem at all in acknowledging that there were lots of better drivers than himself, especially among professional drivers."

Owen Winslow came in with a question. Inquiringly and somewhat perturbedly he asked, "the man who quite obviously wanted to imply that Durwin was inept at finding his way around, what did a person like that do for a living, what was his occupation?"

"He had been in the field of education for many years, and was well advanced in it," replied Collin.

"Wouldn't you know," added Owen, in an aghast manner.

"And how many fine, smart young persons has he belittled and ruined in his lifetime?" asked Gilda Emerson with disgust.

"We have no way of knowing," remarked Collin, "but he was very familiar with the game of belittling."

"Hundreds, perhaps," added Donna Coyne.

"And how many of them went to psychiatrists and mental hospitals?" questioned Albin Anders.

"And yet he would be well covered," said Brett Culver. "He would have many successes to his credit, which he would be sure were obvious to people."

"Yes," said Collin, "he would—the secondary ones so to speak, that he would help to what would be the top for them. But the really fine charactered and uniquely gifted ones he would help send by the wayside without it even being detected. The potential contemporary Lincolns, Twains and Churchills; the possible clergy of world renowned caliber; the modern age latent creative industrialists, business and commerce people; all of genial and genius disposition, and many lesser fine people as well; what happens to these? They could, in time, be operating freely under the moral influence of a mature, unbiased, unprejudiced, undiscriminating church if and where it existed. But because of the undisciplined pride and envious hatred held against them by belittlers who have access to their young lives, they go by the wayside to mediocre positions in life, or worse, to mental hospitals or the open street—a grossly sinful waste of the most valuable of human resources."

Leo Aidan added, "A teacher could help do that as a matter of course without giving it a second thought, let alone anyone else being able to detect it. With young school children it could be done with subtle slights, or by ignoring them at critical times like when they are eager to answer a question, or by down playing a good paper they have prepared."

"Yes, indeed," added Collin, 'belittlers do their destructive work in all of these ways and many more. This group is doing very well with its analysis of belittlers in general.

"Then there was another character Durwin had to contend with. Besides his frequent innuendo and slights meant to belittle, Durwin had to contend with him regarding the congregation's newsletter which wasn't published on a pre-set schedule. He loved to spring the deadline for material onto Durwin with short notice. Durwin would always meet that deadline with an excellent quality writing of a page or so. For the longest time Durwin's presentation of this page for publication drew the sadest look on this person's face. He always appeared disappointed that Durwin could come up with it. Actually, Durwin could come up with such a writing in an hour or so. However, he usually let the finished product lay overnight to see how it read next day. Sometimes it needed a touch-up here and there. Most times it was good as it was. It never brought words of approval from this person; only obvious disappointment."

Continuing with the story, Collin said, "In time, Durwin had little or no effective support at meetings, and was by now having a difficult time finding a way to speak much at all, being continually either cut down or having his suggestions brushed aside as though they were of no value. Especially in meetings where finance was discussed, Durwin was practically barred from participation by grunts and snorts of disapproval from some persons, and by a sheer refusal of others to let him get a word in at all. On one occasion when Durwin had some important information from the church at large to relay to them, he made an appointment with a key member of the appropriate committee for after worship. He sat down with the person and gave him the information verbally. He then told this person the reason for passing on the information through him was that 'many committee members don't like for me to speak at meetings. In order to ensure that his important information gets to them, I am asking you to give it to them.'

"This person knew the game so well that belittling came natural with him. 'Oh well,' he muttered in bits and pieces, 'we don't mind you speaking, if you have something to add to what we say.' Notice the 'if. They were to the point now where they were inferring that Durwin couldn't add to their discussions. Their attitude was he had nothing worthwhile to say anyway.

"By now the belittlers of the local church administration were all openly and brazenly treating Durwin in much the same manner: trivializing, repudating, denying, implying he was inept, implying they were so much superior; in short establishing the fallacy that he wasn't a high caliber enough minister for them. It was a mind-game, being played on Durwin by the 'conspiracy of sorts', as I have called it. Such a game is meant to brainwash, wear down, maim, discredit, and then when the victim's life and character are ruined, get rid of him. It can be deadly, but Durwin was strong.

"However, this local church that had so flourished during Durwin's early ministry there, was on the way down hill—in decline. Discussion on finance by now usually centered around juggling the accounts to ascertain which ones to pay this month, and which to hold off till later.

Any discussion on spending the slightest amount on ideas that might enhance church growth was out of the question. Their emphasis became more and more on saving here, there and everywhere, and less and less on ways for improvement and growth. When a church gets to the point where it continually concentrates on shrinking itself to save money, it is dooming itself to a mere existence.

"This church was now down to that. When they were in good financial condition, they had refused to spend even small amounts on the infra-structure for growth that Durwin tried so hard to put into place. They had shrunk themselves to where their financial position was precarious. They had no money to spend on growth now."

"That too would be blamed on Durwin, I suppose," blurted Leo.

"Well," responded Collin, "when they later asked for a change of minister, they indicated that Durwin was to blame for the church's ills. That may have included its tightening financial predicament. Durwin was never told what reasons were given for their request for his removal. Their reasons were never revealed, but their attitude was easy to discern. Time and again one could read between the lines, 'we are great just as we are; don't try to bring anything new to us; we are perfect; just give us the right minister.'"

Brett could not help but laugh, as sad as it was. "And what would be the right minister for them, Collin?" he asked.

Collin smiled. "It is amusing isn't it—sad but silly. The right minister for them would be something like this: one who thinks exactly as they think, and I mean exactly; one who never thinks of anything they don't think of first; who should have no original thought except what supports and furthers their ideas, and not even too much of that; who never says anything that will ruffle their proud feathers; who does everything they say, and I mean everything, without question, like a good little puppet, even if he has to work twenty five hours a day to do so; and don't do it too well, don't do it as good as they would, because that will upset their pride. Be sure to leave them a little room to look down on you and feel superior to you."

Brett interrupted, "That's impossible, as anyone knows."

"Right," responded Collin, "so they never do get the right minister; and the spiral goes on, with minister after minister walking *their* treadmill and getting nowhere with them.

"However, to support my statements that Durwin was having a difficult time being allowed to participate in discussions, let me tell you of another incident that illustrates the point. It was at a social gathering after a church business meeting. A person was telling the gathering of a business experience he once had. Others in the group were passing remarks about it, mostly favorable, but some pertaining to what might have been if such and such had been done. Durwin joined in on the conversations in a sociable manner. He omitted any hind-sight, but with his analytical mind he made some positive remarks about what had been done. The person whose business experience it was fumed and shouted at Durwin, 'You are insulting me. I'm insulted.'"

"What was insulting him," asked Albin.

"Well," said Collin, "Durwin didn't say anything to insult him. He just analyzed that person's business in a light in which the person had never seen it before. He had been complimented on some things about his own work that he had never thought of before. That's not insulting. The person's silly undisciplined pride was pricked."

"He didn't know how to react to someone smarter than himself," said Brett.

"Right on," replied Collin, "and that is a major problem of these proud belittlers. They do not know how to interact with people they perceive to be smarter than themselves. So their response is, sometimes to run away from them, but all too often it is to turn on them and belittle them, sometimes harshly, sometimes by trivalizing them.

"For some time by now at certain meetings and social functions, Durwin was almost continually the butt of sarcasm and under-the-breath side swipes. Sometimes the content of them was audible to the ear and sometimes not. Most always they came with a glance or glare at Durwin. It was a part of the mind-game to wear him down.

"One of their favorite bits of under-the-breath sarcasm was to the effect that Durwin was in the ministry only for the money. One member of the finance committee usually utilized this one before or at finance meetings where the minister's remuneration was to be discussed. It was a shake-down, not only to prevent Durwin from asking for more, which he never did anyway though most ministers often do, but to make Durwin feel he was already getting more than he earned. Durwin had, on appropiate occasions casually remarked that he had taken a reduction in remuneration by coming from Secundaterra to this church in Terraprima. That only served to harden them all the more against this smart guy with all the answers and who dared to say he was getting more money in other churches than he was in this one.

"They also were told that Durwin paid for postage of all letters going out from his office and personally absorbed all petty cash items as an extra contribution. He paid for all toll phone calls to church members and business places in nearby communities. This was in addition to a weekly offering at worship. Durwin also did all counseling free of charge. He wouldn't dare charge a fee as most ministers do. With these people so anxious and desperate to pin something on him to protect their pride by bringing him down it only incited their hatred all the more. The side-swipes as I call them, and the under-the-breath sarcasms became part of the course at gatherings. It was nothing short of mental abuse."

Collin turned to Dr. Eldren. "Dr. Eldren, once more I am treading on risky ground in a psychiatrist's presence, but again this is something that happens frequently where there is friction between types of people. It is generally labeled people making catty remarks under their breath. Belittlers use it often as one of their many tactics. May I go on with the story?"

"You are clear with me, Collin," Dr. Eldren nodded reassuringly. "The whole story in general supports the validity of the incidents even though they may be unprovable. Please continue. I find it most interesting."

"Thanks, Dr. Eldren," said Collin. "Let me tell of an incident that will illustrate it. A group were planning a Saturday work bee to help in a charitable cause. It was to be physically strenuous work on a building some miles away. Durwin had done much such work in his time. However, he didn't offer to go, because of the high risk of doing physically strenuous work while under the extreme mental stress of working all day with a group of very unfriendly people."

"He could have a heart attack or something, working under such conditions," said Brett quickly.

"Exactly," responded Collin, "and that is why he wouldn't go."

"The under-the-breath side-swipes were plenty at that meeting.

'He's not going. That's for sure, not him', followed by glares and glances at him and then at one another.

"Durwin would loved to have gone on the work bee under pleasant circumstances, but friendliness was totally absent.

"When the project on that building was completed, Durwin attended its re-opening celebration, an event of several hours duration. This was a fitting contribution for a clergyperson. There was no comment on it from the belittlers when Durwin reported it to them.

"I'll tell you now of an incident which is minor in comparison to some of the others I have told," continued Collin. "It illustrates vividly the lack of respect for a minister. There was a social day at the church with attractions for children. A candy floss machine was to be in operation. There were numerous convenient places it could be set up. Durwin and Canda were late arriving due to some pastoral care work that needed doing. They arrived just in time to see the candy floss machine about to be set into action in Durwin's private study at the church to which there were one or two other keys besides Durwins. Not only that, the machine was only inches away from where Durwin's clerical robes were hanging.

"Although nothing surprised him much any more in this church, he asserted himself firmly, reminding them that he was still the minister of this church, and they would have to move their machine elsewhere. They did so very reluctantly. There was much mess in the new location when the operation was over. Had it remained in Durwin's study, his robes and many books and the carpet would have been in a very sticky mess to say the least. There would have been a huge mess in the study which Durwin and Canda would have been left to clean up. There was no apology from anyone, or any admission of error. The atmosphere of the moment indicated that there was every reason for a perceptive mind to believe that this was a deliberate attempt to do harm to Durwin and his possessions. Furthermore, the person who perpetrated it had caused Durwin much difficulty before.

"Relationships came to a head between Durwin as minister, and the administration of the church at a meeting one evening. A business matter had arisen in which some small amounts of unforseen expenses had occurred. It was a small matter really, totaling in the vicinity of a hundred dollars or so. Nobody seemed to have a definite opinion on it. Finally one person said that since these expenses were for items useful to the project concerned, we should pay them. That seemed the reasonable route to Durwin. However, before he could lend his support another person spoke and said we should not have to pay for items not included in the original costs.

"Then Durwin endeavored to speak an opinion, 'most projects of any size, like this one, usually end up with some hidden or unexpected expenses, and—'

"He was interrupted curtly by a belittler before he could finish speaking, 'It is immoral for a church or its minister to accuse this company we are working with of dishonesty in hiding expenses until after the project has been completed,' she said in her usual haughty manner toward the Lawtons.

"From the general attitude that had by now set in towards the Lawtons, and by the tone of the remark, it was observable that this was a slur aimed at Durwin. Here was a mixture of undisciplined pride and ignorance, coming from a person of respected position in the community who had often behaved haughtily towards Durwin and Canda almost since their arrival. Here now was an absurd and brazen attempt from her to label Durwin as immoral towards these business people. The term 'hidden expenses,' meaning unforseen or unexpected expenses, is a common term in business not necessarily indicating dishonesty. Rightly or wrongly Durwin, for the first time during his years as minister of that church, responded with anger.

"It wasn't an uncontrolled anger, but it was very firm and loud. He told them he was tired of being put down in that wayward congregation. He asserted that he was a level headed, faithful minister who was serving them well, and it was high time they took a look at themselves and their attitude towards ministers, not only Durwin but the many ministers they had 'trouble' with before.

"They sat there speechless for a few moments. They didn't have what it takes to either pursue the issue further or to apologize. If they were expecting Durwin to get up and walk out, he was determined not to. He felt sure that while he was there, this was his church as much as theirs. Theology on the universality of the church would bear him out on that. These people didn't know much about theology, nor were they interested in learning. Their pride wouldn't let them do so. Durwin sat there waiting to see what would happen. The chairperson dismissed the meeting. They all left.

"Durwin attended to the church building, lights and doors, then went home alone. Canda was out that evening attending a meeting of a branch of the wider church in which she was quite active and to date well received. Durwin felt well pleased that at last he had put these people in their place for once. He dared to hope that this would be a turning point for good. However, the church at large, in its combination of naivete and utter fear of an often overpowerful laity and its consequent appeasing alignment with them, together with its own inclination to belittle and to align with other belittlers, would see that it wasn't so.

"Later that week, quite by accident, Durwin discovered that there was to be a special meeting of the local church administration with a church official whom they had called in. Durwin hadn't been notified of the meeting, but since he had now discovered it, the church official suggested to Durwin, that after the meeting between the board and the official had taken place, Durwin and Canda be called in to present their side of the case. Durwin agreed. He and Canda waited at home for the phone to ring. It was late evening when finally it rang.

"Canda answered, and a terrified voice that could be heard not only on the phone but around the room, came from the other end of the line screaming frantically, 'It is no good for you to come to the church. Things are not good here. You had better stay away.' It was the voice of the church official, obviously overwrought by an overpowerful laity of the local pastorate—overwrought and sounding very fearful and unstrung.

"Durwin heard the terrified and frenzied tones from the distance across the room, though he could not understand what was said. When the brief and terror-stricken conversation ended Canda hung up and told Durwin what she had heard. They debated whether they should go to the church anyway, but decided not to. Much later, in hind sight, they came to the conclusion that it had been a mistake not to go.

"More than an hour later, when it was getting late into the night, the Lawton's doorbell rang. It was the church official appearing emotionally disheveled, but struggling to keep his composure.

"Now trying to make the impression that there wasn't much to it at all, he suggested to Durwin that if he would apologize for raising his voice at the meeting the matter would be dropped and things should be in good order from now on. Durwin and Canda knew that it would take more than that to set things right in this church. And besides, they weren't called upon to give their side of the story. Only one side was heard—a side based most likely on 'the most warped and twisted' views of the proud and envious. However, out of pity for the church official being so pathetically treated and so obviously overpowered by the laity, Durwin agreed to apologize if the other party concerned apologized to him.

"The church official then rambled on about how when he had a difficult church, and to use his words, 'they used to crucify me, and I used to crucify them.' Then he implied that you have to expect that in the church. This didn't seem much of a solution to Durwin, but it seemed at the time as much as the official was capable of. In fact, it set the stage for the congregation and minister to quarrel with each other as though it was the only way out. It wasn't Durwin's way. "Later Durwin would find there was more to this supposed solution than met the eye at first, because the stage was well set church area wide for the wearing down and/or the wearing out of Durwin. According to the solution offered by the supervisor, there would be continuous confrontation, a whole group pitted against two, and now the Lawton's not even able to raise their voice in defense of themselves. As time went on and Durwin learned the vicious mind-game from experience, he would know in hind-sight what he was in for. He would be continuously antagonized with attempted brainwashing into believing he was inferior to them (the opposite was true) and then relegated to small pastorates, and also obscurity in the wider church. If his health, either mental or physical, was broken, it would be implied that he wasn't strong enough, and too sensitive for the ministry. If he fought back with anger, he would be labeled as bad tempered and told to apologize. If he won out over them he would be labeled as being hard on his people. If he gave up the ministry to seek a better life, he would be labeled as a back slider, not staying with his calling to ministry, or, as not having had a genuine call in the first place, or, not having staying power and unable to see it through. Eventually, much of the wearing out would be done most always by secondary people; that is, people in seemingly insignificant positions, or younger people. If they won a battle, it would be shrugged off as Durwin unable to cope with even these young inexperienced and/or insignificent people.

"A psychiatrist connected to the church at large would bring this wearing down and wearing out matter to the forefront of Durwin's mind in a later tricky interview which I related to you when telling you of the Lawtons' immigration problem. In other areas of Durwin's life, in his relations with the church at large, and in his continuing education experience, this wearing out tactic would also be predominant. The conspiracy of sorts as I have called it was taking further formation. From here on Durwin would indeed be a marked man more than ever.

"The Lawtons learned in time that it is a wide-spread game among belittlers of Terraprima to bring down, to render useless or destroy, people like Durwin and his wife Canda. In this game, once you are marked, it spreads and the conspiracy of sorts has begun. Even belittlers not connected to your work can detect by various circumstance in your life at large that you are a marked person. The conspiracy of sorts spreads even more. A less stronger person would have succumbed to it, but Durwin and Canda both had far above average endurance. All of this that I am saying now may seem strangely sinister, and it is. But the remainder of the story of the Lawtons will bear it out.

"The church official went home seeming pleased. The whole incident proved to be a major turning point in Durwin's life. From now on, Durwin would be belittled and brainwashed by the larger church as well. It would be well under way before the Lawtons became wise to it.

"A short time later Durwin received in the mail a letter of apology from the woman. It was, however, dubiously written. It read, 'If I have said anything wrong I apologize—'. The 'if was very noteable. However, at the next meeting Durwin apologized face to face for his anger, and said he should have handled the incident in ways other than getting angry. He did this without minimazing the problem in any way."

Leo spoke up, "I'll bet the woman who made the derogatory statement was not at the meeting when Durwin apologized."

"She was noticably absent," said Collin.

"So," said Leo, "she does her apology by mail. Durwin does his in person before the board. That says a lot to me about character. How did things go from then on?"

"Subdued," replied Collin. "Things were subdued in tone, but the problems weren't resolved."

"Church officials of the area generally know they have problems in some churches but they gloss it over. Difficult churches they sometimes call them, but they never openly acknowledge it as the major concern it really should be. Nor do they even attempt to analyze and cope with the overall problem. It is beyond their scope and fortitude to do so; also they are afraid of and therefore appease the over-powerful laity so often involved. Several books have now been written on the matter, but little is done about it on a local level. To enable the church at large to hush up the problem, the ministers are to 'put up and shut up, or else', as it is so aptly said in slang. That, in my opinion, is the reason for so many damaged, even ruined personalities in ministry. It is the result of working for years under mental conditions unfit for human employment. Together with other difficult people, belittlers are free to pursue their tactics because of the inaction of the church at large.

"Durwin still wasn't free to perform his own ministry. To please their own pride, the local church lay administration was still trying to create the atmosphere that Durwin wasn't a good minister. They were trying to convince Durwin of that too. In appeasement, and many of them being belittlers themselves, the wider church hierarchy would now support them in the sinister deed. The unspoken philosophy by which these belittlers lived and supported their undisciplined pride was, to repeat again, 'we are perfect as we are, just give us the right minister.' Of course the right minister never comes; such a minister cannot exist. However, there was a brief truce in Durwin's church.

"We are getting well into the Lawton's final year at that church. Christmas Eve came. Durwin had always had an overflow attendance at his midnight service. Extra chairs were always put in place in advance by the ushers. This year there were no chairs put out. People began to arrive. Ushers showed them to the pews. The sanctuary began to fill. Still they did not put out extra chairs. The ushers tried hard, very hard to seat everyone, but could not. Finally, only after numerous people were left standing did the ushers hesitantly and condescendingly bring in the extra chairs. The sanctuary was filled to overflowing as usual. The ushers and some others could not look Durwin in the face. Many others complimented him on the wonderful service.

"The New Year and winter came and there was snow to be shoveled. Durwin had lived in Secundaterra most of his life and was used to snow. He was also very aware, as were most people of Secundaterra, that shoveling snow at middle age and beyond, and more especially heavy snow, could be detrimental to health. It was a major factor in bringing on heart attacks in older people. The caution was, when you reach your late forties you should ease off on snow shoveling. Durwin was in his late fifties. When the residence driveway was heavily blocked he paid to have it ploughed out, shoveling around the door himself. When it was a lighter snowfall he had an electric power shovel which did the work effectively. Once when a snow plough wasn't available, he paid a boy to shovel the whole driveway. The boy was eager to earn money and did an excellent job.

"In this his final winter there, Durwin was approached by the persons generally responsible for church property, and asked if he would do the snow shoveling on the walks and around the entrance to the church each time it snowed. That would mean much more snow for Durwin to shovel than he would have if he didn't pay anyone to do the ploughing around the residence. He turned it down for that and other reasons. A second reason he turned it down was because he went to school in the city early each Monday. If it snowed on Sunday night, that would mean Durwin would have to do about two hours or more of snow shoveling before leaving for school at seven in the morning. At Durwin's age that was too much. Another reason he turned it down was that it would not be a good precedent for any minister to start. It would almost certainly lead him to be saddled with other manual jobs on the church property which, together with his heavy load of usual church work and study, would enslave him.

"Durwin phoned the boy who had shoveled for him before and talked to him and his mother. The boy wanted to start saving money for college. He was willing and eager to shovel snow, mow lawns or whatever. At a meeting Durwin discussed this informally with several people present. 'Oh no,' was their response, 'we will arrange for snow clearing. We have someone else in mind.' To Durwin's knowledge arrangements were not made. Snow shoveling and later lawn mowing was taken care of only sporadically and ineffectively, mostly by a volunteer or two. It all could have been done regularly and well except that Durwin just couldn't be the one to bring it about. The persons to whom Durwin refused to do the snow shoveling, together with others, were later instrumental in asking for his removal as minister of that church.

"You no doubt remember what happened to the first Bible study group. Durwin now arranged another one, this time to be held in the church parlor in the afternoons, with different resource materials than used before. Instead of utilizing the previously used guide book, now they would use the Bible itself, plus two world renowned sets of Bible commentaries; one of them written for lay people, the other a little more scholarly, from which Durwin would draw extra material if and when needed. In this way Durwin could himself guide the Bible study, give it depth and also prevent it from being dominated by overbearing people with their own opinions.

"Several people attended this Bible study group. Some of them, at first, were a little uneasy about the new format, that it might be above their reach as far as Bible study was concerned. The chairperson, as we remember her by that name, paid the study group a visit one day. Whether she intended to join or not we do not know. However, her first remark was, 'Oh, so you are not using the books we always used.'

"'No, we are using these books,' answered Durwin, pointing to the sets of commentaries on the church library bookshelf, and the two volumes from the set that were on the table before him. The chairperson, looking down in the mouth, turned and walked away, and never returned. The books in use were too much for her, or so she thought. She wouldn't be able to take control from the minister.

"The group enjoyed the Bible study tremendously. One member's comment described the atmosphere that prevailed. 'I have never studied the Bible this way before, and it is fascinating. I am enjoying it fully.' The group studied weekly from early winter to spring, when it broke for Easter.

"Springtime came. There were two new housing projects well under way in the area. If there was some appropriate publicity about the church, some of the newcomers in these developments might become interested in attending. The church administration still couldn't agree on any proposals on anything from Durwin. So he and Canda, faced with the options of either doing nothing, or doing something on their own, choose to do it on their own. Whatever they might be accused of, this way at least they couldn't be accused of doing nothing.

"During the spring they worked on the beautification of the church grounds—just the two of them. They cleared the underbrush and trimmed the trees in the wooded lot beside the church. This made the church more visible coming from either direction of the street. They trimmed the hedges and took good care of the flowers, planting others at their own expense. These improvements gave the property a more cultivated look.

"The Lawtons also purchased, at their own expense, additional church directional signs, and Durwin negotiated with the nearby municipalities who gladly agreed to erect them at appropriate sites. They had other plans to attract newcomers, such as printed invitations which could be delivered in one of an assortment of possible ways to the new housing area.

"Durwin will never forget the response he recieved at a meeting when he revealed his plan for church growth into the new housing area, and the arrangements for new direction signs to be placed around the area. There was a look of sheer terror on the face of one of the not very mature belittlers. It was as if he was saying, 'What are you doing to our pride? No way can we let you succeed in this.' Many of the others looked hostile and/or gloomy. There wasn't the slightest interest shown in supporting it, absolutely no positive comment on it. There was complaint about what the cost might be.

"Durwin informed them that the signs were contributed by an anonymous donor, and that the invitations to the new housing area, and follow up visiting could be done voluntarily. There was dead silence on the matter for a moment or two. Then other business was pursued.

"The signs went up, but the remainder of the plan was never completed. Soon, a movement was in process to have Durwin ousted from the church.

"All the while the belittlment of the Lawtons was going on, as I have told you before, various colleagues and acquaintances whom the Lawtons had befriended throughout the area knew what they were up against, and knew the Lawtons to be fine people and good workers. They would say to them on occasion, such and such a church would be nice for you people next, always naming a church where a fine couple would fit in well. The Lawtons as yet had no reason to believe other than the area administration would think of them in that light as well when it came to a move.

"They were in for a shock and a surprise when not only a move became imminent, but Durwin was refused further placement. They would in time also learn that the church at large had no concept at all of placing ministers according as their type and character would fit the general character of the congregation; for one example among many, placing a minister of crude sociability, and with little or no social graces, over a well cultured congregation. Almost always that congregation would decline. Hence there were many misfits, and many declining pastorates.

"Outwardly, the administration of the larger church till now had seemed determined that Durwin was going to stay where he was. The all too powerful local church administration was now determined he was going to move. They made a formal request by letter that he be moved. This being the first time such a thing had ever happened to Durwin, he was dismayed. In his previous denomination to be asked to be moved was rock bottom and only happened for very drastic reasons. Also, as I have said earlier, in his previous denomination when a pastorate wasn't working out it was the expected thing to move to a more compatable pastorate without being asked to do so.

"Durwin was never informed by the supervising church official of the letter to him requesting that he be removed. Durwin was informed of it comtemptiously by one of the persons in the local church who was most responsible for it. He was told by that person that it was a unanimious decision of the committee responsible for that aspect of the church's decision making. At the time, Durwin had no reason to disbelieve that person. A year after he had moved, he was informed by a more responsible person that some of them on the committee had never seen nor heard of the letter, let alone be a party to approving it unanimously. Nevertheless, the letter, a copy of which Durwin was able to obtain, stated that it was the unanimous decision of the committee to have Durwin removed as their minister.

"At the time, Durwin believed the person who first told him about it. That same person also said that the church supervisor told him that Durwin would only be moved if he agreed to it himself. Durwin thought it strange that the church official never counselled with him personally on the matter but rather had to be counselled on such things by a person who had been putting him down for the longest time. By now though he was getting accustomed to strange happenings in this denomination at Terraprima.

"Durwin waited a little, but still there was no notification, caution, advice or counsel of what he should do now that a request had been made that he be moved, and, whether it would be wise for him to agree to it or not. Guided only by his knowledge of the general practice in his previous denomination in Secundaterra and the prospect of getting one of the better churches so often referred to for him by his well wishing colleagues, Durwin wrote to the supervisor a letter of agreement to move; not to quit, but to move to another pastorate. Where communication had been completely lacking before, now it came quickly. Durwin was informed that there was no further church appointment for him.

"Much later, it would be implied by the church area hierarchy that the reason Durwin was being refused further church placement was because he was abandoning his present pastorate. That was a flimsy cover-up indeed. Durwin had said nothing about quitting. He only offered to move to another pastorate thinking they would offer him one, as they were obliged to do in accordance to the terms offered to him to come into this denomination from Secundaterra.

"Belittlers being in character as they are, would not be likely to give the real reason why they wanted to get rid of Durwin as their minister. The reason they inferred openly much later on was to the effect that they wanted a rousing, pulpit pounding, shouting showman type of preacher. This was in keeping with the showmanship concept some of the belittlers had of a preacher. It was in keeping with their own characters. Durwin was not a showman.

"This desire for an extremely animated preacher was also an idea adopted from the television fad of the time. There were a number of T.V. evangelists who either put on an exorbitant show or were prone to get carried away emotionally. Their manner of preaching was not in keeping with the usual practices of this denomination, nor was it of any interest to Durwin himself, as effective as some of these preachers have been at times. But it caught the attention of some belittlers in the congregation who were more interested in showmanship than in content.

"It has been interesting to note over the years," said Collin in speaking of his own experiences, "that a congregation apart from its administration can love the preaching of their preacher, and yet the administration can find no good in it. Why?" The group members waited with interest for Collin to answer his own question.

"The reason is, where that happens, the wrong people are in control of the church. In the administration they may be proud, and looking for the minister to boost their pride. Meanwhile the minister is preaching what will help the people in the pews to grow in grace and faith. These people are looking for something for mind and spirit. Such preaching will at times show people their human depravity. While sincere Christians generally take this in good spirits and use it to overcome their human shortcomings which is what it means to be nurtured in faith and growing in grace, the proud administration want no part of it. They want, not what will help them grow to be better people, but, what will boost their pride and make them feel superior just as they are. Consequently, the better the preacher is at preaching for the congregation, the more the proud administration goes against him. Also, if he is too good a minister, it detracts from their power and control. This they can't stand either.

"This explains why the congregation was happy with Durwin's ministry, while its administration was not, and why the administration had to get rid of him. The desire for a more animated preacher was only an excuse. In the hymn 'All Praise To Our Redeeming Lord,' the first line of the second verse reads, 'He bids us build each other up.' To nurturing Christians that means building each other up in grace and faith. To the wayward proud ones in the church it comes across to them as building up each others pride. Durwin wasn't doing the latter, so the proud ones didn't appreciate his ministry.

"Ironically, this desire for a preacher more lively in the pulpit of Durwin's church was in sharp contrast to the belittlers previous complaints that Canda's church music was too lively. Canda, although not highly trained in music, but always ready to help out when needed, volunteered to play the organ for worship any time the organist was away. Canda believed in lively singing and very definitely had a way of bringing out the best in the congregational singing of hymns. The belittlers complained that they didn't want that kind of music in their church."

"Prejuduce, no doubt," interrupted Donna, "it seems no matter what the Lawtons did, it didn't please them. The music was too lively, the preaching wasn't lively enough. Just prejudice, I'm sure."

"Yes, I agree," added Owen, "when belittlers are down on someone, they find fault with even the best of things. They have to put them down on everything, anything they do."

"Canda was discriminated against and oppressed in other ways as well," continued Collin. "Canda had had a wide experience in the women's work of the church at large for many years. She was often utilized as a guest speaker, and brainstormed for ideas in planning. Now this local church came to a new low. All planning eventually came to be conducted secretly at unannounced meetings in Canda's absence. If Canda was given any role at all in the women's work of the congregation by this planning done in secret by an unofficial committee, it was to be a minor role indeed. For example at a Mother's Day service presented completely by mothers, she was given the role of announcing after the service was over that the men were serving refreshments and all women present were to be their guests—a very minor role indeed."

"I would say that it was moreso the place of the men to extend that invitation," said Gilda quickly.

"Yes indeed," said Donna.

All the group members agreed.

"Canda was further discriminated against that day," Collin explained. "Before the congregation stood for the singing of the last hymn, a woman circulated through the pews with a flower for each woman present. When she came through the pew where Durwin and Canda were sitting she stopped right in front of Canda, passed a flower to a woman in the pew ahead of Canda, then turned around facing Canda, and leaned past her while passing a flower to a woman in the pew behind Canda. She then looked Canda straight in the face and walked away. Upon returning to the chancel she looked straight at Canda again, announcing that there were some flowers left and if anyone wanted one they could come and get it after the service."

"An open snub and a brazenly open insult to a minister's spouse, or anyone else for that matter, and a disgrace to the Christian church," stated Leo.

"Yes, indeed," the others agreed.

"Knowing how openly some belittlers operate, I'd guess she just as brazenly covered herself on that one too, if it did become necessary," said Brett.

"Oh yes," replied Collin. "When another woman in the congregation who, together with some others had seen and were aghast at the incident and confronted her with it, the outwardly belittling woman said it was entirely an accidental oversight. The fact is though that in addition to the way the deed was done at the moment, there were also many lesser snubbings before and after that occasion which verify that woman's attitude toward Canda and Durwin as well. Belittlers always try to cover their tracks, but give them enough rope as the saying goes, or give them enough time and eventually, through their hatred, they will reveal themselves for what they are.

Collin commented some more. "Belittlers are often blatant liars. Some of them think it is real smart to be so. It is part of their mind-game to do their belittling quite openly, and then with a straight face deny it. So convinced are they that it is right to put down big-shots and/or smart-alecks, that they do these evil deeds unashamedly.

"Now to contiue with the dilemma," said Collin, "Durwin firmly protested the lack of an appointment for him. Then he was vaguely offered 'something' in such and such a far away area. Durwin already knew through travelling, and through information previously attained from a friend who had lived there that it was the boondocks, where the chief weekend recreation of the area was drinking and drunkeness. Furthermore, pouting at and belitting nice people was commonplace and taken for granted there. If Durwin and Canda, refined people as they are, were having a hard time surviving in their present position, they wouldn't stand a chance at all in that area. As soon as it was offered, Durwin turned it down and said he would return to Secundaterra. The administration of the local church in Terraprima, as hard as it had tried, could not bring down Durwin and Canda. The church at large, being largely belittlers themselves, and desiring to protect their own against the outsiders, was now attempting to do it for them.

"Indications now were that the church hierarchy wanted to get rid of Durwin—wanted him to leave. Also, though, they wanted to get rid of him in an unfair manner. He was too good for them, more than they could stand. But by insinuation and innuendo they were trying to make him out to be not good enough for them. Their implications were to be to the effect that he was incompetent and unsatisfactory. In the Bible this is called slander. In the law it is called defamation of character. What they were doing was both immoral and unlawful. Durwin wasn't about to leave under such a cloud as that. Later, when he became more wise to them, they didn't want him to leave. They kept him there to destroy his career and his personhood with it."

Gilda Emerson bristled as she spoke. "Didn't you tell us earlier, Collin, that Durwin would only go to Terraprima if he was guaranteed an appointment until retirement time?"

"Yes, that is right," replied Collin, "and to Durwin's knowledge and impression and in accordance with the practices of the church at that time it meant an appointment in the same church area as he now was located. However, now they first told him there was no appointment. You may not be surprised by now, but much later Durwin learned that his standing or status with the denomination had already been changed so they now could, within the church rules, drop him at any time. This change in status was made without any consultation with or notification to Durwin at all. It wasn't until he protested, still unaware of his changed status, that they offered him 'something' out in the boondocks, in a different area altogether."

"Ah sure," said Leo, "they were trying to get rid of him first. He was probably to them a thorn in their side. So when he didn't readily agree to go away altogether, they offered something where he would at least be out of sight, and not only that, but to a place where they would hope he get worn down by belittlers and eventually slip down the drain so to speak."

"I think you are right," replied Collin. "again, for fear of the paranoia label it is risky to say that, particularly in the presence of a psychiatrist, because of the way this church operates. But as the story gets into its next phase, you will be able to discern for yourself whether the wider church administration are a bunch of stupid jackasses or a bunch of crafty belittlers."

"The way they operate?" questioned Dr. Eldren.

"Yes," responded Collin calmly. "This church operated, with Durwin at least, in a secrecy that no other organization I know of does. They can make you out to be wrong anytime by implication only. I suppose many organizations and people imply things at times instead of coming right out with it. They do so for various reasons, but mainly because if they are wrong, or even downright ridiculous, they can easily cover up the mistake. So likewise if the area church administration was confronted with an accusation of trying to get rid of a pastor just to get him out of their way, they would probably deny it, and cover up by saying they really had no place for him. However, in Durwin's case that wouldn't correctly hold for other reasons such as his years of tenure with the church at large, for which he had earlier been given credit."

Collin continued, "Durwin was a thorn in the side of the hierarchy all right. Some of the better people in high places, the relatively few who knew what was going on, were showing some guilt and shame. They were ashamed of their church and what they saw in it as Durwin, by his presence, was bringing out the worst in the envious ones, and revealing what they really were. The hierarchy felt uncomfortable in the presence of Durwin and Canda. Getting rid of them would be a solution - deceitful and cowardly, yet convenient. Their total mode of operation with Durwin was secrecy and deceit. In their dealing with Durwin such secrecy was used for cover up and denying all by implication. In contrast, it should have been communicating, admitting and correcting.

"I say again, every organization has its confidentialities. In their proper context and discriminately used they are necessary, helpful and good. But when such confidentialities are used for the purpose of covering up wrong doings, or to escape responsibility for it, or to make the other person out to be wrong, yes, and even to destroy a person, then that is immorally deceptive. Furthermore such secretive operations often make it impossible for a person to defend himself. Justice is not done. It is ironic in churches that portray themselves as champions of justice."

In an aside from the story Collin remarked, "Durwin once told me that the church administration of the area had more secrets than the C.I.A, the F.B.I, and the K.G.B. all put together, at least in their dealings with Durwin. Strangely enough, in an interview for publication, the C.E.O. of that area remarked that among the requirements for leadership in its administration was the need to be 'candid, open, up front!'

"As I have already said, secrecy can make the other person out to be in error when really he is not. Sometimes it can make him out to be a liar or a stupid person, or even worse again, making him out to be, in the eyes of a psychiatrist, a person with impaired perception and imagination, who is in need of therapy of one kind or another. The psychiatrist can then label the person with some type of deranged thinking which often can be attached to a diagnosis for one of the mental disorders. A person may be at high risk to try to explain to a psychiatrist what had been done to him under such secretive circumstances. These are reasons why so many people would not dare to talk as we are talking in this group."

Dr. Eldren shuffled in his chair, forced a little smile, nodded and said, "I see the point you are making Collin. I hope we can discuss it more fully some evening after we have heard the complete story of the Lawtons. Then perhaps we can get a clearer perspective on it."

"That's fine with me," replied Collin, "secrecy, innuendo and hair splitting deceit are major factors in the attempted bringing down of Durwin Lawton, but for now I will continue with the story.

"A friend interceded to the C.E.O. on Durwin's behalf. Soon another friend was informed that they had a 'nice' church in mind for Durwin, leaving the impression upon the friend that it really was a nice worthwhile place. Note that this was taking place without any direct communication by the hierarchy to Durwin."

Owen Winslow, who himself had some years of ministry in the pastorate, interrupted the story. "Was this 'nice' church they had in mind for Durwin a country church?"

"Yes it was," replied Collin.

"Seems to me" said Owen, "that they were taking advantage of the old, old fallacy about the country church; the old myth of the nice peaceful country church. This is, no doubt, what they were implying to Durwin's friend that they were coming up with for Durwin. In reality, of course, such peaceful little country churches for people like the Lawtons are just as rare as peaceful big suburban or city churches. Country churches also have their share of belittlers; some congregations are dominated by them. Country churches also have their share of problems and problem ridden people to deal with, including belittlers who come down hard on fine, intelligent people. If there was a rural church that the Lawtons could fit into, it would be in a rural area that had become largely a residential area for either retired or active business and professional people with a minimum of belittlers among them."

"I agree with you, Owen," said Collin. "Also, nowadays, statistics are telling us that rural areas of Terraprima have, per capita, more crime, drug/alcohol and related abuse than do cities and suburbia. If there was any notion or pretense of putting the Lawtons in a nice peaceful rural community where life would be easy and pleasant for them, it was either deceitful or downright silly and naive, and may have led to catastrophe for them. However, I am convinced there was more to it than that. The Lawtons had been badly maligned. The hierarchy wanted to be rid of them instead of tackling the problem. As you hear another phase of the story two weeks from now, I think you will see ample implications of that."

Collin continued, "There was a shroud of secrecy surrounding Durwin's appointment to this 'nice' country church. Before it took place, Durwin's supervisor was still acting very congenial toward him, as though he appreciated Durwin's good ministry. Yet here Durwin was being re-appointed to the far reaches of this church area at a greatly reduced salary. He had refused to go to the boondocks. Now he was being appointed to as near the likeness of it as was possible and still remain in the same church area. Although the placement was supposed to be the responsibility of a number of people acting together, they would normally do so taking into consideration the references of the immediate past supervisor. Durwin would be under a new supervisor in this new appointment, by the way, but he wondered if the present supervisor was being two-faced, yet at the time he didn't seem to be that kind of person. Later experiences would convince Durwin that the supervisor was being smooth and nice to him while leading him down the garden path to destruction. He too was playing a mind-game."

Collin interjected an insight into the story. "What Durwin didn't know at the time is that belittlers have a ploy they use which utilizes the nice country setting. It goes this way: belittlers like to cover their dirty work by intimating that it is the big city or busy suburban atmosphere, not their underhanded tactics to undermine you, that causes people like the Lawtons and you and I to falter or fold. They imply that we are too ambitious for our own good, and we should be satisfied with the little country places, because it is as much as we can handle. It is one of their foremost ploys to put a fine, smart person down and out of the way. I've had it tried on me a number of times. However Durwin wasn't yet fully wise to their mind-games.

"Just before his move was effected he attended a large gathering of the wider church. A lay person was required to attend with him, so one of the foremost belittlers went along. It made for a very tense day. To make it worse, another key official of the church was very cordial to the belittler accompanying Durwin, while completely ignoring, not even speaking to Durwin. Obviously the church hierarchy as a whole was now going negative towards Durwin—birds of a feather flocking together. No way were they going to let a couple from little Lower Secundaterra show up a congregation of theirs. Not that that's what the Lawtons were trying to do. But any such persons as they were, and from a place like that, had to be lower than the least common denominator of Terraprima. Durwin was beginning feel for sure now that he was labeled in the wider church administration as well.

"As time went by, this labeling would be affirmed by the continuing attitudes taken toward Durwin by a significant number of people in high places and low from there on. Durwin was only beginning to know what a marked man he was, and just how many in high places and low and in between, would be playing this mind-game on him."

Gilda Emerson fumed, "Wouldn't the fair and respectable thing to do be, if there were derogatory reports about Durwin's performance, to confront him with it. Even if it were true reports of some weak area in his work, wouldn't they confront Durwin with his weak areas and help him with them—a pastor to pastors interaction?"

"That sounds like the right thing to do," replied Collin, "but it didn't happen that way. There was a complete shroud of secrecy over the whole matter.

"I ask you to consider as we go along," Collin continued, "was it merely a relay of false and prejudiced information that had caused Durwin to be treated so badly. Or, was it as Durwin later concluded, that an age old and vicious game of systematic destruction of smart guy Durwin had begun amid a sinister secrecy and deception that appears to be in practice throughout much of this church in Terraprima, and in much of secular Terraprima also; a game played cruelly and brutally to protect the pride and hide the envy and tactics of belittlers. If it were the former, that is, false information, then as the story continues to unfold, you will hear of some of the most ignorant stupidity ever performed by educated leaders of humanity. To say it is the latter, that is, a vicious and destructive mind-game, is to risk being told it is unprovable, and that it is utterly paranoid to think it was an intentional attempt at the destruction of a person and/or his career."

"Well said," Gilda replied, wide eyed and eager to know more. "I will keep an open mind on it."

"Me too," was the general and exuberant response from the other group members.

"Another question: why didn't Durwin go back to Secundaterra?" asked Donna Coyne.

"There were several reasons," replied Collin.

"Durwin was not one to give up easily on anything. When he was told about this 'nice' church, he was also told there was some growth there. Durwin had a record of building up churches. With growth in the area he thought he would be able to do so with the church here and redeem his career in ministry. He was also told by the supervisor that 'the best offer for appointment comes first, if you turn it down, the next one is not as good.' Also, both Durwin's and Canda's main family connection was in Terraprima. He wanted to stay if he could."

"You will tell us about his experiences in the new church also, won't you?" asked Owen Winslow with concern.

"Yes, of course," said Collin. "It is a part of the total dismal picture I want you to have. I will tell you about it at a future meeting. For now, I wish to finish up some odds and ends concerning the Lawtons' experiences in the church we have been discussing here tonight, and I think that will be enough for this meeting.

"Durwin still performed the excellent ministry he was credited with much earlier. His performance was superior to the end. Durwin and Canda continued as always to remain courteous and friendly toward the belittlers in the church he was about to leave. He continually ministered to them as though they were receptive to his ministry in a friendly way. Except for the one incident of anger I told you about earlier, Durwin patiently and with great perserverance ministered to them lovingly and caringly. It didn't break through the crust with which they had surrounded themselves. They looked upon it only as weakness that opened the way for them to abuse the Lawtons all the more.

"Time and again Durwin tried to assure them that they were smart people, and that they had good ideas. That only encouraged them in their ever present rivalry and disire for credit, power and control, and to feel superior to Durwin. He tried to get through to them that a minister, due to his training and his experience in other churches, was bound to know more about ministry than they. This was implied by them to be boasting. Under all and every circumstance they were down on their minister, and in rivalry with him for credit for all attempted progress, and for power and control of the general oversight of the church. These belittlers could not look up to anyone. They could only look down and were not content unless they were doing so.

"Durwin was a calm, strong and gentle person who gave a superior performance. The belittlers did not know how to react or interact with someone like that; someone who they perceived to be so different from themselves. So they portrayed him in their insinuations of gross malignment as harsh and difficult, with no other basis for it other than he occasionally expressed opinions different from theirs, and they in their over-sensitivity felt hurt by it. It shook their sense of hollow pride and false security. This caused them to actually believe that Durwin was doing something harmful to them."

"They were paranoid," exclaimed Leo quickly.

"Sure they were," responded Collin, and continued, "these people often expressed opinions different from each other. But when a different opinion came from a person like Durwin, then they reacted as though Durwin was actually wronging them.

"In the immaturity of their own faulty, but solidly entrenched mind-set, it was as though they expected Durwin to express no thoughts different than their own. This was an impossible expectation of course, which if allowed to be pursued would rob Durwin of all personhood, destroy his capacity to think as a human being, and relegate him to mental incapacity fit only for a mental institution or the open street. It was not only the local church that treated him this way, but by now major parts of the larger church, as you shall see as the cruel story of oppression continues to unfold.

"Another aspect of the scenario was that because Durwin didn't succumb to this expectation, they acted as though he wasn't adjusting to their land and really didn't like their land. Ironically, when Durwin and Canda each bought a new car, they bought vehicles made in Terraprima. Soon thereafter there was, by strange coincidence, a rash of car buying among the belittlers, some of whom unwittingly bought foreign cars. At a time in conversation when a belittler was extolling the superiority of Terraprima to Durwin as though he needed to hear it, Durwin politely replied 'Yes, that is why Canda and I bought Terraprima made cars.' The belittler sputtered in embarrassment, 'Oh well, my car is foreign made, but there are times when foreign is better, sometimes you know.'

"Time after time, through Scripture readings, sermons, hymns and Bible study, Durwin emphasized the Apostle Paul's concept of 'varieties of gifts, but the same spirit.'(I Corinthians 12:4, R.S.V.) It never was able to penetrate the faulty mind-set of these people.

"Durwin had always been a fast worker, well organized, able to produce in abundance, and with good results when it wasn't all blocked by belittlers. His work day was usually fourteen to sixteen hours a day except for Saturdays and Sundays when it was reduced to about half of that. There was an occasional hour or two out for shopping each week, and an occasional evening to visit family or to eat out, usually on the week-end. This time schedule included his ministry and his continuing education to continually update his ministry. For all that, he was often side-swiped with insinuations of laziness and incompetence as well as harshness. That's the way they wanted to see him, so that's the way them made him out to be and thats the way they wanted to brainwash him into thinking about himself. Their insinuations didn't make sense, didn't stand to reason. Nevertheless, after the notorious meeting of the supervisor with the church board, with the following request for apologies, this scenario of attitudes and inuendos intensified and became noticeably evident not only in the local church now, but among many in the wider church, particularly its administrators. The Lawtons were never given a chance to counteract or to speak for themselves on these matters, neither at the notorious meeting nor any time thereafter."

"Collin, was there any change at all in any of them over all that period of time?" asked Gilda Emerson, "do such people change at all?"

"There were traces of change here and there," replied Collin, "but when unchecked pride is in the way change is hampered. There was one person who began to see the depravity and the distortion of her character. Had she accepted the fact, even if only to herself, that she had been deficient, and then corrected herself, she could have continuously grown in grace to become a lovely, good-natured person. She already had many nice qualities. Many more could have been added.

"But no, as she began to correct herself, she also began to deny to herself, and to others by implication that she had ever been deficient in character. The implications included that the pastor was treating her badly. Actually, all he had done was, by his presence and character, make her aware of her deficiences.

"It is Durwin's opinion that it may well have been this person's warped and twisted implications that caused the turning of the tide for him in the wider church."

"There's gratitude for you," quipped Leo. "Durwin causes her mind to be opened to better, and she turns on him for it!"

"That is a typical reaction from their kind," said Collin sadly. "I will give you further instances of this in later parts of the story. Their pride is still in the way of completing the change of mind-set. So they take one step at a time, covering up as they go, making it a very slow process —sometimes years, especially if the person stays in the same location. If pride was out of the way their growth could be continuous."

"On the other hand, if that person were to go away to another local church in a new setting totally away from the old, chances are, in the new setting she would behave very well in her new found self. In the old setting she would put the blame on Durwin. She may behave very well indeed in her new church, denying to herself and perhaps to others that she was ever at fault in Durwin's church."

Collin contined, "I would again like to impress upon you, because it is so important to the point we are trying to make in this group, that it was a relatively small number of people who were displeased with Durwin's ministry; only the belittlers and a few others who couldn't see through them. The majority of the congregation were dismayed when they heard the Lawtons would be leaving. Much displeasure was now openly expressed at what was being done to this fine minister and his likeable wife.

"Still for all that, there was no point in Durwin staying on there. He had tried time and again, each year in fact, to get a change of officers. Each time he had been turned down by well meaning people who could have done the job well, but who were afraid of the egotistical belittlers whom they could not see through nor understand.

"Had there been people willing to take over the administrative positions of the local church, a different secenario would have developed. Then, because of just the presence of Durwin's strong, quiet, unassuming character, some of the belitters would have relegated themselves to the back pews, so to speak, where they could do no harm. Belittlers shy away from victors over them, often waiting for another opportunity to strike. But I am sure most of them would have left this congregation altogether when they saw they weren't going to get their own way in everything, or be in control, but the decision to leave would be their own. If this had been feasable it would have left the congregation sufficient peace in which to allow it to do its work and to grow.

"However, had that happened, later indications are that in this instance, and in this church area, the belittlers would make a case for themselves out of that too. Even though the decision of the belittlers to leave the congregation or to take a back seat would be their own decision, Durwin would be blamed for driving them away. In reality, all he ever did was try to defend himself, his wife and his ministry from them. These people were not mature and objective enough in their thinking to realize that. Already Durwin had received a blast from a person of some account outside the church altogether for what he was 'doing to that nice person' (the chairperson). Actually, all Durwin was doing was trying to defend himself and his ministry from her. Again, if Durwin had been able to recruit other leaders and turn things around, and some belittlers left the church, later indications are that the wider church administration, being belittlers themselves, would have upset it on him. For indeed there came one day a mysterious phone call from the area office, from someone unknown to Durwin, questioning whether a certain family was leaving the church of their own accord, or whether these people were leaving the congregation because of Durwin's treatment of them. Durwin assured the unknown person that the decision was the family's own.

"Durwin could stand no chance at all of making a success of this congregation and his ministry in it. To dislodge the belittlers, even if it were possible locally, would be to bring repercussions from the administration of the church area. Indeed, as I said, many of them were belittlers themselves, and I think you will agree as the story continues to unfold.

"Again let me say I do not wish to leave you with the impression that the Lawtons' ministry was a total loss in this church and community. On the contrary, many people showed much friendship and affection for Durwin and Canda, and they received it well.

"Besides having friends within the congregation, Durwin and Canda pursued a social life within and outside the community. They were continually invited to many secular social functions which they always atteded and participated in to the fullest extent possible. They were well received at these functions, and were well respected.

"Some people in the church implied that Durwin's decorum was too cold and impersonal. However, it was intentionally that way except with people he knew extremely well. Let me tell you why.

"In many congregations it was becoming the custom of the time to display a great deal of personal affection, members with other members, and particularly between a minister and his people. This affection was manifested through hugging, patting on the arm or shoulder, placing one's arm around another's shoulder or waist. This was all done in affectionate gestures that were meant to develop a bond between people. In the school where Durwin was studying in the big city it was particularly well developed and utilized. In Durwin's congregation it was utilized some, and also at meetings of the church at large. But Durwin remained very cautious of it."

Gilda Emerson interrupted, "But if Durwin had utilized it more fully, wouldn't it have enhanced his position in the congregation, perhaps including its administration. Wouldn't it have thawed out the belittlers?"

"It would be very risky business, Gilda," replied Collin. "An affectionate and well meant hug can mean several different things to different people. To a well adjusted person, it means simply what it is, an expression of affection. To a poorly adjusted person it could mean a power trip or a conquest or the like. Durwin utilized it some with people he knew to be well adjusted. With belittlers, he already knew that they could manipulate it as a means to get their own way in matters of the congregation. Indeed, to some it would be a means of outright control over others, an avenue to personal power. On the surface of things one would think that to show such a sense of affection would win the cold belittlers to friendship. It is not necessarily so. Some belittlers would see it as an indication of weakness, as giving in to their desire for power and control over the minister in his dealings with the administration of the congregation.

"Ministers not perceived as a threat by belittlers could practice this display of affection quite readily, and not expect any backlash from it. But anywhere where there are belittlers present, together with a person they wish to belittle, then there is risk for that person in the practice of hugging and other expressions of affection. One of the foremost weapons many belittlers are prone to use is to find a sex scandal or create a suspicion of one in a smart and fine person's life.

"Belittlers mutilate people like us continuously with their oppression, rivalry, snubbing, hostility and hatred emanating from their pride and envy. They see no sin in this, regardless of all the damage it does. But sex! They sometimes behave as though fornication and adultery are the only two sins of any consequence. No doubt about it they are sins. Or rather, they are a part of the total sin of humanity; that is, a part of the total estrangement of imperfect humans from perfect God. That total estrangement includes, no less than the above mentioned sexual sins, pride, envy, jealousy, and the vicious harm often done by them in the practice of belittling and diminishing other people. There are times, depending on the context, when the actions of the envious are far more devastating than the actions of fornicators or adulterers, doing far more harm to people. Yet many belittlers in their quest for weapons of belittlement, sometimes treat this illicit sex as the one and only unforgivable sin.

"In this congregation Durwin did practice, just a little hugging and similar gestures of affection, as much as he would dare in such an environment as he was in. He showed this genuine affection to all those who had shown the same to him. He showed it not nearly to the extent suggested by the helpful little book he found so reassuring, "The Hug Therapy Book" by Kathleen Keating. (Compcare Publishers Minn. MN. 1983). Even at that there were some innuendos from some of the belittlers about the minister and pretty women.

"On the other hand, some people, both in and outside the congregation chided Durwin for being so cold, telling him to loosen up. Durwin already knew that when a belittler had concocted reason to come down on a person, even well meaning affectionate gestures would in their minds be turned into something derogatory. Belittlers could not be entrusted with such delicate behavior, even though if they could, it would be therapeutic for them. So Durwin played it safely. As I said earlier, he had accurately surmised how some belittlers, even though presently welcoming and enjoying a hug or a pat on the arm or back, might later turn it against him, as you shall hear later. Then, out of envy, or, out of a desire for power and control—often a derivative of pride and envy—or, because of a perceived loss of power and control, they would utilize the gestures of affection as a weapon. As I said, one of the deadliest weapons some belittlers seek to use is a sex scandal, create a suspicion of one, or, even attempt to set one up."

"Set one up?" questioned Gilda Emerson.

"Yes," explained Collin further, "I have heard of instances where unsuspecting people, were either or all of lured, nudged, led, or conned by implication only, seldom in explicit words, to in some way fall into sexual misconduct where the victim would be caught and exposed. Durwin was aware of the danger of that game, and not only protected himself well from it, but also, often, without their knowledge, took steps to protect his good friends from such contrived suspicion or scandal.

"But so much for sex now," Collin interrupted his own thoughts. "It isn't a major part of this total story, so I'll go on with other aspects."

"Before and after the Lawtons left the community, many people in the place asked why they were leaving so soon. Durwin always felt duty-bound to protect the image of the church. He would answer vaguely, something to the effect that ministers sometimes get moved often in our denomination. Some wanted the name and address of the

C.E.O. so that they could contact him and keep Durwin there. Durwin would simply put them off and avoid the matter. On their occasional visits to the area thereafter for social or unfinished business reasons, Durwin and Canda were frequently confronted with the same question, 'Why did you leave here?'

"The few belittlers and the several others under their spell had thought they were doing a wonderful thing for everyone by getting rid of this smart guy; this too nice a person and his smart aleck wife. Little did they know it was for only themselves, a very small minority. Yet they so often get their way amid the naivety and the lack of knowledge that belittlers exist, and that these belittlers play havoc with any society.

"There is one incident Durwin told me of that came out in expressed words as it seldom does. One belittler was talking to Durwin gloatingly about Durwin's coming departure.

"'I've given this church a good and intelligent ministry,' said Durwin to this belittler."

"'Intelligent,' snarled the belittler as he lost control of himself and revealed his true mind-set. "Ugh! That's it, you can be too smart,' he growled as he put his head down some and glared upward at Durwin. 'We had a smart guy where I work, but I'll guarantee you he's not there now. I took care of him.'"

Collin remarked to the peer group, "Here was a person who could not stand to have anyone around whom he perceived to be too smart. Being smarter than him is what constituted being too smart. Not only that, he thought everyone was the same way about smart people. This belittler really thought he was doing everyone around a great favor by getting rid of smart people."

Owen Winslow broke in, "Supposing everyone took that attitude, get rid of smart people. The smarter people of the country would end up beggars in the streets. What a waste of human resources and God given talents!"

"Exactly," said Collin, "and that's what belittlers in the church were doing to Durwin. Many have tried to do the same to me. Some of them never can see so far as to visualize what the end result would be for the belittled, although many do see it and intentionally try to bring it about. Many are not mature enough to think beyond their foul deeds to what would happen to these fine smart people if everyone treated them as the belittlers did.

"On the other hand, and I would emphasize this, there are indeed many belittlers who are consciously brutal enough to belittle and brainwash a person right into a mental hospital, or wear him down to become homeless and destitute in the street. What happens to a wife or children the belittled may have, matters not an iota to them."

Leo Aidan gasped, "Even many hardened criminals wouldn't harm a child. It is taboo among them."

"Many belittlers do, though," said Collin somberly and then continued, "Durwin and Canda were determined not to allow themselves to be pushed out among the homeless and destitute of Terraprima by supposedly Christian people who viciously practice their own destructive sin of belittling that is so overshadowed by their self-love, hollow undisciplined pride, and the ensuing envy; 'the most warped and twisted of human emotions.'

"This local church that was being so hard on the Lawtons, had a record of being hard on ministers dating back for many years. The members of its administration were the cause of it. They were power and control belittlers. They had been extra hard on the Lawtons, because of the special kind of fine people the Lawtons are. But proud, belittling people are hard on most good ministers. Durwin was determined to break that trend in this local church. The church at large had never done anything about it. How could they when many of them were the same kind of people? The thought of still another minister being appointed to the mental abuse of this congregation was something Durwin could not leave unattended. No matter how effective or ineffective a minister is in the performance of his duties, no one had a right to deprive that minister of his personhood, personal dignity and integrity; not undisciplined pride as they had, but basic human dignity and integrity and a sense of personal identity as to who and what kind of person he really is. That is what this kind of church does to people. It is as immoral as any other sin ever written about, and does a lot more harm than many of them.

"On his last Sunday at this church, Durwin simply told them in firm strong language that the record of their treatment of ministers was widely known, often talked about, and was a disgrace to the Christian church. He told them he would forecast that in another two or three years they will be looking for yet another minister.

"It sowed a seed which took hold during the process of the next ministry. The next minister of this congregation, over a period of time, came to be well treated by the administration, and reports indicate that he had a good ministry there. Of course, Durwin knew the belittlers would make him out to be wrong in his forecast. They would not ask for a replacement this time. Not surprisingly, Durwin's infra-structure was working now, and they did have some influx of new members sometime after Durwin left. It was a part of the influx that Durwin and Canda were preparing for, and the administration didn't even see coming. Sadly enough though, and not surprising, most of the new people dropped away again. Such a congregation seldom grows. However, to my knowledge, the next minister was not ill treated."

"Some communication did reach Durwin to the effect that the new minister could take the punches better, thus insinuating that Durwin had been too sensitive. But that is not so. Durwin had rolled well with the punches, far more than is normal. He stood them well and not only survived them but remained on top of things in his own life. The new minister may not have had everything rosy, but from other communication it was clear he didn't have to put up with the kind of abuse Durwin had taken. So even though the outcome was not in his favor, Durwin took comfort in the fact that he had helped protect a colleague from mental abuse and brought about at least some improvement to the behavior of a congregation's administration."

Collin paused in his story telling, and with satisfaction and relief, commented, "This takes me in the story to where I wanted to get tonight. It has been mind-draining. I suggest I cut it off here and continue with it next week. Will that be okay, Dr Eldren?"

"That will be in good order," replied the doctor. "Just let me know in advance when you require a longer session, and I can adjust my time schedule in advance."

"Thank you, Dr. Eldren, I will do so," said Collin.

"I will welcome it again next week," remarked Owen, "It is very important to my future."

"It is helpful to us all in gaining insight into our unique circumstances," added Brett.

"Okay then," concluded Collin. "At next week's meeting I will begin to tell you of other of Durwin's experiences such as with his new church, with his denomination at large, and on the ecumenical scene. Also, the following week I wish to tell you about Canda in the world of business."

The meeting ended, and it being late, the members chose to forego a social gathering at the coffee shop. They went straightway downstairs, and with the usual good-night salutations on the way, proceeded to their cars in the parking lot nearby and drove away.

CHAPTER VI

It was another Wednesday evening, and the support group members were standing around Room 405, talking; all except Brett Culver, the usually tardy participant whose more than busy business schedule kept him running just a little behind more often than not; a common characteristic of many people building up a business for themselves.

Dr. Eldren, of course, had not yet arrived. He always made his appearance right on time, within a minute of starting time, then in a very accomodating manner would linger around with the group to await Brett's arrival.

The members stood in a cluster, with Owen Winslow speaking, "You have caused me to have some second thoughts about ever going to live in Terraprima, Collin. I'm keeping an open mind on it yet, but I wonder seriously about the wisdom of such a move."

"Don't make up your mind yet," replied Collin, "you have several things in your favor that would give you a good chance of success in Terraprima."

Albin Anders gave a chuckle that revealed his lack of confidence in himself. "I don't think I would ever make it down there," he said. "I'd best stay where I am. It's tough enough here."

"I think you are right for now," replied Collin straight-forwardly. "Don't let me be discouraging to you, but also don't say never to venturing down there. Establish yourself well here in Secundaterra first, Albin, learn the ropes well. Then when you are older, more seasoned, and adequately educated and if some particular opportunity opens for you, it may be possible for you to do well there. All of you keep an open mind on these things until this group has done its work and then decide."

Attention now turned to Dr. Eldren who was entering the room. He shook hands with everyone, asking them how their week went. Then to Collin in a jovial manner, "and what do you have in store for us this evening Collin. Will it be dismal or will it be enlightening?"

Collin smiled and shook his head, "not much enlightenment yet, Dr. Eldren. Sorry to say, but it has to get worse before it gets better." Subdued laughter arose from the group.

Collin remarked, "You see doctor, we are able to laugh even in the face of the many dismal aspects of our lives."

"That's enlightening," said Dr. Eldren.

Brett Culver arrived. "I heard laughter," he said, as he joined the group. "What am I missing?"

"Just that things are going to get worse in this story before they get better," quipped Leo Aidan.

"Oh well, what else is new," responded Brett, "might as well laugh a little, and accept our lot in life."

Dr. Eldren then directed the members to the chairs and the group meeting. Collin was to continue with the story of Durwin and Canda Lawton in Terraprima.

"In previous sessions," Collin said to the group now in session, "I have told you of the Lawtons' experience with the government immigration department and also with their first church in Terraprima. You may have wondered by now about Durwin's interaction with other clergy members and some like minded laity in the church at large, of his own denomination, and on the ecumenical scene. I am very sorry to say that the ministry of the church has more than its share of belittlers and other proud people who do not know how to live in a proper manner with people whom they perceive or imagine to be a cut above themselves. I once read an article by a veteran minister stating that 'throughout his ministry he had had more trouble with other ministers than with any other group of people.' (Pulpit Digest, May-June 1981, Page 36). Needless to say, a minister of such considerable experience had encountered many, many people throughout his ministry and life. His remark does not speak well for the ministry. I am inclined to think he was very right when it comes to the ministry of Terraprima. However, there are also well meaning ministers, numerous in some areas, but many of them not wise to belittlers.

"As a prelude to Durwin's story of experiences with other ministers in Terraprima, I would like to repeat, as a classic example of their behavior, the story I told you last semester of the experience I had with a high profile Terraprima minister-professor who was invited to Lower Secundaterra when I was a minister there. My telling it again will enable you to relate it to Durwin's treatment in Terraprima, and you will be able to discern that it is a common, taken for granted treatment of fine people by many clergy there.

"This Terraprima professor of high standing, from a renowned school of theology, was invited to Lower Secundaterra to present a continuing education course on preaching. Advanced instructions had been given to all who registered for the course, me among them. We were to have certain readings done and a sermon prepared on one of a choice of topics. I went to the course well prepared, but would eventually find my preparation was of no avail. The professor, I would soon discern, was a belittler to the Nth degree. From the beginning he showed no friendship towards me as he had to the others.

"During the week of the course, the previously prepared sermons were presented at intervals, interspersed with discussion and other teachings on the art of preaching. The professor chose to begin with the student who sat directly opposite me on the other side of the oblong table, and then work his way around towards me. On the morning it had become the turn of the person sitting beside me on my right, I fully expected to be called upon after him. The person on my right made his presentation and there followed the usual evaluation of it. It was not yet mid morning, and time for two more presentations. Now the professor quite openly and brazenly went back to the starting point at the side of the table opposite to me, and asked the person to the right of the starting person at the beginning of the course to make his presentation. From there during the remainder of the week the presentations continued around the table in the oppostie direction, working towards the person on my left. I knew I was being snubbed of course, it was easy to tell. He avoided me during the socializing each day before class began, and his eyes continually shifted away from me during class. I reconciled my mind to being last. As the week ended, however, I was to learn that I would not even be last. The professor worked his way around the table until the person on my left presented his paper and the follow-up discussion was through. Then with gross impudence he announced that was the end of the course, that we were through more than an hour early, and we could go. A new vice—a new evil—had been introduced to Lower Secundaterra.

"If there were any in the class that day in Lower Secundaterra who were glad I was treated that way, it wouldn't have been more than two or three at most of the more than a dozen attending. But here was this brazen Terraprima professor behaving as though it was the natural way of everyone to treat fine people that way. That's the atmosphere that predominates among Terraprima ministers in the mainline churches. Is there any wonder their churches are decreasing in membership.?

"My path crossed with that belittling professor only once more. At another time soon after, he was invited to preach at a large combined Lenten gathering of a number of our churches in Lower Secundaterra. Because of the way this event went for me, I acquired the impression that some church officials, with good intentions, may have, after the preaching seminar, consulted with him about me. It seemed they had spoken to him about my peculiar circimstances as a fine high caliber person as some of them were getting to know. I cannot be sure about this. I do know it was a custom of the Lower Secundaterra clergy to consult on a variety of matters, with visiting dignitaries. Anyway, there was some change in his attitude, resulting in his awkward cover-up of his previous behavior.

"The incident I have in mind made the event a memorable occasion for me. At one point in his sermon, he stuck his eyes into me as I sat in a pew near the center of the church and he said introspectively and sulkily, 'I guess I am a coward of a sort, eh! Yes I suppose I am, since I don't stand up to those troublesome and obnoxious people in the church, but avoid confrontation, in which case they generally get their way.' He made it look like a foul deed was done because all the others wanted it that way. Such tactics were unknown in Lower Secundaterra.

"As he spoke, I thought to myself, *my dear man, you are not merely one of the cowards, you are one of the most obnoxious of people. You need a whole lot more introspection yet before you get the matter into proper perspective, instead of shifting the blame for your bad behavior to innocent people.* Outwardly, I just smiled at him and he abruptly changed the subject, turning elsewhere in the congregation, and not looking my way again. I knew this was his cover up. These people often use the pulpit for such mind-games. Another cover-up would come after the service.

"Following the service, I purposely stood in line to greet him, wondering how he would behave in close quarters. As I attempted to converse with him, his eyes got shifty and he said, 'I have never met you before. I don't know you.'

"I replied, 'yes, we've met on occasion. God bless you,' and I walked away, thinking, *why else would he single me out among four hundred people, all strangers to him to tell me he didn 't know me, other than to cover himself for his shabby behavior.*

"Here was a belittler from Terraprima, of the most seasoned and openly brazen kind. As I would learn much later, they play the belittling game there in a much more sophisticated and skilled manner, and ever so much more dirty and destructive than it has at any time been played in Lower Secundaterra, or in Secundaterra either for that matter. As I have said before, in these latter places, belittling was practiced by individuals and in a haphazard way only. In Terraprima, the game is highly developed into a widespread, vicious, destructive weapon. Here was this *Christian* professor spreading his discrimnatory and poisonious venom into territory where it had never before existed.

"I will add here that, in my travels around different parts of North America, by far the gross quantity and craftiness of the discrimination against fine people is practiced mostly by people from what I call Terraprima, and more openly by its church ministers. They seem to think it is the proper way to be and that most everyone agrees with them on it.

"Now I will tell you of various experiences Durwin Lawton had in Terraprima with other clergy, first on the denominational scene and then on the ecumenical scene. You will see similarities to the story I just told you and understand it is a way of life there.

"Durwin gave the congregation of his first church in Terraprima an excellent ministry from beginning to end, regardless of the problems encountered which we have already covered. His first summer in Terraprima would pass and there would be little contact with other clergy until early fall. Durwin would then find out what he was in for in his associations with them.

"So when fall came there was a major special gathering of both clergy and laity of a very wide area of Durwin's denomination. Durwin and Canda were up in the early hours of the morning to find their way and drive the considerable distance to this major gala event. They were excited about it. On their many prior visits to Terraprima, some of them at special church times such as Christmas and Easter, they had marvelled at the creative, innovative ingenuity displayed in the few of the larger church celebrations they had attended. Now they would participate in one. Upon arrival, they separated. Canda went to the huge church sanctuary to sit in a pew among the many hundreds attending. Durwin, with his clergy robe, found his way to where the clergy were to vest. After donning his robe, he began to look for the group with which he was to process. The hundreds of other clergy present were all strangers to him of course. He introduced himself to several clergy, one after another, asking them where or with what group he should be for the grand procession. Some simply said, coldly, they didn't know and with a shrug walked away. Others brushed him aside before he could even ask. Eventually Durwin spotted a church official whom he knew. No doubt this man would see that Durwin was taken care of. In Durwin's experiences in his previous denomination such a shepherd of the flock would take a stranger in hand and introduce him to some appropriate peers. Seeing he was a stranger and without friends they in turn would welcome him into their company for the event.

"This church official came hurrying in. As Durwin approached him, he barely paused.

"'Can you tell me where I should be and with what group?' Durwin asked.'

"'Oh just jump in wherever you can,' said the official, and went on his hurried way."

Leo Aidan interrupted Collin's story telling. "Social illiterate," he fumed.

Collin continued, "Well, for a moment or two Durwin thought perhaps the official was in a hurry to take care of something special, so he decided to take his advice and step in wherever he could. He approached a little cluster of five robed clergy.

"'Okay if I process with you people?' he asked. "Four of them paled as though they had been confronted by the devil himself. The fifth paused in his conversation, turned very briefly to Durwin, 'if you want to,' he said with a shrug of his shoulders, then back into conversation with the other four. Durwin stood there for a minute or two. Not being spoken to again, nor welcomed into the cluster, he walked to another cluster, and then out of curiosity, from cluster to cluster, getting a similar negative reaction in each case."

"Social illiterates, plural!" fumed Leo again.

Collin went on with the story. "Durwin, standing alone, looked around. There they were, standing in their little clusters all so busy talking meaningless small talk, that they had no time, nor thought, to be hospitable, the church official included; he was there in his little cluster also. Obviously, he had no official duties to take care of that morning. Social illiterate he was, indeed, Leo."

Leo persisted with his previous remarks, "seems to me, social illiterarcy was widespread among them."

"I think you are right, Leo," said Collin supportively. "I think you are largely right. Durwin, in looking around, spotted one other person standing nearly alone, just on the outer fringe of a group of about a dozen clergy. He was a short tiny man with a physical deformity in his shoulder and back. Durwin approached him very casually, introduced himself, and explained to him that being new here, he did not know what part of the procession he should be in."

"'Well,' said the friendly little man, 'we are a group of lay-ministers. If you wish, you can join us.'

"'Thanks, I will,' said Durwin readily. The two carried on an aimiable conversation for the ten minutes or so till the start of the procession. Then they processed into the great sanctuary together."

"Durwin didn't get much of a welcome, did he, Collin?" commented Gilda Emerson.

"Welcome only from one person out of hundreds," replied Collin. "No doubt you can note the similarity of this large scale snubbing to the similar treatment I received from the Terraprima professor in Lower Secundaterra. Durwin was completely left out on a multiple scale, as I was on a single scale. Imagine a fine person, dedicated as he might be, being treated like that on his first attendance at a church. He would never come back a second time. And they wonder why the denominations membership is decreasing, and its finances with it."

"And their aloofness at that point was based solely on Durwin's appearance," added Donna Coyne.

"Yes," replied Collin, "he was smart and distinctive looking but they gave him absolutely no opportunity to prove his character to them, whether he was a good natured person or not. Durwin recognized what he was up against. He figured that in time, he may be able to prove his genuineness to these people and break down the barriers that surely existed.

"An opportunity for this came at a later date. There was to be a social gathering of clergy and families the purpose of which was to welcome new ministers of the denomination to the immediate area, a much samller area of the church this time. There were about thirty people present. Introductions were made, and Durwin and Canda split up to meet and talk to as many people as they could, each on their own. Some of them talked fairly well, though often tense in doing so. Others tried hard to avoid them. Others would speak a few words of greeting and then join in the games that were going on. Durwin eventually decided to participate in the games as it might be a good way to break the ice, he thought. That, after all, was what the games were designed for, to get people mixing and break down barriers among strangers.

"They were simple, enjoyable games, like relay races with a ball on a spoom, or a human wheel barrow race, or bean bag toss. Durwin tried most of them, and like everyone else, won some and lost some. There were belittlers present who could not hide the dissatisfaction showing on their faces whenever Durwin won a game, especially if he won it outstandingly.

"Meanwhile Canda and some others stood looking on, talking and getting acquainted. At one point as they looked on, Durwin won a game. One of the leading persons in the group with whom she was talking pointedly asked Canda of Durwin, 'Is he hard to get along with?' He asked the question in such a manner as though he was hoping to find something wrong with this seemingly all around fellow. Canda thought the question a weird and inappropriate one for a stranger to ask a woman of her husband. She assured him and all in the cluster that he was not hard to get along with, and that Durwin and Canda had and are having a wonderful marriage.

"The Lawtons wondered at the time if it was just probing to find fault. In later years after more experience with these people, they came to realize that it was the beginning of a shakedown, a mind-game to bring the victim down to falling in line beneath them and becoming a yes-man to them, or else, be regarded as hard to get along with. This man who asked the question later acquired a high office in the church.

Collin paused in the story to analyze. "By way of comparison and contrast let me surmise from years of observation what goes on in the mind of belittlers in a situation just described. First of all let me say that a normal person would observe Durwin in some of these ways: there is something unusual about that person. He is not only different, he is smart, friendly, confident. He may even be exceptional in some ways, perhaps gifted. How nice, how interesting, or even how admirable in cases that warrant it. Here is a unique person. I must get to know him. I would like to know such a person. It would be a pleasure, and surely there are things I can learn from him.

"The belittler looks at the same person and thinks in his mind: that person is different from us. What's wrong with him? Look how he plays that game. We've got a smart alec in our midst. We'll fix him and put him in his place. Who is he to be here showing us and making us feel small? He can't do that to us and get away with it."

"Aren't they the paranoid ones?" asked Albin Anders, curiously.

"Yes, many belittlers are paranoid," replied Collin, "they actually believe that we are behaving in a superior manner just to put them down. It is a projection or reflection of their own behavior. It is the way they think themselves. Many of them are paranoid in that manner. Then with regard to friendship they keep their distance and await every opportunity to do their dirty work, their putting us down, their belittling.

"There are some belittlers who never become openly damaging to the fine and/or exceptional person. But still, they are saddened and negative at the appearance and performance of one. They find no joy or delight in the gifts and graces of others. These are belittlers just the same. They belittle by default.

"To illustrate," continued Collin, "over coffee, I once told two ministers about a very exceptional performance I had attended. It was a one person performance in which the performer had entertained more than two thousand people with classic literature including Shakespeare, in such a manner as to keep them spell-bound for nearly two hours—no mean feat given such material as classic literature of a serious as well as comical nature.

"It was very noticeable that one minister's face dropped into sadness at the mention of it. His undisciplined pride was pricked and his envy aroused. The second minister joyfully said, 'wow, I would loved to have been there to see it. It must be wonderful to be able to do something like that!' The gloomy faced minister, as if partly awakened to awareness by the comment of the other, mumbled, 'Yes, I guess it would be.'

"Nevertheless, his first inclination was negative towards the outstanding ability of another. It was for him a natural inclination. He had probably been taught by example since early childhood to be down on people he deemed to be a cut above him in any way. This person wasn't a hostile type. His belittling would be done silently. Simply by his negative facial expression and lack of positive verbal expression he would belittle many people throughout his lifetime; people he deemed, in his mind, to be superior to him in any way.

"When the more active belittlers see, or perceive in their minds, a person to be an all around fine, gifted person, it bothers them to the point where they are just bursting to find something, or make something wrong with him that will enable them to look down on him. When they can look down on him, they feel superior again. But it doesn't stop there. Each success the belittled attains, causes the belittler's undisciplined pride to be pricked again, so he has to keep finding fault in order to keep feeling superior.

"Durwin and Canda did make a few friends at the gathering that day by the way. They felt the ice had been somewhat broken, and they were encouraged. However, the question, 'Is he hard to get along with?' would later come to mind when in time it was often inferred that the Lawtons were indeed hard to get along with. This atmosphere arose time and again when the Lawtons wouldn't step in line with every Tom,

Dick and Mary who tried to make them dance to their drum. It is another ploy much used by belittlers and control freaks in the congregation and elsewhere.

"Let me tell you now of a couple of minor continuing education events that Durwin attended. On another night I intend to go into more detail about Durwin's more major continuing education experiences, because they are quite significant to the story as a whole. I will tell you this one now because it illustrates still more barriers that Durwin was confronted with.

"During the year there was a continuing education event for clergy of the denomination, held one evening weekly for several weeks in the parlor of a centrally located church. About fifteen ministers attended. None of them were friendly toward Durwin. None of them were hostile either, and that was somewhat helpful. Time after time, week after week, Durwin tried in vain to strike up conversations with them, either singly or with a group. When trying at times to do so to persons singly, these persons would be so up tight that Durwin practically had to drag words from them. The conversation just wouldn't go for long before the person would look for some reason to move elsewhere. When trying to participate in a group conversation, the group participants would simply talk to and look towards one another, as if Durwin was not even in their presence. When he spoke his words were ignored. They were frightened half to death of him. His appearance, presence and personality which was openly friendly, were thus far the only factors that could be affecting their behavior towards him."

"Sensitive, sensitive, all too sensitive," interjected Leo quickly.

"And much moreso," added Collin. "Their sensitivity was displayed even greater as time went on. Each week one of the class members did a devotion before the class work began. Durwin wondered if he volunteered to do a devotion one week, would it make things better or worse. Need I tell you it made things worse.

"Durwin carefully prepared a devotion consisting of Scripture, prayer and a meditation of about half the length of a sermon. The quality was good. Durwin felt confident about this aspect of a ministers work. He had had sermons published in high caliber religious publications and was always asked for more.

"On the designated evening, Durwin presented his devotional period. You remember," interspersed Collin, "how when on the grounds of his local church Durwin showed a man how to properly saw a limb off a tree, and the man went away with a sad and drooping face? Well, that was mild compared to this. As Durwin sat and presented his devotion, looking around at the others for effect he was dismayed at the sad, sad faces he was looking at. Some of them, you would swear, he was stabbing in the stomach with a knife. Perhaps you have seen such scenes in the movies, the face goes sad and sick looking. The corners of the mouth drop down, the head droops. The intellegence and ability factor had now entered into their attitude towards Durwin.

"What am I doing to those people?" Durwin frantically asked himself in the midst of his presentation, as he almost came to the point of terminating it. Then, just as quickly, he got a hold on things. *I'm not doing anything wrong to them,* he told himself, *these people are sick, and they don't even have a half-measure of mature adult self awareness to know it.*

"When Durwin completed the presentation of his devotion, a strange, eerie, and prolonged silence followed. No one spoke. Durwin glanced around. The whole group looked as though they had had something terrible done to them. There was not an iota of comment. Eventually the lecturer of the course arose slowly from his chair, went to his lectern, fumbled for the longest time with his papers, then began his lecture."

"No expression of thanks or appreciation, or anything like that?" asked Owen.

"Not a word," replied Collin. "So Durwin finished out the weeks of the course in that atmosphere and tried not to let it bother him. He planned to keep working on those barriers, to try and break through them, but there was a difficult road ahead.

"On another occasion Durwin attended an all-day seminar consisting of a lengthy morning lecture by a figure known throughout the denomination nationally, and followed by an assortment of smaller work-shops from which a person could choose three to attend in the afternoon. Among those chosen by Durwin was one presided over by the morning lecturer.

"During the course of this work shop the discussion for a period centered on worship and Sunday Church School. The lecturer stated strongly that he favored Sunday School at a time other than worship time, so that children, youth and teachers could attend worship. Durwin had always favored that position, but having proposed it in his present church, he had run into strong opposition to it. So during a question and answer period at this workshop he raised his hand, as did others, to ask a question. The lecturer noticably avoided looking in Durwin's direction. He would respond to someone's question, then point to someone else and say 'next', or okay this person over here', but kept glancing away from Durwin. If you have ever witnessed anyone doing that, you will know by their guilty glancing that an obvious avoidance game is being played."

"I've seen it lots of times," remarked Brett, "You can usually tell when the omission of someone is accidental or intentional."

"Easy to tell," added Gilda.

"Okay," said Collin, "so you know what I'm talking about. "Durwin kept his hand up high until everyone else had been answered. With only one hand left up, the lecturer had no choice but to respond. But instead of saying, 'next', or 'this person here,' he simply looked straight at Durwin, cocked his head up quickly and waited for the question.

"Durwin handy about knew what was going on in this man's mind. Very tactfully he expressed his question, 'How would you handle the usual and very frequent objections of people to having Sunday Church School at a time other than worship? Some teachers say they don't have time to spare to attend both worship and Sunday School on Sunday morning. Many parents say it is too long a period for their children to attend both worship and Sunday School in one morning.

"'Ugh,' snorted the lecturer in a contemptuous manner. 'They do it during the week in day school don't they?' he snapped, and then went to his lecturn to prepare his papers for the next topic of discussion."

"An educated ignoramus," quipped Leo.

"Educated, but with no culture," added Brett.

Collin continued, "A dead silence fell over the work-shop. Many people were stunned by his attitude. It was a logical question concerning one of the most frequent problems encountered in any local church. The lecturer gave a rude answer in a rude manner. Some may be inclined to say that maybe he was put on the spot by a troublesome question. However, by his mannerism he was rude to Durwin before the question was asked, when there was only appearance to go by. The fact is, this man was a belittler. During the course of his lecturing career, numerous students, some of them very good students would pass through his lecturing, not only unscathed, but with his whole hearted support; but never would there pass through his class unscathed, a student whom he would perceive to be different in a fine sort of way, and who wouldn't fit into his mold, yet who may well have the potential to be an exceptionally creative person, minister or otherwise.

"As Durwin was leaving the room with the others at the end of the work-shop, he was approached by one of the few church officials of Terraprima who had shown a fair interest in him since his arrival. This man said to Durwin, 'It looks like you are going to have to tread very lightly and look out for yourself very carefully here among us.'

"Durwin smiled and replied, 'It seems so, doesn't it? Thanks for your interest,' then undaunted, he went to another room to attend another work-shop. Throughout his years in Terraprima he did experience a few pleasant seminars and work-shops. On the whole, at this all day seminar I have just told of, Durwin did make acquaintance with some friendly people. Many people noticeably avoided him as though he had the bubonic plague. But during the breaks and at lunch time, Durwin, by his persistence, did befriend a few nice people and made some meaningful acquaintances. This made his new life quite bearable.

"In contrast to the unnatural, uncultured and unchristian reception Durwin received from the lecturer at that gathering, let me tell you about another. Months later, Durwin attended a much larger seminar presided over by a different person who was nationally known throughout many denominations for his teachings and numerous writings. This man took note of Durwin as well as others throughout the session, and included him in the discussions with respect and glad acceptance, giving credit where such was warranted. This and similar times of inclusion served to re-affirm Durwin as being an acceptable person in the eyes of those who really count.

"Over the several years that followed, Durwin would have to get used to often being shunned or omitted. He was nearly always the last to have his hand responded to in the question periods of various area meetings of different levels and sizes; sometimes at smaller meetings, sometimes medium and occasionally larger gatherings. If before he went to Terraprima, Durwin hadn't been well seasoned, with a good awareness and knowledge of himself and of belittlers, he would no doubt have taken on quite a problematic complex about himself, which of course is always a goal of the more active belittlers."

Young Albin interjected, "I find myself wondering what is wrong with me under such circumstances. That is my first inclination but then I catch myself and say, no, it is not me, it is them."

"I know how you feel," said Collin. "It isn't natural to have so many people negative towards you, so it is natural to wonder about yourself under such circumstances. However, you must never give in to that. If you do, they won't stop until you are in a mental hospital or a beggar in the street. Some would do this unawares of the end result of what they were doing. They don't think ahead that far. They live in the present moment and put you down without thought of the far reaching consequences for you. Others do it intentionally, playing a vicious mind-game knowing full well that they are ruining a life. It will be a continuous battle of your mind, especially when you are still young, to not give in to it. If you take good care and train your mind to react positively towards yourself and discerning towards belittlers you will survive. Keep well rested as much as possible. It will be a continuous strain, sometimes a hell, but it can be done.

"On the other hand I have known older people, in their middle years or later, perhaps late bloomers or some in a new job, being put down more harshly than ever before in their lives, and over a prolonged period coming to think there is something wrong with self. To make matters more difficult, there are times when we have to look at self, for we are not perfect, and have to keep growing and adjusting. So you also have to learn to discern between legitimate self-examination for personal growth, and introspection caused by the wrecking of your self esteem by belittlers.

"The more you learn about belittlers now in your younger years, and find ways to deal with it, the better it will be for you as you get older. Don't look forward to a time when it won't be there, or you will surely be disappointed. Just learn all you can about it, watch what you get yourself into, and get a good education or training for your chosen way of earning a living. That should open up doors for you in life."

"Thanks Collin," said Albin somberly, "I find it a little scary at times though."

"I don't mean to scare you," replied Collin, "I'm just trying to prepare you. Forgive me for parting from conventional counseling methods and being blunt about it, but I just mean to be straight-forward. I assure you that with the help and understanding of this group you will be better equipped to handle it well. An improved capability of handling this way of life that you have inherited will grow on you over a period of time. By the time you graduate from this university you should be very good at it."

The other group members spoke assuringly to Albin.

"We will explore the various professors and help guide you through, help you choose classes with instructors who will be accepting of you, Albin," said Owen, summing up the helpful intentions of all the group members. "No more nervous breakdowns for you," he concluded.

"Let me tell you of other experiences of the Lawtons," Collin continued. "The churches of Durwin's denomination met as a group on several different levels. There was the smaller area, then a larger area and on up to a very large area. They met periodically to discuss, plan and administer the appropriate business allotted to the various levels.

"I wish to tell you now of the smaller area, or the lower area on the scale if you wish. It was the more intimate area, because it was less structured and less formal. People attending were drawn together by very common concerns for the near immediate area in which they all lived. Meetings were held monthly, on an evening, and attended by clergy and lay representatives numbering about thirty when attendance was good. Durwin and Canda both attended regularly.

"In the discussions at these meetings, Durwin was treated strangely, to say the least, by some of the participants, the chairperson in particular and his young sidekick, another minister. When Durwin tried to participate in any meeting discussions, he was many times crowded out by these two people who obviously thought it in proper order for them to dominate the proceedings. Durwin tried to maneuver a little. He would wait till others would join in the conversation, then join in himself so that he would be only one of many participating. It didn't work. In fact it was implied that Durwin had no business interferring. It is true that some of the problems being discussed had been around before Durwin arrived, but now he was supposed to be a part of the fellowship. According to some he wasn't. Durwin often wondered why a certain familar hymn was in their hymn book. It reads: 'In Christ there is no east or west, in Him no south or north; but one great fellowship of love throughout the whole wide earth.' According to some people in this as well as other area levels, this didn't include Durwin and Canda, but only those whom certain warped personalities could look down on in condescension.

"Then there was a very highly educated layman who attended these meetings. Durwin tried several times to befriend him. He wasn't a hostile or active belittler, but he would become frightened near to death each time Durwin tried to talk with him or join in a discussion in which he participated. He would actually become nervous, upset, and frightened. Here was a talented man with a serious personality problem. He could not look up to or deal with in any way, people whom he deemed to be a cut above him. This man dealt with numerous adults in his secular employment in the education field. Durwin often wondered how many people with fine or exceptional potential this man turned away from himself and from the vocation they wished to follow. Durwin eventually gave up on him.

"Canda, one of the few clergy spouses who attended these meetings regularly, was well able, with her friendly outgoing way, to befriend many of the women participants. Durwin also made significant inroads in befriending both lay people and some ministers, mostly during the fellowship and refreshment hour that followed the meetings. Whereas Durwin was practically barred from discussion at the meetings, he was free to circulate and participate in the fellowship hour. Altogether, Durwin and Canda drew respect and friendship from many members of the gathering. They were making headway in breaking ice. It was of no help to them in their local church because no members of that church attended these meeting, or very little of anything else regarding the church outside their own congregation.

"An interesting and revealing incident was the planning of an annual combined special worship service by the several churches involved in this smaller area. Such a service had been taking place for some years, and now it was the turn for it to be held in Durwin's church. At the first planning meeting it was decided early to have an emphasis on music and singing this year. The chairperson suggested that Durwin as well as readying his church, would see to it that an organist was available. Durwin expressed the opinion that he felt sure his organist would be available. He would check it out. A belittler's rivalry immediately set in as the chairperson's side-kick expressed the desire that his organist play for the service and he could arrange some special music with her. Durwin had no desire to enter into childish rivalry over the music issue."

Brett was amused. "If there was to be something special about the music, someone other than Durwin Lawton had to get credit for it, right?"

"That's it," said Collin, "Little children have to be able to say, 'look everyone what I am doing.'

"As the meeting proceeded further, the topic of music came up in more detail. The side-kick said he would discuss the proposals made at the meeting with his organist. Consequently, Durwin saw no reason why he would need to contact the side kick's organist since the side-kick was going to talk to her himself.

"At the next meeting a month later, the planning was being completed. When the topic of music came up, the side-kick looked across the room at Durwin with an unfriendly countenance, 'Did you make arrangements with the organist?' he growled.'

"In surprise, Durwin replied, 'Well no, you said you were going to talk to your organist about the music.'

"'You are supposed to ask her if she will play?' he growled again. 'Did you do it?'

"'No I didn't,' replied Durwin, 'I didn't think it would be necessary when you said you were going to discuss the music program with her.'

"The young side-kick growled again, this time louder, as if looking for a quarrel, 'You were supposed to contact her.'

"All eyes were on Durwin. Even though it could have been humiliating to a person like Durwin who was always thorough in his work and in doing his part, he was not about to quarrel over such a matter of either oversight or buck passing, whichever it was. Besides, if he did quarrel, he would be quickly labeled as hard to get along with, a trouble maker. He simply and calmly replied, 'I will call her now.'

"Durwin left the meeting room, found a phone and called the organist. She informed him that her minister, the side-kick, had indeed discussed the music program with her. At that time she informed him that she would let him know later if she would be available on the date of the service, but they hadn't had contact with each other about it since. She then informed Durwin that she would be available to play at the special service. Durwin returned to the meeting with the information that the organist was available. Still growling, the side-kick simply said he would discuss the content with his organist later."

"Childish deceit," blurted Leo in his characteristic manner.

"And buck-passing too," added Gilda. "Either he or she had neglected to call the other to affirm whether or not she was available for the service. Then he blamed the lack of information at meeting time on Durwin."

Brett added, "Being a minister doesn't guarantee humble admission of an error, does it? There was no honesty to self or others shown by the side-kick; only envy, rivalry, incompetence and belittling all covered by childish deceit."

"And the way he growled at Durwin! You say he was a young side-kick," remarked Owen. "Obviously he had no respect for age."

"Not in the least," agreed Collin. "Durwin was more than old enough to be his father. He had absolutely no respect for age and as for honesty, well!"

"Another social illiterate," quipped Leo again.

Collin added, "On other occasions this person attempted many times to belittle Durwin in the more usual ways. I tell you of this incident to illustrate the childish deceit and buck-passing that belittlers so often use to protect themselves and their undisciplined pride.

"By the way, at the planning meeting it was also decided to invite a special singing group from outside the denomination, to bring a program of special contemporary music and song to the service. The side-kick readily stated he would make the arrangements with the group. Consequently, the service was publicized throughout the participating churches as having special music.

"Durwin in his immediate area publicized ecumenically the special music, as well as a unique guest preacher. This brought extra people out from Durwin's area and it was one of the better attended such services in recent years. However, the music part of the service was near a complete let down. The special group had been invited all right, and they were there, however, no prior planning had been done with them. On invitation by the conductor of the service, they came forward and sang one brief song. That was the extent of the special music that had received so much publicity. There was the usual couple of choir numbers in addition to the hymns. The 'special' music was almost non-existant. Although the lack of special music was a let-down, the guest preacher saved the day to a large extent.

"There is yet another revealing incident that came about through Durwin's acquaintences in this same area. You may remember that I previously told you how Durwin's church turned him down on buying a photocopier, and Durwin bought his own. Well, when Durwin was looking around for a copier, he had heard of a layman of another congregation who was employed in the copier field. At a church function Durwin approached the man and expressed his interest in acquiring a copier. Durwin told him how he had heard it was possible to get a rebuilt copier for around four hundred dollars. The man told Durwin it was indeed possible to get an older yet quite efficient rebuilt copier for that amount of money. He named several makes available through him, and suggested he have his church decide which one they would prefer. The man appeared proud to be the one to do this for the church. He was puffed up about it.

"Durwin then informed the man that his church felt they could not afford a copier, so Durwin himself would buy it and use it for church purposes as well as personal use. In a matter of seconds the man did a complete about face. He began listing the different makes and quoting prices. In a matter of a minute the prices went from four hundred to eight hundred to twelve hundred, to sixteen hundred dollars. 'I can get you a pretty good one, not too bad, for sixteen hundred dollars,' the man said.

"'What about the four hundred dollar one?' Durwin asked.

"The man brushed the question aside, 'I can't do any better for you than sixteen hundred dollars,' he said curtly.

"'That's more than I can afford,' said Durwin.

"A smug look of satisfaction came over the man's face as Durwin walked away.

"You can see this man's attitude towards a minister of caliber," said Collin to the peer group. "At first he was proud and puffed up that he and not Durwin was to be the one to get a copier for the church. When he found it wasn't to be for the church but for Durwin personally, he turned on Durwin and put him down. It is an example of how belittlers often regard protestant ministers, especially the good ones, with a desire to have power and authority over them. I will discuss that matter with you later.

"Durwin needed a copier in order to keep up the high caliber of his personal ministry and keep in tune with the way the church at large was operating. He phoned the sales office of a well known manufacturer of quality photo copiers and introduced himself to the sales manager.

"'I hear it is possible to buy an older rebuilt model for around four hundred dollars,' Durwin asked,' is that correct?'

"'Yes it is,' replied the man helpfully, 'but not from us.' He explained further, 'you see, just as car dealers wholesale their older trade-ins to other car lots, so we wholesale our older trade-in copiers to used copier dealers. Some of them they rebuild and some of them they use for parts to do the rebuilding. If you get a copier from a careful rebuilder, you can do well with it.'

"'Can you suggest a dealer?' asked Durwin.

"'Yes I can', said the man, eager to help. 'We have a young man working here whose father is in the used copier business. This young man is out on the road now, I'll have him contact you when he comes in. In the meantime some models are better than others,' the man continued with his helpfulness. He named three or four models. 'Watch for one of these models and you should get a good one that will last for years.'

"Durwin thanked the man, and within two weeks had a very efficient four hundred dollar copier that with only minor servicing lasted him throughout many years."

Collin now came to another phase of this part of the story. "You may remember," he said, "that I told you earlier tonight of the different levels of area meetings that took place in the church at large. We have just finished discussing the lower, smaller level. Now let me phase you in on a higher level, moderately larger and more authoritative than the first.

"We are covering a wider area of the church at large now. There were such gatherings as business sessions, special worship events, seminars, work-shops, a variety of lectures, celebrations of special church days or events, social gatherings at special seasons; a whole variety of educational and informative events. Some ministers attended a few, most ministers attended several, a few ministers attended nearly all of them. Durwin was among this latter few, seldom missing an event. Over a period of time he was able through persistence to make friendly acquaintance with a number of ministers and also with lay people who attended many of these events as well. He was able to make enough friendly acquaintances to help him feel comfortable, and more or less a normal part of the gatherings."

"A normal part of the gatherings?" questioned Gilda.

"Yes," said Collin, "earlier tonight Albin mentioned that he often catches himself wondering if the problem is with him instead of with the belittlers. Well, Durwin, by making some friends and acquaintances was able to keep himself assured that he was a sociable being. When people like us get under circumstances where there is not at least some worthwhile social or professional acceptance of us as we are, then indeed we may eventually be worn down to where we would think, even be convinced that the trouble is with us. Watch out for that, group members. I say again, don't let them do it to you!"

"I see," said Gilda with satisfaction. "That rings a bell with me. When I told my story to this group, I told you of a doctor who began convincing me that I was the problem. I got out from under his spell!"

"Right," said Collin, "and Durwin was doing his best to prevent it from happening to him by different means in a different setting.

"Durwin didn't back down. He attended meetings and all other gatherings almost without fail. It wasn't easy. When he tried to participate in a question and answer period, the resource person conducting it, usually a minister, often kept looking away from Durwin if his hand was up in the air. When he did by persisting, get the attention of the speaker it was often in a curt, unmannerly way, quite distinctly different than the way others were generally attended to. When the speaker gave the answer, it was at times in a curt, quick, incomplete sometimes garbled or trivializing manner that singled out Durwin from the other participants. Still, Durwin did not succumb and give up in the face of this inhumane, dignity shattering treatment. He had enough past successful experience, and present friendly assurance to know that the problem was the belittlers and not himself.

"Regardless of this, Durwin, rightly or wrongly, was of the same opinion as was expressed to him by the friendly and concerned church official at the large seminar, one of the first Durwin attended in Terraprima. That opinion was that he would have to tread lightly and watch his step. This he did.

"When the ministers of the area were called upon to submit to the head office a resume of their experience on church committees and in various offices, Durwin played very low key. In the past, he had not been one of the most ardent wider church administrators or politicians, but he had come from a church where every minister had a goodly share of it. Durwin could have submitted a reasonably impressionable resume, but he intentionally held back on many things. For example, at that particular time the highest church officer of this area came into church news as a participant in the larger church's study of human sexuality. Durwin in his previous church had already spent two years on a committee meeting monthly, studying human sexuality and formulating an extensive report on the same. He had served on many other committees but only listed some of them on his resume. He was already being slighted enough, without upsetting the top people.

"Also, Durwin made no pretense at being a public, spur of the moment debater on the floor of a large gathering. However, he knew from previous experience and present confidence that he could well give a prepared report on the floor of any gathering, answer questions on it, and defend or correct it if necessary. No opportunity would ever come for him to do that in the church in Terraprima."

Donna asked of Collin, "Do you think, if Durwin had submitted a better, more complete resume, he would have been given a better opportunity to participate in the larger church?"

"It is debatable," answered Collin, but mostly I don't think so. A better resume would have stirred up the defence of their undisciplined pride all the more. I base that opinion on my overall experience with belittlers. Especially with Durwin coming from another denomination with more experience in some ways, than some of the officers and many of the clergy of this denomination, they would have shunned him all the more. Durwin did list some worthwhile experiences in his resume. Only once was he called upon by a friendly person to participate, and that project was terminated before very long. Termination of a project is one of many ways belittlers use to block the progress of a fine person.

"Furthermore, a later statement by the same high officer who had been a participant in the human sexuality study, supports my opinion of the advisability of Durwin playing low key with his resume. At a large gathering of clergy presided over by that high officer, Durwin, after going through the usual ritual of being last to get attention to his raised hand, tried to bring the church to task for its weakness in reaching out to middle and upper middle class business people, as they already did to certain middle class professional people. The high officer's response was that they felt ill at ease with business people. He then emphasized there is no other reason involved, 'we simply do not feel comfortable with them.'

"Durwin had at a time previous to that spoken to another officer of the church about the shunning that existed in the church by people who perceived other people as being a cut above them and received a vague reaction. Now in this later instance the high officer, speaking directly to Durwin from the floor, was being defensive, about a similar matter. Durwin was getting to know that on the part of many, both clergy and lay people, there were more complexities behind this estrangement from business people than feeling ill at ease with them. There were more complex reasons than that and our stories bear it out. They felt ill at ease with Durwin and Canda too because the Lawtons were high caliber people of whom they were envious. Durwin also knew there was no use trying to get through to the clergy belittlers on the matter, at least at this time.

"Overall, Durwin's first and foremost interest was in the local church. He wasn't alone in that. There were some highly successful, low-keyed ministers in the good parishes of Terraprima, and surviving well there even though they seldom if ever participated in the church at large. However many observers know that usually the better parishes are given to those who tow the well established line, and also get themselves involved with the administration of the church at large. There may be some merit in working the system that way, but only some. For one thing, not all administrators make the better pastors of congregations and vice versa.

"Regardless, Durwin wasn't given much opportunity to prepare himself for participation in the church at large. Heads all too often turned the other way when his hand went up to ask a question or make a comment. Those heads turned because they felt uncomfortable in Durwin's presence, and more. They also wanted to belittle him to bring him down and this because they perceived him to be a cut above them. I am convinced a better resume would have turned their heads away all the more."

At this point, Collin again changed course in the story. "Durwin was an ecumenically minded person. I will bring you now a few of his experiences on the ecumenical scene as related to his first church at Terraprima.

"During his early weeks at his first church, Durwin by chance casually met two or three of the other clergy of the town, and there seemed at the time to be no problem with them. They seemed pleased to meet him and invited him to attend the ecumenical monthly meetings that would begin again in the fall.

"Before the fall meetings began there was in the town the grand opening of a major public facility to which the public was invited, and with invitations mailed out to notables, including clergy. This would be Durwin's first public event in the community. He was pleased about it, and arrived at the scene in plenty of time as was his usual custom. There was seating for four hundred people. He looked around for other clergy and there were none as yet, so going about half way down the aisle, he sat in a chair at the end of a row where if other clergy came in he could easily connect with them.

"When the seating was about half filled, two other clergy appeared on the scene, one of whom Durwin had casually met previously. He approached Durwin, beckoning the other minister to come with him. Durwin stood and shook hands with the familiar minister, who then introduced him to the other minister. The second minister gave Durwin only a cold, loose, perfunctionary hand shake, without speaking, and almost immediately began to walk away. The familar minister pointed to the empty chairs beside Durwin and motioned for them to sit down together. The other minister now some steps away, and continuing to move further away, curled his mouth contemptously, 'naw', he said to his accompanying minister, 'come on, he's only a—' and his voice became undiscernable in the widening distance. It was a snub, stirred up by Durwin's appearance only.

"As often happens the friendly minister followed the proud impudent belittler, almost dutifully. They walked to the front of the seating, where they turned around and stood facing the gathering crowd. There the proud belittler stood looking around as though he were the main person present, stretching himself upward vehemently as he turned this way and that, trying hard to make himself a towering figure over the other people. Durwin could not help but smile, even though the man's ignorance was so pitiful. Durwin also knew, there and then, that he would have to be careful with this unabashed belittler, and not give him any chance to put Durwin down. This belittler treated Durwin very haughtily for the remainder of the time they both were in the community.

"A later incident that has bearing on the Lawtons' story is worth interjecting here. With all the beating and hammering belittlers were inflicting on Durwin everywhere he went or turned, it began in time to affect his sleep. He knew from previous experience that if his sleep was affected for a prolonged period, he would eventually be worn down to where he would lose his considerable energy and vigor. He had heard of a Christian family physician in the community who gladly looked after the medical needs of clergy. Durwin went to him. He was a good, helpful, well meaning type of person but alas, like many people, including doctors, he was not wise to belittlers. I will explain.

"Durwin asked this doctor for a prescription for a tranquilizer that Durwin was familar with and had used sparingly before. Durwin would take only one twenty-five milligram pill each night at bedtime, he told the doctor. It was an idea I had passed on to Durwin some time previously. The doctor told him, 'it is just as well you put it under your pillow as take that small amount. The average dosage is ten to twelve times that much, usually two hundred and fifty to three hundred milligrams per day.'

"'I know,' replied Durwin, 'but twenty-five milligrams at bedtime is all I need to ensure my sleep. I don't need any medication during the day time. My work won't be affected as long as I get my sleep.'

"'What is keeping you from sleeping?' asked the doctor.

"'Anxiety,' replied Durwin, 'I am that kind of person.' He wouldn't dare go into it any more deeply. He would be labeled paranoid or over sensative right away, he knew for sure.

"'How about having a talk to my minister about this?' the doctor suggested. He is a good Christian helper. I can arrange for you to talk to him about it.'

"'What's his name?' asked Durwin.

"The doctor told him and Durwin shuddered. It was the same minister who had been treating him so haughtily, beginning at their first meeting at the public gathering and still continuing.

"'Perhaps he won't like me,' responded Durwin.

"'Oh, but he's a minister too,' replied the doctor in obvious innocence and naivety.

"Durwin had been told by now from another source that this minister, as well as being pastor of a very nice local church, also belonged to a religious group that some people saw as a cult. That is all Durwin would need—a would be counselor involved in a questionable religious group, and who had from the beginning, without even knowing him, treated him as though he had something wrong with him, which is a deadly weapon of belittlers.

"Durwin had had more than one deep religious experience in his life, and then twenty years of ministry on top of that, with sound theology, as well as training in counseling. To accept help from this would be helper-minister would be a catastrophe. Ironically he was wanting this pill, this very minimum amount of medication because of the cruel treatment he was getting from ministers such as this *helper,* and some other *Christians.* Needless to say, Durwin politely turned down the offer.

"The amiable doctor wanting to be helpful, gave him a prescription as he had asked for, and had it run a lengthy time before requiring another visit to the doctor. This event is a vivid illustration of medical doctors not being wise to belittlers, and how different things could be if they were.

"A remark made to Durwin much later, by still another minister, revealed that that minister at least, had heard that Durwin was on pills. The implication at the time was that he thought Durwin couldn't stand up to the regular rigors of ministry. Nothing was further from the truth. Durwin was merely preventing himself from being worn down and out by the belittlers with whom he was surrounded and plagued every way he truned. As I have indicated earlier in this story, Durwin was not only capable of keeping up longer than average hours of ministry, but also an above average load of continuing education with it.

"This doctor, by the way, remained a well meaning friend. If it was through him that news got around to the clergy that Durwin was taking prescription pills, then that doesn't surprise me, and I know no harm was meant, even though much harm may or may not have been done."

"It doesn't surprise you?" queried Donna.

"No," replied Collin. "You see, for example, I know of another minister, new in another community, who went to a nearby doctor to get established with him. This doctor also was happy and pleased to be a doctor to ministers. During the course of a thorough medical examination the doctor readily and openly told this minister of three others of his colleagues in ministry who were also his patients. As the one-sided conversation proceeded, this doctor would say, your colleague, so and so, has such and such wrong with him, but it will be okay in time, nothing to worry about. Before he was through his medical, this minister knew the medical history of his three colleagues, and he also surmised that the other three would know the same about him. He never went back to that doctor."

"Why would a doctor do a thing like that?" asked Donna again.

Collin explained, "Well it is one of those rare and naive situations where a well meaning religiously oriented doctor assumes that the ministry is one tight knit near perfect brotherhood and sisterhood of highly compatiable people who can completely confide in one another. Little do they realize the belittling, and the rivalry that emenates from the undisciplined pride and envy that exists in some segments of the ministry as well as elsewhere in society. Some very high caliber professional people are naive about the realities of life in the outside world.

"Continuing with this experience, Durwin was able to avoid an open run in with the haughty minister. However, he did have occasion to preach in that ministers church one Sunday morning when there was an exchange of pulpits among the local churches. The haughty minister was to preach somewhere else. He must have been late arriving there, because he remained at his own church till the last minute, fluttering around running interferences as Durwin called it, making sure that Durwin didn't talk to any one person for more than a few seconds, and still stretching himself practically out of his shoes trying to look as a person of towering importance. Just a minute or two before the service began he departed to the church where he was to officiate. Immediately after worship time he was back again for the refreshment period that followed, doing much the same as before, and not once joining in a conversation with Durwin."

Brett chuckled, "And he was the one the doctor proposed to try to find what was wrong with Durwin?"

"Ironic," added Owen, "the man had more wrong with himself than he was aware of."

"A fine mess he would have made of Durwin," quipped Gilda.

"Mess is right," said Collin seriously. "More lives are ruined than we know of by pseudo counselors who have more wrong with themselves than is wrong with those whom they try to counsel. Always beware of them.

"When Durwin attended his first ecumenical monthly meeting of the clergy of the immediate area, he chose to sit beside a clergyman of middle years like himself, whom he hadn't met before, to try to socialize before meeting time.

"The clergyman didn't speak to Durwin, nor even look his way at first. So Durwin spoke to him, introducing himself. Then the clergyman turned somewhat towards Durwin and glared at him coldly without speaking. To try to break the ice, Durwin repeated his own name again and told which church he was now serving in the area.

"The clergyman, still glaring, asked abruptly, 'Where are you from?'

"Durwin calmly replied that his original home was in such and such a place in Lower Secundaterra. The clergyman's glare turned into a front on stare, but no words were forthcoming.

"'I wouldn't expect you to know where my home town is,' said Durwin in a mannerly way. 'But it is near such and such an airport.'

"The clergyman continued to stare directly at Durwin. It was close quarters, but Durwin held his ground and added, 'that airport used to be famous during World War II, but I don't suppose it is well known around here now.'

"The clergyman was moved to speak, but in a very curt and cold manner. 'Yes,' he snapped, as he nodded his head with a quick jerk, 'I know where that airport is.'

"Durwin smiled a friendly smile at him and he looked away. There was no further conversation between them for the evening, but Durwin stayed right in the same chair for the duration of the meeting."

"What a welcome!" remarked Leo.

"What was his motivation for that kind of behavior?" inquired Gilda, curiously.

Collin explained, "Durwin didn't fully realize at the time what it was all about, but with time and more experience he would come to know it is another ploy used by Terrapriman belittlers to stare you down, make you cower in front of them, and overall make you feel inferior to them. To their way of thinking, Terraprimans must be regarded as superior to all. Outsiders, of the Caucasian white race especially, and of the caliber of Durwin Lawton must be brought down below the least common denominator of Terraprimans and feel inferior to them all. Or, to put it more to their liking, see themselves all as superior to all others.

"How not to endear outsiders to your country!" exclaimed Donna.

"No wonder it's 'Yankee go home' in so many parts of the world," commented Leo.

"I notice you mentioned the Caucasian white race in particular. What's the significance there?" asked Owen.

"A good question," said Collin. "You see, ethnic minorities, no matter how high caliber or low, will be well treated by Terraprima 'Christian' belittlers. It boosts their pride to be able to say we do not discriminate against minorities. They give themselves a pat on the back for it. But fine, high caliber people of the Caucasian white majority will be put down mercilessly and by belittlers mostly of the Caucasian white race, but including some belittlers of the minority races."

Collin then added, "With those Caucasian whites who could be exceptional in one or any number of different ways being treated so, it is noticeable that in many spheres of life, Caucasian whites are becoming less and less in numbers at or near the top of the scale in any given occupation.

"I must add a positive note to the incident I just related to you," remarked Collin without delay. "In time, that clergyman I last told you of, whom Durwin would later come to know better, was regarded highly in his denomination. He would eventually be friendly and kind towards the Lawtons. Over a period of years he and some of his people would have social interaction with the Lawtons which would change his mind on his behavior towards them. He is one of very, very few belittlers who ever change their ways towards any fine, high caliber people."

"Well what do you know, a positive note from the belittlers of Terraprima!" exclaimed Leo with a chuckle.

Collin continued, "One other minister in the ecumenical setting caused problems for Durwin. This minister didn't come across as hostile. In fact he often acted very friendly toward Durwin or so it seemed. However, each time Durwin would try to speak at a meeting, this minister would react in a very insecure manner. It was as if a combination of Durwin's voice, together with the content of what he said, would upset the security of this otherwise compatible minister."

"Another case of a person not knowing how to react to someone he perceives or imagines to be a cut above him in some way," interjected Gilda.

"That's it," said Collin. "This minister had much going for him. He was very effective in his work; but got jittery each time Durwin spoke. He soon devised, perhaps unconsciously thought Durwin at the time, an almost constant and automatic reaction to Durwin speaking at a meeting. When Durwin got a few words of an idea out, he would speak up, take over the same idea, and discuss it with the other ministers, mostly the doctor's haughty minister who was always most willing to crowd Durwin out.

"Over the years this almost continuous reaction, together with always being the last hand to be responded to during the question and answer periods at most denominational gatherings and then being answered curtly or vaguely besides, had its detrimental effect. Added to that was the problem of being snorted and grunted at in meetings within his own congregation, as I mentioned before. Altogether, it caused temporary damage to Durwin. He developed a hesitancy and a quiver in his speech. This conscious, yet almost uncontrollable reaction on Durwin's part may be likened to reactions catalogued by the Russian physiologist, Pavlov in his studies of reflex behavior with dogs almost one hundred years earlier, and which have since had influence on behaviorist theories of psychology.

"Durwin, like Pavlov's dog when it ate, in effect was being snapped at each time he spoke or attempted to speak. Over a period of several years, it could not help but have an adverse effect on him. Also, he tried his best to lessen his verbal impact on those proud, insecure souls, by softening his voice when speaking to them or in their presence. This also over the long period helped do temporary harm to his speech and conversation skills, but it did help a little to deter the insecure ones and the paranoid belittlers from labeling him, harsh, heavy handed, hard to get along with and the like, even though some of them continued to do so.

"At one point in time, Durwin took the trouble to, in a friendly manner, confront some of these people about their shabby behavior towards him when he tried to speak. Each of them brazenly denied ever having done so.

"As I indicated a minute ago, Durwin at the time was of the opinion that this continuous taking over of and/or crowding out his conversation was done unconsciously, or inadvertently, although he did wonder about the ignorance and complete lack of culture and decorum of it. As time went by, however, and as his experiences with many belittlers of Terraprima expanded, Durwin would come to know that many belittlers use that tactic very consciously and intentionally as a ploy to belittle and maim, and to crowd their victim out of everything. It couldn't be just ill manners and ignorance because they were not like that with other people around at the same time. Their denial of it is also a part of the ploy.

"There is another incident worth recalling. There was to be a series of mid-week services during Lent. On this particular night Durwin and another minister were to conduct the service between them in Durwin's church. This minister was a dramatically inclined sort of person. Indeed, he was very good at dramatics, except that he liked to use them to his own ends, whether or not it belittled anyone else, as you shall see.

"Durwin asked this dramatic minister or dramatist as we shall note him, to get together with him and plan the service. He kept putting it off, saying, 'O, I can just come along to the service and do my thing.'

"Durwin knew what that would mean. It would be that the dramatist would come in at service time, take over the whole show, and that's what it would be—a show, a one man show. He would crowd Durwin right out of the picture, and Durwin's people would then wonder why he hadn't participated, perhaps even surmise it was his laziness or his incompetence as they were indeed trying to brand him by this time.

"When the day of the service drew near, and Durwin had received no cooperation, he planned the service himself, informing the dramatist afterwards that the planning was done and the dramatist was to be the preacher. He could do his thing there, Durwin told him.

"Durwin knew that this minister may still come barging in and take over the whole show, so to speak. Durwin's photo copier I have told you about earlier arrived the day before the service, just in time. Durwin printed bulletins with the order of service using his newly bought copier. At service time the next evening, he was present early, distributing the bulletins personally to all the congregation to ensure their distribution.

"As he fully expected, the dramatist minister came rushing in just shortly before service time.

"'I came and forgot my sermon notes,' he said, 'so I've decided to do a religious drama with hymns and message and all, all by myself, he asserted. It's just a one person thing, you can sit back and take it easy,' he said authoritatively.

"Durwin calmly replied, 'You can do your thing as you wish during the sermon time, but the congregation already has in their hands, the order of service with both you and I participating.'

"The dramatist's face dropped. He paused for a moment, 'I guess I had better run home and get my sermon notes.'

"'Okay,' said Durwin, 'I'll delay the service a little, but I may have to start it before you get back. But that's okay, the sermon is later in the service.'

"The dramatist returned with his sermon notes in good time. The well planned service went very well with both ministers participating.

"During the fellowship that followed, one of Durwin's parishoners stood talking with him. She was not a belittler. In fact she was a very nice and efficient person, but she was naive about belittlers; could not see through them at all.

"'It was a lovely service,' she remarked to Durwin. "Durwin thanked her, and then by way of small talk he told her how he had planned the service, and how his newly purchased copier had arrived just in time to print the bulletins."

"'Oh, so it was your service!' she exclaimed with surprise.

"'Yes,' said Durwin, frankly, 'It was my service. We couldn't arrange a time to plan it together.'

"The look on her face was one of astonishment," said Collin, "and why?"

Then Collin answered his own question. "Durwin had been giving this congregation what had previously been described by officials as an excellent ministry, and superior performance, yet this nice person was surprised that Durwin could put together a service such as they just had. By now after some years the belittlers of the congregation had worked on Durwin's reputation vehemently. This nice woman, and some others like her had been brain-washed by the belittlers into thinking Durwin wasn't a capable minister. It began the first day the Lawtons arrived, with the complaining by one person about them being one half hour late on a several hundred mile trip.

"Also as I have already told you last week, Durwin had reason to believe that this brain-washing had also extended via the back door, so to speak, to officials of the wider church. And of course the belittlers there would welcome it. Belittlers were indeed doing Durwin in, just as his friends from Secundaterra had warned him they would.

"It bothered the belittlers that Durwin now had a copier. He played it low key while still using it as much as necessary to do a satisfactory job. Later when Durwin bought his own computer to enhance his church work, one of the belittlers upon learning of it, actually was seen going away crying. In time, Durwin would get to know more fully of the envy and over-sensativity of these people.

"Now to bring this part of the story to conclusion, I wish to say that several other ministers, priests and rabbis in the area did Durwin no harm. In fact he had very good rapport with some of them, especially at community social functions where the belittlers were not usually present."

"Why were belittlers not usually present at community social functions?" asked Albin.

"Simply because many of them are social misfits," replied Collin. "Outside their own familiar turf, they are not capable of fitting in. Normal people can quickly adapt to almost any public circumstance or social function. The belittlers feel very uncomfortable in any circumstance with which they are not very familar and not already on top of. They therefore become masters of their own domain, but are misfits and lost when it comes to participating outside that domain."

"They really are inferior then, aren't they?" questioned Leo.

"Yes, they really are," affirmed Collin. "Next week," he said, "I will tell you some things about belittlers at work in the Commerce and Industry of Terraprima. At this point I suggest that we adjourn for the evening."

Dr. Eldren agreed.

After the usual making and confirming of arrangements for the following week, the group adjourned for the evening. Dr. Eldren departed to go to other duties. The group members decided to again gather at the Corner Coffee Shop before going home.

CHAPTER VII

On this next Wednesday evening, when the support group was seated and ready Collin led them into a different aspect of his presentation. “Being a minister of the church, I guess it is natural that I have concentrated so much on belittlers in the church,” he started. “However, I would not have you think that belittling is a characteristic found in the church only; far from it. Although in the church, due to more birds of a feather flocking more closely together, the belittling becomes a near organized conspiracy, to maim and/or destroy. It is therefore a more concentrated and extremely cruel phenomenon.”

“Could you elaborate on that a little more,” asked Dr. Eldren, uncomfortably, “the near organized conspiracy part?”

“Of course,” replied Collin with self assurance. “There are many belittlers in the church, both clergy and laity. The mind games and belittling in the church are very familiar to most of them. By innuendo, implication by voice inflection, by derogatory gesture and other such ways, the game that may be being played on a victim is passed from one belittler to another, one catching on from the other, until they are all treating him in much the same belittling and unchristian manner.”

“Well explained, and well taken,” said Dr. Eldren, amiably.

Collin continued, “Establishments in industry and commerce as well as in the church get overwhelmed with belittlers at times. Also, at times in industry and commerce it may be a single powerful belittler and his supporters who cause problems for exceptional people. When such a person is rooted out in time, the integrity of the organization is protected. Let me illustrate both concepts further.

“In the industry and commerce of Terraprima, this malady, this wayward characteristic, is abounding to the point where it frequently near paralyzes businesses and all too often causes them to fail altogether. This frequent cause of business failure has never been explored. Let me illustrate to you how belittlers not only ruin personal careers, but whole business operations as well.”

Brett Culver perked up. “Now you’re getting into my field.”

“And mine,” added Donna Coyne.

"I experienced early in life the sting of belittlers in the work a day world. They make life miserable for people like us. I was not aware though that they bring businesses down too," said Albin Anders.

"Let me tell you a story that illustrates it vividly," said Collin. "This is another experience of Durwin in Terraprima. You may have surmised by now that since belittlers were so domineering in Durwin's church they were a major factor in the surrounding community.

"The area in which Durwin lived had, in recent years, grown from a quiet little town to a bustling suburban community, with middle and upper middle class people in very large numbers. To compliment this a large supermarket chain moved in and built an ultra modern store with top quality facilities to meet the needs of the very, very busy career people that now were a major portion of the population. In addition to the aisle upon aisle of the usual grocery and other items of an extra large supermarket, there were such services as elaborate delicatessen and gourmet quality prepared or unprepared food in a large variety. This was welcomed in the fast pace life of the now suburban area. A person could pick up a meal of high quality cooked or uncooked food in a few minutes. The facilities were there for one stop world class shopping. People flocked to this new store as soon as its doors were opened. This supermarket did a tremendous business—for a while.

"Durwin shopped there at times. It was actually an exhilarating place to be at first, always busy and bustling, with people talking excidedly about the wonderful store. One day as he was shopping, he noticed an encyclopedia of several volumes was coming on stream to be sold a volume each week as such stores sometimes do. Up to the third volume was already in stock, so Durwin picked up the first three volumes together with some groceries and proceeded to the check-out as usual.

"There was a young man operating the check-out to which Durwin went. He appeared to be characterless as he checked out the nicely dressed, nicely spoken obviously high caliber woman ahead of Durwin in the line. In hostility towards her he slapped her groceries across the check-out, tossed them carelessly in the bags and was unresponsive to her friendly manner, not even saying thank you or have a nice day, as would be usual.

"Durwin placed his groceries on the check-out. The young man handled them in the same manner as with the woman, careless and unconcerned. Lastly, Durwin placed his books up for check out. The clerk pretended he didn't see them, and totaled up the groceries.

"'These books are mine as well,' said Durwin politely.

"The clerk flicked them aside with his fingers, obviously miffed by a fine person with a cultured thing such as encyclopedia books.

"Durwin spoke more firmly, 'I wish to have these books please.'

"The man pushed up his lip in contempt, rang the books up on the cash register, practically snatched the money from Durwin's hand, handed him his change, bagged the books and pushed them at him, and did the same with the few groceries; altogether obnoxious behavior in which, in a matter of minutes, the check-out clerk shunned and treated shabbily two fine, high caliber people, the kind of people for which this store was designed.

"Durwin, at home that evening, told Canda of his experience. 'I'm not sure yet,' he said to her, 'but that business may fail, it may be just an isolated case of a belittler getting hired, and he will be dismissed later, or it may be that belittlers are getting the upper hand there. I will see in time.'

"Durwin continued to shop there over a period of months and observed what was happening. He would pause at the end of aisles nearest the check-outs to observe the employees. He would go to the various extra high quality deli counters for service or observe them from the aisles nearby. Sure enough, what a belittler would refer to as 'ordinary' people, were being treated well, with the best of service. The many fine higher caliber people, whom belittlers refer to as 'big shots,' and for whom this store was designed, were being shunned with slow and/or unmannerly service. Belittlers were now domineering in this store.

"How could such a thing have happened in so short a time? I will tell you next of another incident that will illustrate how. Meanwhile, within a year this fine, high caliber supermarket had failed and was up for sale. True, the competition of the area improved their existing services to meet the new needs of the expanding community. But there was still more than plenty of room for this business as well had the belittlers not ruined it.

"Most observers, even those who know business well, would simply say, these employees were not good workers, they were lazy, they didn't understand business, or such reasons as that. The few people who are wise to this reaction to 'big shots' put it down as ignorance, which it is, but which term does not define it well enough to analyze it. It is a particular type of 'ignorance.' It is belittling, born out of envy and its accompaning hatred and contempt for people whom the belittler sees as persons a cut above him or her self.

"Let me tell you now of an incident that will illustrate how such a high class business could become dominated by belittlers and ruined in so short a time," Collin continued.

"The Lawtons had a friend living in a city not far away to where they used to drive and visit occasionally. A new department store opened in that city, so the friend went to work there. It was a store catering to the higher priced tastes of the middle to upper income people. Many of the customers would be cultured people of quality, connoisseurs, and promoters of that quality and culture. Then, of course, there would be what I would call the followers of such people; that is, people without culture, giving themselves a continuous ego trip by materially keeping themselves up with the cultured. However, that is beside the point. Mainly this store had goods and services that attracted high caliber people.

"That being so, many good quality workers, including the Lawtons' friend flocked to this store to obtain employment. These were also people of culture, not wealthy as many of the customers would be, but nevertheless, fine cultured people who wished to work in a compatable atmosphere. Also, there were again the followers of these fine workers. The followers seeking a job here were looking for the glitter, excitement and ego exalting of working among the wealthy—together with the supposed opportunity of making more money off the rich.

"At the opening of the store, the fine cultured workers were in the majority there. Sadly, however, it soon became apparent that the manager and some other people at the top, were not accustomed to working with fine employees of caliber, and did not know how to react to them or handle them; nor did they want them around. These fine people, these good, responsible workers did a marvelous job, far beyond the call of duty, in preparing for the store to open on time and making it a grand and gala event. They outshone the management by far.

"Were they complimented for their extraordinary feat? Was any appreciation shown? Not a word. They were told there was always room for improvement, that they could do better. The management did not have what it takes within them to compliment people who were by far a cut above them. So they belittled them, even openly criticized them. There were no smiles, or 'good mornings' at the beginning of a day, no 'good-byes' or 'have a nice evening' at the end of a day. There was coldness, silent stares and shunning—to the properly motivated, cultured people, that is.

"To the others, the followers, who were there on a money making, ego trip, and who were far, far less responsible in their work and in their responsibility to the business that was employing them, it was altogether different. For these there was the better shifts on which to work, the better lunch hours, no pressure to obey the company rules, no pressure to do better, favoritism in every way. These people were no threat to the management, who felt at ease with them. These were the kind of people the management wanted around.

"So the inevitable happened. Before very long at all, the fine, hard working, responsible employees began to resign, one by one. They had no choice. It was not healthy psychologically to stay in such a negative environment for long. It would be harmful to themselves to do so. These people were not soft or oversensitive. They were simply looking after their mental health and employment reputations. If they stayed too long, they would eventually be degraded by being labeled with an unsatisfactory work record, as well as having psychological harm done to their characters.

"In this store I am talking about, only the wrongly motivated, many of whom were belittlers like the management, were left there to do business with fine, high caliber people. It just couldn't work.

"To give an example of the behavior there, a customer was making a large purchase in the many hundreds of dollars. As she was choosing her several purchases a fine saleslady attended to any help she needed.

Then at periods when the customer was in the fitting room trying on clothes, the saleslady, responsible person that she was, would spend the time arranging or tidying other goods nearby.

"Another salesperson also stood nearby, watching the whole proceedure, doing absolutely nothing to make herself useful in the store. She watched closely, and at the crucial moment sprung like a leopard. As the customer appeared ready, the crafty salesperson crowded in, I'll check your purchases out for you now,' she said in a pushy manner; so she checked the customer out and thereby captured the credit for and the commission on the sale. The fine saleslady complained to a member of the management. He shruged his shoulders, smiled a greasy smile and replied, 'Oh, she is just being aggressive.'

"The fine sales person soon resigned, as did many others, until the store, within months, was dominated by belittlers and other inferior employees. These were no threat to the management, but neither could they carry on a good rapport with the kind of customers for which that store had been created. Consequently, as the fine responsible employees dropped away, so the fine better customers did likewise.

"To conclude this incident I will tell you of the reaction of one customer who had just been taken care of by the Lawtons' friend before she resigned. This humble, genuinely cultured connoisseur type customer thanked the Lawtons' friend for her efficient and cordial service saying how such service is often a rarity nowadays. Then the woman went on to say, 'I had hoped this store, with all its seeming fineness would be, at last, a store in this city where nice people would work and shop, and enjoy quality and culture at its finest. But I'm not so sure this is it. Already, I detect a strange atmosphere here. I don't think they are going to make it. I've seen it happen in other stores. I don't know just what it is. It is very strange, but it happens.' Time will tell how accurate that woman's concerns are, and whether the store will catch on and change, or go under.

Collin moved into another phase of the story. "Let me tell you now of some of Canda Lawton's experiences in industry. Before moving to Terraprima, Canda throughout the years had held several high caliber jobs in the offices of some of the largest business organizations in Secundaterra. During the course of her business career, she also, for these companies for which she worked, did business for them by telephone, correspondence and in person with many other nation wide industries of the largest size and complexity. Canda was an exceptional person in any office, and also in personality and the ability to work with people in all walks of life from top to bottom. Now in Terraprima, after only a few months of familiarization and adjustment, she was ready for the world of business and industry of her new environment.

"Canda went to work in the general office of a nation wide industry, in one of its departments with a dozen or more employees under one person's supervision. After only a few weeks, Canda had mastered all the work included in her job description, and with time to spare each day. A little later, when one employee dropped out to work elsewhere, Canda was able to absorb that person's job with her own, without any undue sense of stress or rush. She thought it would eventually be appreciated. As time went on, business increased in the department, and Canda took on still extra work, well able to take it in her stride. Such was her natural ability.

"In time, Canda learned the inner politics and workings of the company. Although this foreign owned, foreign managed business was known to be very discreet in its business practices, it had many Terraprimans in key positions, some of whom were belittlers to whom the present management was not wise. The supervisor of Canda's department was a Terraprima man of great pride but of little ability. He didn't know the workings of many parts of his own department. The other employees carried him.

"He had attained his position by downgrading others, or belittling as we call it, and by manipulation. He was bluffing his way along now, with some other senior people in the department actually carrying much of the load of his office and making many of the decisions. Usually the only time they heard from him was when there was room or reason for him to assert himself and come down on someone with discipline of a sort. He was a manipulator as well as a belittler and he had slipped himself into a key position in an industry that was not generally under the domination of belittlers.

"Over the two year period that Canda worked there she received the usual periodic reviews and salary increases that others of the department received. Then the company posted a job opening in another department. It was a more responsible position with higher salary. According to required procedure, Canda told her supervisor of her intention to apply for this job opening. He told her he wanted her to stay in his department, at the job she now had, and therefore he would not recommend her for the new job. She protested and rightly said that this was unfair treatment. In an effort to work around him Canda went to the personnel office on a Thursday afternoon, the day before the deadline for aplications, to apply for the position anyway, only to find that the Terrapriman personnel officer was a belittler also."

"A deadly position in which any business could have such a person," said Brett. "A person like that as a personnel officer can do untold harm to an industry, depriving it of the better employees that would otherwise come its way."

"Right you are," agreed Collin. "Let's see what happened.

"When Canda went to the personnel office and made known what she was there for, the personnel officer was very cold towards her. She nastily told her that she had to leave early that day, right away in fact. If Canda wished to fill out the application and take the tests she could, but the clerk would take care of it for her.

"The personnel officer left immediately and sternly. Canda under the oversight of the clerk went through the procedure without problems. The next day, Friday, the deadline, she hoped to hear from the personnel office, at least an acknowledgement of her application and the results of the tests. When by mid afternoon there was no response, she phoned the personnel department only to find that the personnel officer had not come in that day.

"On the Monday following, Canda went to the personnel office in person. The personnel officer was there, as cold and severe as ever. She told Canda that she hadn't gotten her application in on time. Monday was too late. The position had already been awarded to another person. Upon further inquiry elsewhere in the offices, Canda was to find out that the person to whom the position was given had, according to the corporation rules, not been with them long enough for promotion, or even to have her first review and appraisal. She was not long out of school, had little previous business experience, and lacked almost any knowledge of business machines.

"Needless to say, Canda left that company immediately; she would not allow herself to be abused and humiliated by such people. After she left, her department had to hire three people to take her place. They shuffled the jobs around a little to cover up, but there were three new employees in the department shortly after Canda left.

"This corporation as I said earlier, was a discreet foreign owned business, not partial to people like belittlers. However, so little or nothing is widely known about belittlers that it often takes a long time for their deeds to catch up to them. Some time later, when a new foreign general manager came into office, Canda's department supervisor's job was phased out and he was given a mediocre job elsewhere in the company. The personnel officer conveniently retired. The supervisor who hired the unqualified employee to his department was dismissed for many infractions of rules—but Canda had long been out of a job by that time."

Gilda asked, "Was there not any recourse at all that Canda could have taken to get fair treatment from the corporation?"

"None at all," replied Collin. "She knew that the management of that general office was not at all astute when it came to human behavior. The belittlers had them completely hoodwinked. It wasn't until a new management took over, that these people were recognized for what they were, a liability to the corporation.

"You can also quite easily notice from this story that belittlers do not reward exceptional work. In fact their character make-up would never let them acknowledge it, even though they know right well in the back of their minds that it is there. They will deny it sometimes even to themselves, while still utilitzing such work and taking advantage of it in the meantime. There is no reward or appreciation from belittlers for good or exceptional work. The better the work the more they put down the worker of it.

"By the way, there were several other top quality people leave that corporation before the new management came in. For example, one person who had been there many years and had given excellent service, asked for some new equipment for her office. Her work load had grown over a period of time and with her outmoded office equipment it was difficult for her to keep up with it as much as she might try. She explained to her supervisor what the latest in new and affordable office equipment could do, and how a new system would allow her to keep up with the work quite readily.

"There was no question that this corporation could easily afford all the latest and best in equipment. But her request was refused. She was told she would have to work a little harder. It was insulting and abusive to one who had worked so long and faithfully over a period of many years. She resigned and found a job elsewhere. A person was hired to take her place and was immediately given the equipment she had been refused."

"Rats," exclaimed Leo, "a bunch of rats."

"Why wouldn't they give the new equipment to the original person?" asked Albin.

"Pride and envy," replied Collin. "It was her idea and not theirs, and that bothered them. She had a whole new process devised that the new equipment could do for them. It was a masterful plan, but alas it was her idea and not theirs. When the new person came in they were able to bring in both the process and the equipment as their own idea. Little did they realize how many others knew the right story of it. They are not capable of thinking that far on such matters."

"Thieves," remarked Leo again.

"Deceitful little children!" remarked Brett.

"This kind of thing is abounding in Terraprima industry and commerce," continued Collin. "Let me tell you of another person working in a branch plant office of a major manufacturer of a line of building materials."

"I'm all ears," said Brett, perking up.

Collin began the story of yet another victim of belittlers. "This woman whom I shall refer to as the 'woman', had been working in this branch plant office for approximately thirty years. She had seen the plant through its better days, many years of them, but in later years the place had become infested with belittlers, and as happens under such circumstances business was on the decrease.

"This woman, in a key position, had built up an excellent rapport with customers all over the continent. Generally, a nation-wide network of sales staff kept orders coming into the plant. When orders were slow coming in, for example when salespersons were on vacation, this woman would get on the phone to the customers and take orders from them for materials. In doing so, she often averted temporary lay-offs in the plant. This woman, whose major function was to resolve problems between manufacturer and customer, had done such a masterful job of it, that the customers were only too happy to place orders with her.

"Over the past several years, belittlers had crept into positions in the operation, both in management and down through the ranks of office and plant staff. Correspondingly, over these years more and more complaints about errors and insufficient service kept coming into the office. This woman continued to handle the complaints graciously and effectively, making the responsible departments, now either under the control of or infested with belittlers, to make good on the customers problems.

"Needless to say, belittlers don't like such action. They prefer under such circumstance to simply turn to their hollow undisciplined pride and claim that they are doing things quite well, its just that the customer is too fussy, and the woman doesn't handle them right or the woman herself is too fussy. Consequently, the woman became quite unpopular among much of the plant and office personnel in her final years there.

"She continued to persist in her excellent customer services, and in keeping orders coming in during the lean times. As much as this one woman's effort helped to keep the plant going, you might surmise that the business gradually deteriorated over a period of five years or so.

"It was during this period that Canda Lawton, working with a temporary employment agency, went to work in the same office with the woman on a temporary basis. Canda and the woman, having so much in common concerning efficiency, effectiveness, and fairness in business, soon became good friends. Before long, Canda could see what a predicament this business was in. She talked to the woman about it, and the woman began to confide in her about how things had deteriorated there in recent years, and also how she was now unpopular for trying to keep things going well.

"One day the woman also confided in Canda, 'you know, most of my years have been good here, but I've been working under adverse circumstances here these past few years, and at times I really do get on the brink of thinking that the problem is with me and not them. I guess I'm gradually being brainwashed. I really do know the difference. It's easy to observe their inferior workmanship, their carelessness and callousness, and their attitude toward people like us, but still, I've been in it for so long now it is affecting me. Do you think it is me?' she asked Canda, 'do you think I am the problem and not them?'

"'Certainly not,' Canda assured her time and again. Canda felt that any level headed, properly motivated person could easily see that this woman was a genuinely good and fine person, exceptional in many ways. Obviously she had always been a strong person, but the strongest of people, under severely adverse circumstances long enough are affected to varying degrees.

"For the remainder of her time working there, Canda's ministry was to assure that woman that there was nothing wrong with her. She would point out to her examples of how Canda herself could see that the inferior belittler employees were doing damage to the business with faulty products, service and human relations, for which they were unwilling to make restitution if they possibly could get away with it.

"Let me illustrate how this woman was discriminated against. There was another woman employee in the plant office, in a senior position. She took advantage of her position continuously. Her usual was to come into the office twenty minutes to a half hour late each morning; then get herself coffee and with it read the morning paper. Then she would go to the wash room and put on make-up. On her return to her desk, quite often she would do such chores as balance her personal check book, or make phone calls to friends. She would then do a little work before taking much more than the allotted time for lunch break. Her afternoon work load was very casual and light, and usually ended with her leaving a little early, with or without an excuse or reason for doing so.

"One of her tasks was to make arrangements for visiting company officials, or for local officials going elsewhere for meetings and so on. She was a master at this but also at spending the company money lavishly for it. They loved her for it, and she manipulated the situation for her own popularity and ease. In comparison to this, the woman who is the main object of this story, and who was almost single handedly keeping the plant going was being ignored, shunned, passed over, belittled in other words, almost continuously.

"Eventually, this plant, losing money for the corporation, was sold to a foreign owner as a losing business, and was moved far away to another part of the country. In the months during its sale, and before it passed into the hands of the new owner, the woman discontinued bringing in orders to keep it going. Business all but dried up. She was sorry to see that happen, but it proved her worth to herself. Many customers called her to thank her for such good service over the years and she received gifts and flowers from many of them. When the doors finally closed, she was able to walk away feeling she had served faithfully and well. She would never get recognition for that from the company, but she could feel good about herself."

Owen remarked, "It is amazing and almost unbelievable how the belittlers dominating this corporation could close their eyes to the good woman's work and be so taken by the wayward woman's work, or lack of it."

Collin explained, "The wayward woman vaunted their undisciplined pride by making them feel important with all her lavish arrangements for them. The good woman pricked that same pride by doing for the business what they, lacking foresight, initative and personality, could not do. What each of these women was doing for or to the corporation didn't matter to the belittlers. It was what they did to them and their pride that was their concern."

"Unbridled selfishness," remarked Gilda.

"Yes," said Collin, "the belittlers' concerns were completely self centered; no concern for the well being of the corporation that was feeding them. By the way, the corporation in its new location eventually failed because the new owners took so many of the belittlers with the business.

"Allow me to illustrate further the vast difference that exists between the proud and the practical, by telling you of an experience Canda had with a temporary employment agency.

"The local branch office of this employment agency was staffed by two personnel officers. The two were as different as chalk and cheese. The one was proud and biased, but with not much know-how and perception of people and the kind of employment situations they would fit into well. The second, the senior of the two, was practical, with keen perception of personalities as well as their skills.

"Canda went to this office with a resume that showed an outstanding employment record, some of it earned through another branch of this same employment agency. Canda, as always, was modestly but tastefully well dressed, well groomed, and pleasant and down to earth in personal behavior. That was her natural way. It so happened that she was waited on by the proud personnel officer who almost immediately, and more emphatically after reading her good resume, treated her with guarded disdain. In her overly sophisticated dress for office, she vaunted herself over Canda with an overly proud, overly sophisticated manner in order to belittle Canda beneath her, naming several specialized jobs for which Canda would not qualify. Over the next several weeks she offered Canda several temporary jobs, such as taking inventory in department stores, delivering samples from door to door, but nothing to utilize her qualifications. Canda did not take such jobs but rather protested to her. One day she offered Canda a two day job in an office of several employees. 'You had better dress very professionally for this job' she told Canda, 'a good business dress. There is something special going on there.'

"So Canda arrived on the job very well dressed, only to find the other employees modestly but tidely dressed, and wondering what kind of person Canda was to be so overdressed. After an hour or so, when Canda had made acquaintance with them she explained why the dressed up appearance. They laughed. The next day Canda came tastefully and modestly dressed, her usual, and was well received by all the staff.

"Soon after that job was completed, the proud officer still acting overly sophisticated, offered Canda another temporary job. 'You'd better wear jeans for this one,' she said, 'its a constuction company. Canda ignored the suggestion on clothes, went dressed similarly to the second day at the previous office. She was very well received there from the start by just being herself.

"One day Canda had occasion to visit the agency office when the proud one was on vacation. Now she was taken care of by the practical one, who was from the start, pleasant, open and down to earth. She reviewed Canda's resume with her. Some of Canda's recently acquired skills gained through night school and that she had reported to the proud one were not noted there. The practical one now added them to the resume. Canda discussed with her the behavior of the first officer towards her. In return the second officer revealed to Canda that other complaints had come in to the same effect.

"Before long Canda was being offered employment more compatible with her qualifications and experience. This second officer was basing her impressions and decisions on rational reasoning, whereas the first officer had been motivated by the haughty type of pride and the envy and bias that usually goes with it. Within a month or so, the proud officer was no longer employed with the agency. The practical officer was still there, but with a practical helper. Not all corporations get overpowered by belittlers. Some weed them out in time.

"Canda worked at many different places through the temporary employment agencies. Over a period of time several of them wanted to take her on to their permanent staff, but they were seldom willing to pay her any extra salary for her exceptional ability and capacity; the reason being they were fearful of offending those of lesser ability by offering Canda higher salary. I tell you this because it is one more instance of how the fine and exceptional people are short-changed. "One such company, with whom Canda had worked for several months as a temporary employee, wanted her to stay on permanently. However, they offered her only the same salary as employees who had worked with this corporation only a short time as Canda had, but had never done similar work before. There was no allowance made for the wide and varied experience Canda had in numerous other types of business, which most of the other employees did not have. Neither was there any allowance made for Canda's exceptional capacity, which was a result of her wide and varied experience and her personal natural ability. Care was taken not to offend the employees of lesser ability. Canda did not take this job that was offered, and again after she left they had a general office shuffle and hired two extra people to take up the work load."

"They shuffle around to save face, eh?" observed Leo.

"Yes," replied Collin, "with many people there is no such thing as acknowledging exceptional ability. Some people, including belittlers wish to take advantage of it if they can do so without acknowledging it. When they can't, they just wish it out of the way and out of sight, period. In this latter case they use various means, fair or foul, to get rid of exceptional people.

"Nevertheless, there are some who do recongnize, acknowledge, appreciate and reward fine and exceptional ability. Canda did work under one such person in a corporation that was not under the spell of belittlers. It was a large corporation who's work largely required that people learn it from the bottom up in order to master it well. They generally hired younger people.

"Canda worked in their general office as a temporary employee for a while. Her well cultured, fine woman supervisor recognized Canda's exceptional ability and trustworthy personality. She went to bat for her, had her hired on permanently and for above usual salary. Canda did well there and from the middle position in which she started, learned the job towards both ends, so to speak. She was able to take it well in her stride with no undue stress or over concern. Such opportunities for fine, exceptional people are rare indeed.

"Discrimination against fine, exceptional people knows no sure barriers of race. An experience Canda had while working temporary at another large manufacturing concern will illustrate. A fine young white man of very pleasant and likeable character worked in the general office of this corporation. He had been there for seven years when a new supervisor had been brought in, and would have supervision over the section in which the likeable young white man was working. The new supervisor was a black man, a graduate in accounting, but lacking in experience. Since graduation, he had held only one mundane job in a small concern for less than a year. He had no experience in supervision, and, as was soon to be seen, he lacked the character to learn it gracefully.

"This young but experienced and also well educated white man would have been quite capable of taking on this supervisory job. He never realized why he didn't get it, but it was because the department head was a belittler. Canda observed this as she worked there. The belittler wouldn't give a job like that to such a fine person.

"Although disappointed the fine young white man very graciously took upon himself to show the new black supervisor the workings of the office. He very patiently, day after day, helped the supervisor through the various procedures, files, communications, etc. of the department. The supervisor was quite capable of learning them. Sad to say though, once he had mastered them well enough to get by, he turned on his helper and enabler in a most cruel, arrogant and ruthless fashion. At every opportunity he turned on the white man; complaining whenever he could fabricate some reason to do so, snapping orders at him when there was no reason to be snappy at a willing worker, giving him disturbing and glaring glances for no reason at all. All of it together was nothing short of mental cruelty.

"The young white man was getting upset more and more as time went by. He made a complaint to the department head. The response was, 'You will have to adjust to your new supervisor. Look how well he is doing. He has been here so short a time and he knows the job quite well already. That man is going to do a lot for this company. Just fall in line with him, that's all.'

"The young man was dismayed. He had always been a good worker, willingly taught the new supervisor the system, and was always ready to take on new procedures or whatever. But there was nothing new being brought in here except a proud, envious, arrogant belittler, as a new supervisor.

"Canda had been working there as a temp when this was going on. She knew what was happening. Whereas the others in the department were afraid to show support for the young man, Canda, being temp, had nothing to lose. She befriended and supported him with empathy. As time went by he revealed to Canda that he was losing sleep over the matter, awakening in a startled manner very early most mornings. He was also losing weight. Canda recognized the symptoms as a danger signal. He told her how he had given seven faithful years of service to this company, and had hoped to make his life's work there. Now it had come to this. He asked Canda if there was anything more he could do to make things better.

"'Well, since you're asking me', said Canda, 'I don't mind telling you what I think about it. This corporation is headed for the rocks sooner or later down the road a ways. The wrong type of people are taking over, and bringing in more people like themselves. You are only young yet, not married, no children; in other words you are free to take your chances on finding an even better job. There are good companies out there where with your personality you can fit in well. You have good training and experience. Get out of here and find a better place. From what I hear this was a good place in bygone years, perhaps when you started here, but you can't judge a place by its past glory.'

"The young man replied, 'I guess when you're working in a place for years, you don't really notice the changes that have taken place over the long period. Now that you bring it out, yes, this was a good place to work when I started here, but you are right, it has gone down hill a whole lot. It is time I looked elsewhere.'

"Canda's temporary work in that office terminated. About three months later she met the young man on a city sidewalk. He was looking the picture of health, and was pleased to tell Canda of his pleasant new job where everything was going extremely well for him in a progressive corporation. He told her he was sleeping well, eating well, and feeling good about life again. It was another of Canda's ministries fulfilled. Not many years passed before news was out that the faulty plant's profit margin was very low.

"Discrimination against fine, exceptional people knows no barriers of age, or gender," Collin went on without stopping. Another place where Canda worked temporarily was also becoming laden with belittlers in high places. In this instance a man in his later years, had given most of his work life to the corporation in which he worked and was looking forward to retirement in two or three years. He came under the supervision of a severe belittling woman supervisor. She made life miserable for him in the usual belittling ways, putting him down at every turn. For this man to leave, it would cost him his pension. He was stuck there and had to take it. That is not easy for an older person. His blood pressure went sky-high, his heart nearly pumped out of his body at times, his sleep was disrupted, it was difficult to eat properly at times. In order to save his pension he was taking a chance on losing his health. That man had to stay there. He might have a stroke, or a heart attack, by which he might be maimed for life, or die. However, it seems such thoughts as that would never enter the mind of this vicious, belittling woman who was bent on putting him down. As I have said many times before, such people are often not capable of thinking ahead to the end result of their misdeeds. They just need to feel superior, with power and control over others, and they do so by putting other people down."

"Brutal bitch," remarked Leo, furiously, "not fit to be loose in society."

"Trouble is," added Donna, "whereas there are laws against harming anyone by physical means, this woman may well be doing physical harm by psychological means and there is no protection against it. It is not even recognized by most people in management positions."

Collin felt he was making much progress with the groups understanding. "Let me tell you of another instance where belittling knows no barriers of gender. This time the victim is a fine young woman.

"Durwin was on location to receive a sizeable truckload of paper supplies for an organization with which he was involved voluntarily. The truck of the largest size short of a tractor trailer pulled up beside the ramp and was readily and very capably put in position for unloading. Then the driver, a very fine, well groomed woman of about age thirty stepped out of the truck. After the usual preliminary exchanges of where to pile the boxes of goods, she began unloading in a very capable manner. At that time it was still somewhat unusual for a woman to be making a living at truck driving.

"Durwin felt obliged to help her. After all, this was a woman, he thought in a traditional manner. Of course, he would pitch in and help a man also if need be. Such was his character. But being a bit older and what some would now call old fashioned he felt even more inclined to help a woman. As they together slung heavy cases of paper, Durwin inquired of the obviously fine, well culture young woman, 'What's a nice person like you doing with a job like this?'

"'I'm appreciated at a job like this,' she replied.

"'Have you worked at other jobs where you were not appreciated?' asked Durwin curiously.

"The truck driver obviously felt a good rapport with Durwin and began to confide in him. 'I'm a secretary by training,' she revealed. 'I am a graduate of such and such a secretarial school, one of the best in this part of the country. I have had some good jobs, and I know I do exceptional work. However, one does not get ahead by exceptional work nowadays. You have to fight your way up or manipulate your way up, and I do neither. Some day I may be a secretary again, maybe. In the meantime I'm a truck driver and I'm appreciated for the quality of my work.' When the unloading was done, Durwin signed for the goods, and the very fine woman whirled very efficiently away in her truck.

"Durwin saw her once more after that. It was at a county celebration type of function. She was tasteful in her dress and social mannerism, and as Durwin already knew, a well trained and very capable person. He thought to himself, *another life being lived at much less than full potential; but then, she is preserving herself, and finding satisfaction in doing so.*

"In another experience, Canda witnessed the attempted toppling of a boss of a branch office. This smart, fine young woman of integrity was the envy of her older employees, both men and women. They gave her a rough time through the usual tactics, among which was not following her discipline at the office. She was strong and keen and was able to hold her own against them. As belittlers do when they are outsmarted, one by one they dropped away, and new employees were hired in their places.

"For a while there was only one belittler left. He was planning to leave on a certain date. In the meantime an executive from the head office was to pay a visit to the branch office. So the remaining belittler planned with his accomplices who had now left the company, to bombard the executive with a derogatory report on the supervisor and giving her as the reason they all left the company. One of the better employees heard them several times talking about it on the phone. In their exeuberance over it they got carried away, allowing their voices to become loud enough to be overheard by this better employee.

"Immediately the better employee took the initative, and without the boss's knowledge of it, wrote a letter extolling the boss's abilities as the wonderful supervisor she really was. She circulated around the office with it and most people there signed it. When the executive arrived she presented the letter to him. The high caliber boss's job was saved. The remaining belittler left the next day.

"Belittlers are at work in all spheres of life, including the health industry and services. They are not particular what damage they do to a fine person. In a routine check-up, Canda had occasion to have a mammogram at the outpatient services of a well known hospital. This hospital had the reputation of being efficiently managed by high caliber people who generally hired quality employees like themselves. Alas though, because so many people are unaware of belittlers, their motivation and tactics, they slip into the best of places.

"As you may already know, the process for a mammogram requires that the woman patient's breasts be set firmly in the equipment but not overly tight. It can easily be done without discomfort to the patient. However, Canda, fine clean cut looking person that she was, for this mammogram had to face a belittling technician of cruel proportions. The technician showed by her facial expression a dislike for Canda as soon as she appeared on the scene. Added to that, when Canda removed her clothing sufficiently for the mammogram, a set of well cared for breasts, in exceptional condition for her age, was revealed. The technician noticeably soured her face. Envy had set in now. She very curtly set up the mammogram, and began tightening the machine on the breasts, tighter and tighter and tighter. Canda Lawton is no chicken, but this was getting to be too much. 'Stop,' she said, 'that's too tight already.'

"'It has to be tight to be any good,' snapped the technician sadistically, and continued to tighten the equipment. Tears came to Canda's eyes. As I said, Canda was not a delicate person, but the technician continued to tighten the machine until Canda cried aloud. The technician quickly completed the process. Then with an air of victory about her, sent Canda on her way.

"Canda had very sore and tender breasts for more than two years after that. When the tenderness didn't go away after three months or so,

Durwin wrote the president of the hospital corporation, with a complaint about the incident. In a short time he received a very well meaning reply, with an apology, and stating that the technician had been further instructed in the use of her equipment and in the necessity of being more careful with people.

"It was a concerned reply, but also a naive one with regard to the technicians motivation. It was obvious to Canda's seasoned observation that the technician knew her equipment well. Canda could also easily observe that the tecnician was spiteful and hateful toward her from the moment she saw her, and that spite and hatred continued to increase to the end of the process. Canda was a fine person. To the technician she was a big shot to be despised. It made no difference that irrepairable physical damage might be done; just put that big shot down beneath her.

"Canda avoided a mammogram for two years after that. By that time the tenderness was beginning to subside. Then, in another city and with another doctor, she was to go to an independent laboratory this time for her mammogram. There, as bad luck should have it, she was confronted by another belittler who disliked her at first sight and who gave her much the same type of treatment. Again, the machine was tightened until Canda was brought to tears. Again the technician concluded the process with an air of mastery and victory over a person she perceived to be a cut above herself.

"Canda's breasts became sore and tender all over again. This time she reported it to her doctor who put in a complaint about it. Nothing was heard about it after that. The following year, at the doctor's request, Canda went to the same place for another mammogram.

"'Have you been here before?' asked the receptionist.

"'Yes, last year,' replied Canda.

"'Okay, I'll just bring up your record,' said the receptionist, as she worked the computer. Then she left and went to another office. Upon her return, the receptionist said to Canda, 'We have no record of you ever being here before.' Canda knew a coverup job had been done. However, she went ahead with this new mammogram. It was done well by a pleasant and careful technician.

"Canda's breasts never returned to normal. Some of the soreness still remains, together with a lump in each breast which is presently being monitored by her doctor. These lumps are located in positions where the stress of the severely administered mammograms were felt the most at the time of their taking."

"Owen commented, "Belittlers sure need to be weeded out of such places, don't they?"

"Yes," added Brett, "but there is not enough public knowledge about them to do so."

"I wish to add," continued Collin, "that there are belittlers in the medical field as much as anywhere else. However, medical doctors are very wary of being sued. Often, the worst we can expect from them is cold but efficient service. However, sometimes their staff members do their dirty work for them, by messing up appointments and other gimmicks to drive you away. So while the risk is lessened the annoyance is still there. Nevertheless, there are some belittling doctors among them who will push their game as far as they dare, according to circumstances.

"Canda was referred to a heart specialist by her congenial family doctor. She was to have a not uncommon procedure done to evaluate the heart area. It was cause for concern, so before it was begun Durwin and another family member were at her bedside. Canda introduced them to the doctor, who merely nodded his head towards them as he went about checking Canda.

"As the nursing staff came to wheel Canda away, they told Durwin and his family companion that as soon as the process was over, Canda would be returned and the doctor would come and explain the problems, whether it was serious and so on and what should be done from here on. This doctor is always good at that, they were told.

"Canda was returned in due time, but the doctor never showed. They waited more than an hour but no word. Canda needed rest so the two left and decided to go to the hospital cafeteria to eat. On the way back to Canda, now nearly two hours after her return, they were walking along the hallway when the doctor came out of a doorway and nearly bumped into them. Startled, he told them in a frenzied manner that he was just returning from an emergency. Caught off guard, this belittler's characteristic inferiority to anyone he perceives to be a cut above him in any way, was showing through very plainly. He then in his continuing frenzy explained Canda's condition to them, some of which was different from a later more official report. Overall her condition wasn't too bad but still cause for concern.

"Durwin wondered at the time if the doctor really did have an emergency, and if so did it take all that time. *Perhaps he did,* thought Durwin so for now he would give him the benefit of the doubt. However, when Canda later went to him for her follow-up check, he gave her a quick report of her condition, and a perscription for medication to take indefinitely, but no instructions as to diet or exercise as I have heard others usually get; just "come back and have it done again next year." The Lawtons knew that was careless advice. It wouldn't necessarily need to be done each year. The advice was just a concluding nicety to cover the previous shabby mannerisms shown by the doctor. This is a common ploy of belittlers - to do something nice to their victim at the end of the encounter. It is supposed to confound the victim's perception of the matter.

"Before long, in the course of his ministerial hospital visitation, Durwin met that doctor three different times in the hospital's hallways. Each time he would quite noticeably turn away as if to snub Durwin. One of these times, they were each walking down a long empty hallway towards each other. As they met in a space with nothing to look at on either side, the doctor turned his head at a right angle toward the wall until he got past Durwin. It was obviously an intentional snub meant to belittle. Why do you suppose he behaved that way? I'll tell you what I think. Although he was known to be an up and coming good heart specialist, he had the appearance of a rough hewn, saucy squirt which he couldn't accept. And Durwin stood out as a fine person of clean cut stature, which the doctor couldn't accept either.

"This doctor, a specialist in his field, was highly spoken of by the hospital staff, and by some other acquaintances. He was known to treat his patients meticuliously well. But he discriminated against the Lawtons. With such a good reputation already established with many people, he would know he could do as he pleased with the Lawtons and get away with it. Then again, he could be one of many who think that everyone is like that to fine people. If so he would have felt quite unabashed about his behavior towards them.

"Another doctor Durwin tried he dropped after only a brief period. This doctor, after doing a physical examination of Durwin, returned briefly to his genital area. He pulled the lips of Durwins penis apart to where it caused a sharp, needle-like pain. Then the doctor quickly ended the examination, and left the room and his staff came to take blood samples.

"From that time on, and still today, Durwin occasionally experiences that sharp needle-like pain. It usually happens when sitting on a particular type of chair, sofa, or car seat that is inclined to pull his trousers tight into his crotch. It gets a bit embarrasing at times because it makes him jump a little when it happens. Also he has to somehow, without being unsociable, get his pants loosened some from the area. It is more of a nuisance than anything.

"This doctor may have been very pleasant to most other people. When Durwin appeared before him, he kept looking at him with a glare, and was obviously taken aback. In reaction to it he did the damaging deed on the spur of the moment. It showed his wayward bent against fine people like Durwin.

"Still another family physician Durwin went to seemed to be aimable for the longest time. Eventually, on what would normally have been a regular visit, a conversation between them centered on a non-medical topic with which Durwin was more experienced and knowledgeable that the doctor. As the conversation proceeded, the doctor's countenance changed from pleasant to disturbed, until he eventually refused to talk about it anymore. This doctor didn't know how to look up to or respect anyone more knowledgeable than himself even on a topic outside his own expertise altogether. The result was near tragic. This was no backroom doctor. Here was a practicioner of prominence. But envy can be a powerful force on a proud but immature mind.

"The doctors own health was somewhat of a shambles. He now tried in every way to find major problems with Durwin's health, sending him to this and that specialist, but it all came to naught. Meanwhile, he ignored some minor matters that Durwin brought to his attention, and which in time could become serious. In fact, one of them did become serious, later requiring two lots of surgery by a more amiable doctor.

"Also this wayward doctor now began to play mind-games on Durwin to, by inflection and tone of voice, try to make him suspicious of evey specialist doctor he had sent him to over a period of time. Actually, only two secondary doctors had tried to belittle Durwin. Some of the others were among the nicest people Durwin had ever met, and they had been very friendly to and respectful of Durwin.

"But the now very envious primary doctor also intentionally tried to make Durwin suspicious of him as well. He frequently inflicted unnecessary pain on Durwin during the course of examinations. When Durwin would speak about it, the doctor would brush it aside with an unmeaningful remark such as, 'Oh that.' On two occasions, Durwin heard coming from another room, this doctor becoming spiteful and whimperish as a nurse questioned him concerning his work with Durwin. That is a common characteristic of belittlers when their game is not working their way. They show a mixture of spitefulness and wimpering, as would an undiciplined young child around six years old or so.

"Whether this doctor did Durwin any permanent physical harm Durwin was unable to find out. He did question one unsuspecting and well-meaning doctor about one matter, but without any examination this doctor passed the opinion that such a condition usually comes about with older age.

"So it could be that the belittler doctor was just trying to make Durwin suspicious of him. That too is a major ploy used by belittlers—to instill paranoia into their victims, get them labeled, and then if they are green enough to fall for it, pack them off to a psychiatrist.

"It took considerable time for Durwin to get wary enough of this doctor to stop going to him. He always had to be careful of the paranoia factor in his dealings with doctors. However, as time went by the evidence became clear and fool-proof.

"For example, the doctor on numerous occasions would tell Durwin to exercise more for better circulation in his legs. In a startling sort of way he would tell Durwin to use his legs or lose them, even though

Durwin exercised regularly. Later, high tech examinations revealed that Durwin's legs and their circulation were in excellent condition for his age.

"On one visit to the doctors office, the doctor and a nurse did a sigmoidoscopy on Durwin, (an internal examination of the lower bowel, using an invasive technical device). The examination was painless until just before withdrawing the device, the doctor pumped it up so high that Durwin felt his lower abdomen was about to burst. Durwin quickly cautioned the doctor who then defleated the device, took it out completely, and almost immediately told Durwin he had a diverticulosis condition and had to refrain from eating nuts, raisins, corn and numerous other things. He told Durwin that this condition would be for life. Durwin hasn't been able to get a second opinion on the matter.

"On another occasion the doctor and staff told Durwin that his lung capacity was lacking greatly. Detailed examinations by a specialist in the field revealed that Durwin's lung capacity was well over one hundred percent in all the various tests given.

"After each semi-annual physical, Durwin was told he had an enlarged prostate. Later examinations by other doctors proved this to be wrong.

"On another occasion he was told that a rash that was moving over his thigh was caused by blood poison. It turned out to be something almost harmless.

"Eventually Durwin had enough tangible evidence to make for good reason to break away and go to another doctor. This new Doctor, after obtaining Durwin's record from the now dubious doctor, handled Durwin very cautiously at first, but then very humanely, all the while covering for the previous doctor by evading Durwin's questions about his health."

Owen interrupted Collin's story telling. "What would possess an otherwise reputable medical doctor to put himself out on a limb like that, and so openly."

Collin replied, "Envy is a very powerful force in a self-centered belittler. His erroneous conception of Durwin was, I believe, a projection of the belittler's own personality magnified many times. This was inciting the belittler's hatred and rivalry for Durwin.

"Such a belittler would think somewhat along these lines. He sees a fine, smart person and says to himself something like this: 'I'm a pretty good caliber person myself, and I think a lot of myself for it. But his fine, smart person must really think too much of himself—far too much. He really must be overly conceited.' So the belittler thinks he is doing a wonderful thing in bringing down and ridding society of this supposedly grossly conceited person. Hence the bullying and belittling becomes quite open and the perpetrator of it is often very proud of what he is doing. Such is the envious mind—a mind with the "most warped and twisted of human emotions." (William Barclay, The Daily Study Bible, The Letter to The Romans, 1966. The Saint Andrews Press, Edinburgh. Page 28.) "Actually, conceit has no place in the character of a fine person."

Collin added, "Since there was no large scale attempt made by the belittling doctor to make money off his erroneous diagnoses, Durwin has the belief that they were items intended only to disturb Durwin's peace of mind and keep him down with worry. It did not work that way on Durwin because from observing the doctor's attitude, he suspected all along what the doctor was up to."

"I might add that the dental profession too has its share of belittlers. I will be telling you about that some evening in the near future, as it will fit into the total story better then.

Collin continued, "Of all the service industries there are, the one that is most hazardous for people like us is the auto repair industry. In Terraprima, it can be an ordeal to keep your car on the road without letting them drive you broke. In the Secundaterras it isn't always easy either. When I was younger and cars were more simple, I largely got around the problem by doing most of my own repairs, including some complicated things like wheel alignment. Cars being much more complicated now, we are dependent on garages and their mechanics. If through trial and error you find a good place, large or small, for repairs, you have it made in that sphere of life. The process of finding such a place can be hazardous and expensive.

"Some belittler garage owners and/or mechanics shun a fine person outright; others do unnecessary repairs and overcharge for it. Of course this practice is not always confined to fine people only, but we are sure targets for it more often than others. Still other belittler mechanics do plenty of work on your car, necessary or unnecessary, charge plenty for it, and your car never works right again. As I indicated, other types of people also have such experiences as this, but people like us eventually detect a growing animosity toward us by either small garage owner/mechanics, or, large garage service advisors who delegate our work to belittling mechanics in their employ.

"In Terraprima, Durwin had the experience of getting repairs done over a period of time with a small garage owner working alone in his own garage. After awhile he began to have doubts about the man's attitude toward him, so he eventually decided to look elsewhere for repairs. Before he had occasion to go elsewhere, while driving one day his car engine suddenly cut out on the road. He had it towed to another garage, a medium sized place he had been contemplating using. It was located in the center of a medium sized city where people of all walks of life worked daily and would use their services. He thought he might be safe there. The service manager delegated the car to one of the mechanics, by chance a very mature and congenial type of man. He examined the car and reported to Durwin that a major artery of a set of several wires had burned off. The wiring had been obviously worked on before in a doubtful manner, he informed Durwin in an open, honest and concerned manner with obvious respect for a clergy person. He further stated the opinion that had certain other conditions come into play, the car could have caught fire.

"Durwin had not authorized any wiring repairs to his car previously. All evidence weighed, it could be reasonably established that his car had been dishonestly tampered with. The honest mechanic repaired the wiring in a satisfactory manner. As Durwin was completing the business and taking possession of his car, the mechanic began to discuss his concerns about it again. The service manager shut him up by rudely and curtly interrupting the mechanics speech and stating that such things happen all the time. 'You can't be too fussy about cars,' he said as he shrugged it off and put an end to the conversation.

"At the time, Durwin interpreted that as the service manager just being careful not to get involved in what might, for all he knew, turn into a legal problem. In time, however, Durwin would learn that this service manager was also a belittler, and so we see birds of a feather, even though they do not know each other, and have no connection to each other, flocking together in their dubious maneuvers against people whom they perceive to be a cut above them. This is one facet of the 'conspiracy of sorts' I have referred to.

"Durwin went back to this latter garage once again a little later, for another repair job. There being other people in line ahead of him, he was able to observe that this belitter service manager treated what he would term 'ordinary' people in a manner that would keep their repair expenses at a minimum. For example, he would say amiably to a customer, 'You can have all of this done for such and such a price, but if you want to save some money, you can try to get by with such and such. Its up to you.'

"When it came time to estimate Durwin's repairs, he very arrogantly came up with a figure in the five hundred dollar range. Durwin turned it down, went elsewhere and had the job done for fifty eight dollars. On that visit Durwin also found out that the honest mechanic who had diagnosed and repaired his wiring problem, was no longer working there. My guess is he was too good a person to be working under a belittler.

"By the way, another fine person had an experience with the same small garage owner I first mentioned. This person had a car of several years old, but which had always been in excellent condition. The engine, well serviced over the years, was as smooth as could be. Upon recommendation of a friend, he left this car at this small garage for minor repairs. Soon after that, the engine of the car developed a knock. Diagnosis of this from another garage established that for some reason, a knock had developed in the lower part of the engine, and that by now serious damage had developed. The person had to trade the otherwise good car.

"You see how belittlers can drive us bankrupt through our cars," commented Collin. "In each case, the burnt wires and the knocking bearing, the garage owner had nothing to gain in repair business. With such extensive potential damage, both cars may have had to be discarded. Neither was the mechanic connected in any way with selling new or used cars. In both incidents it was an envious, spiteful and meaningless act to destroy. Durwin eventually got established with a large car dealership where they were accustomed to dealing with high caliber people. There, he was treated well and received excellent service that wherever possible was money saving.

"There may be room for doubt about foul play concerning the car with the knocking bearing. The car was getting old. But there is room for suspicion just as well. The car had been serviced regularly. Also the engine problem developed rather quickly and not over a long period of time. As for the car with the burnt wiring, there is no doubt the wires had been tampered with without reason or authorization.

"Let me caution you though that not all car dealers including some selling fine and expensive cars, are accustomed to dealing with fine people properly.

"Durwin went to one such dealership located in a large suburb of a respected city to see if he could find a hard to get spare wheel for his car. He explained to the parts supervisor that he was going on a long, long, trip that included much isolated wilderness area in rugged country. He needed to have a regular spare tire. His temporary spare, or donut tire as some call it, might not be sufficient, and besides, it may do well to have two spares. The supervisor's manner turned cold. However, he did say he could get the wheel and it would arrive in two days. Durwin had the size of the wheel written down on a piece of paper. He offered it to the parts man. The parts man brushed him aside on it. Durwin held it in front of him. He refused to look at it. Doubtful though he was Durwin ordered the wheel.

"Durwin couldn't get back for the wheel on the second day, but he did on the third morning. The supervisor told him that he had it ready for him the previous day but now it was at the bottom of a pile of parts to be stacked on shelves during the day. He suggested Durwin come back that afternoon. Durwin did so, and was told it wasn't yet available, but if he'd sit in the waiting area they would call him when it was ready.

"Durwin sat in the waiting area leafing through magazines for the longest time. Eventually he decided to go to the counter and inquire. The supervisor, as cold as ever, said 'your wheel is ready. We called you three times and you didn't come.' Durwin knew that wasn't so. Besides, Durwin was in sight of him all the time. If they did call and he didn't respond, someone could have easily walked across the room and told him his item was ready.

"Anyway, Durwin paid for the wheel. He then went to a tire shop to get a tire put on it, discovering there that it was the wrong size wheel. What Durwin suspected from the cold attitude, he now felt sure of. This was the tormenting trickery of belittlers, who may have thought he was going on his trip real soon and they would delay or spoil it. Regardless, Durwin had made it known he was going on a rare trip. The supervisor and his cronies were envious and were playing tricks on Durwin, antagonizing him with come ons and put offs, and hoping to either send him away empty or delay his trip. Worse still they could send him away with a wheel that didn't fit, and hopefully have him stuck out in the wilderness. Durwin took the wheel back, gave them a disciplinary blast that made them cower, as such people do when smoked out, and quickly got his money back.

"Upon returning home, he looked up the yellow pages, found a nationwide parts dealer that could have a wheel delivered to his door in three days, for only two dollars more than the cost at the city dealer he had just finished with.

"After Durwin had caught on to their trickery that day, he took a good look around the place. They were selling what is termed as fine and expensive cars all right. However, the majority of their customers, what there were of them, were not fine cultured people. They impressed Durwin as the kind of people who are trying to keep up with fine people. They most likely were, as I have often termed them, not rich, or successful or fine people, but poor people with a lot of money, as the belittlers would view them and therefore cater to them. These would get good service at this dealership. It is the nice people with a lot of money the belittlers like to turn against. Needless to say the place was far from flourishing. Not long thereafter, Durwin read that the dealership was for sale.

"Durwin got the wheel, but getting a tire on it is yet another story about the craftiness of belittlers. Durwin went to a tire dealership to have a set of four new tires installed on his car for his unusual trip. The best one of the tires to be replaced was to be put on his new spare wheel. It was a good tire with low mileage on it.

"After watching the installation of the four new tires Durwin reminded the man to install the good spare, and then went to the office to pay the bill. There he also socialized with the manager for a while. Upon his return to the shop, the installer affirmed the spare had been placed in the tire well and all was ready to go. The man looked sheepish. Durwin thought perhaps he was expecting a tip and so took out his wallet from which he gave him three dollars. During this little transaction a look of sheer hatred came over the man's face, as he quite literally snatched the money out of Durwin's hand, turned and walked away.

"It looked strange but Durwin gave it no more thought until months after his unusual trip. He was going over his car one day, and decided to check the air pressure in the spare. As he took the tire out of the well to do so, it was then he noticed he had been given a ragged looking tire that obviously had been run on considerably while flat. It had gobs of rubber missing from around its edges, and wire hanging out in the spaces. The tire wouldn't have lasted five miles had Durwin needed it on the roads over which he had traveled. And there were only two gas stops, with no other services for as long as three hundred miles, with only an occasional other vehicle passing by on the way. To be stranded in such country would also leave people open to attack by wild animals not accustomed to humans, and therefore all the more dangerous to them.

"Fortunately, Durwin and Canda had not needed that spare tire on their trip, but they came close. Somewhere along the way they picked up a small nail which caused a slow leak that wasn't noticable until after they reached their destination where they were able to get it patched.

"Some time later, Durwin brushed with the same tire installer at another tire shop. The man's hatred was strong. He and an accomplice tried to pull a similar tactic, but Durwin recognized him in time to prevent any further harm being done.

"One day Durwin was in the service area of another garage. There was a rattling noise coming from the air conditioning unit of his car. The service manager and two mechanics stood in front of the car with the hood up to listen to the noise under various conditions. They suggested Durwin sit in, put the gear in drive and speed up the engine a little. To do so of course, he had to put his foot hard on the brake pedal. After doing this for a half minute or so, the brake pedal began slowly to sink to the floor. Noticing what was happening, Durwin immediately turned the motor off. Stepping out of the car he asked the three men if they did anything to the brakes. They told him they had not. Looking underneath the car they discovered a pool of brake fluid that had just leaked out on the floor beside one of the front wheels.

"'You people are lucky the car didn't lunge into you,' Durwin said.

"'Yes, and you are lucky that didn't happen as you drove through the fast and busy city thoroughfares to get here,' they added.

"The brake problem was repaired there and then and Durwin was informed a brake line to the front wheel had been cut. Durwin hadn't been driving anywhere or over anything to have it cut accidentally. He previously had repairs done in another garage, an unfriendly place so he found when he was there a week or two earlier."

Without pausing, Collin said, "I'll wind up the stories concerning industry and commerce with two more stories, the first of which shows that fine couples, when together in public often get discriminated against. To illustrate: Durwin and Canda were accustomed to eating occasionally in a particular good quality restaurant chain. One evening they went to a restaurant of this chain that they had not been to before. It was in what appeared to be a well to do neighborhood. They waited to be seated. Several of the staff saw them there, including both hostesses. All would look at them from a distance, then continue with their work. The Lawton's stood there for the longest time until it became obvious they would not be seated. Then they left, drove four miles to another restaurant of the same chain where they had been treated exceptionally well for some time, and enjoyed their meal. Some months later, just for curiosity the Lawton's went back to the restaurant where they had been refused seating. This time they waited even longer. There were tables available, but nobody would seat them.

"White niggers, eh!' blurted Leo.

"It amounts to the same thing," said Collin, and continued, "Durwin, while studying in the big city, also experienced much the same thing. There were many, some just very plain and ordinary places where he could eat, and in some of them, even in the big city, became known and liked there. There were other places where they wouldn't serve him."

Brett spoke, "No doubt you have often noticed, in many restaurants, even in some good ones, how a particular server is down on some people, and will serve others well and cheerfully."

"Yes," agreed Owen, "with a friendly server you can enjoy a meal. If the server is a belittler and can't help but show it, your meal goes down in lumps and your stomach ties up in knots, that is if you let her or him do that to you. I've learned to control the situation for myself, but still it takes the joy out of a meal. You don't usually go back to such people again. Customers are lost because of the belittlers."

Collin spoke again. "I'll relate just one more experience tonight. On a visit to Durwin in Terraprima, he took me grocery shopping with him with a purpose in mind. First we shopped at a supermarket six miles away from where Durwin lived. It was where he usually did his grocery shopping. The employees there were friendly and courteous to him even in this busiest of times.

"Another time we went to a supermarket of the same chain, but this time only two miles from where Durwin lived. As we approached the store, Durwin said, 'you may wonder why I don't shop here regularly, it being so much closer to home. See if you can tell me the answer when we come out of the store.'

"We went in and shopped. Many employees were not only cold, but actually snooty and unmannerly to Durwin. When we were outside the store again, I said to Durwin, 'I see what you mean. Belittlers are in control.'

"'Right,' replied Durwin. 'Now just a half a mile from here is a supermarket of another chain. Let's go there.'

"We did so, and there the employees were courteous and friendly. There was no snootiness at all.

"'Now,' said Durwin, 'about eight miles from here, in the vicinity of the first friendly supermarket, there is another store that belongs to the same chain as this latter one. That store is cold and unfriendly. Belittlers have gotten in there. I won't bother to take you there now, because you already see my point.'

"'Sure do', I replied.

There was a pause among the group. Then Collin, as if thinking out loud, spoke in a different vein. “It is still somewhat early. I could continue tonight with another aspect of Durwin’s experience in Terraprima, but it would keep us very late. I leave it with you Dr. Eldren, could you make a suggestion?”

“I’m glad you asked, Collin,” replied Dr. Eldren. “I haven’t adjusted my schedule to allow me to stay late this evening, so we had better stop where we are for now. Also, I would like to ask if you still think you can finish the story of the Lawtons adequately in this semester, even a little early if at all possible. Can that be done?”

Collin pondered for a moment. “Yes indeed,” he then responded. “I will aim at that for sure. It can be done.” He then wondered why Dr. Eldren, usually so patient, was in a hurry to complete the story-telling. By now, however, he completely trusted this fine charactered psychiatrist.

The meeting adjourned, with Dr. Eldren departing as usual to other work, and the remaining group members going for what by now, after group sessions, had become a much enjoyed late evening time of relaxation and fellowship at the Corner Coffee Shop.

CHAPTER VIII

On this Wednesday evening, again designated to continue with Durwin Lawton's experiences in ministry in Terraprima, the support group members, including Dr. Eldren, were settled down in Room 405 and prepared.

Collin Seldon now alerted them to another area of life for Durwin in Terraprima. "You remember," said Collin to the group, "I told you previously of an experience Durwin had in his first continuing education unit and how difficult it was for him to break the ice there and be received into the group.

"Now I will tell you of a different type of experience. I will describe in more detail the program in which, as I previously told you, Durwin sought to improve his expertise in pastoral care in order to fulfill the type of ministry he had in mind.

"Durwin enrolled in a school in the big city that specialized in pastoral care and counseling especially for religious workers. There would be courses in psychology, pastoral care, and counseling, and also supervision for any consultation or counseling cases in which the student became involved in his parish. As further preparation for this kind of work, there was also a required peer group. In it all of the students had opportunity to look at themselves, their own lives, their work and their approaches to it as much as possible, with the view to getting their own house in better order, so as to improve their helping skills for other people.

"Before I go into the details of the school experience, I must tell you of an incident Durwin had getting home from his first day at the school. Durwin had traveled into the city school by bus the morning of his first day of attendance. It was opening day and after the first day of classes there was a social gathering to better facilitate getting acquainted. One of the results of this was that Durwin arrived at the huge city bus terminal too late for the usual rush hour buses. Arriving there just after seven o'clock, he found that the next bus would be nine p.m., and one last bus for the night, near midnight.

"Durwin purchased his ticket and sat on a bench near the gate from where his bus would leave. It was a long wait. Finally, just before nine the bus was put into its loading place. Durwin was first in line. Almost immediately a line of about a dozen or so formed behind him. The driver stood in place to take the tickets and as he looked around and began to open the bus door, it was as if he suddenly changed his mind, shut the door closed again and walked away. In about two minutes he was back again, walking around aimlessly near the line, but making no attempt to facilitate loading. Durwin stepped toward the driver a little and telling him his destination, asked, 'Is this the right bus for that destination?'

"The driver glared at him viciously but didn't speak. An obviously more seasoned bus traveler two people behind Durwin in the line, was growing impatient. 'Of course it's the right bus,' he shouted. I ride it most every night.' Then to the bus driver, 'what's your problem? We're tired and want to get home. Open the door.'

"The driver sulkingly walked up to the door, opened it and reached back past Durwin and the person behind him, taking the ticket of the man who had shouted at him. Durwin then held out his ticket. The driver ignored it reaching to the person behind Durwin, and then as these two boarded the bus, the driver continued to reach past Durwin to the next person. When this fourth person came up, he held out his ticket. As the driver opened his hand to receive it, the person hesitated, quickly looked at Durwin and then nodded towards the driver's hand. Durwin quickly pushed his ticket into the driver's hand and boarded the bus. The fourth man followed behind and sat in the seat directly across from Durwin as if to care for and support him. When all in the line were on board, the driver himself boarded, with a pouty, defeated look on his face. The fourth man, sitting across from Durwin, said in a very firm voice, 'Driver, we're a few minutes late leaving. If you don't procrastinate any more we should be able to make it up, eh?'. The driver immediately got the bus rolling. The fourth man looked across at Durwin, winked, settled down in his seat and closed his eyes to rest.

"The second day at school, some class members were discussing about getting to school on time and how each one did so. A student, without knowing of Durwin's bus experience of the previous evening, told him how he could travel by train more conveniently than by bus, taking into account his location and the location of the school. From there on, Durwin taveled by train and to his great pleasure and satisfaction was always treated courteously by the train crew, sometimes very respectfully when they got to know him traveling back and forth."

Leo Aidan startled the group, "Hallelujah," he shouted. "Someone in Terraprima is being nice to Durwin."

"Yea," added Donna Coyne, "the train crew are treating him like a human being."

"And the fourth man in the bus line!" chimed in Albin Anders.

"From my experience and knowledge," commented Brett Culver, "bus terminals are often in the inner city, which is not a good place to be at night. Think what could have happened to Durwin had he been stranded in the city overnight, or even till midnight, with muggers, robbers, murderers and all sorts of creeps around."

"It could be very gruesome indeed," responded Collin. "In fact there had been a news item throughout the media of the area that shows what could have happened to Durwin that night. A young man, visiting the city had been, no one knows how, stranded in the city overnight. He was chased to his death in the city streets. No explanation was ever given for it."

Leo Aidan was aghast. "Does the church realize the extreme results of *its* belittling—the trends such as this they are setting for society?"

"It is hard to answer that question, Leo," said Collin, "but yes, this denomination of Terraprima does, in effect at least, support such action in society by practicing similar, if not so drastic, themselves throughout their church.

"I might add, in fairness, though," added Collin, "that that big city has since been cleaned up in many remarkable ways. But belittlers haven't yet been openly identified for what they are and how dangerous they can be. In actuality, this big city is beloved by many people, including myself. I love to go there. But no city or country has all good people in it. Crafty belittlers are among them always, like the bus driver I just told you about."

Gilda Emerson bristled, "Do belittlers like that bus driver realize the extent of the damages they do to people?"

"Some of them do," replied Collin, "and it is a sadistic sport for them. Others see only the immediate moment and never think ahead to the cruel consequences of their belittling."

"I would say," added Owen Winslow, "that the ones who do know the potential extent of the damages they inflict are the most dangerous."

"Yes," said Collin, "because most of their belittling, rather than being a spur of the moment impulse, is calculated and crafty. They make us as gladiator victims in the arena of life, and it is every bit as cruel as in ancient Rome; the difference being, the cruelty we have to go through is mental cruelty, and sometimes prolonged over a lifetime. In the ancient Roman arena, mental agony not overlooked, the physical cruelty was the outward and predominant factor, and often brought life to an end swiftly. Yes, there are many belittlers who know what damage they are inflicting. In fact, their intent and purpose is to maim and/or destroy. They know full well what they are doing. It gives them a sense of power, protection for their undiciplined pride, an outlet for their sheer hatred of anyone they deem to be a cut above themselves, and a warped sense of power and victory in life. Later in this discussion you will be able to see what I mean."

"You mean we are going to see this even in continuing education for Christian ministers as well?" questioned Leo, painfully.

"Yes, that is what I mean," nodded Collin somberly, "calculated, intentionally inflicted mental cruelty, with the intent to wear down, discredit, maim, and for all intents and purposes to destroy the victim. The victim may or may not, under the prolonged and severe stress, remain well and alive physically, but regardless of that, his life as it was and could be, may be destroyed."

"And the belittlers would rejoice in that and feel victorious!" commented Leo, in a more somber mood than usual for him.

"That is my opinion," said Collin firmly, "and I will let you people form yours as I tell the story. However," continued Collin, "this next part of the story began as one of the brighter spots in Durwin's experience in Terraprima. Since that time, Durwin has had cause to wonder about the latter part of the experience which in time we will cover.

"The building which housed this school was situated in a major business area of the big city. It occupied three floors of a high rise office complex that includes some commercial business offices. The location, and the building exterior and interior were satisfactorily impressive and gave the impression of a well run school inside it. In this school, Durwin was among people who were interested in looking at and analyzing their own lives as well as that of others. Consequently, there was a high degree of maturity there among most of the students and instructors who gave the various courses. Most classmates and faculty showed respect and friendship towards Durwin. It was like he was in another world, not enirely, but by far mostly. It is a pity I cannot dwell on the positive aspects of this segment of Durwin's life. He really enjoyed the counseling and consultation training which enhanced his pastoral ministry so much. It was like a touch of heaven for him to be in the company of so many people who were friendly to him, and treated him like a normal human being. It supplied him with the human touch that every person needs to keep their life normal. It was lacking in Durwin's church, but he could withstand that now, because he was keeping in touch with normalcy here at the school. Disappointment would come later, but for the present it was going well.

"Circumstances hadn't yet reached their worst at Durwin's church during his early period at the school. In time when it did as I will describe more fully later, Durwin made a risky attempt to discuss his local church problems before the class. The instructor garbled it over some and then let the matter drop. At the time, Durwin took this to be another example of the naivety of many psychologists about the adult world of reality. A few street wise psychologists and psychiatrists may be up on it from personal experience, but the psychology books have nothing to say about such problems as Durwin was experiencing.

"I emphasize again that about three quarters of Durwin's time at this school was a bright spot in his experience in Terraprima. However, for the purposes of this group, I must dwell on its short-comings.

"To begin, there was a class in child psychology with emphasis on the formative years and how the adult years may be affected by them.

The instructor knew his subject and presented it well. Durwin thoroughly enjoyed it, but the instructor was scared skinny of him. As he presented his course, the instructor would quite easily look around at the others in the class, by-passing Durwin for a while and then pausing to make a concerted and quite noticeable effort to look at Durwin and even stare at him for a brief moment before going on with the course. Durwin over a period of time praised both the course, the way it was presented and the instructor presenting it. This did not help. Here was a person who had a problem with people whom he considered to be a cut above himself in some way.

"This man was not a belittler, as far as could be ascertained; he meant no harm to Durwin. He was only trying to protect himself from his imaginary problem. It made circumstances tense for Durwin at first, until he felt sure the man meant him no harm. We should take note though," said Collin to the group members, "that here was a man steeped in psychology and very efficient in it, yet unaware of the common difficulties of life that existed for a person like Durwin Lawton in adulthood; difficulties that could and would cause him grave problems that had little or nothing to do with anything that may or may not have happened to him in the formative years of his childhood. Such a concept has not yet been discovered by psychology. Only the perpetrators of belittling, and some street wise people, not all of them, are aware of it.

"Well into his second year in this study course, Durwin, having been well received and well treated to date, dared to bring some aspects of his by now severe parish circumstances before the class. I am referring here to Durwin's first church in Terraprima after it had gotten severely difficult. No doubt you remember my lengthy discussion on it. Durwin had gotten along very well with the efficient instructor and the other students involved. Now he described to them three difficult people in his parish and how they were treating him. The instructor seemed to show a mind-set of having difficulty understanding why anyone would treat a minister in such a mean manner.

"After much uncertain discussion, the consensus established by the instructor, seemed to be that Durwin shouldn't let such people have key positions in the local church administration. The trouble with that, from

Durwin's point of view, was that these people already had control of the church even before he became minister there. What's more, there weren't any street wise people in the remainder of the local church administration who were wise to them. Only some of the less active members of the congreagation at large were wise to them, and in various quiet unnoticed ways had let Durwin know so.

"However, Durwin had now revealed the problem looming before him in his congregation. The response, or lack of it, was causing him much stress, as it threatened to undo an otherwise very pleasant continuing education experience. When the instructor brushed the matter aside, Durwin did not press it any further, reasoning to himself that people cannot learn of such things through his explanation of it. One has to learn such complex things either through years of experience and becoming street wise, or, read it in an authoritative book or other writing. Such a writing had not yet come into existance.

"This incident was, to date, Durwin's big disappointment in this study course. Belittlers in his church were working hard to wear him down, label his ministry as insufficient, cast doubt on his abilities and person and generally discredit him. Here he was among a group of people well trained in psychology, and seeming of good and pleasant character. Yet they could do nothing to help him."

"Couldn't or didn't want to?" questioned Leo, suspiciously.

"Yes, I was wondering the same thing," added Albin. "I am wondering if this is your conspiracy of sorts setting in. Durwin's taking his problem to the school, makes him a marked man there among belittlers."

"I know what you're getting at," replied Collin, "but it was hard for Durwin to tell at this point in his experience in Terraprima. As it was, Durwin could see no one on the horizon in the wider church area to help him either. In fact in time he would try for such help only to find, too late, that the hierarchy of the church in that area would side with the belittlers in his local church. In that area, his denomination was under the dominance of belittlers, and as I said before, 'birds of a feather flock together.' Durwin and Canda were beginning to find out that they were alone in their struggle for survival. They didn't know yet how severe that struggle would get. It may be a good thing they didn't.

"In future, Durwin avoided bringing up the matter again at the school. However, it was getting into the final semester, and there was, on the part of some, noticeable change of attitude towards him. In this final semester, one outstanding problem arose with a new instructor placed in charge of the class peer group sessions.

"As this instructor presided over the group sessions, it became noticeable to Durwin that when he joined in on the discussion, the instructor ignored him, seldom turning his way, and often, when he spoke, the instructor would continue on as if Durwin wasn't there at all. Durwin experimented. On different days he would sit at different places in the room, on different sides and different angles to the instructor. It made no difference to the instructors behavior. Wherever Durwin sat, he avoided looking in that direction. When Durwin spoke he was not only ignored, but crowded out by the instructor taking over the conversation and turning it to someone else in the class.

"Durwin also noticed that this was happening to one other person in the class. She was an extremely knowledgable person of beautiful character. Durwin talked to her about what was happening to them. She said she was very aware of what was happening to her and Durwin. With this support, Durwin made very obvious and louder than usual attempts to enter the conversation. A few times he received such brief, trivializing replies from the instructor as, 'I see,' or 'is that so?', or more often, 'no, I don't think so,' and then he would turn to the others and either change the thrust of the topic or set the class off on a new topic."

Albin Anders chimed in with a firm voice, "Collin, all this negative attitude looming up on Durwin at the school is enough to make me suspicious of there being a connection between it and Durwin's experiences elsewhere. He was being barred from conversation at local church meetings, at wider church meetings, including on the ecumenical scene, and now at the school. The whole thing is church related. There could have been a connecting link somehow between all these birds of a feather acting together. If there was, then it was not only a 'conspiracy of sorts' as you have called it. It looks to me like a conspiracy, period."

Collin answered, "You could be right Albin. There is indeed quite a grape-vine throughout the church. We have no way of knowing for sure if what you suspect is so, but there certainly is circumstantial evidence of it. Or, at the school, just from the little bits that Durwin had told them of his church problems, they could have surmised what he was up against, and being belittlers themselves, joined in on the negative treatment. Either way they would be belittlers. And discouraging and preventing a victim from participating in conversation is a much used ploy of belittlers. If they were not belittlers, then they must have been very unqualified for their jobs, having no knowledge of such a common problem. It is significant that it happened in the last semester of the course. Another often used ploy of such belittlers is to try to make the victim drop out of the course just before finishing time, after they have his tuition fees, and have picked his brains all they could.

"Durwin complained about the matter to the Dean of the school, with whom till now he had had a friendly rapport. Durwin, knowing such people from experience, was concerned, and rightly so, that if he didn't do something about this, he may very well be appraised as not participating well in the class. This he wanted to head off. The complaint received a vague response at the time. Sometime after that, in another gathering, the Dean made a negative appraisal of Durwin, something he had never done before, and including in it the old belittler ploy about Durwin being oversensitive. Durwin, not being very sensative or concerned about such things in what had been a generally pleasant atmosphere, didn't press for an explanation at the time. He did wonder about it later while he was still being ill treated and put down by people outside of this school, and still learning more about belittlers' tactics.

"By protecting himself from being discredited for not participating, he got himself discredited for being too sensitive. Durwin paid no attention to it at the time. But in further experiences of defending himself against belittlers he would hear that term often—he was too sensitive. As time went by he would come to know this is one of the chief, if not the foremost weapons of belittlers. They practice some of their tactics on you until it gets under your skin a little. You protest to them and they brand you as over-sensitive. But not only that. From there on they work on you all the more, often quite openly when circumstances are favorable to do so without them being exposed, with the purpose of making you all the more sensitive, and implying further that they did nothing to you, but you were always like that. Then they tag you as whimp, which is what they are in a crunch. They turn it around and say you cannot stand up to the rigors of life. In the church, that means demotion, or, you have to get out of it altogether to avoid being ruined. Then they imply you were not strong enough for the ministry as they are. This makes them feel superior to you.

What it adds up to overall, according to them, is that if you are bothered by the facts: that your livlihood is being purposely put in jeopardy, your studying in preparation to improve your livlihood is being stymied intentionally, your character is having negative shadows cast on it, perhaps even being destroyed, your family may suffer because of all this and often more—if your bothered by it you are over-sensitive. Out of pride and envy this is the belittlers' game with fine exceptional people.

"Let me tell you something pleasant again," said Collin, changing the tone of the atmosphere. "There is a little aside that has bearing on the resourcefulness of Durwin Lawton. At lunch times some of the students of this school went out to lunch in clusters, some alone or in couples. Durwin sometimes went along with a cluster, or sometimes with an individual or two. It was enjoyable and the conversation was usually about the courses and their application to parish or other similar work.

"Durwin liked variety in life. Having worked in business and industry before going into ministry, he was able to talk the language of people presently working in business and industry. Being a stranger in a foreign land, he was able to strike up a good rapport with other people from foreign lands. So, quite often Durwin walked alone to a particular fast food place in one of the busiest parts of the city where at lunch time people flocked in large numbers. The unique thing about this place was that although there was a large amount of seating space, there was also a larger number of people. Consequently it was the practice that customers sat wherever there was a place at a table to sit, until all places were filled. That is, a person, or even a small group of persons, didn't have a table to themselves. It was shared with others.

"More often than not, people would find themselves sitting with complete strangers. This intrigued Durwin. He would pick up his food at the counter, then proceed to sit beside an interesting looking person of any age, race, color or sex and start up a conversation. He was careful in the conversation not to ask where anyone lived or worked. That would be interfering with their privacy and may scare them off. He did often talk about what they worked at, what country they or their ancestors came from, what their feelings were about the country of their roots, compared to this country in which they now were, what hobbies and leisure they pursued, and numerous miscellaneous topics. In his two years of going there, of all the various people Durwin chose to sit beside and talk to, only once did someone turn away from him, just once. When there were no belittlers to interfere, Durwin had a wonderful way with people, more especially when it was a one on one or two encounter."

Owen spoke, "It's too bad Durwin wasn't able to utilize that gift in the church somehow."

Collin shook his head, "It wasn't possible. In a fellowship gathering at his church one day, just to participate by trying to add some interest to the fellowship, Durwin began to tell of some of his experiences at this eating place in the big city. He was quickly shot down with a negative snarl and a growl by a pseudo psycholgist/minister in competition with him, and had to sit through the meeting listening to others tell of their experiences."

"The church's loss!" commented Brett.

"Durwin actually felt quite at ease in the big city didn't he?" commented Gilda Emerson.

"Yes he did," replied Collin, "yet he came to know it would be foolhardy for a person such as him to ever try to live there with belittlers and belittling being so prevalent. To commute or visit there during hours when there were lots of people around was well within his stride. Yet even being at ease with that, he was always wisely cautious there, given his circumstances as a fine person, but he was not fearful. And that reminds me of another incident that emphasizes Durwin's circumstances and also the naivety or otherwise of the psychologists concerning it.

"Durwin had a terminally ill parishoner in one of the outstanding inner city hospitals. He planned to visit her and so at home with a map of the city, ascertained just where the hospital was in conjunction to the location of the school. It looked as though it was within walking distance on streets with numerous people on them during business hours. This would be safe.

"It was common for students to bring such cases before the class in order to receive the supervision of the instructor, and thereby gain new techniques for pastoral care ministry. This Durwin did one afternoon, and then informed the class and instructor that he would visit the hospital after classes late that afternoon, which he did.

"At the next session he reported his visit to the class, saying it went well, and also happened to mention that it wasn't as far away as he thought; it was only a twenty minutes walk and he had figured by the map that it would be half an hour.

"'Why did you walk?' asked the instructor, 'why didn't you take the subway or bus?' she asked in critical tones that implied timidity on Durwin's part.

"Durwin replied, 'well I have had no reason or occasion to ever use this city's public transportation, so I don't know it at all.'

"'You could have asked any policeman or bus driver which route to take. Its easy,' the instructor said.

"Durwin thought to himself, *easy for people who are reasonably sure they are going to get reliable instructions, but not for people like me.* Then out loud to the instructor and class, 'its no problem. If I hadn't walked over to the hospital, I probably would have gone home and taken a long walk for exercise, which I do quite frequently.'

"The instructor then to the class extolled the city's transportation system implying it was easy and nothing to be afraid of.

"Actually, in his younger years Durwin had used the public transportation systems of three major cities of the continent, learned them so completely that he could find almost any nook and cranny in these cities. In this present 'big' city as I call it, he frequently drove his car all over it in a quite relaxed manner. If he ever did have to utilize the public transportation he would find ways to get to know it. However, he already had enough experience with bus drivers and policemen in

Terraprima, two of which I have told you of, to know that for people like him, their directions may or may not be dependable.

"This instructor, a seemingly very nice person, highly qualified in psychology, appeared at least to know nothing about that. From her attitude concerning this incident she seemed to imply that Durwin was too timid to utilize the transportation system. Actually it wasn't fear that would keep Durwin from asking directions if he wanted to. Rather, it would be calculated and reasonable caution; the good sense to protect himself from the bogus directions of belittlers."

Leo commented again, "You say the instructor seemed to be a very nice person. I wonder was she really, or, was she belittling Durwin for not taking the transit system?"

Collin replied, "Again it was hard for Durwin at that time to discern whether such a person is naive or tricky. Experienced belittlers can cover themselves well at times. Durwin was accustomed to holding his opinion on such a matter until there was more sure evidence."

Brett commented, "According to his previous experience with a police officer and a bus driver, Durwin could well have gotten a wrong steer from someone, and it being so late in the day, he could well have ended up in an isolated part of the city after dark. I've heard of awful things happening to people that way."

"Exactly," said Collin. "It would have been foolhardy for him to take the chance. He was being wise, not timid. The instructor was giving him either naive advice or an intentional bum steer, either of which was unbefitting her position of instructor in a school of psychology."

Collin told of yet another experience in Durwin's life at that time. It was not only to some bus drivers and policemen that Durwin was prone to be the object of belittling in the big city.

"Durwin and one of his friends from outside his class decided to attend a two evening once a week seminar on how to get published. This was a legitimate short course, one of many offered throughout the city by the city's education department. The course was to be held in another part of the city. The friend had his car so they would drive to the location, have dinner nearby and attend.

"The first session of the seminar was in the form of a lecture in which the participants were informed as to what publishers' requirements were from prospective writers; how to get in contact with a publisher; what to submit for preliminary appraisal; how to negotiate an agreement; the requirements necessary when submitting a completed manuscript; what to expect in the way of sales with the various size publishers and varying types of books. It was a very informative class.

"Towards the end of the class an assignment for the participants was set to prepare at home for the second class which was to be held the following week.

"As the instructor was explaning this assignment, he began to pay more attention to Durwin than he had previously. Durwin wondered, 'does he see me as a person with promise and is trying to help out, or, does he see me as someone he can take advantage of for his own ends as many belittlers do?"

Leo expressed the puzzlement of the group members. "What's coming now?" he asked with a wry smile.

"I'll explain," continued Collin. "The instructor paying much attention to Durwin, explained the assignment. For next week the students were to prepare an outline of what they wish to get published. They would read these outlines to the class for discussion. Then the instructor would pass an opinion as to chances of getting such a writing published, and which publishers were likely to be interested.

"After explaining this, the instructor focused his full attention on Durwin, saying, 'now the publishing business is not a sleazy business, so unless you're paranoid you will do this assignment as I have asked.' He repeated himself in near the same words three or four times, all the while looking straight at Durwin who held himself steady and unruffled. Looking around briefly at some of the others present, Durwin could see four or five of them looking his way. One woman in particular, well past her middle years and so probably well seasoned, looking at Durwin, tipped her head affectionally. Durwin knew he had one supporter there and probably more.

"Durwin wasn't paranoid, but he wasn't a sap either. During the following week instead of preparing an outline of what he would really like to publish, he prepared a careful outline of a religious social-political topic that was current at the time. Remember, this was a time when militarism of any kind was very unpopular in much of the mainline church. It was a topic that was sure to sell if anyone dared and could write on it adequately. Durwin went to the next class well prepared.

"At the second session the instructor asked the students to present their outlines as they felt moved to. Durwin refrained from being first. Four presentations were made. There was a variety; a trade book, a how to book on finance, a children's book, a romance. Then there was a pause. The instructor remarked, as he glance at Durwin, 'put aside your paranoia now, and lets hear what you have. Durwin ignored him for the present, looking around to see who would present next. There was another presentation, a book of poetry after which, before there was any further request by the instructor, Durwin volunteered his. It was a deep and difficult, yet currently hot topic.

"After Durwin finished reading it, what he was half expecting came; that is, nothing except an expression on the face of the instructor which was difficult to discern whether it was a smile or a smirk as he looked away from Durwin and all around at the other participants. The woman who the previous week had tipped her head in affection to Durwin now came to his support, 'That will sell,' she said very emphatically, 'its sure to, especially in religious book stores. Three others present supported that opinion.

"The smirk part of the instructors expression disappeared and a forced smile replaced it. Then as if he couldn't find the right words, said, 'aah, err, we-1-1, trouble is I don't know where you can publish such a writing. I can't help you on this.'

"This seemed to be a surprise to many. Religious publishers are numerous. But in this instance the intent of the instructor to belittle a fine person was made obvious by his mannerism. He had also used the paranoia ploy, a frequent trick used by belittlers who are up on psychological terms. Other belittlers simply us the term 'nuts' or 'crazy, but they use it the same way. Durwin had been singled out with the paranoia bit and he had not been helped in the end. He was inclined in this case to believe he was first of all getting a shake down to reveal his subject. Secondly, when he revealed a topic and outline not useful to the instructor, there was no comment from him as to what he thought of it as there was in other cases presented. If the others present hadn't supported it, he most likely would have smirked to belittle Durwin. But when the support came, he forced a smile to camouflage his real self. Also, belittlers don't easily give in, so he offered no help about publishers for Durwin's topic, even though religious publishers are plentiful."

Owen asked, "What about the friend who had gone to the seminar with Durwin, did he see what was happening?"

"No," answered Collin. "He didn't. He was a very highly intelligent person, well up on most things in society and the world, but no, he was younger and had very little awareness yet of what I am describing here tonight, although he was developing it and would come to know it more fully as he gained more experience."

Brett commented, "Even if there are no sleazy publishers out there, there are lots of sleazy people who would like to be published even if they have to steal someone else's topic."

"That's why Durwin chose a topic that wouldn't interest sleazy people, even the sleazy writers in the church who might get hold of it," commented Collin.

"Sleazy writers in the church! Wow, that's saying something," said Leo in awe.

"Just stay tuned," responded Collin, and then continued, "Durwin had tried his hand at writing, had been published in a small way each time he had tried to be, and was always asked for more. Later, I will tell you of one attempt Durwin made to be published and also how he mentioned in class at the next school he was attending for continuing education, that he would like to publish a small book on a church topic. I will let you know what the repercussions were, and let you decide for yourself about sleazy people in the church.

"Let me say, before I conclude this episode, that on the whole, Durwin thoroughly enjoyed and found helpful his studies in pastoral care and counseling. It was helpful to his career and particularly for his plans for his pastoral care ministry in his local church at the time, as I have previously described. On the negative side, the response for help from this school with the serious problems of his pastorate was disappointing, and in the final semester he had been mistreated in the school itself. Overall he regarded the courses and the sizeable expense of it well worth while in many respects for his career and for his person as well.

"I say for his career and his person as well. In time belittlers tried to imply and impress upon Durwin and others present, that Durwin's major purpose in going to that school was for badly needed self-improvement. This was not so. It was another attempt to belittle him. When Durwin started there he was a well adjusted, confident person. His main and major interest was to learn more about pastoral care and counseling, with self improvement always a welcome by-product. However, in future, time and again, crafty belittlers would be quick to imply that Durwin went to that school for badly needed self-improvement. It became a weapon for belittling.

"Had Durwin remained at this school for another semester he would have been able to discern more accurately just who were naive and who were belittlers, and which of the two carried the most sway there. At the time, he was still learning and just getting wise to the mind-games Terraprima belittlers play. However, his two year course ended and he pursued other plans. As it is, he has pleasant feelings about the first three semesters, a year and a half, but mixed thoughts about the final six months. That he was mistreated during the last semester, he has no doubt. And besides the overall course wasn't helpful to the circumstances of his pastorate where he was also by now being very openly mistreated. Formal psychology just wasn't up on this frequently experienced psychological problem of adult life.

"Whether naivete or belittling was the predominant factor in this school, Durwin wasn't there long enough to find our for sure. Either way, it lowered his estimation of the school and he wanted nothing else to do with it. Later stories, coming from other than Durwin's experience, convinced him that belittlers and mind-game players were indeed a factor to be reckoned with there in this school of psychology. Whether the C.E.O. of the school was one of them, or was not wise to them, Durwin lacked the needed interaction to tell. But either way, their psychology was wanting in its dealing with adult human behavior."

After a brief pause, Collin said, "I will now take you into the interwoven finale of the Lawtons' experience with the church and life in general in that area of the continent I call Terraprima and more preferably, occasionally term it 'Terraprima fallen.'"

"At this time and over the next three weeks or so I will combine several spheres of Durwin Lawton's life, namely, his second church, his continuing education, his treatment by the church at large, and how it all affected him and his wife Canda.

"As Durwin told me of his experiences in Terraprima, he also told me how it grieved him greatly to tell such a story about the church, but also how he felt it had to be told. Durwin, during his experiences, gave the church every opportunity to turn itself around and begin to treat him as a human being, one of God's people.

"The change never came however, and it became more and more obvious that his overtures of friendship and peace were only looked upon as weaknesses to be exploited further. Fair play would never come to Durwin Lawton from the church in Terraprima. A vicious, inhumane mind-game would be pursued to the end of his experience with them. It was a way of life with the belittlers of Terraprima. They couldn't rise up to better; it just wasn't in them to do so.

"To pursue the story, I am going to take you back to different points in time which concern this denomination in Terraprima. First, a recent happening, and then two events away back beyond Durwin's experience. First, remember the second interview of Durwin with the psychiatiist for immigration purposes. At the beginning of the interview, the psychiatrist came down hard on Durwin, asking bluntly and even harshly why he had 'gotten moved to a church away out there', what went wrong at his first church, what had he been doing, and so on. Had Durwin been vulnerable under such bombardment, the psychiatrist would have been able to establish, in his own mind and purpose at least, that Durwin had been demoted by the church for his unsatisfactory performance one way or another. But Durwin held his ground in the interview so then the psychiatrist did a flip flop, easily establishing that Durwin had been given the second church with more members than his first, which made it look like a promotion. Actually it was a demotion of which it could be said indeed there were more members, but with far,

far less salary, and even less opportunity for a full and vibrant ministry such as Durwin had in mind. It was, in Durwin's opinion, one of the most unprogressive churches in which he had ever ministered."

Collin paused briefly, then spoke dramatically and emphatically, "And there in that encounter with the phychiatrist you have revealed to you one of the most degrading mind-games played by this denomination in Terraprima. I will show you that they have been playing it at least for generations and decades. The essence of the game is this: when there is a minister whom they wish, out of envy, to belittle, degrade, knock out of action, get rid of, disgrace, and for all intents and purposes destroy, they place him in a pastorate that is mainly far inferior to his previous pastorate. Mainly I say, but they are always sure there is a way to cover themselves in case the dubious deed backfires. In Durwin's case they could say his new church had more members. It would look that way in the books. In reality it was a dead end with near nil potential for improvement. For various reasons it was not at all compatable with the training in counseling Durwin had acquired which training was inclined more towards urban and suburban ministry. It would reduce Durwin's efforts in studying to a waste of time and effort. Remember also that the psychiatrist now questioned Durwin about taking pills for depression. If Durwin had fallen for that he would have been labeled as sick. Be assured though, neither Durwin, nor Canda let this drastic demotion depress them.

"One evening at a previous support group meeting I mentioned two cases from many years ago of two fine ministers being belittled severely. I said then I would go into more detail about them later. I will do so now.

"Let us go back approximately seventy years, and you will see how long this game has been played. This is a story I investigated myself more than thirty years ago when there were still people around to shed light on it. It is the story of an exceptionally fine, clean cut, well cultured young man with a lovely wife and small children. After partly educating himself, he went into the ministry of Terraprima and in the service of a nice pastorate. From there he intended to work his way through the remainder of his education for a lifetime ministry in the church.

"Each time I heard about this man, I realized there were conflicting assessments of his ministry there. On the one hand there were accounts of lovely people and a popular and exceptional ministry. On the other hand there were accounts of harsh, and what I now call belittling treatment to the minister. Upon investigation of this man's life and ministry, it was revealed to me that this young man and his family were indeed popular and well liked by the better people of this lovely community. There was evidence that his ministry was indeed well received there, both within his congregation and ecumenically. As I visited, people were overjoyed at the mention of his name, and inquired very enthusiastically about him and his family.

"Why then the corresponding accounts of harsh treatment?" Collin asked himself and the support group.

"It is because the belittlers were at work," blurted out Leo disgustedly.

"You're right," exclaimed Collin, "not much trouble for us to tell now is it? Yes, belittlers at work! From all indications at the time of my investigation, the man, his ministry, and his family were all more and more highly regarded by the better people as time went on. That being so, of course, it also meant that as time went on, the belittlers turned on him all the more.

"From this church, the man was eventually posted to another church, which from my observation, was a little larger, but in a community where there would be few, if any, people of similar caliber, interests or social qualities and there would be a whole lot more belittlers. It is not that this minister would shun or remain aloof from these people of lesser quality; far from it. He wasn't that kind of person. It is that some of them would shy away from him; others would shun him; others, the active belittlers, would stymie his ministry in all or some of the ways we have discussed in this support group.

"The normal people would accept his ministry respectfully and graciously but out of necessity for their own peace and well-being in the community in which they would most likely have to live for a lifetime, they would have to be silent supporters, very silent. This man's ministry was being ruined on him.

"It was obvious, belittlers in the hierarchy of the church had sided with the belittlers in the first congregation in putting this man down to a lesser congregation. They sided with these belittlers even though they were in a minority, and also because they were belittlers themselves —birds of a feather always working together. The man had a young family to consider, so he had no choice but to get out of the ministry in order to take control of his own life again, and deal with belittlers in his own way. Another exceptional minister was lost to the church out of the undisciplined pride and envy of others. Is there any wonder that such a denomination has been losing membership!"

"He escaped," remarked Leo, with his usual wit.

"Yes, that sums it up well, Leo, he escaped," responded Collin. "This man went on to a successful Christian life in business and politics, was very highly regarded in a wide field of life. One of many person's descriptions of him to me sums up the high respect better people everywhere had for him: 'he was as honest as the sun, and a perfect gentleman.'

"Belittlers still rode him hard throughout his lifetime, but now he dealt with them on his own terms. Now he didn't have a church hierarchy to pull the rug from under him."

"Tell me more," remarked Owen.

"Sure," replied Collin, "just come forward thirty years or so, and visualize another young man, experienced in all phases of life, a world traveller, and well educated in some of the best colleges and seminaries on the continent at that time. He worked his way through all this on his own. Parental or other help was not available to him. His story of bettering and educating himself was one of outstanding accomplishment. He married a beautiful, talented and cultured young Christian woman. He then came to Terraprima to make a career in ministry in this same denomination that Durwin was in later.

"The treatment received by this cultured couple went from bad to worse. Every young person going into the ministry, expects to have to rough it at first and start at the bottom end of the scale. However, in this story, the same pattern evolves; moving from one place to another place where it can always be said there is something better about it, but which actually, on the whole is, worse. Anyone can take that for a while.

Eventually though, it eats into your culture, and your character, if you let it, and sooner or later, depending on your strength, may bring you down. That is the purpose of the game.

"This man had some advantages. His education for ministry was already complete. He did not have a young family yet. He 'escaped' to another denomination, and to another part of the continent where regardless of whether the people running this church were of good character or not, due to its different structure, he could by God's Grace, control his own destiny more fully. With his beautiful and talented wife beside him, he went on to build up, from zero beginnings, a mega-church complex of which he remained the senior pastor for many years. Another exceptional minister was lost to this denomination of Terraprima."

Gilda remarked, "And now forty or so years later they are still treating Durwin Lawton the same way. They haven't grown any in that regard in all that time."

"That is correct," replied Collin, "and Durwin found the church in Terraprima to be backward in more ways than one; stuck on first base as he called it. In time they would try to vaunt themselves above him in rather artificial ways, and simultaneously put him down as though he was the backward one. This will be further illustrated to you throughout the remainder of the story.

"Of course if this wayward denomination were to ever be openly confronted about these cases I have told you of, they would very simply and callously cover themselves. They would respond in a manner like this: Oh well, the church is made up of humans you know, and we make mistakes and sometimes people get hurt."

"No conscience about it at all!" remarked Gilda.

"None that I've ever noticed," replied Collin. "Furthermore in Durwin's case it would be absurd for them to try to say it was a mistake. Durwin stuck it out against them so long that it would have to be mistake after mistake after mistake, on and on and on; supervisor after supervisor, professor after professor, minister after minister, lay person after lay person, all making the same kind of mistakes. It is not possible for it all to be mistakes. It is a way of life developed by belittlers. Their usual cover wouldn't hold up in Durwin's case.

"Now to continue with the story, Durwin took up duties in his second church in Terraprima. The church building was located on the edge of town, with the secondary highway that ran in front of it, separating it from the edge of the town itself. It was also on the edge of a multi-acred flat plain where farmland came to the edge of each side and the back border of the church property. The building looked and had the characteristics of a typical country church, a tall steeple rising above the white siding of its walls. It was a well kept building outside and inside. It had extensive renovations done in the not too distant past. The minister's home was located in the town itself.

"Regardless of the good condition of the church building, the Lawtons would soon discover that the congregation had many of the symptoms of an unsuccessful church. The first of those was they had trouble with previous ministers, and likely they would eventually create trouble with the Lawtons. Among some troublesome members there was evidence of much doubting of the integrity of ministers generally, and a continual seeking out their faults to support that doubting, even to the point of seeing no good in them at all. The other symptoms you will be able to see as the story unfolds.

"Congregations of other denominations in the area were prospering. Durwin surmised, and accurately so, that his congregation was hoping for the right minister to do as they say and command, thereby filling their church in a very short time without the powers that be in the congregation having to change anything one iota. Of course, that never happens; the church never fills under these circumstances, so the minister takes the blame. Before long they are looking for another minister.

"Early in his ministry in this second church, Durwin set about to try to cure the congregation of this and its other misconceptions. He decided to do this mainly through a study group of people who were interested enough to volunteer to analyze and resolve the problems.

"Furthermore, having completed the year of part time class work required for a Doctor of Ministry program before coming to this present congregation, he decided he would make his work, with and through the study group, a project by which he would complete his degree program. With the consent of the seminary involved, he embarked on this program with its two-fold mission—to help this congregation become healthy, and to complete his doctoral program. Before I go ahead with the story of the congregation, I need to fill you in on Durwin's experience at the seminary at which he attended the Doctor of Ministry program.

"The seminary was not related to the denomination, but was recognized by it as an accredited school. It was located in the big city to which there was the usual commuter service by train, which Durwin preferred, or bus, which he seldom used, or, by driving his own car, which he occasionally did to accomodate the sometimes unusual hours for special occasions, and/or to take other people with him.

"The building which housed the seminary was located on a moderately busy part of one of the main city thoroughfares. It was an older type three story brick building taking up a relatively small corner of a city block. It was dwarfed by the other buildings surrounding it, yet large enough for a fair sized seminary.

"When Durwin made application for admission to this seminary, he filled out the usual forms and gathered the usual transcripts. As was also required he submitted a lengthy statement of theological, social and political convictions and adherence. Over the two year period of his previous continuing education event in pastoral care and counseling, he had joined with the others of his class in being open in discussion to the point of baring oneself moreso than one would comfortably do in most spheres of life. Now in his theological, social, and political statement he did the same, opening his thoughts and convictions to the faculty of this supposedly educated and Christian community. He would later find they were not trustworthy to have such personal and privileged information in their possession.

"In his statement, Durwin stated, unabashedly, as he would to anyone who needed to hear it, that he believed in moderation in all things; that in both his theological, social and political convictions he was near middle of the road, but not quite. This was by no means a fence sitting position. He was a little right of center in all of these, yet for example, he belonged to no political party. If a governing political party went too far to the right, he would change his vote to the other party, if it were not too far to the left. Right of center was his firm and long standing conviction, and remains so to this day. In an accepting interview with a seminary official, no problem or concern was expressed with his statement or his educational background. He was received into the doctoral program of the seminary."

Leo quipped, "Gauging from Durwin's previous experiences in Terraprima I would guess that instead of being received in, he was 'taken in'!"

"Taken in, he was," agreed Collin, "as you shall hear.

"This seminary publicized a number of different facets from which a student could choose, including a degree in pastoral care. This was the logical one for Durwin to choose. It was one of the facets that attracted him to this seminary in the first place. After all, he already had two years of it in his previous continuing education course at the school of psychology, plus previous seminary training in it. Whatever else was taught at this present seminary, was of minor concern to him. He would concentrate on pastoral care, so he thought.

"The first semester began with an overnight retreat. The class and some members of the faculty met at a retreat center several miles outside the city on a Sunday late afternoon. A get-acquainted meeting was held in the relaxing atmosphere of a large family style room. After each faculty member and student introduced and told a little about themselves, the Dean asked for a student to volunteer to conduct an opening devotion. There was a long pause with no one volunteering. Then Durwin spoke up and said he could offer a take off from this morning's sermon in his own church, together with a prayer and an appropiate hymn or two. The offer was readily accepted.

"Hymn books were passed around. Durwin asked the students to choose a beginning and an ending hymn, which they did. There was a Bible nearby. Durwin always like to include a Scripture reading in worship.

"They sang the first hymn. Durwin then read a scripture passage, Acts 10:34 (RSV) the essence of which was 'God shows no partiality' among people. He then read the story of the 'widow's mite.' (Mark 12:41-44 (RSV). Then he did a summary of his morning sermon. The topic was, "God Shows No Partiality". Durwin stated that the person of average means who does not give anything at all of resources and/or self and service to God's Kingdom, is just as deliquent spiritually as a wealthy person who gives nothing. They all should be giving according to their means. Everyone can make a contribution of some sort to life, to God, and to God's people. A prayer then followed, the theme of which was asking for God's guidance for each of us to give of our means and ourselves in helping to make a better world, according as our means, material and personal permit. Then a closing hymn was sung, followed by a benediction.

"There were no comments on the devotional, and Durwin wasn't looking for any. He just assumed everything was okay. Soon, at the evening meal he would be shown otherwise. Durwin would learn that in this school, people of average or poor means are automatically all good and right; well-to-do people are automatically all wrong and bad. There are no bad poor people, and no good well-to-do people, so Durwin Lawton was about to begin to learn.

"When the call for dinner came, the students, Durwin with them, made their way to the dining room and the large circular table at which they all sat. There were some vacant chairs, one of them next to Durwin on his left. The professor of Christian Ethics came and sat in it. As Durwin tried to strike up a conversation with him, he turned, noticably, shoulder and all to the persons on the other side of him, ignoring Durwin, and carrying on a conversation with them. Worse than that, the dishes of food, as they were passed around the table, went away from Durwin's right in a counter clockwise direction. Durwin managed to get food from a couple of them before they circulated, but by and large the dishes went around and came to a stop at the hands of the professor of ethics, who helped himself, and then pushed them in the opposite direction where they came to a stop mostly in one little area out of Durwin's reach.

"Durwin thought to himself, the professor of ethics is either a social ignoramous, or he is giving me the shaft; I don't know which just yet. Durwin ate a little of the bit he had, then said to the professor, 'could I have the dish of carrots please?' The professor did not pass the food, so Durwin still giving him the benefit of the doubt, thought perhaps he didn't hear. Then Durwin tapped him on the shoulder that was so turned away from him, 'could you pass me the carrots please?' he asked.

"The professor abruptly picked up the dish of carrots, plunked it down hard in front of Durwin and immediately turned away from him again. Durwin tapped his shoulder again, 'would you pass me the meat please?' The professor of ethics passed the meat platter in the same abrupt manner as he had passed the carrots. As he began to turn his back again, Durwin quickly added, 'while you're at it, you can pass me the potatoes too please.'

"At this the professor bristled, turned red in the forehead, passed the potatoes even more abruptly than before, turned his back on Durwin once again and talked continuously to the other students. "At the free time that followed the meal the other students shyed away from Durwin as though they didn't want to be seen with him. Needless to say, there wasn't much sleep for Durwin that night at the retreat center. He lay awake pondering what had happened to him. Here he was among a group of strangers, supposedly Christians, and didn't yet know just what he was into or in for. It is an accredited seminary, he reasoned to himself, so I'll see it through some more before deciding either for or against it. At this time he still wasn't fully wise to the complexities of mind-games belittlers of Terraprima played, but he was learning.

"The next morning after breakfast, there was a brief period of free time again. Durwin knew he was visibly tired. However, now some of the students made brief overtures of friendship toward him, as if recuperating from whatever fear had kept them away the night before. The friendship seemed genuine.

"I'm making progress, Durwin reasoned again. *I've been belittled worse than this before and made my way. We shall see!"*

"The morning free time was called to an end and the class again sat around on the sofas and easy chairs of the family-style room. Another professor, an obviously close associate of the professor of ethics came and sat beside Durwin with a smile on his face. 'You'll do all right,' he said, in a friendly manner, 'perhaps some day you will be able to help the poor of the inner big city, with your gifts and talents, according to your means.'

"Durwin should have taken his direction right there. Being the type of person he was, he knew he would be no more suited to that kind of ministry than he would to flying space rockets. Considering his background, his age, and his previous experience, he knew that it would be extremely difficult for him to fit into a ministry like that at this stage in his life. Besides, he had his own idea of what kind of ministry he felt called to.

"As time went on Durwin would learn that it is a much used ploy of belittlers of Terraprima to have some person of lesser significance plant an idea, usually a goofy and unfitting idea, in a prospective victim's head. Then the other accomplices, by the pressure of much innuendo and implication, try to brainwash him into it. It is one of their favorite and most lethal means of destruction.

"However, keep in mind that Durwin wasn't yet wise to their mind-games. Again in his trusting way, he reasoned, *I have already had a lot, a whole lot of dumb experiences with clergy in Terraprima. Now, it seems, the professors here are no brighter, so I'll just have to forge my way through this phase as I have done so often since coming to Terraprima, and to a lesser extent in my experiences with ministers and churches before coming here. There is the pastoral care thing they publicized. I will find out more about that, see it through further, and maybe I can make something out of this yet.*

"As the class now sat around the room, the various courses of study were outlined, as well as the options students could choose. There were some basic courses for everyone, then some options, including pastoral care. Durwin felt from that he could indeed get his degree in pastoral care. He could take the other required courses and sift through them for himself. Surely these highly educated broadminded Christian people as they are supposed to be, these professors, if necessary would allow for a well reasoned theology that might be a bit different from theirs. After all, these are Christian teachers and they did accept my resumes and applications. How wrong Durwin was in that early reasoning, and how meager would be the pastoral care studies compared to that which he had learned in his previous years of study in the subject!

"In addition to the aforementioned reasoning, Durwin also reflected in his mind that back in the very beginning of his career with the church, he had to push his way into the ministry against the wayward behavior of belittlers. When he finally got to know enough of the right people on the inside of the church structure, he had no problem being received into the ministry. Until he established that proper inner contact, the belittlers blocked his way. *Perhaps I will have to do the same thing now,* he reasoned again. *It is something I have had to do practically all my life.* So Durwin decided to attend classes on the part time studies schedule of the seminary.

"From Durwin's perspective, it turned out to be a poor program at best. In time also, the belittlers would play havoc with him no end, or attempt to do so. Durwin was strong. Though somewhat scarred in the melee of life, he had always been able to bounce back to fullness of life again in a very short time. Through the inner workings of the Grace of God in his life he had an extraordinary resilience. This is something foreign in the life of proud belittlers, and they can't understand how it can happen to a dedicated Christian like Durwin.

"The major classes of the doctoral program were based mainly on Old Testament theology and contemporary economics, the two of which they had shabbily woven together. A very definite bias was taught in favor of the poor, but also an even greater bias was taught against the rich. God is like that, they taught, biased in that manner, with the implications that we should be that way also.

"No thought was given that there were good stewards among the rich in Biblical days, including some of the foremost of God's chosen in Old Testament times. There were also many who were not good stewards. Their theology gave no thought to the fact that there are many wealthy good stewards, both Christian and non Christian in society today. There are not as many as we Christians would like. One major reason for that, in my opinion, is that wealthy and/or well-to-do people have been driven away from the influence of much of the mainline Christian church by its adverse theology, laden with bias against the wealthy. I might add a note here, that there are, likewise, many good and many not so good stewards among the poor and average people of society. No thought was given to that either.

"Altogether, the supposedly Christian theology of this school was, in Durwin's opinion, and I agree, very error riddled indeed. The prevailing attitude was, away with all rich people, up with all poor people. It was an immature and ill-informed attitude, to say the least. Durwin knew and knew of many rich people who were honest to goodness Christians through and through, not perfect, but living under the guidance of the Grace of God. He also knew many people of average or poor means whom he would not trust as far as he could throw them. The faculty of this seminary were out of touch with the realities that existed so plainly out there in the world for anyone who was living in it in an unbiased, objective and mature manner.

"Another part of this wayward attitude was that the rich business people were to blame for all the country's ills. These rich people were thought of in essence as having money no end, a bottomless pit from which they could come up with money to employ all the unemployed, house them, and all. There was no appearance of any thought that business people and corporations also have their limitations. It was naive thinking to say the least.

"Durwin spoke against all this and stood his ground of being right of center in the various aspects of his philosophy of life, including business. A professor took up belittling him before the class. Durwin put a stop to that one day by simply stating in general conversation before the class that one of his main concerns when considering this seminary was how he would be treated in a school here in the big rough and tumble city. This shamed the professor temporarily. He blushed and acted remorseful for a while after that.

"One day Durwin was asked pointedly, how he would resolve the unemployment problem. Durwin first reminded the professor who asked the question, together with the class, that the present time is a period of great prosperity. Unemployment is at a very low rate. Mainly, the unemployed at the present time are people who are unemployable; they would be detrimental to any employer and his business. These presently unemployed people need to be taught such things as culture and decorum, honest behavior, the need to do a good days work for a good days pay, and how business and industry are dependent on them when they are employed with them. They have a responsibility to take seriously these basic fundamentals of life. Then they also need to be taught a technical skill. Where the church can help is with teaching the culture and decorum part, and when these people have learned well rounded skills of living they will be employable. When they learn a technical skill on top of that they will be employable in even better jobs.

Of course the employer has responsibilities as well, but that wasn't a part of this particular conversation.

"The professor who asked the question in the first place made no comment. Durwin knew that first of all the church in Terraprima had to regain its lost culture and decorum for itself before it could pass it on to others. He knew also that many leaders of business and industry were lacking in a different aspect of culture and decorum. These had to learn how not to squander prosperity in outrageous and greedy living, often funded by too much credit, or too much dipping into the profits for personal squandering, or by avoiding taxes by all means, thereby crippling the nation, and so on.

"The church could do a great deal of work here too, if they were not at so great odds with the whole system, and if they had sufficient clergy who were up to the task, which they did not have at the present time. Many of the present clergy of Terraprima were not able to take their place beside the leaders of business and industry. They did not have it in them to do so, thus they faulted the system.

"Durwin believed in making the present system work better through the reforming of individuals into a religiously correct spirit of responsibility. Being a well oriented Christian himself, he naturally saw possibilities for this throughout the Christian church.

"The professor on the other hand was advocating changing the system—away with all the wealthy people, up with all the poor people. Durwin questioned what would happen to any poor people who might eventually do well and become rich. Would they then be turned away. There was no answer forthcoming. Soon thereafter the professor of this Christian seminary declared himself to be a Marxist.

"The professor's stated case for Marxism was simplistic and in Durwin's opinion naive. For example the professor one day said to the class, that he had this notion of he, and say about four others, under Marxism owning a nice sail boat and sharing it together.

"Thought Durwin right away, *and three or four of you -would sail the boat and the other one or two would do all the upkeep work on it.* However Durwin didn't debate the point that day. He didn't think it was worth the trouble.

"In his early teens, he remembered, he had given some thought to Marxism and rejected it after less than a half hour of thought, and then felt foolish that he had even considered it. The few pages of assigned readings of Marx he had ever read, he had considered a waste of time, for it reminded him simply of a person with a chip on his shoulder against the whole world and everything in it, and not really worth the paper it was on."

Collin briefly broke with the story, "It amuses me to think of a Marxist belittler; the Marxist theory being, 'from each according to his ability and to each according to his need.' The belittler tries in every way possible to prevent people like us from exercising our full ability. He is envious of it. He doesn't want us to have much for our needs either. He is envious of that. It just makes me wonder if the whole belittler's concept of Marxism is based on envy and hatred for those he deems to be a cut above.

"Some days after the declaration of Marxism by the professor, however, a homework paper was set for the class on economic systems. In his answer to one of the questions, Durwin stated that 'from each according to his ability is a noble concept, but, to each according to his need will never, never work because it does not take into account human incentive, that very necessary characteristic to wholeness of life for people. Soon after that, with still a couple of months to go, Durwin announced before the class that he would finish out the year of class work, but would not be doing a paper to complete his degree. He didn't explain why, but his personal reason was he just wouldn't give much credibility to a degree from such a place.

"By the way, some time later, that professor while still upholding socialism acknowledged that before it could work, the human incentive problem had to be resolved."

Collin continued: "Another factor that came into play in this seminary and in the wider church as well was South American theology. Whether South American theology fittingly applies to South America we need not debate here. Durwin in telling his story, had no doubt however, that from the little he knew of it, South American theology does not fit North America and therefore has no logical place in the life of Terraprima.

"For a person to visit or live in South America and be moved to action by the poverty there is one thing. To come back to North America and having been moved by the South American economic scenario, also armed with South American theology and expecting to tackle the North American economic woes with it, is absolutely ludicrous in my opinion. The two economic systems are absolutely different. In South America, people are more or less stuck in their position in life; the poor remain poor, the average wage earner remains average, the well-to-do remain well to do. At least, this is the picture some theologians present.

"North America, including Terraprima, has always been known to be a place where anyone, yes any person, can go to the top if he/she has the ability, the desire, the drive and the incentive to do so. It is true, problems have arisen in the North American economic system at times to hinder, but never to stop this wonderful process. Nevertheless, we don't destroy a good system simply because it has occasional problems. We tackle the problems.

"Durwin had had enough experiences with some of the South Americans who had come to Terraprima armed with their belittling trickery to put down the rich and the well to do. I will relate a couple of those experiences to you.

"There was a department store on the edge of a large well to do town. It was part of a chain of discount department stores, but this store was rather exceptional for its class. It was an extra large store with good layout, pleasant staff and quality goods for its class. It was a busy store, efficiently managed and catering to the middle and upper middle income people of the immediate area and beyond. Durwin and Canda had shopped there often at one period in their lives.

"Then they moved away from it, and on a visit back there two years later Durwin went there to shop again. To his surprise the whole atmosphere of the store had changed. It was drab and poorly kept now. Of the small number of customers there, few if any were from the well to do community nearby. There was a complete change of employees now, all South and Central Americans. God bless them, they had found employment. More power to them, as the saying goes, but, what else had they done? The remainder of this story will illustrate.

"As changed as this store was, Durwin still did his shopping there that day, picking up many of the usual bargains in his shopping cart. When he had finished shopping and the cart was nearly full, Durwin decided he had better go to the washroom before checking out because he had a long drive to get home. Parking his cart beside the washroom door he went inside for only a short length of time. When he came out his shopping cart was gone. He looked all around the area, but it was not in sight. He explored other nearby parts of the store including the check outs, and customer service counter, but the cart was nowhere to be seen.

"Durwin approached the woman at the Customer Service counter, told her how his shopping cart full of goods had disappeared while he was in the washroom. She shrugged her shoulders, pushed up her lip, and went on with other work. 'Look lady,' said Durwin firmly, 'I spent a lot of time picking up those things. Are you going to try to retrieve them for me?'

"She grinned a saucy grin and asked, 'would you want to speak to the manager?'

"'Yes I would,' answered Durwin.

"She picked up the house phone and spoke something into it that Durwin was not able to hear, then hung up. Durwin waited and waited. Finally he asked, 'Is the manager coming?'

"'He said he would,' was the callous reply.

"By now she and the nearby checkout staff were exchanging glances and grins. The manager didn't show. Durwin decided there and then that this store was no longer for people like him. It had been ironically turned into a 'poor' people's store only, to serve people who alone did not have the money to keep it going. Well to do people would be discriminated against. All the symptoms were there for the failure of this business. As Durwin walked out of the store empty handed, a chorused laugh went up from the staff at the service counter and nearby checkouts. *That's enough demonstration of South American Theology for me today,* thought Durwin to himself. *No way need the church try to teach that garbage to me in this country.*

"About three years later when Durwin was visiting that area again, he purposely and curiously visited that store once more. He wondered if it had closed up by now, but no it was still open. He entered and did some shopping around. The whole staff and atmosphere had completely changed again. Except for three out of dozens, the staff was not made up of South and Central Americans. Now it was made up mainly of enterprising, highly motivated people of both Oriental background, and North American black people, all obviously well cultured, courteous, and energetic. The remaining three South or Central Americans were doing equally well, no doubt having thrown off their former attitude. The store was alive with customers of all classes, the well-to-do and the average, spending according to their means. Durwin was heartened to see that this exceptional store had survived and rebounded."

Collin continued with another story of South American theological influence. "Only a few miles away from that store was a car dealership from whom Durwin bought a slightly used car sometime before the store experience I just related to you. South American theological influence was only beginning to get a foothold in the area of the dealership.

"Durwin obtained an extra good deal on this better than average model car. As a condition of buying a car from this dealer, he was assured of good service from their service department, both before and after the purchase. The car received the usual going over any reliable dealer would give. Some minor repairs were made, and Durwin took possession of the car with which he was pleased.

"Sometime after the short term used car warranty had run out, Durwin returned to the service center with which he had become somewhat familiar during the purchase of the car. He wanted a new sun visor put on to replace the one that was flopping down. He fully expected to pay for this now. There were two connections in the sun visor, the one nearest the car's body causing the floppiness. The service manager had the visor replaced leaving the loose connection at the body of the car still unreplaced. After trying the visor and finding no improvement, Durwin complained to the service manager. He winced and whined and in his accented English reluctantly ordered the visor replaced right from the connection onto the body of the car.

"On this same visit, Durwin also asked to have the transmission oil changed. The automatic transmission was acting up, not changing into high gear at times, especially when it had been sitting overnight after a long run. The service manager again made excuses for not changing the oil. 'You may need a new transmission,' he said nevously. Durwin had already checked the oil, it was discolored and old looking. He ordered the oil changed, and the service manager complied, partly that is. Over the next three days Durwin tested the car again, but the problem with the transmission was not corrected. Undaunted, Durwin phoned an area number of the car manufacturer that he found listed in the car owner's manual. There he was informed that there are two separate compartments, not one, requiring a transmission oil change.

"'How many quarts of transmission oil did they charge you for?' the manufacturer's representative asked.'

"Durwin checked the bill and told him.'

"'They only changed the oil in one compartment," he answered. 'Go back and tell them to change the other compartment, and make sure the filter is changed also,' he recommended. 'Then if it doesn't work out, call me again.'

"Pleased with this information, Durwin returned to the service manager with a request that the oil in the other transmission compartment be changed also. The service manager winced and whined again, making excuses. 'It will do no good sir, you will need a new transmission.' Durwin wasn't ready to give in to that yet. He went to the salesman from whom he bought the car. The salesman responded, 'well that's a used car you know, you have to expect things to go wrong with it.'

"'That's not my concern,' replied Durwin, 'I fully expect, at this point in time to pay for the servicing, provided it is the right servicing. But your service manager is being obnoxious with me.' The salesman shrugged his shoulders, 'we find him alright.'

"Durwin went asking for the sales manager, but he was not available. They said he wasn't in at the time. Durwin then returned to the service manager, and pressed him, 'are you going to change the oil in that second compartment for me, or not?'

"The man winced again, this time with tears coming into his eyes. 'Sir,' he said, whiningly and in his accented English, 'you're a clergyman, and I hope you will be able to forgive me for the way I'm treating you, but I have to do that you know.'

"Durwin guessed at the problem. 'What country are you from?' Durwin asked him curtly so as to ensure an answer.

"The service manager told Durwin which South American country he was from.

"'And you belonged to the church there?' asked Durwin, pressingly.

"'Yes,' replied the man.

"Durwin knew it was a church of that country whose left-wing-liberal theologians of the time had been promoting social activists against the economic systems of some South American countries.

"'I thought so,' said Durwin, then turned away, sat in his car and drove off, never to return to that garage again. He found another dealer in another town to service his car; had the transmission oil changed in both compartments, together with a new filter. It took care of the problem, and Durwin drove that car with satisfaction for several years with only the usual upkeep and servicing."

Donna asked, "Collin, supposing Durwin had gone to the management of the dealership, could he have gotten better service?"

"Maybe, and maybe not," replied Collin. "You see, the service manager was, by Durwin's appearance, taking him to be a member of the wealthy class. This man was so brainwashed against the wealthy that gauging from his behavior he may have been willing to risk his job rather than treat Durwin well. On the other hand, as indicated by the salesman's response, it is not likely any of the sales or management people would be wise to the devious behavior of the service manager and his reasons for being that way.

"Durwin went to a town of well-to-do people which had not yet been much affected by this type of belittling. If he hadn't gotten away from the infected dealership, he stood to lose several thousand dollars on what would eventually become designated as a worthless car, and his credit rating may have become seriously damaged, none of which Durwin could afford. To put it briefly, Durwin's financial reputation may have been adversely affected. Durwin did right by getting his business out of that place."

"I agree fully," said Brett, "you just can't let a nut like that tamper with your life."

"I see your point," said Donna, "of course, I know from experience that different types of people often get different qualities of service in different business establishments, including car dealerships. People have to shop around to find out where they fit in. I agree now, Durwin handled it safely."

Owen spoke, "I guess it was so much for South American theology in North America for Durwin, after these experiences.!"

"You guessed it right," replied Collin, "I could tell you of other similar incidents, some of which are even more blatant, but I think I have made my point already, so I will continue with Durwin's seminary experiences.

"In response to another assignment, Durwin brought to class first hand, irrefutable evidence that unintentionally toppled one of the seminary's pet premises. In their teachings, the professors' overall implication was that all rich people were greedy after more money, and glorified their riches, while the average people, the common people they would call them, were rightly only interested in making a good living.

"Durwin's research established that the majority of students in a particular college were mainly interested in getting the best paying job they could find, and someday strike it rich so that they could live 'high on the hog' as the saying goes; in other words live extravagantly as they supposed all of the wealthy class do. Durwin established in his research that it is not only the rich who could benefit from learning Christian stewardship of the world's resources, but also the average people need to be brought under that same umbrella. This research further upset the seminary's premise that all rich people are bad and all 'common' people are good. Durwin could put aside bias and see objectively that all people are in need of, and can be given wholeness of life by the experience of God and His Word in their lives.

"A professor's response to Durwin's research was that it was too difficult for the class."

"What?" retorted Owen, "too difficult!"

"Yes," replied Collin. "The mind-game was in play now. Anything worth while Durwin did had to be played down. His confidence had to be wrecked, so they could brainwash him into the way they wished him to go, and that way was down. There was indeed another crunch to this particular incident. It was a woman professor who said the topic was too difficult, implying it to be so in both content and language usage. Actually, Durwin's project was quite ordinary, in easily understandable concepts and everyday English language."

"Then what was the problem," Gilda pressed further.

Collin explained, "As Durwin learned more about the trickery and mind-games he found he was supposed to have listened to her, and scale this and all his other work down until it was all trivial. Then later the other professors would disqualify Durwin's work for being of inferior quality. If Durwin were to claim the woman professor led him that way, they would imply that he was silly to let a woman lead him astray."

"You're kidding!" exclaimed Gilda.

Collin added, "To make it sound more ludicrous, it was coming from a school that now championed equality for women. And here they were, in a new age, still using a generations old item of trickery to try to lead a sound mind astray.

"And speaking of seeing things objectively," Collin continued, "in still another class discussion on the unemployed, this same professor's assumption was that if those rich people would loosen up on their money, they could employ all these people and nobody need be out of work. Durwin's response was that business and industry do not have a bottomless pit full of money. The matter has to be looked at objectively, especially with regard to their employability and what the church can do about that. The professor seemed puzzled and did not respond to it at that particular class. At the next class the following week, the professor did respond by saying that one cannot look at such a problem objectively because there are poor, hungry people out there. Durwin did not bother to debate the point. He knew he was dealing with subjective sentiment, rather than with reason."

Gilda asked, "Why did it take a week for the professor to respond in that manner?"

Collin replied, "I asked Durwin the same question. He is of the opinion that the professor didn't know the difference between objective and subjective thinking."

"I can believe that," added Owen, "given people who are of a caliber to think that God is biased and that they must be too."

"Another professor sometimes lectured them on the formulation of the final dissertation. His lectures were, in Durwin's opinion, a hodge-podge of inferior writing suggestions, social activism, about which he most wished us to write, and the occasional out of context slurs against 'big shots' and the rich. He rambled profusely on various social activism projects of others, usually of a decade or two previously, and seemed to take great personal delight in them as evidenced by the smiles that would break out on his face. It seems it had never dawned on him that class members were more interested in the present. He would sometimes present a plan that would totally contradict the previous weeks ideas, leaving the class members perplexed, that is if they would let it do so to them.

"One week he talked about a water conservation project in a nearby state. He talked of how it was blocked by a quote 'big shot politician' who was living in the area and didn't want it to go through. Durwin knew the area well, and knew that the politician mentioned, a national right wing figure by the way, did not live in the area, but lived sufficient miles away to be in another, and much more minor watershed altogether. A few minutes afterwards the professor talked joyfully about a poor man who got a million and a half dollars for his land in the project. Then a sentence or two later he places this poor man's property many, many miles away from the project. Some people may have swallowed the propaganda, but Durwin ignored it because he knew the difference as would any school child who knew the geography of his home state."

Leo remarked, "It was okay for the poor man to have a million and a half dollars, eh!"

"Oh yes," replied Collin, "he would not be branded a rich man, he would simply be a poor man with a lot of money. They make a distinction between the two."

The group members laughed aloud.

Albin, sounding perplexed and anxious, asked, "Collin, I can't imagine a professor being so wishy-washy and dumb as you describe. Was he in all this purposely playing a mind-game with Durwin for any one or more of various reasons; was he trying to mislead Durwin into wayward avenues of thought, thinking he was naive enough to believe it all; or was he trying to confound Durwin, simply to wear him out; or was he just trying to anger Durwin so that he would quit the seminary and go away mad, giving up like a drop-out?"

Dr. Eldren shifted around uncomfortably in his chair. It caught Albin's attention and he addressed Dr. Eldren, "Doctor, I'm not very experienced yet, but I just can't believe a professor would behave like that except he had some ulterior motive and was doing it on purpose."

Dr. Eldren looked all the more uncomfortable. He didn't want to be analytical of this younger member of the group, at least not at this time of learning for him. Looking to Collin, he said, "I do not think it is an appropiate time for professional opinions on these matters yet. Would you care to comment on Albin's speculations?"

"Sure," said Collin, "I cannot speak professionally, but I can speak from experience. Belittlers do try all these things Albin mentioned, mislead, confound, wear out, anger, make them quit and brand them as quitters, and more besides. Albin, in my opinion, it is quite in order for you to have such speculations, as long as you keep them under control. Get carried away with them and it may lead to either paranoia, or, to the accusation of being paranoid. I would suggest that for the present at least, you keep an open mind on it as to whether it is a mind-game or gross incompetence. More evidence is needed to make a decision on it. As more of the story unfolds you may decide that this professor was indeed incompetent, very incompetent. On the other hand, you may believe there is enough room to surmise that he was indeed blatantly playing mind-games on Durwin before the whole class.

"We cannot read another persons mind, but given enough evidence, even circumstantial evidence, we can speculate, sometimes with a good degree of accuracy, on what a person is up to. However, I give you two precautions. First, don't speculate with someone who is not society wise and who doesn't really know the world of reality for people like us. Secondly, as I said earlier, don't get carried away with it in your own mind. Keep an open mind on it until there is evidence enough to convince you that either there is or there isn't a damaging ulterior motive involved. Remember, through all this, you are on the brink of allowing one of the main weapons of belittlers do its work on you. Paranoia is what the more skilled belittlers would like to brand you with."

Collin turned to Dr. Eldren, "That's my opinion on the matter, doctor."

Dr. Eldren, now more at ease raised his eyebrows. "Well done and well taken," he said.

"Thanks, Collin," said Albin appreciatively.

Collin then said, "I think this would be a good time to break for the evening before I boggle your tired minds too much. Is that okay with you Dr. Eldren?"

"A good idea," replied Dr. Eldren.

Dr Eldren soon departed to other work. The group members, by now enjoying their weekly relaxation and fellowship at the coffee shop decided to go there again this evening. Collin called at the library for his wife Vita on his way.

At the coffee shop they put two square tables together in their favorite corner, where the large plate glass windows met overlooking the brightly lit busy city street corner. There they all snacked and talked.

Albin, showing an apology for the way he had talked towards the end of the support group meeting, said, "I guess I stuck my neck out too far this evening, did I Collin?"

"Not too bad," replied Collin. "Dr Eldren doesn't always go by the book or jump to conclusions. You're safe."

Albin remarked further, "I can see why Vita doesn't get involved with the group. It would be bad enough if someone without much experience in real life labeled Collin with abnormal psychological tags. If both husband and wife were to get labeled they would be in quite a predicament."

Vita Seldon replied with a smile, "It's as I told you last semester, I never leave myself open to that, particularly after what Collin has been through in his lifetime. One of us has to be looked upon as legally sound in order to live a normal life."

From there the conversation went to a lighter vein as they all conversed about their extracurricular activities, and then in time dispersed to the nearby parking lot to drive home.

CHAPTER IX

As Collin Seldon and his wife Vita walked into the foyer of the Arts building of Quilibet University on the next Wednesday evening they paused for a moment.

"Be careful what you are getting into," said Vita affectionately.

"No problem with this group and Dr. Eldren," he assured her.

Collin went on his way to another support group meeting in Room 405, as Vita went to read in the library while awaiting his return.

The support group convened as usual and Collin continued with the Lawtons' story.

"Now I must tell you of the continuing education class in which Durwin had the most interest; the course, the publicity of which helped attract him to this seminary for his Doctor of Ministry program in the first place, namely Pastoral Care.

"The once a week class in Pastoral Care was a little more than an hour in length; hardly sufficient, in Durwin's opinion, to qualify the claim of the seminary that it offered a degree in the subject. Most of the total Doctor of Ministry Degree teachings were by far in the area of Old Testament studies and the social and economic factors the faculty had attached to it with their obvious biases.

"The total Pastoral Care class consisted mainly of exploring and analyzing case stories in short term counseling; cases brought before the class from the experiences of the instructor, together with a few cases from the experiences of the students. This was, in Durwin's opinion, far short of what the requirements should be for a degree in the subject, and rather paltry compared to what Durwin had experienced in his previous studies on the same subject.

"Pastoral Care covers a whole broad spectrum, ranging all the way from informal conversations with parishoners on Sunday after worship, to hospital and home visitation, to more formal meetings for exploratory purposes, to determining the need for futher counseling, and then setting up the counseling itself with a qualified long term counselor.

"The part-time instructor who taught this course, what there was of it, seemed to know his work well, showed no bias, and made no attempts to be persuasive with theological, social or economic bias. Regardless of its shortcomings, because of the competence of the instructor overall Durwin was able to accept the format of the class, as much as there was to it, that is.

"There was, however, one experience in this class that to Durwin was revealing as to a weakness in the character and knowledge of the instructor; a weakness very familar to all belittlers, especially in Terraprima, but also to some others who do not practice belittling openly.

"This instructor had for some time shown no ill favor towards any of Durwin's work for the class, neither his papers presented, nor his participation in discussion. But then one day, in one of the papers distributed to the class for teaching purposes, there was mention of the significance of dreams and their interpretation. Durwin made a request to the instructor, asking if he would utilize the class time one day to demonstrate with case studies the significance of dreams and their interpretation so that the class members might become more familiar with the topic.

"The instructor said he would do so the following week, and he did. During the discussions the next week, Durwin showed keen interest and insight into the topic of interpreting dreams and the skill required to handle it properly. At one point, this weakened the instructor to a childish whine and a comment about Durwin's analytical mind, as though it was bothering him that Durwin was able to grasp what only seasoned therapists were supposed to be able to handle. 'Don't you go practicing that,' he whimpered, 'that's in our domain.' "Durwin assured him he would never practice such a delicate art after only an hour or so of instruction. He only wanted to become familar with the topic as he thought would be appropiate for someone involved in pastoral care and at times referring counselees to highly trained therapists.

"Durwin related this story to me," said Collin, "because he was convinced that due to the atmosphere and the nature of the instructor's behavior in this instance, it could be seen that he was deeply bothered that Durwin, a student, showed so much skill in the various topics of Pastoral Care that the instructor had obviously studied extensively. This instructor did not know how to respond to someone he deemed to be smarter than himself, in this case in analysis, in a way that could be healthy for both student and teacher.

"This story illustrates a common problem people like us have with teachers, and more especially with belittling teachers. In this case the friction was of a mild sort and not disconcerting. This instructor was not a belittler. Nevertheless, even though he was a seasoned psychologist and therapist, he did not know how to effectively co-exist with someone like Durwin Lawton.

"In some cases, usually over a longer period of time, similar incidents can become very severe to the detriment of the student, all because these people do not know how to react to someone they perceive to be a cut above themselves in some way! This is a very common, and sometimes very severe characteristic of many of the people of Terraprima."

As his custom was, Collin paused for a moment, then changed the course of the story telling. "Let me revert back now to the time when Durwin announced to the class that he would finish out the class year but not write the dissertation for graduation the following year. A little later he made reference to that statement in class again and added that he was toying with the idea of writing a small book on church behavior matters, for publication. There was no comment on this statement by anyone at the time.

"About a month later, with still a month of classes to go, the professor who had been making the hodge-podge lectures on dissertation writing, made a startling statement to the class. He announced that the dissertation requirements were now changed to allow anyone who wanted, to by-pass the previously established methods and do the paper in the form of a straight essay of an appropiate but reduced length that could be later published if the candidate so desired.

"He said this with what appeared to be at the time a friendly grin, and although he didn't make the statement to Durwin personally, Durwin at the time took it to indicate that this would accomodate his desire to write a book, and at the same time gain his doctorate by it. Durwin assumed that since the proposal was made to the whole class there may have been others show an interest in this method since he had mentioned before the class his desire to write a little book.

"Immediately as the professor was finishing the announcement before the class one of the students, a very amiable person indeed, lowered her head slightly and gave the professor what obviously was an upward glance and glare of reproval. Durwin saw it and thought to himself, 'that's out of character for her. She is such a lovely, good natured person, she would normally want to see anyone accomodated this way. But Durwin wasn't yet aware that a deceitful mind-game had begun. He later drew the conclusion that the always amiable student saw through it at the time as a mind-game and silently but emphatically rebuked the professor for it right on the spot.

"Durwin kept the professor's offer in mind. There had been some signs of change in theological thought in the seminary. How much was difficult to tell. Perhaps, thought Durwin, it was worth another try. Maybe they would give him his degree on his own terms; utilizing his own theology that is. Later when the time came for him to try to lay the ground work to change his new and second church from a chronically unsuccessful church into a successful one, he decided to take the professor up on the deal.

"Having completed the year of classes, and having later moved to what I will continue to refer to as the second church—the second church for Durwin in Terraprima that is, Durwin made arrangements to do the project in his church and to write the dissertation on it. Then with some editing of it, have it published as a small book.

"The professor who proposed the idea in class, I will refer to simply as the professor. He suggested by phone conversation that Durwin first write a sketch or a little more than an outline of what he intended to write. This posed no problem for Durwin. He wrote it up and sent it in. The main negative comment about it when it was returned was that it smacked of a heavy handed minister. This surprised Durwin. The whole essence of his paper was that unsuccessful churches were that way for the opposite reason—the minister wasn't permitted to be properly in leadership. Besides, anyone who knew Durwin, as the professor should have by now, could not logically say he was a heavy handed person.

"Durwin phoned the professor and discussed the matter with him, suggesting that his outline also showed that there was a very real place of authority for lay people also, in his plan for peaceful, well ordered administration of a congregation.

"'Go ahead and write up the whole paper,' suggested the professor. Durwin took this to mean approval thus far, and quite logically so. He took a period of time, about three weeks to write up the paper in the rough, a skeleton of what the final paper would be. Then, according to instuctions, mailed it to the professor's home, and awaited a reply. The reply never came. Durwin phoned the professor's home frequently, at the times of day or evening previously designated to all students by the professor, when he would be at home. There was never any answer. He tried at different times of day and evening, week days and weekends. There was no answer. He phoned the seminary to ask if the professor was away, or if he had a new phone number, and was told by the unsuspecting receptionist that neither was the case."

"Oh Oh, I smell a rat," quipped Leo Aidan.

"Me too," added Albin Anders, "did he pick Durwin's brains and then try to dump him?"

"He's just a common thief, if he did," retorted Leo.

"Easy, easy," cautioned Collin, "while belittlers do those things you say, we have not yet explored the whole story.

"I must admit though," continued Collin, "that Durwin, at that time, became somewhat suspicious of this sudden lack of communication with the professor. So you see, group members, this suspicion happens to all of us, but we have to keep it under control, sift it out for evidence or lack of it to establish whether it might be so or not, and do so without letting it wear us out. Let me illustrate.

"Durwin Lawton was a person with very concrete ideas for books of good quality floating around in his head quite often. Another factor made Durwin suspect something more in the aforementioned case, and it could possibly have been very real, or very unlikely. You see, early in his time at this seminary, and quite apart from the seminary work, Durwin had been in correspondence with publishers about another book he had already written while still living in Secundaterra. In his resume to the publishers Durwin had quite naturally stated he was a minister of a mainline church and also that he was in the process of working on a doctoral program. These publishers would easily have the means to check that out if they wished to do so. Consequently there were times when Durwin wondered if the publishers indeed had some contact with the seminary and his denomination as well, over his attempt to get published. Perhaps now the seminary staff were not only trying to pick his brains on the little book he had mentioned in class, but on the big one he had previously tried to publish. They may or may not have thought it was one and the same book.

"Further along in his dealings with these people, Durwin became more certain that one of their mind-games was to scab what information and ideas they could off a person like Durwin, insinuate to him it was not good, and then try to put it to work in other areas of the church.

"Often it did not work well for them because they had neither the full concept, nor a sound understanding of it, as they would have received had Durwin been able to write more completely, perhaps under their guidance, his own concepts of the matter. Furthermore, by doing it their way it did not reach far and wide as a book may have done. Also, they did not possess the Christian character to make it work.

"But no way were they going to let Durwin do it. Overall, it became a case of suppression of knowledge the like of which reaches back beyond the Middle Ages. Under these conditions Durwin's studies with them turned out to be a waste of time and effort.

"If picking his brains was their objective it was short sighted on their part. If they had properly estimated Durwin for what he was, outside their own hatred, envy, and hollow, undisciplined pride, they would have recognized, guided and encouraged his creativity."

Albin Anders was bursting to speak. "I guess being so young I haven't much experience in these matters yet, but I see the possibility indeed of a connection between the publisher Durwin had correspondence with, and the seminary. They could quite well have inquired of him for a character and ability reference. It would be the logical thing to do before putting up money on a possible publication. Had the seminary been able to handle it properly, it could have worked out well for all involved.

"That is a rational point you are making, Albin," replied Collin. "There were some incidents that have pointed to that, but only some. Since they are insufficient it prevents both you and I from saying there was a connection. As I said, take it easy Albin, and if later in the story there are any further indications, we can perhaps have a better idea then whether they were picking Durwin's brains on this small book he intended to write, or, on the larger book he had already written and tried to publish, or both."

"A good and safe suggestion," commented Dr. Eldren.

"Incidentally," added Collin, "Durwin became so absorbed with his now questionable studies and ministry together that he had no time until much later to make further attempts to publish his previously written larger book, originally completed in Secundaterra. It would be long after he had finished with the seminary, that he would have time to write some new revisions to update and make the book more current."

Collin continued, "Getting back now to Durwin's dealing with the professor, he tried in vain over a considerable period of time to contact the professor or have the professor contact him. Later, he tried to contact the dean, but was told the dean was away on six months sabbatical. Durwin then sent a part of his paper to the Principal of the seminary explaining his circumstances and asking for action. He followed up the letter with a phone call asking if the principal himself could oversee his paper, at least until the dean returned. The principal informed him that it could not be so, but he had assigned him to another professor whom Durwin had never met, and that this professor would be Durwin's mentor. It was left to Durwin to contact this mentor and set the process in motion.

"At first opportunity, Durwin contacted the mentor, and set up an appointment with him in his office at the seminary in the big city. It would utilize the better part of a day for Durwin to drive into the city from the longer distance where his second church was located, have the interview, utilize the library, and return home. Durwin wanted to make the most of the trip.

"'Do you have the copy of my paper?' asked Durwin.

"'Yes I do,' replied the mentor.

"'Will you have time to read it before the appointment?' asked Durwin again, 'or should we set the appointment for later?'

"'I will have it read,' came the reply.

"'Okay, I will see you at the appointed time,' said Durwin, feeling he was well on his way this time. But it was just a feeling, and it wasn't to be so."

"I smell that rat again," quipped Leo a second time.

Collin smiled. "As sad as it is, I cannot help but smile. We will see about your rat as time goes by. In the meantime Durwin kept the appointment.

"The interview with the mentor turned out to be a complete shake down from beginning to end. The mentor was cold and calculating in his attempted discouragement of Durwin. He started out by telling Durwin how his own wife had attained a Phd. with him as her mentor and editor. He emphasized several times that he was the editor of his wife's thesis.

"Durwin's immediate and quite rational thought was, *the guy has a problem with his wife's attainment. He wants to make it known to me that he is responsible for her accomplishment. That doesn't quite sit properly with a seminary that teaches equality of women in society. I wonder though is there some other reason for his behavior towards her today"?* Durwin would later come to a different conclusion; the mentor was vaunting himself above Durwin in preparation for belittling. In the same interview he also belittled Durwin by criticizing and trivializing Durwin's work.

"After he impressed upon Durwin a half dozen times or so that he had been his wife's editor, the mentor questioned, 'They tell me you plan to publish a book from this dissertation you are doing. Is that so?'

"Durwin answered, 'If the paper that fulfills the requirements of this seminary for a degree is compatable with what I would see as publishable in a book, then I may try to have a book published.'

"He appeared not to be pleased with that reply. He then said, 'there is not anything new to be written on the topic of problems in the local church, nothing that hasn't been already written.'

"'Oh, I see,' said Durwin curiously.

"'That's right,' he continued, 'and one of your classmates,' calling him by name, 'has already written his paper on the topic you have chosen.'

"'Is that so,' replied Durwin calmly. 'That classmate had already chosen a different topic than that before the close of the class year. Did he change his mind?'

"'He has written on this same topic you have chosen,' the mentor repeated.

"Durwin found that very odd, because the classmate mentioned was in Durwin's opinion, an upright person. He would never knowingly take someone else's topic for his own. If he did indeed write on it, it would be because he was talked into it without him knowing that it was someone else's plan to do likewise.

"'I find that strange,' said Durwin.

"'His paper is on file in the library,' said the mentor further. I'd suggest you look it up before you go home, and read it for ideas and so on.'

"Durwin thought that a very strange suggestion indeed. He didn't want to quarrel with this man. He remained silent for a moment.

"The mentor layed it on some more. 'In your own paper you ramble a lot. Your style of writing needs much improvement,' he said more harshly, coming down harder now that Durwin had not butted up against him.

"Durwin held his peace, knowing full well that one of the favorite tricks of belittlers is to send you away angry and then label you a drop-out.

"The mentor became more openly down on Durwin. 'there are dozens of books written on the topic you have chosen. I would like for you to read them.'

"'I have already read many books on the topic of problems in the local church, all the latest in fact. They were recommended to me by the Dean and other staff members of the seminary and cover the topic well.'

"'But you should know about these other books,' he insisted.

"Durwin became curious. 'Okay,' he said, 'I have pen and paper. What are they?'

"The mentor reamed off quite a list of books and authors. Durwin wrote them all down cooperatively. This visibly perturbed the mentor, as he revealed his thoughts with the curious question, 'Aren't you discouraged?'

"'Oh, maybe a little,' said Durwin lightly. 'But I'll just get these books and read them over the next month or so. I can't help but notice by the titles though, a few of which I have read already, that they are not books about trouble in the church between pastor and laity or between laity and laity, but rather they suggest the special harmony that exists between them, and suggesting an almost idyllic atmosphere. That is the exact opposite to the general theme of my paper.'

"The mentor seemed stuck for words.

"'Have you read my paper?' Durwin asked him pointedly.

"'No I haven't,' he replied. "I developed a cold and didn't get it read.' Then he stammered out, 'well I read enough of it to know you ramble in your writing.'

"'And you didn't phone me to change the appointment. I came all the way in here to receive direction for my paper and you haven't read it. So what am I to do now?'

"'Well,' he said, 'I'd like for you to read these other books and include them in your paper.'

"At this point Durwin was just a little suspecting. But trusting person that he basically was, he wasn't quite sure whether he was dealing with an academic idiot or a seasoned belittler, or some of each. It turned out later to be some of each of the two, with a third element added. He was also a stooge - the man set out front to do the dirty work.

"Knowing that he was wasting time, Durwin politely terminated the interview, and went straightway to the library. A search by the librarian and her assistant showed no trace at all of the dissertation Durwin was told had been done by his classmate. There was neither a cataloging of it in the files, nor a copy of it on the shelf where such papers would normally be. Nevertheless, Durwin, mostly out of curiosity now, picked up the eight books suggested by the mentor, took them home and over the next month read them.

"Each of those books was in the opposite direction to Durwin's paper. They were much older books than Durwin was using. Most of them extolled the harmony and the special respect that existed between minister and laity. Durwin knew this didn't exist any more especially in the troubled churches he was researching and writing about. He was being led in a different direction altogether, so he decided to await the return of the Dean in five months time before pursueing what might turn out to be a fool's errand.

"Meanwhile, an opportunity arose for Durwin to do a unit of Certified Pastoral Education in a nearby hospital. This also would be a part time proposition and it would be of six months duration, finishing soon after the seminary Dean's return, when Durwin would again look into the possibility of completing his degree course.

"Durwin had a particular interest in this Certified Pastoral Education Course or C.P.E. as it is commonly called, because after his retirement from ministry in the pastorate not many years ahead, he might like to do part time work as a minister of visitation.

"I will review with you as briefly as possible, some of Durwin's experiences, both positive and negative as he worked in this hospital with several other clergy of various persuasions, and under the tutelage of the hospital Chaplain.

"The hospital was located in a suburb of a city within convenient commuting distance from Durwin's pastorate. The impressive greyish white cement building rose high above the other mainly residential buildings of the area. It consisted of several sections some of which looked newer than others, indicating how it had grown over the years. It was now a progressive medium size establishment, highly regarded for its quality health care. Durwin was happy to be attending there for his C.P.E. unit.

"It was the overall plan of the course to eventually expose the students to all areas of the hospital, thereby encountering patients with almost every type of illness and learning to deal with them effectively. At the same time, each student would choose an area of concentration to last throughout the total length of the course. Durwin chose the several Intensive Care Units as his area, and in doing so brought down upon himself the first dose of negativism for this continuing education venture.

"Immediately as Durwin chose the Intensive Care Units, the Chaplain remarked to him before the class, 'Oh-h-h-, that's quite an assignment *for you* to take on!', with emphasis on the you.

"'And why is that quite an assignment for me any more than anyone else?' Durwin inquired.

"'We-l-l-l, you just don't seem to be the kind of person for that,' came the reply from the chaplain.

"Durwin knew what the basis of his remark was. Durwin was an easy going, easy speaking, for the most part, quiet type of person, what the Bible would call a meek person in the positive sense of the word. Today's macho people, proud, loud and showy, have the very wrong impression that meek people are weak people. The fact is, it is very often the proud, loud and showy machos who break down and whimper like babies when under stress.

"'I have no problem with Intensive Care Units,' asserted Durwin.

"'Then its yours,' conceded the Chaplain, reluctantly.

"Throughout the duration of the course, Durwin worked the Intensive Care Units, attended classes, interviews and discussions faithfully, and when his turn came each week he covered the whole hospital for a nine hour period ending at midnight. He fully enjoyed this work as a ministry of compassion and care. Even with all the pain, suffering and death he encountered, it brought inner satisfaction to him because of the very real need such a ministry was fulfilling.

"Durwin became generally respected throughout the hospital, by patients and staff, including some of its administration whom he had opportuntiy to get to know. One incident describes how people reacted to Durwin's ministry of visitation. A doctor, doing his rounds, reported to a nursing station in Intensive Care that a patient he had just visited was in a very depressed and disoriented way. He asked if the Chaplain could visit with her and try to cheer her up. Durwin was called and spent considerable time with the woman. Shortly after, Durwin was at the same nursing station going through the files before visiting other patients. The same doctor came by again. He remarked to the nurse, 'that patient is okay now.'

"'Yes,' replied the nurse, 'this minister here spent some time with her. He has some sort of magic with people around here you know.'

"The doctor simply responded pleasantly, 'H-m-m-m.'"

Owen Winslow asked, "Collin are you about to tell us that Durwin Lawton struck a good place and situation at last?"

"I'm sorry, but it cannot be so," replied Collin with a sigh. "People like Durwin Lawton and you and I will scarcely know a time or place in our lives where someone will not be trying to bring us down. However this was one of Durwin's better situations in Terraprima. Some of the students befriended him; others looked on him as a curiosity but could find no way to label him adversely. Only one openly tried to bring him down. She was a young clergy from a religious persuasion other than Durwin's. The first evidence of her envy of Durwin was noticable when she blurted out to him angrily and tearfully before the chaplain and a number of students one day, 'Don't you ever break down and cry when you see them in pain and suffering?'

"Durwin calmly replied, 'My dear girl, I've been doing this for many years now. I feel deeply for these people, that is why I spend more time with them than do most ministers, but no, I don't break down and cry over them. It'sjust not my nature to do so.' The whole group remained silent on the issue and dispersed.

"Durwin made attempts to befriend her but to no avail. At times she accused him of being arrogant. This is a typical reaction of some belittlers regarding the performance of an exceptional person. She tried frequently with verbal side swipes and innuendo to shake his confidence. If Durwin or a person like him ever did the same to her or others like her some of them would probably cry religious discrimination and take the matter up with authorities to have him thrown out. Durwin took it for what it was; her undisciplined pride was shaken and her envy stirred. She felt Durwin to be a threat to her and she had to try at least, to destroy him. Durwin saw this as a minor matter compared to what he had been used to all his life, and ignored her. She even tried to make a case out of that, with inferences that Durwin was shunning her.

"How did the Chaplain view this?" asked Brett Culver.

Collin replied, "He refrained from discussing it before Durwin or the group. Whether he discussed it with her in private we have no way of knowing. Openly he was always very amiable towards her."

"Was he always openly amiable to Durwin?" asked Brett further.

"We-l-l-," said Collin, yes and no, or rather, as much as many Terraprimans can be to a person they see as exceptional. At no time was the Chaplain visibly unkind or nasty to Durwin. But let me tell you of an incident that reveals, to a mind that is discerning on the topic, the weakness of so many people when it comes to dealing with people like us. You will see again, they just don't know how to react to people they perceive to be exceptional in some way or ways.

"Durwin was on evening duty at the hospital from three o'clock to midnight alone as far as pastoral care was concerned. As his usual custom was, he covered the whole hospital first, to take care of any existing needs. At meal time he went to the cafeteria and ate. Just as he was finishing he was paged, and a very unusual evening and night set in. From around six o'clock to midnight, he was to be paged for no less than six deaths.

"There were family members present for some of the deaths; other families had to be called in; some deaths had been expected, others were a surprise and a shock; some family members took it fairly well, some members were distraught to varying degrees. All had to be consoled. Durwin was able to deal with all this while still having regard and respect for the several different religious denominations involved. In some cases, he called in their own clergy, consoling them personally until their clergy arrived. There were absolutely no complaints from families or hospital staff about Durwin's performance that night. He handled the task well, just finishing up with the last family as his replacement arrived at midnight.

"Three days later, just prior to class meeting time, the Chaplain and Durwin met in the hallway.

"'Did you have much work on your last evening shift?' the Chaplain asked Durwin, casually.

"'Oh boy,' responded Durwin, 'six deaths for the evening. At one point I was dealing with two families at once, going from one to the other.'

"'Oh, I see,' remarked the Chaplain in a passive and disinterested manner.

"'Yes, its written up in the log book, didn't you read it,'" said Durwin.

"'No, I haven't read it yet,' replied the Chaplain casually and walked away.

"This seemed odd. The Chaplin always kept up on things in the log book. Furthermore, such matters were routinely discussed before the class as a means of exploring and improving methods of handling them. This one never was. Durwin never heard of it again. You see," said Collin to the group, "some people, whether they are active belittlers or not, cannot bear to acknowledge the accomplishments of others, particularly any accomplishment they perceive to be exceptional, and might shake their own or others pride and stir their envy; or as the more common saying puts it more mildly, any person or accomplishment that they perceive, in their oversensativity, to be a 'threat' to them or their friends or acquaintances."

"Of course," said Gilda Emerson, "if it had been discussed at class it may or may not have ruffled the feathers of the Chaplain, but definitely more certain the feathers of the clergy person who was already putting Durwin down. So if the Chaplain refrained from bringing it before the class only to protect that clergy person, and not himself, that is still shortchanging Durwin the exceptional person in order to accomodate the belittler. That is another way people like us are discriminated against."

"You are very right," said Collin. "In Terraprima, exceptional persons are often stiffled in order to protect the feelings of others. It is wrong, it is discrimination, it is injustice. But it happens all the time. It is a common ploy of belittlers to conveniently and purposely overlook the accomplishments of their victims.

"There was one other thing Durwin noticed in this course, as well as in some other church related events in which he participated at various times over the years. Whenever Durwin did an activity exceptionally well, that activity would be eliminated from the program, or be curtailed in some way so as to restrict Durwin's doing of it. In this course, Durwin actually enjoyed visiting his patients regularly. To him it was much better than hanging around talking small talk. One day he was informed, not by the Chaplain, but indirectly by the other students, that regular visiting was to be no more. We were to visit only when called. As I said, Durwin had experienced similar curtailments and cancelations on occasion as he participated in other spheres of church work.

"However, Durwin finished this C.P.E. unit unscathed, and feeling good about himself at having helped so many people. He knew he could have a sense of a job well done because of the positive response of the patients themselves, and because of the approving smiles and cooperative spirit of hospital staff. What was or was not present beyond that didn't matter an iota to him except it taught him all the more about the peculiar behavior of many belittling Terraprimans.

"About the time the C.P.E. unit was winding down to a close, Durwin received a letter from the dean of the seminary. The letter expressed in glowing terms the recent successes of the seminary, that such a large number had just graduated, and how he wished he could see Durwin graduate the following year. He invited Durwin to again take up his work with them and complete his paper in the coming year.

"Durwin thought about it for awhile but did not respond right away. A couple of weeks later he received a phone call from the dean, again inviting him to pursue his paper. 'Your mentor meant for you to come back you know,' he said. Durwin wondered why he would so obviously say that. There had been no action or mention on Durwin's part that the mentor was trying to drive him away. It was almost like an admission that the mentor had indeed given him a rough time.

"Durwin informed the dean at that time that he was just completing a C.P.E. unit, shortly after which he would be going on Summer vacation. 'Why not come and talk to me about the paper in early September,' came the response. The invitation from the dean seemed so sincere, Durwin replied, 'perhaps I will,' as the phone conversation ended.

"But Durwin was beginning to wonder by now, *is this just another game of a manipulator smoothly, very smoothly leading me down the garden path to some sort of dubious conclusion, even destruction. On the other hand there could even be some change of heart and even change of theology on their part. There had been some signs of that before classes had ended. Maybe in time they will find their feet on the new ground they may be breaking. If for no other reason than just to follow my curiosity, I will keep an open mind on it and follow it through to the end, whether it is a game or stupidity or whatever. It will be interesting to see what they eventually do to me. Obviously they are not content for me to just drop away. They have had their chance at that.*

"If they are seasoned belittlers, they will not only want to put me down, but they will want to capitalize on that other characteristic of their kind. That is, they will want to get as much money from me as they can, tuition money in this case, so if they can string me along for another year, they can get another year of tuition before my time with them is up. These people deal in the lower categories of money, but they deal in it just as craftily and greedly as any wayward big business man whom they despise so much. But I can take whatever they may be planning to deal out if indeed they are planning any dubious deed at all. Such was Durwin's thinking to himself.

"Over the next day or two, Durwin recalled a story the dean had told in class one day. He spoke of a woman who had attended classes there and had apparently had some conflict concerning her personal faith and what they were teaching at the seminary. The dean said she had accused them of attempting to wreck her faith. The dean said he told her they weren't trying to wreck her faith, but rather to give her a more sound faith. As the dean told the story to the class he emphasized noticably that it was a woman inferring she was a weak person. This implication was very questionable coming from an official of a school that very ardently supports equality for women. He continually placed emphasis on the word *she.* Durwin knew from experience that this was an old ploy of belittling tricksters, to brand as feminine and therefore soft and oversensative, anyone who complained about their belittling trickery. If it was a ploy, it was an ironic story indeed to be coming from, as I said, the dean of a seminary that considered itself a champion of equality for women."

Collin turned to Albin Anders. "You see Albin, here we have Durwin Lawton pondering over delicate and complex circumstances. He has come to no conclusion on it, and will not for some time. It would be premature and foolhardy for him to definitely surmise that it was all trickery. On the other hand, given his experiences in life, it would be just as foolhardy to ignore the symtoms of belittling that were there, and perhaps be taken in completely and led to a dubious conclusion.

However we cannot wisely discern such a matter until the evidence and attitudes give a good indication of which way it really is.

"Of course, if all of this didn't mean much to Durwin, he could take the attitude that there is nothing worthwhile in this for me, and walk away from the whole matter, having nothing else to do with it. There are times in life when it is best to do just that rather than expend your energy for no significant purpose. Anyway, the point I am making is that you can develop an excellent process of discernment in such matters without either being labeled as, or actually becoming paranoid."

"Whew," said Albin, "I'll give it my best."

"Good," encouraged Collin, "And now I would like to change the emphasis of the story for a few minutes. It would be helpful to our purpose to know more about Durwin's second church and what he had been doing about it for the nearly two years he had now been there. This second church, as I will from now on refer to it, had for some time been an unsuccessful church in comparison to the churches of other denominations in the area; unsuccessful in its general growth, its program, its fellowship and as you might now surmise from this, in its rapport with its ministers, one after another.

"With the help of the many books he had chosen on the topic of conflict in the local church, and with his own wide experience, Durwin, early in his ministry there, had set up a study group to try to turn this church around to becoming a successful church. With all the hodge podge of dealing with the seminary there was absolutely no direction coming from them on the matter. The truth is they had been so long detached from the local church scene they knew very little or nothing about it. In time, Durwin would find out, they didn't want to know or learn about it or accept what existed there.

"Durwin set up his own project in this second church, and with the help and support of the volunteer study group he held a series of meetings and seminars that did indeed turn the church around. It worked well and there was harmony among the congregation members and with Durwin the minister. The project worked very well, for a while that is."

"Oh, oh," exclaimed Leo, "here we go again, more trouble!"

"Not just yet," Collin said as he smiled, "we'll hear later what happens to it when some new people who were not involved in the meetings arrive on the scene. Meanwhile it is sufficient to know at this point that Durwin's project brought peace to the congregation early in his ministry there. It was this project Durwin planned to write on in his paper for the seminary work for his degree. The project had long been completed, in action, and working wonderfully well when the dean made his latest overture to Durwin.

"In the course of bringing peace to the congregation, Durwin also set about to change it from a cold church, to a church of warmth and friendly fellowship. During his first church services there Durwin and Canda could not help but notice that most people of the congregation did not even shake hands to each other after the service. Indeed, he was astounded to notice that before he could make his way to the exit door at the end of the worship, many people had already left the church. Durwin changed this by publicizing a time of greeting and fellowship following the service and not at some point during the service. Then he made arrangements for himself to be at the door before the service actually ended. This way he delayed the people from rushing away, circulated among them and soon they were circulating among one another and enjoying it. Instead of the church being nearly empty a few minutes after the end of the service, many people now lingered for a half hour or more.

"In the interests of further breaking down the barrier of estrangement that existed between people and minister of this congregation, Durwin also initiated something else. He had, for safety reasons, largely refrained from it in his previous church, even though it was a commonly accepted practice in congregations throughtout the wider church. His decision on it came about one day when he was talking with one of the middle aged women of the congregation. She was the austere type. In the conversation she remarked to Durwin disgustedly how the previous minister, a woman, used to go around 'hugging all these old women, and they lapped it up.'

"Durwin smiled and commented positively, 'I suppose they liked the warmth and caring of it.'

"'Well, I suppose,' she muttered awkwardly, 'I suppose its all right,' she continued, as though trying to please the new minister.

"With that, Durwin said, 'I have to go now,' as he reached forward and gave her a hug of medium warmth, with a tiny peck of a kiss on the cheek as he retracted from the hug. Obviously it was a new experience for this austere woman. She stood motionless, awed and goggle eyed as Durwin smiled and left. He continued this hugging of her, as he did with others of the congregation mostly on special occasions. She got to like it well, and seemed delighted to be included in the warmth of the congregation, many of whom she had been previously at odds and quarreling with. Durwin continually treated her with decorum and with cheerful acceptance.

"In time, this woman confided in Durwin how she had previously been a difficult person in the church, and siding with other difficult people. She admitted that when Durwin came and brought peace to the church, she may have had to leave the congregation and go elsewhere were it not for Durwin's acceptance of her regardless of her past austere and friction producing character. She remarked that this has been her church for a long time, and it would have been hard on her if she had to leave it. At the time, her appreciation was genuine."

"Oh, oh, at the time, you say," remarked Leo with a chuckle of sadness. "Don't tell me this one goes awry too."

"Oh, yes, just you wait and see," answered Collin assuredly. "From here on, with peace established throughout the congregation, Durwin felt it safe for him to utilize the hugging he had mostly refrained from in his previous congregation. In many local churches this was now considered normal among both ministers and laity every Sunday.

"Some people may get carried away with such things temporarily, at least a little, once or more in a life time. No need to condemn or brand such people for life, or burden them with lifetime guilt for such a mistake so easy to make. Durwin usually limited his practice of hugging to special occasions such as Christmas, Easter, birthdays, and other occasions for celebration. He did this openly in the congregation, including with the austere ones. He did so, still in accordance with the practices outlined in the little book, 'The Hug Therapy Book, by Kathleen Keating, (CompCare Publishers, Minneapolis, 1983), only a little more mildly than sometimes recommended in the book, and with a peck of a kiss on the cheek added, according to an old inherited custom. This worked well, that is until some new comers, pied pipers of a sort, came on the scene whistling another tune.

"It was from this transformed congregation that Durwin went to the dean of the seminary in September, at the dean's invitation, to seek to prepare the way for writing a paper on this project that had worked so well.

"Durwin took his wife Canda along for this interview so that she would be able to affirm with Durwin, and reassure him of what he had heard and didn't hear in the interview.

"At the interview, no mention was made of Durwin's past paper. 'What you need to do,' said the dean, 'is to do a formal outline of your paper first, in accordance with the regular methods of this seminary.'

"'I'm willing to do that,' responded Durwin, 'if I have someone to give me direction on it. The mentor is leading me in a different direction altogether than I previously planned.'

"'I will supervise your writing of the formal outline,' said the dean. 'Then when it has been approved, your mentor will take over again.'

"'What if I do the outline one way, and he leads me in a different direction, what then?' asked Durwin.

"'That will be okay. All you have to do then is revise the outline,' replied the dean in a gentle, out of character manner for him. In fact throughout the whole interview the dean had been uncharacteristically mild. From his considerable experience with belittlers, bullies, cowards and the like, Durwin knew that the dean was subdued that day just because of the presence of a third person, Canda. Bullies are always cowards when everything is not in their favor. It doesn't usually take much to bring out the cowardice in them. On the other hand the slightest opportunity brings on the belittling and bullying again.

"Durwin and Canda came away from the interview skeptical of what the outcome would be. The seminary probably wanted the tuition money all right, and they would pick his brains to the end, but whatever else they wanted with Durwin remained to be seen. The Lawtons were skeptical that a degree would be forthcoming. Durwin decided to carefully play the game to the end, more out of curiousity than out of the expectancy to obtain a degree.

"He also put aside the idea of publishing a small book from the paper. With a formal outline and all, it would not now be a narratively written paper, at which Durwin knew he could do well. Rather, it would be a scholarly paper, at which Durwin felt, with some direction, he could do well on a student level, but had no desire to attempt to try a scholarly publication of any sort.

"Durwin went home and began work on his formal outline and before long submitted a preliminary copy of it. The dean returned it with plenty of criticism but very little, and vague at that, suggestions of how to improve it. As Durwin had come to suspect, it was to be a guessing game. He would get no actual tutoring from them.

"Durwin had access to other outlines. By referral to these he eventually was able to guess what needed to be done with his own. After several attempts he finally whittled the dean's criticism down to one. Durwin hadn't defined the term analysis, the dean claimed. Analysis had hitherto been acknowledged as one of Durwin's exceptional abilities.

"'Where would I find help with that?' asked Durwin of the dean on the phone.

"He informed Durwin that it could be found in such and such a book. 'It's in other books as well, but its in that one. It was one of the main books Durwin had used for his project in the local church, but also one of the books the mentor had played down. The dean gave no indication of what chapter the definition might be found in. So Durwin read the whole book again, yet neither the definition, nor anything pertaining to it was to be found there. He searched elsewhere, but to no avail. After losing more than a month on this one item alone, Durwin got an idea. He simply looked up the word analysis and analyze in the dictionary. Having studied these, he phoned the dean.

"'I looked up the words analysis and analyze in the dictionary, and…'

"Before Durwin could speak further, the dean quickly cut in, 'Yes, to analyze means to criticize. That's what we want. Now you have it.

Let me have your revised copy soon.' Then he said 'good-bye for now,' and the conversation ended.

"Because of the lack of real guidance and leadership, and the presence of this vague and hazy kind of suggestions it took Durwin four months to complete his formal outline alone."

Owen was aghast. "After suggesting it could be found in that book or one of the other books, he is satisfied with Durwin merely looking it up in a dictionary. Had he not thought of the dictionary he could have read several books in his search for it. You can't tell me now that the dean wasn't leading him down the garden path to destruction."

"Cruel," remarked Gilda.

"Mental brutality, nothing less," added Leo.

Albin added his opinion. "I remember how the psychiatrist asked Durwin if he was going to stay in the country till they wore him out. So now the seminary is simply trying to wear him out."

Collin nodded, "You have it right. Durwin was convinced now that it was a vicious destructive game they were playing. He decided he would follow it through as far as was safe to do so, to learn more of the game and tactics of these master belittlers.

"In time Durwin would come to realize more fully that from the beginning they had no intention of ever giving him a degree. They would teach him nothing about writing his paper. They would pile as many books on him as they could for a threefold purpose - to pick his brains and get his views on their subject matter, to wear him down, and to steer him as far away as possible from his original plan for his paper so as to have more reason to discredit him. In the meantime he would be paying tuition, and they love to take us for our money; they wouldn't want to overlook that aspect of their belittling.

"Durwin had a number of quality dictionaries in his study, and had access to others, They all more or less agreed that to analyze was 'to separate a thing, idea, etc., into its parts so as to find out their nature, proportion, function, interrelationship, etc.'(Webster's New World Dictionary, 1986), or 'to determine the nature, form, etc., of the whole by examination of its parts.' (Funk & Wagnalls Standard Desk Dictionary, 1969). That is what Durwin had always been good at, exceptional in fact. Remember how the Pastoral Care instructor whimpered when he referred to Durwin's analytical mind. Durwin had often had friendly and unfriendly people refer to this aspect of his thinking ability."

"Ah," said Leo, "I smell a rat for sure. The dean was attempting in a crude way to belittle Durwin's exceptional analytical abilities by making him think he didn't even know what it was all about."

"Referring to the dictionaries again," continued Collin, "only some of them gave as one of the meanings of analyze as being to criticize, and then only in a secondary way. For example, 'to examine critically or minutely.' Then again, according to these dictionaries, one finds such meanings of criticize as 'to judge severely;' or 'to analyze and judge as a critic,' or 'to judge disapprovingly; find fault with,' or 'judge as a critic, especially adversely.'

"Durwin had no intention of letting anyone con him into becoming a severe critic, or a fault finder, or a disapproving judge. To him that is what Marxism had done. He would have no part of it. He was merely trying to root out 'a thorn in the side' of unsuccessful churches by offering constructive remedies for their shortcomings.

"Durwin had heard the white dean state in a judgementally critical manner in class one day. 'The white race has made a mess of this world.' Durwin would have no part of such bigotry concerning the white or any other race. There were good and bad among all of them. Durwin, and we here in this group are concerned about belittlers and the harm they cause people, no matter what the race.

"Since there was no direction forthcoming from the dean on just what they expected in the way of analysis except criticism Durwin decided he would stay with his own analysis methods in accordance with his own mostly moderately conservative practices concerning the church over the years. Durwin had never been a severe critic of the church. Neither would he now take up a liberal/critical view of its solid traditions just to get a doctorate. In fact he had always sheltered the church from criticism. But he would do now as he had always done; he would analyze ways in which some people, only a minority, were causing some churches to malfunction, and he would offer ways to correct the malfunctions. This is a normal means of renewal in any worhtwhile organization. It is a far cry from judging severely and disapprovingly or from aimlessly finding fault.

"Terraprima is a part of a country of which its people generally speak of as being the best country in the world. Yet for all that confidence and esteem for one's country, there are continually being new laws passed, old ones discarded, flaws being recognized and corrected, acknowledged shortcomings being overcome, to make it an even better country. Durwin visualized the same for the church. In time, he was to learn the hard way, that the powers that be in his denomination of Terraprima, expected its ministers to see the church only through rose colored glasses; to callously bear the harsh brutaltities and at the same time pretend that such just isn't there.

"When Durwin finally received official approval of his formal outline of thirty pages or so, he was informed that his mentor would be the same person as previously, and that he was to contact him personally. Durwin phoned him almost immediately, and informed him he was still to be his mentor, and that he was ready to begin the paper. The mentor whimpered as bullying belittlers usually do when they feel they are in a tight spot. 'I haven't been informed that I'm still to be your mentor', he whined like a child, 'perhaps you can find someone else who can be of more help to you.'

"'That's not for me to do,' responded Durwin. 'It's not for me to find a mentor, it is for you people to designate one. Now if you don't want to be my mentor, then I'd suggest you inform the dean, and let him take it from there.'

"'No, never mind,' replied the mentor, disgustedly. 'Mail me a copy of your outline.'

"Durwin knowing he had an unwilling mentor, warily mailed him a copy of the formal outline. Many days passed by, and then Durwin phoned again. 'I mailed you my outline,' said Durwin, 'I'm waiting for direction from you.'

"'Go ahead and write up your paper,' the mentor replied in a half interested manner.

"Durwin paused, waiting for more, but none came.

"'Well, what do I do,?' he asked, 'send you each chapter as I write it, or send the whole lot at once.'

"'You can send each chapter as you write it, if you wish,' came the uncertain reply.

"'Then I'll wait till I receive each one back with corrections and comments before sending another,' suggested Durwin.

"'That will be okay,' replied the mentor. Then there was another long pause.

"'Is that all?' asked Durwin.

"'Yes that is all, you can start writing,' said the mentor, and brought the conversation to an end." Such was his mentoring.

Owen commented, "He was very reluctant to be Durwin's mentor wasn't he? And even reluctant to give him any more direction except to start writing."

"I'm wondering which one was the mentor in that conversation," said Gilda.

Brett remarked, "Collin, you questioned before whether this mentor was an academic idiot or a seasoned belittler, or something more; I believe he was something more. It think, as you said, he was the out front man designated to do the dirty work; a stooge, reluctant to take it on, but with not much choice. He looked to Durwin for a way out by suggesting he get another mentor. When Durwin turned that down he reluctantly accepted."

"I think both of you are right," agreed Collin. "He was to be the stooge, the man out front, as you say. If the mind-game worked well in their favor, he would be supported by the others and perhaps be rewarded in some way. If the game went against them, the mentor would have to take the blame personally. That is my first speculation on it, and we will see whether or not it is borne out.

"Anyway," continued Collin, "Durwin wrote a paper of approximately one hundred and thirty pages, over the next four months or so. He would write a chapter, mail it in, then work on the next chapter, but before mailing it in would wait for the previous one to return to see how he was doing. At times they were slow returning, and Durwin lost several weeks because of it. But when they did arrive there was very little criticism on any of the chapters; mainly a few corrections of errors in composition, together with the occasional remark about something needing a little more elaboration. Durwin assumed from this that he was doing well, and was given no reason to think otherwise. It was going so well, or so it seemed, that all suspicion of being taken in was put in doubt. After three to four months of writing, part time of course, the paper was nearing completion.

"Near the end of the paper one of the chapters was heavy theologically, and as Durwin's custom was with such a writing, he would first block together his case by quoting the views of the major writers on the subject. Then in a second review of the writing he would critique it, inserting his own views and preferences on the subject and why.

"However, before he had time to go over it a second time to do this, he received a request from the mentor to have a copy of the whole paper in by a particular date. It was to be within two days. Durwin was now very pressed for time. He had already done all the corrections and additions requested in the previous chapters except part of one which needed correction of errors in composition and a weak area, one of few ever indicated by the mentor. But there would not be time to review the difficult chapter and add his own critique and views to it, even though these views would be mostly positive.

"When the request came, by telephone, the first time by the way that the mentor called him throughout the whole process, it was to have, as I said, a complete copy of the paper sent in. At the time, Durwin asked the mentor 'does this mean it is possible for me to graduate this spring?' He replied, 'I didn't say anything about you graduating. I just have a request from the staff here that you have a completed copy of your dissertation in by the date given.'

"Durwin protested, 'but with all my other work to do as well, I need another two weeks.'

"'Better send it in as is,' came the reply.

"So in order to meet the deadline, Durwin would have to send his paper in with at least one of the final chapters not up to even his own par. One other chapter could also use a little touching up. *Since there is no graduation involved at the present time, and since I have had so many delays, not all due to my own tardiness by any means, surely I will be able to get an extension of time; just two weeks or so is all that will be needed,* reasoned Durwin to himself. That is not too much to expect seeing I lost six months because of the dean's absence, another four months doing the outline without good direction, and several weeks due to chapters being returned late by the mentor. So he mailed the paper in, and awaited a reply.

"Before we continue with the matter of the paper," said Collin, changing the emphasis as his custom was, "you need to know now what is meanwhile happening at Durwin's second church. During his first two years there, you no doubt remember, Durwin through his project had established peace, progress and friendly fellowship there. In the third year, however, some new people arrived on the scene; people who hadn't been through Durwin's peace process.

"Some members of the congregation came upon the opportunity to acquire the services of a new organist for the church. This was something for which they and the Lawtons had been looking for some time. At Durwin's suggestion the available organist was asked to submit a resume for consideration, which she did. The resume showed adequate training in music, but her main experience as a church organist had been in a church of a minor denomination whose general practices and theology emphasis would be quite different than those of Durwin's denomination. However, in her past she had a connection with another mainline denomination that would be compatible with Durwin's. Always willing to give someone a chance if they were anywhere near qualified and open to improvement, Durwin was instrumental in the organist being accepted.

"The first Sundays with this new organist were disappointing to Durwin. Her style became obvious; the hymns played very softly and slowly, and the anthems much the same way; the overall tone being one of sentimentalism, or, as the vernacular would put it, the tear-jerking type. This was in sharp contrast to Durwin's desire for a generally lively, celebrative type of music. Starting with the hymns, Durwin soon began to nudge her, just by a word here and there to speed up the hymn singing, which she did to some extent.

"Soon, the special Christmas services came along. For one of them, the organist asked it be publicized that she would have a period of preludes before the service. The publicity was gladly given, and many people arrived early for this special Christmas music. Durwin arrived at the church shortly after it had begun. When he entered the sanctuary he couldn't believe his ears. The music coming from the organ was, slow, low, and mournful, like a funeral. In fact, someone approached Durwin and remarked aghastly, 'Is this a funeral?'

"'Not supposed to be,' commented Durwin, 'but perhaps she is just warming up to it.'

"'She's had time already for that,' replied the other person. 'I don't know about this,' he said with abandonment and went to sit down.

"Durwin waited for some lively, joyful Christmas music to fill the sanctuary, but it didn't come. He began the service on time, and when after a greeting and prayer he announced the first hymn, he said very emphatically to the congregation, 'now people, we are celebrating this evening, so let's sing as though we are indeed celebrating—let's sing loud and lively and joyfully.

"The congregation sang the hymn just the way Durwin asked them to. The organist, after only a line or so put on more volume and speed. The experience set a new standard for her. From then on she had lively music, very lively and outstanding in fact, for the choir more especially. The hymns I will talk about later. She had caught on, and became a popular organist among the congregation. Both Durwin and Canda were pleased and happy about this, befriended her and socialized with her and her friends.

"At about the same time this organist came on stream, another woman came with her and became a member of Durwin's church. She told Durwin she had tried many churches to date in her lifetime, but had found no satisfaction in any of them, until now in this church she felt good about it. This made Durwin dubious about her past seeking and not finding fulfillment of some degree in any of them. Nevertheless, he had no reason not to accept her membership, so he did. She was well received by the congregation, and being a singer was a good friend of the organist, and close to her at all times.

"So here we have Durwin and his peaceful church; everything going very well indeed. We will see what happens to his church and to Durwin over the next several months, and how undisciplined pride and envy play havoc with it all.

"Let me first tell you about the supervision Durwin had in his second church of Terraprima. In this his second church in a different area altogether than that in which his first church in Terraprima was located, Durwin now had a different supervisor. This supervisor was not at all warm toward Durwin, spoke to him very little and in general kept his distance at church meetings of the wider area. One Sunday morning, however, he turned up in Durwin's church for worship. This was a custom of some supervisors. He arrived at the door barely in time for Durwin to greet him before getting into the procession that began the service. The supervisor, by his own request was left to sit in a pew and worship with the congregation. This was no problem at all to Durwin. He conducted the worship as usual, with confidence and reverence.

"The sermon, however, was on the topic of living victoriously, even under adversity. At a point in the sermon toward its ending, Durwin emphasized that with God's help, and by God's Grace, life can indeed be lived victoriously regardless of adversity.

"At this point the supervisor noticeably tossed his head high into the air. This, as you know, is a custom of some people everywhere. In Terraprima you see it more often. There mind-games are played more frequently than in most places; so much so, as a matter of fact, that it is a way of life there.

"Durwin could not help notice this toss of the supervisor's head that morning in church. It could be taken one of two ways; either positively, indicating the supervisor liked the sermon and its assurance, or negatively, indicating the supervisor did not like the sermon at all, especially coming from Durwin who had been put through so much adversity with this denomination, and now daring to preach about living victoriously.

"Either way Durwin knew he had a worthy sermon as always. Regardless of what this supervisor, who had till now been so distant from him, thought of his sermon, Durwin had his own self assurance. He had had sermons published with a quality publisher and had been asked for more. He had also previously been published in area newspapers for special church occasions, and had received very positive response.

"After the service ended that morning, the supervisor mingled with some people for only a few minutes, then casually and cooly gave Durwin a brief handshake, and was on his way, without comment either positively or negatively."

Albin came quickly with his usual type of remark, "I'm wondering if the supervisor somehow knew that Durwin had a sermon on that particular topic for that day and showed up because it may be an opportune time to somehow put him down further."

Collin responded with his usual caution, "Albin, there were ways that the supervisor could know beforehand the title of Durwin's sermon for that day and be riled up about Durwin daring to preach such a sermon after all the denomination, including the hierarchy, has done to set him back. Otherwise it could have been a coincidence—quite a coincidence, but nevertheless just that."

Owen commented, "If that head toss was meant to be negative, I would say it was a supervisor's duty to remain behind and discuss with Durwin what was wrong with the sermon. Likewise, if the head toss was meant to be positive, there could have been, at least, an encouraging comment at the time of the farewell handshake, if not indeed a favorable discussion on it."

"Its the mind-game all right, no comment at all from the supervisor," added Brett.

"Yes, it is the mind-game indeed," affirmed Collin, "and negative at that, as you shall see by the very next incident I tell you of."

"Tell us quickly," said Donna, perking up in her chair disgustedly, "what cruelty is coming now?"

Collin continued, "Since arriving at this second church, Durwin had been having some discussion with various church officials about the drastic cut in salary he had been handed out at the time of his move to this second church. Shortly after the visit of this cold, cold supervisor, Durwin received a letter from him stating that his salary would be cut down even more; to the salary level of a beginning minister on his first year in the ministry.

"Durwin returned a letter of protest and rejection. He already had several years of experience in Terraprima. He had many years of experience in Secundaterra where in many ways the church generally was away out ahead of this denomination in Terraprima; much more progressive, tremendously more cosmopolitan, and more socially literate. He now told the supervisor he would rather return to Secundaterra than accept such unjust treatment. He asked to be informed whether he would receive at least the minimum salary in accordance with his total number of years of experience in Secundaterra and Terraprima combined. If not he would make plans to return to the church in Secundaterra. He never received a reply. However, neither did he hear any more about the matter of taking the lower salary. As it was though the salary he was now receiving in his second church was still far, far lower than he had been receiving in his first church of Terraprima, which in turn was lower than his Secundaterra salary.

"In time, with more of their mind-game experiences behind him, Durwin would come to his own conclusion that the whole matter of the supervisor's visit, the head toss, and the following attempt at the further reduction in salary, was a crafty attempt to destroy Durwin's self confidence. It was the same game as is often used in spousal abuse cases - break their confidence. If it had worked on Durwin, it would have been only a matter of time before they pushed him down still further. It was becoming obvious from here on they didn't want him to go back to Secundaterra. He knew too much about them. They wanted to wear him down and out where he was.

"Durwin's only other brush with the supervisor was at a large gathering of the wider church at which the supervisor spoke. Durwin and Canda attended together. After the program there was to be a reception line by the supervisor and his family. Durwin and Canda knew they wouldn't be welcome at that part of the event. They started toward the parking lot, as did some other people as well.

"A well respected senior minister of the area, who according to Durwin's knowledge was unaware of the intense politics of Durwin's situation, spotted the Lawtons leaving and moving quickly toward them, sincerely invited them to remain for the reception line and refreshments to follow. The Lawtons now had little choice but to remain, rather than appear to be uninterested in the wider work of the church, or seem to be unsociable.

"They reentered the large hall and stood in the reception line. The supervisor was there, standing tall and immaculately dressed, next to him was his wife who was first in line. On the other side of him stood his grown children, mostly inappropiately dressed, looking tacky and red necked, as the vernacular would say, and ill at ease in their greeting of the Lawtons. As the Lawtons went through the line, the supervisor gave each of them a quick, cold handshake without speaking, then looked quickly away from them towards the next in line, reaching out to them with greeting and warmth.

"The Lawtons proceeded through the remainder of the line, with smiles and warmth toward the supervisors family. Most of them practically shrivelled up and were not at all sociably capable. These family members would not know anything about the Lawtons, but they simply just shrivelled at the site of such people of caliber. They had no idea of how to respond to, or behave with people they deemed to be a cut above themselves.

"In the second year of Durwin's term at his second church, a new supervisor came on duty over Durwin's area. Early in his tenure as supervisor, Durwin and Canda attended a large gathering over which the supervisor presided. His main message to the gathering was essentially his platform and the approach he would take toward the church as a supervisor. Speaking what amounted to a lot of left wing theology he set himself up in a very uninspiring manner as a champion of the poor. This was okay as far as it went except there was no fresh outlook on the matter, as much of the remainder of the country was having. He also championed the ethnic minorties but left no place anymore for the well to do white majorities in the church. There was no emphasis on any other aspect of the churches' ministry; in fact it was as though none other existed. The majority of people there to hear him came away feeling there was nothing in the church anymore for them. They came away showing a sad countenance, and expressing remarks to the effect that the church we have worked so hard to build up does not include us any more. Likewise, the early newsletters written and sent out by this supervisor carried much the same message of social bias commonly carried by the church, but with little or nothing by the way of inspiration for those who had been successful in life and who had for years been the foundation of the local churches.

"Durwin and Canda attended regularly and faithfully the meetings over which this supervisor presided. He was less than friendly towards them at all times, as though he was afraid of them and nervous in their presence. The Lawtons were very familiar with this scenario in Terraprima by now, other clergy nervous in their presence, afraid of them.

"For example, at one meeting during which the supervisor presented a new plan of action for local church committees, there was a period for questions and answers. The Lawtons were sitting to the far left of the supervisor, on the edge of the gathering. Durwin put up his hand as did several others. The supervisor chose people to whom he would answer, from all over the gathering except the left side, where he refrained from looking. His head turned to the far right, but not to the far left, where Durwin and two others held up their hands.

"After considerable time, ten or fifteen minutes, the supervisor had no choice but to answer the questioners on his left side, they being the only three left with hands up. He answered the other two first, then obviously reluctantly, he looked Durwin's way, cocked his head up as the signal for Durwin to speak. There was no comment for Durwin, such as, 'yes, this person here,' or 'yes, Durwin, your question,' as he had done for the others' just a cold, very impersonal and rude cock of the head into the air.

"Durwin asked the question, 'what method would you suggest for us ministers in the pastorate to get the contents of this meeting down through and accepted by the rank and file of the congregation?' It was a logical question, because, as Durwin knew by now that getting the rank and file informed and active on anything new was a major task.

"The supervisor nervously stumbled over his garbled, undecipherable answer. Then ended it with 'oh well, its very clear cut you know, just tell it to them as it is.' He very quickly brought the meeting to a close.

"Durwin and Canda continually tried to be friendly toward this supervisor, and his family when they were present. Several times they extended an invitation for them to come and visit. There were things they wished to talk to him about concerning ministry, they informed him. They also wished him to get to know them, and hopefully he would be able to accept them as friends in ministry. He never came, not until nearly two years later, when it was too late.

"Meanwhile the Lawtons seriously wondered by now, whether there was any place at all for them in the church at Terraprima. Through friends and connections in Secundaterra who had visited and saw for themselves what was happening to them, they received an offer for a large city church in Secundaterra, at just a little under double of what Durwin's salary had now been whittled down to. It was a church with which Durwin was familar, and felt he could do well with. The Lawtons pondered it seriously. Then one day Durwin met his former supervisor whom he had when a minister in his first church in Terraprima. In conversation, Durwin asked him, point blank, 'Why did you people place me in such a church as you did, after all my years of ministry, and after my giving such a good ministry in my first church here?'

"The supervisor, without showing any trace of facial or verbal uneasiness, which was in accordance with his usual character as Durwin was learning by now, answered, 'It's because you haven't officially transferred your membership into our church.'

"'Oh well,' replied Durwin, 'You know that with the immigration problem I couldn't do that before, but soon I will be able to do so.'

"The supervisor spoke no more, but nodded his head in what seemed to be an assuring manner. Durwin would later surmise that his nodding was just a part of the deceitful mind-game.

"Durwin knew, and the church supervisor had known all along also that Durwin could not yet cut off his connection with his church of Secundaterra. There were several times when he very nearly had to go back there due to his difficulties with the immigration department of Terraprima. However, church officials now made an appointment for him to appear before them where he would have to offer either to transfer his membership in or be left without a church. This placed Durwin in a quandry. He could not let go of his membership in Secundaterra, because he had not yet received his permanent resident status for Terraprima. It looked like he might have to step down in

Terraprima and return to Secundaterra to get a church and continue his career there.

"I might interject here," said Collin, "the only reason why Durwin would now have to transfer his membership is because his status with the Terraprima denomination had unknowing to him been changed and downgraded after he had been there considerable time. Even before his arrival in Terraprima he had been told of, and was given a standing of permanence with which he was satisfied, and which gave him all the rites of their own permanent ministers, except that he would not be able to vote on certain matters. Somewhere along the line all this had been mysteriously revoked and disappeared from view, without Durwin being informed or consulted on it.

"At the time of this most recent quandry with church and immigration, Durwin had been told three months previously that his permanent resident status would soon be coming. He had more reason to believe now that it really would. Nevertheless, he had also been strung along on the matter for nearly five years. He could not take a chance on it until it was officially secured. He decided he would go to the meeting expressing his desire to transfer in, but asking for a little more time to see if the immigration department would come through with his papers. However, on the night before the meeting, Durwin received a phone message from the friendly woman at the immigration department that finally his permanent resident status had been granted and that the papers for it had been mailed to him that day.

"With that assurance Durwin attended the meeting with church officials the next morning. It was a strange meeting. Five church officials were in attendance to interview several people. Durwin awaited his turn by socializing with some of the others to be interviewed for various purposes. As he appeared before the five they met him with a 'good-morning', and shaking of their heads, all five in concert. Durwin almost laughed, yet he knew it was something serious on their part. *What are they up to now?* Durwin thought to himself. Obviously it was something that had been planned, for all five of them did the silly head shaking so harmoniously. Durwin gave them a moment to express themselves in words that might have some bearing on the head shaking. None came.

"He then explained to them that his permanent resident status had come through, and that he was ready to set in motion the procedure to terminate his connection with his former denomination in Secundaterra and place his membership with this his present denomination of Terraprima. He insisted that he be placed on the salary scale as an ordained minister with full credit for his years of service, including those in the Secundaterras. This would be as he had been offered before moving to Terraprima. If it were otherwise now he would not transfer. They informed him they would let him know in a few days whether he was to be accepted. One of the church officials present also told Durwin that he didn't have to do anything himself regarding the transfer. They would take it from there. The C.E.O's secretary would set it in motion and initate contact with the denomination in Secundaterra. This seemed very odd to Durwin. However, by now he was used to odd things happening in this church.

"More than a week passed, and Durwin heard from no one on the matter. He then phoned one of the five church officials and asked whether or not he was to be officially accepted into the denomination. She replied unenthusiasticlly that he would be accepted into the denomination at Terraprima with full recognition of his standing and years of service in his previous denomination at Secundaterra.

"Concerning Durwin's original membership standing given when he first decided to come to Terraprima, he thought they had been generous enough in the first place in giving him partial membership, with which he was satisfied. But they had taken it away unknown to him, and gave him a lesser standing. Now they gave him full membership for which they had previously told him he was not academically qualified, and which standing was still not necessary as far as Durwin was concerned. Durwin was of the opinion that, among other tactics, it was done to cover the official who had told him the phony reason as to why he had been appointed to the meager out-of-the-way place of his second church.

"The phone call just mentioned was the only word Durwin ever heard on it. There was no official acceptance or welcome either by letter or by recognition at any meeting, nothing whatever. Durwin was beginning to sense with certainty now that they didn't really want him, but they didn't want him to go back to Secundaterra either. However, being a person like us here in this group, he was used to being not wanted, and it no longer bothered him. He would see it through and find out how they would deliver on a better church for him now that he was in full membership of this denomination.

"A little later, thinking the C.E.O's office had by now effected the transfer, Durwin, with his inclination towards proper decorum decided he would write his former denomination affirming his action to transfer to the church in Terraprima. He also thanked them for all their thoughtfulness to him in sending him newsletters and other communications by which he was able to keep up on events and happenings. It seems that it was because of this letter from Durwin, that they removed his name from the rolls of the church in Secundaterra.

"There has never been any visible evidence that the denomination of Terraprima had ever had any contact with the denomination in Secundaterra concerning the transfer. Of course, in keeping with the tactics of belittlers, that could be easily blamed on a person of relative insignificance, the C.E.O.'s secretary. The church of Secundaterra apparently acted because of Durwin's letter to them, and consequently they removed his name from their rolls. The result of this removal was that an important door had now been shut to Durwin. It would not be impossible, but very difficult for him to return to the church of Secundaterra if he had to; there would be a lot of red tape. As far as Durwin was able to ascertain amid the shroud of head-shaking secrecy in which he was now enveloped, the church of Terraprima did nothing official to effect a transfer, except to have his name placed on their roll, which they could have done any time previous."

Owen spoke, "I am anxious to know what kind of church was offered to Durwin after the supposed transfer."

Collin laughed and said, "There is good room to be anxious about it, Owen, but I will ask that we adjourn for this evening, and I will take care of your anxiety about it next week."

"I expect there will be some more anxieties and concerns to replace those about immigration and membership that have now been taken care of," replied Owen.

"Guaranteed," affirmed Collin.

The group members and Dr. Eldren agreed to call it an evening. There would be the usual gathering at the coffee shop.

CHAPTER X

The following week the support group met as usual, same time, same place, and by now no longer surprised that there is more abuse and gross mistreatment in store for the Lawtons.

Collin Seldon continued with his presentation on the Lawtons in the church of Terraprima. "They offered Durwin a church in accordance with the game I previously indicated they had been playing for decades, the better but worse game I will call it. It was a larger congregation; that was its good point by which they could claim, if necessary, that it was an improvement. This church they offered had nearly twice the congregation. However, the salary was the same as the much reduced salary he had, after a struggle, retained at his second church. Geographically it was even more isolated than his second church. He would have more than twice as far to travel to visit hospitals, nursing homes, and attend ecumenical events. Yet there was no travel allowance. Canda would have more than twice as far to travel to her employment. Under these circumstances she would have to buy another car much sooner than planned whereas the old one would last considerable time under more favorable circumstances. The whole set up would spell financial disaster for the Lawtons.

"Furthermore, they would have to practically kill themselves to make anything worthwhile out of the environment there. The church building was dingy and musty, a hazard to health in the Lawtons opinion. The parsonage, also dingy and musty, would be disheartening to say the least to a couple who liked and were used to bright, cheerful surroundings. The carpets also smelled badly of cats and their excretions. It was a place for a young, healthy and physically strong minister to flex his/hers wings and gain basic experience in ministry; not for a couple for whom it would probably be their last church before retirement. The congregation also had a reputation of quarreling, so they were told by a source knowledgable on the matter. Durwin knew he would have no support from the hierarchy in dealing with that and the many other matters that obviously needed attention.

"Durwin turned down the offer for these and numerous other reasons. He then wrote a letter to the church official who had told him of his reception into the church. He explained to her the necessities they needed in an appointment to a church in order to have a proper retirement later on. One of these requirements was that they be placed in or near a suburban industrial area where there was satisfactory employment possibilities for Canda in office and secretarial work.

"The Lawtons had been planning carefully for their retirement for many years. This denomination of Terraprima had played havoc with their plans, and the Lawtons were now giving them a chance to set it right again. Surely they would respond to such a reasonable request, was their opinion.

"The next offer of a church would have had the Lawtons accepted it, placed them in a far, far more isolated place than ever. If one would take a map of the whole church area and search it in detail, one could not find a place further removed from places of employment for Canda. The house, if one could call it a house, they would have to live in was reeking with mold and mildew, and with water actually running in through the basement walls. The Lawtons' furniture would not fit into the house. The rooms were of much smaller than usual size, allowing insufficient space for the usual furniture one would use in an average house. The awkward stairway and narrow hallway would not allow their bedroom furniture to pass through. The Lawtons had, for some time, been gathering good furniture for their retirement home. They were not about to give it all up now just a few years from retirement, or, put it into storage for a long time where it would be at the mercy of an environment controlled sometimes by careless people. They turned down this offer also.

"Quite noticably there were new ordinands being place in far better and more central churches than was being offered Durwin. The church official responsible for these offers was behaving toward the Lawtons as though he was doing them a great favor by offering them even these churches, each of which were of the 'better but worse' type as I call them; that is there is always at least one thing better about them, but on the whole they are much worse than the *victim* previously had. Again I say, the church official behaved as though he was doing the Lawtons a great favor. He was the 'stooge' the 'nice' guy doing the dirty work in the front line with a smile on his face while leading them down the garden path to destruction."

"As I have said before, the stooge was betraying the Lawtons with a kiss," remarked Leo.

"Same thing," added Owen, "imagine a *Christian* practicing that kind of infamy, when Jesus himself was betrayed by it."

Albin Anders, the younger member of the group spoke up, "I've been bursting to ask a question, Collin, but hesitated to do so because of my reluctance to border on paranoia in my thinking. But now I must ask it."

"Go ahead," replied Collin, "you're among friends here."

"The way I see it," said Albin determinedly, "first, there was what looks like a coincidence in the timing of Durwin's immigration papers coming through just in time for him to be able to accept a church transfer. I am, however, prone at times to wonder if it is a connection rather than a coincidence. It's obvious," continued Albin, "that the church didn't really want Durwin, but the way I see it, they didn't want to let him go either where he might succeed elsewhere, so they were keeping him in bondage so to speak till they could wear him down and out. So my question is, did the church carry any weight in the government whereby they could have arranged for his papers to finally come through at the appropriate time?"

Collin kindly smiled and replied, "That is dangerous thinking Albin, but in my opinion it is okay to think that way until you have thought a problem through. Then when there is a lack of concrete evidence to support your thinking, you have to put it aside as not definitely so. In this case, many Christians would believe it was Providence that caused the two events to happen simultaneously. I believe in Providence that way myself in many instances. But to answer your question as to whether the church carried any weight in government, I think there are individuals in the church who carry weight with individuals in government, where, I would add, the law is not being transgressed. Let me give you an example: a church had been fulfilling faithfully its obligations to the Income Tax Department in sending in the employers portion of employee deductions. But the Department had been, in error, crediting them to another church in another part of the country. Meanwhile they were threatening this church in question with legal action and confiscation of property, eventually including personal property of members and minister. The minister and a local church official tried for months to have the error corrected but to no avail. Finally, the minister wrote a letter to a high church official explaining the problem in detail. The problem disappeared immediately. There was never another word about it. So the church could and did have connections when it wanted to.

"Then again," continued Collin, "if some mind-game playing belittler, somewhere, someday, had a harmful connection concerning you and your business, it would be very detrimental for you to accuse that person of such unless you had tangible evidence to support your claim. There are people who would see you ruined, destitute in the street, or branded for life as paranoid before they would admit they were interfering with or harming you in any way. That, after all, is part of the game they play. And they would love to keep us guessing at it to wear us out."

"Are there people in the church who would go that far?" asked Albin, wide eyed.

"Oh yes, I think so, and know so," emphasized Collin. "There are people anywhere and everywhere, who if they could get away with it, would do so. There are many belittlers who are not mature enough to think ahead to the end result. All they see is putting you down at the moment, and from moment to moment to hold on to their undisciplined pride and placate their envy. But there are others who are very calculating indeed and know full well what the end result might be for a victim. They derive a sense of power from contributing to that end result. This in turn helps the belittler to feel stronger and better than the belittled. A sense of power keeps them feeling on top."

"So," said Albin, "in this case I have brought up, it is conceivable to be a possibility that the church arranged to have Durwin's immigration problem solved at a crucial time in order to keep him in Terraprima."

Collin chuckled, "You are putting me on the spot here before Dr. Eldren, Albin, but yes, it is a possibility."

"So, if I keep an open mind on such a matter in case some day some concrete evidence does come into the picture, then that is okay?" asked Albin.

Collin replied again, "Provided you don't let it wear you out, and provided you don't let it become a general way of thinking for you, so that you become a totally suspicious person, I would say that is healthy." Then to Dr. Eldren, "If you wish to state otherwise, Dr. Eldren, I won't be offended."

Dr. Eldren seemed at ease with the situation. "Your questions and statements Albin and Collin, are sufficient for now I would say, and once the story is complete, we will take plenty of time to explore it more fully."

Collin continued with the story. "While all this was happening to the Lawtons, Durwin continued to faithfully attend the wider church area meetings of various sorts. He knew now that by transferring his membership he had been taken in, not received or welcomed in, but taken in, in the vernacular sense of the term.

"At this particular point in time, Durwin hadn't yet had return contact with anyone in his denomination at Secundaterra to know for sure that his name had been removed from the church roll there. He was now hoping against hope that it had not, and he would consider returning to Secundaterra. He already had two offers of a church there, from people who knew him, but who didn't know he was having trouble in Terraprima. They just wanted him to come and be their minister.

"So Durwin tried to telephone a person he knew in a church area administration office of Secundaterra, to explore in a preliminary way the possibility of his returning to Secundaterra. The person he knew, and felt he could talk to humanely was no longer in that office. Another person whom he knew not as well but who was a person who knew all the rules and regulations, took the call. In the conversation, Durwin was informed, much to his disappointment that he was no longer a minister of that denomination. His name had been already removed from the rolls. On the spur of the moment Durwin thought of telling this person by phone, the details of his predicament, and ask if under these extreme circumstances the action could be reversed or annulled so he could remain on the rolls of his former church. But then he thought differently.

He figured, rightly or wrongly, that this person was the type to most likely stay with the rules to the letter.

"At the time, this was a grave disappointment to Durwin. It wouldn't be impossible for him to be re-established in his former denomination, but as I said earlier, it would entail a lot of red tape. However, in only a short time he would recover from the disappointment and decide to pursue his battles of life from the ground on which he presently stood.

"In the interlude, soon after this call, which was also soon after the first offer of the disappointing church, Durwin attended an area meeting. I guess disappointment was still showing in his face at this time, which was unusual for him, being such a positive person. At the social gathering over coffee prior to the start of the meeting, Durwin was talking to another person who was revealing to him how attempts were made by the hierarchy to pressure him into taking churches with substandard conditions, including housing, and how some friends came to his rescue with support.

"As they were talking, the supervisor and one of his accomplices stood a short distance away gazing at them. The accomplice remarked aloud and contemptously to the supervisor as they both gazed at Durwin, 'look at those eyes, just look at those eyes this morning!' Durwin could tell the remark was aimed at him and that it was a part of the intensifying negative attitude towards him. However, Durwin was becoming more fully wise to them now. He quickly pulled himself out of his downward trough that morning, and from then on continued to live victoriously amid a sea of belittling. He was becoming more certain that he had few friends, if any, among the total administration of the church area; also that he had some friends among the rank and file, and they were being careful and sometimes silent in their support of him. Occasionally and unsolicited he heard stories from them of unfair treatment. They trusted and confided in Durwin.

"Shortly after Durwin turned down the offer of another church, the new supervisor changed completely his tactics toward Durwin, becoming openly harsh, even hostile at times toward him. Durwin didn't let it shake him down, but kept inviting him for a visit and a talk.

He didn't come, nor did he invite Durwin to come to his office for an interview.

"Durwin did telephone this wayward and difficult supervisor one day to talk to him in an attempt to prick his conscience and appeal to his better side. In the telephone conversation, Durwin emphatically stated that since he had now transferred his membership into this denomination, he had, by doing so, placed his life and career in their hands, and they now had a responsibility toward him to treat him well. As usual there was no conversation from the other end; just a faked, sentimental type of 'Oh-h-h-h-,' which was really a mockery considering the type of treatment the supervisor had been giving Durwin to date.

"In this same telephone conversation, Durwin made a further attempt to appeal to any better side this wayward supervisor might have. He explained to him how, having lived in Secundaterra the greater part of his life, most of his retirement benefits to date would be from that country, and would therefore be subject to the exchange rate discount which presently had become very unfavorable. He explained further, his necessity to earn as much Terraprima retirement benefits as possible. The only response from the superivsor was a cold and uncaring, 'oh, oh.'

"When Durwin first moved to Terraprima, and even before he had moved, he was very aware of this exchange rate on his Secundaterra pension funds. He and Canda had made careful inquiry of Terraprima government and church pension plans, and calculated very well, that they could make a go of it considering the salary and total monetary support they had first been given to come to Terraprima. But as you will remember, Durwin's salary had now been cut drastically at the time of his move to his second church in Terraprima, with attempts to cut it even more. The cut greatly affected his pension accumulation in Terraprima. In the event of a large increase in the exchange discount of his Secundaterra pension, Durwin and Canda could be hard pressed in their old age if they were to remain in Terraprima.

"Now with Durwin trying to appeal to the human side of his supervisor with this potential problem, he was met with no conversation except a cold and curt, 'oh,-oh.' There was no one else to whom Durwin could appeal. After writing a letter to another high official of the administration and being snubbed on it and after receiving dubious offers of 'better but worse' churches from the smooth guy with the smile on his face, the front man, the stooge, and after time and again been shunned in his approaches to the C.E.O. and now receiving nothing but a meaningless 'oh-oh', Durwin was in a state of isolation in his relationship with this denomination of Terraprima. Isolating the victim is one of the chief tactics of belittlers so that their victims will have no one of significance to tell his side of the story to.

"Without spending too much time on this supervisor, let me tell you of one incident that illustrates how no matter what Durwin did, he would be put down by this wayward character. At the next meeting after the phone call I just mentioned, there was a meal served. Durwin purposely sat at the same table and directly across from the supervisor. The same accomplice as I mentioned before as having remarked negatively about Durwin's eyes, sat next to the supervisor. They began a conversation with each other as to how they could speed up the process of a series of group meetings. Durwin joined in the conversation, suggesting that the area senior ministers be asked to help by each one conducting a group. They looked at one another, but as usual there was no comment to Durwin. In a short time, however, Durwin's idea was put into action. Senior ministers would conduct the meetings, with the supervisor floating around from group to group in a supervisory and consultative manner.

"Durwin was invited to chair one of the meetings, an unusual happening for sure. In his former denomination, with its different polity and organization, Durwin frequently chaired meetings of this and similar sort. He was very familar with it. He knew he could perform the task well without even trying hard. However, he would put his best into it, as he did with any task, and he would conduct the meeting using his own good decorum, together with his years of experience in such matters. At similar meetings in the Secundaterras, Durwin recalled at this time, the church for whom he was conducting a meeting quite often expressed the desire for him to be their next minister; remarking frequently, 'that's the best meeting we have ever had,' and the like. That could not happen here, Durwin knew, because of a different procedure of placing minister. Nevertheless, he would conduct the meeting in his usual effective way, without show or pretense, but also with confidence and self-assurance.

"The first meeting Durwin was requested by the supervisor to chair was for a medium size church with a minister typical of many of the belittler type of that denomination in Terraprima; lacking in self confidence, over-sensative, pouty, and, in order to supposedly defend himself in all these his own shortcomings, a belittler; not a powerful, overbearing type of belittler, but nevertheless a belittler, as I said, the pouty, sulky kind.

"Durwin began the meeting by drawing attention to the printed agenda and report after seeing that everone present had a copy. He quickly noticed the pages of the report were not numbered. This could make it awkward for the members to refer without loss of time to any report that may be discussed through the course of the meeting. To remedy this Durwin asked the members to follow him through the booklet, each person numbering the pages in their report as Durwin called them out and numbered his own copy. Everyone seemed pleased to do so, except the minister that is. His mouth dropped very noticably and his forehead became a bed of horizontal wrinkles, as if he was about to cry. Durwin went straight ahead with calling the content of each page and giving it a number.

"As the procedure continued through to about the half way mark in the booklet, and as Durwin called the content of a page and gave it a number, someone in the group responded, 'Perhaps you have missed a page.'

"Durwin, without a ruffle, calmly asked the group member to call the pages in that area of his booklet. When he did, Durwin responded, 'okay, there is a page missing in my booklet. I'll just make allowance for it with the numbers. The minister of the group looked needlessly mortified. In an attempt to reassure him, Durwin remarked calmly, 'it's no problem, It happens all the time in a report of this kind.'

"The minister's face dropped all the more. 'I've got some extra pages; here take this one,' he said, as though some drastic crime had been committed against him.

"Durwin thanked him for the copy, fitted it into his booklet, and before he had a chance to continue, the minister, with a quivering voice brought the attention of the meeting to the first item on the agenda and began to give a report on it. As he did so, the members half listened to him and continued to number their pages themselves. Durwin let the matter go. He knew he was dealing with babylike gross immaturity; the 'I want my own way' kind.

"Before very long, the supervisor, now circulating from group to group, appeared on the scene. He stood beside the minister who talked to him privately. Durwin, sitting at a table on the other side of the room could not hear what was said, nor did he try to hear. As their conversation continued, however, the supervisor began looking daggers at Durwin, and did so each time he was present during the remainder of the meeting.

"For the remainder of the evening, in order to avoid the fuss of open confrontation, Durwin allowed the minister to call attention to the various reports according to his own desire. This was something the minister could not have done had a supervisor been conducting the meeting. However, Durwin still largely conducted the meeting, first by telling from his now numbered pages where the participants could find the report at hand, and also mediating the discussion, calling for voting, and for attention to the next topic, allowing the babishly mortified minister to name what the next topic would be, thereby giving him the sense of control he obvious felt he had to have. All those present at the meeting showed pleasure at the way Durwin handled the meeting, difficulties and all. Only the minister and the supervisor showed displeasure.

"Together with several other senior ministers, Durwin was later scheduled to conduct another similar meeting. As he prepared to leave his home to drive to that meeting, he received a phone call from someone at the church where the meeting was being held, asking him why he wasn't there already. Durwin replied, 'but the meeting is scheduled to begin two hours from now.'

"'The time of the meeting was changed,' came the response, 'didn't you know?'

"'No, nobody told me,' said Durwin.

"'Well, you can't get here in time now. The meeting is about to begin. You may as well stay home.' said the caller.

"'I will stay home,' agreed Durwin.

"At a ministers' gathering some time later, a friendly senior minister assured Durwin that he was not at fault in missing the meeting. He showed Durwin his appointment book. 'See,' he said, 'I had the time of that meeting noted here for 6:00 p.m. It was changed to 4:00p.m. and neither was I notified. I found out accidently about it from another minister. If you need help on that anytime let me know and I can verify it for you.' Later, however, when Durwin spoke to the supervisor about it, the supervisor coldly, and angrily blamed Durwin by telling him he could have double checked on the time of the meeting.

"'I had no reason to double check,' replied Durwin. The supervisor responded only with a cold glare.

"A little later a notice came to Durwin of another group of such meetings. In the typed letter from the supervisor, the time of the meeting was doubly underlined in red. It could be anybody's guess whether the double underlining was meant to emphasize the time to Durwin, as though that was needed, or, whether the supervisor was angrily or otherwise correcting himself. This time, however, Durwin did not depend on the supervisor for the accurate time of the meetings. Some hours before the stated meeting time, he phoned the church where the meetings were to be held, obtained the time of the meetings, and the time of the worship before the meetings. He was present in plenty of time.

"This time the meetings were held in a very large church where the core of the governing body of the congregation were obviously not belittlers. A small group of these people of faith from this congregation gathered early around Durwin during the fellowship and coffee period before the worship and meetings, stayed with him through the worship, and again associated with him closely during the refreshments after the meeting. Being genuine people themselves, they knew a genuine person when they saw one, so they had taken to Durwin right from the start.

"It is noticeable," said Collin, "this is similar to what has happened to me, and to Durwin, in Secundaterra many, many times, and nearly always with a request that we be their next minister. However, these people in this Terraprima church would not have the occasion to witness Durwin in action. Some other minister would be conducting the meeting of their group. Durwin would be conducting a meeting of a group from another congregation meeting in this church, as were several groups this same evening."

Owen Winslow interjected, "Having taken to Durwin so well that evening, wouldn't these people later make inquiries about him to the powers that be, with the idea in mind that he might be able to be their minister some day?"

Collin replied, "I have information that such things as that happened to both Durwin and I in Secundaterra. Whether it happened concerning Durwin in Terraprima, we have no way of knowing. Even if it did, it would be down played most emphatically. The powers that be of this denomination of Terraprima were belittlers of the worst kind, and Durwin and his career were slated by them for destruction. There is no way such an inquiry or request would get past the belittling hierarchy. In addition, Durwin had no opportunity again for contact with the friendly group of people after that evening. He would never be able to ascertain from them whether they pursued an interest in him or not."

Collin continued, "Now let me tell you about the group meeting Durwin conducted that night. It was a group from another congregation, led by a young minister who had been educated, not in the usual local theological seminaries that most of the ministers there had attended. Rather, he was a graduate of one of the nations outstanding, and most renowned universities. Even at that there was no pretense about this obviously genuine, high caliber, down to earth, open minded truly Christian person. The many hang-ups so predominent in the clergy of the area were not present in this person. He was a delight to work with. The meeting went wonderfully well right from the start. The parishoners present openly showed delight with Durwin and his handling of the meeting. There were smiles of approval, and nothing but pleasant response. They too were obviously free from inferior hang-ups. Obviously this was a case of minister and parishoners as near perfectly matched as can be.

"Then the supervisor appeared on the scene and began immediately to put his hang-ups to work. With a severe scowl on his face he began to glare his eyes at Durwin in an oppressive and hostile manner. Durwin ignored it and went on with the meeting as before. In time a question was asked concerning the correct parliamentary procedure on a matter in the local church. Out of courtesy to his superior, Durwin turned to the supervisor to see if he would care to answer. The supervisor's scowl intensified, so Durwin answered the question himself, knowing he had a legitimate answer. Immediately he gave the answer in the affirmative, the supervisor growled a loud and emphatic 'no-o-o-.' It put a damper on the otherwise jolly meeting. In the weeks that followed, Durwin made inquiry about the validity of his affirmative answer that night. He found that he was not only right, but that the supervisor afterwards tauntingly admitted to others that Durwin was right, and that he knew it at the time."

"Just putting Durwin down in hatred for no reason at all!" remarked Brett Culver.

"Just another ploy in the attempted destruction of the career and consequently the real person of Durwin Lawton," added Collin, "and he did it quite openly, knowing that Durwin by now had no support and therefore no recourse in this church area."

Albin's curiosity became stirred into action again. "But he was doing his belittling so openly now. Why would he dare do that? Were there not some good people there?"

Collin replied, "One reason, because he thought he was doing a brave and wonderful thing for everyone—putting this smart guy down beneath the lesser gifted minister. It is such a regular practice in this part of the denomination that he thought everyone would automatically be delighted about it. Also, most probably he had hoped to infuriate Durwin and make him out to be a bad tempered and therefore a bad charactered person - the opposite of what he really was. It was another attempt to destroy a fine person, and furthermore to openly make a sport of it."

"A sport!" exclaimed Albin in astonishment.

"Yes," responded Collin. "Eventually, in their over-confidence, they came to think they had Durwin cornered, with no way out from under their oppression. So their belittling came to be more open, and in mockery, with jeering, cheesey smiles and 'oh-oh's and all. It became an open game with them.

"Incidentally, that supervisor went on to even higher office. His field of action diminished greatly under him.

"Durwin suspected by now, and rightly so, that they were trying to discourage him from any acitivity that would make him known in the wider church; to drive him into obscurity, so that very few if any would question about him, whatever may happen to him in the end."

"Savage beasts," exclaimed Leo Aidan angrily.

Collin concluded, "that ended the series of meetings for that year. Durwin wouldn't be around for similar meetings the following year."

"Did they kill him?" asked Leo with perturbed excitement.

"No," replied Collin, "he was too tough for that. They would harm his career and affect his life greatly but he would survive them. Stay tuned.

"Previously I have told you," said Collin, "how Durwin made a peaceful and vibrant congregation out of his second church, and how well his plan worked. Now I will tell you how that accomplishment was torn down by hollow undisciplined pride, envy and the ensuing rivalry of others.

"Remember, there are two new people in popular positions in the congregation now who were not there during the implementation of Durwin's seminars and peace project, the organist, and her singer friend.

"Under the purposely obscured prodding, nudging and tactful suggestion of Durwin, together with her own abilities, the organist was now producing lively music that was extremely well liked by the congregation. The new singer had sung spectacularly a few times some numbers she could handle real well. This endeared her to the congregation, even though, generally, there were many shortcomings in her singing abilities. Her volume was her foremost asset. The organist and the singer were popular. This pleased the Lawtons as it fitted so well Durwin's plan and project for a peaceful, progressive church. They were pleased that the organist and singer were so popular and they accepted it with delight.

"It is astonishing to know, however, how difficult it is for many people, belittlers in particular, to accept the popularity of others side by side with their popular selves. Durwin and Canda had till now been both well received by the congregation. This was to come to an end. Signs of rivalry appeared. The organist in particular, popular though she was, could not allow for the minister to be popular as well; as though there wasn't room for both of them in the church.

"The first sign of trouble Durwin detected, was when the organist had some special music at one of the regular church services. Remember that till now Durwin and Canda had been good friends with the organist, visited her in her home, had her into their home, gone places with her and her husband, eaten out together with them and so on. Now after this special music, Durwin, asked her to come out from the organ and be acknowledged by the congregation. She came forward and they gave her a big hand. Then Durwin, as he had at times been doing throughout the congregation reached forward to give her a peck of a kiss on the cheek. She blocked the kiss completely by tipping her head on the side as though she had to protect herself. Durwin knew that it was a way women had of preventing them being kissed lustfully on the neck. There was absolutely no need here for that defensiveness.

"Durwin always practiced good decorum in public and private. Besides, in the culture in which Durwin had previously lived many years ago such behavior as kissing lustfully on the neck was not a practice, so such behavior was foreign to him. Obviously, the organist had had experienced otherwise. It could have been transference that had made her respond as she did. Her needless defence was an embarrassment for Durwin at the moment. Later attitudes would indicate that most likely it was a public slur made during a reverent church service. Only a crude, warped and twisted mind could do so. Much worse, it was the beginning of the belittling of the Lawtons by a group of people in the church, all ardent friends of the organist by now.

"The organist soon became an authority on all church matters, contradicting the minister on decisions that should be no concern of hers. As the choir and prelude music became more and more lively and exhilarating as Durwin had originally encouraged, the hymn music and consequently the hymn singing was slowed down to a drone, thus reflecting adversely on Durwin's worship services, while making her part of the services look good.

"Soon the organist was protesting two special events that Durwin had planned, and which was his place as minister to plan and promote. The one, involving the choir she squashed altogether. Another, having to do strictly with a special worship service, she protested vigorously. The date had been set for it for a long time. Now, with her rivalry increasing, she protested that she wanted to have a special musical service on that date. Durwin overcame her on that one.

"The organist planned a musical service for a later date and left Durwin out of it altogether, inviting another minister to participate. The power and control aspect of this person was becoming obvious. By the way, this other minister, out of courtesy, or out of delayed courtesy I should say, asked Durwin shortly before the service, and long after it had been publicized, if it was all right with him that she be there. Durwin, in the interest of avoiding an open fuss for which he would be blamed anyway, gave his okay. Please note it was a woman minister that the organist invited. In a minute or two I will tell you why this is noteworthy in the story.

"At an opportune time, Durwin had a firm talk with the organist. I say firm, and it was firm, and straightforward, but not angry nor anywhere near it. During this interview she tried to imply that Durwin didn't know anything about church music. Durwin responded that in seminary, courses in church music were required; that he wasn't a musician but he had a knowledge of church music, and also some personal opinions as to what options he preferred in his church. She became defensive and pointed out that Durwin had as one of the hymns on a Sunday far removed from Easter, the hymn, 'Rejoice, the Lord Is King.' 'That hymn is never sung except at Eastertime', she snapped with a demeaning snarl.

"Durwin calmly, but firmly replied, 'In some hymn books that hymn is indeed placed in the Easter section of the hymn books. In other hymn books it is placed in other sections. In the hymn book of this denomination it is placed in a section other than for Easter.'

"'They have made a mistake,' she snapped defensively. 'That hymn is meant to be sung only at Easter time. There are a lot of mistakes in that hymn book.'

"Durwin had no desire to argue with her. Quietly but firmly, and more with a tone of pity now, he said to her, 'you have disagreed with many things in our denomination over a period of time, the most notably of which was your denounciation of women speaking in churches, when I was having women participate in the worship with me. The Bible says we are not to, was your reasoning. I told you that the Bible was open to interpreting, and I offered to discuss it with you. Your reply was 'no interpreting is necessary on that one. It's as plain as can be in the Bible. Women shouldn't speak in church.' Then a little later, without my knowledge, you invited a woman minister to speak at your special music service. How am I supposed to take that? Was it wrong for me to have women of the congregation participate in the worship services, and okay for you to invite a woman pastor to participate, and without my knowledge at that? Now you don't wish to accept our very popular hymn book. Think it over for yourself. Perhaps you shouldn't be in this denomination, perhaps you are not compatible with it.' She didn't reply to that, and soon the conversation ended.

"Shortly after that conversation, Durwin received notice that a particular board of the congregation wished to have a meeting to discuss Durwin's ill treatment of the organist. Durwin went along with it, and at the meeting he saw the warped character of a belittler at bay and in full action; the orgainst, not mature enough to deal with the truth about herself and others. She accused Durwin of addressing her in their private conversation in a frighteningly angry manner. Actually, as I told you, Durwin had talked to her calmly but firmly. She accused Durwin of telling her she shouldn't be organist of this congregation. Actually, as I told you a moment ago, Durwin had questioned whether she was compatible with the whole denomination. Then she told the board that Durwin had accused her of bad-mouthing him throughout the congregation. There was no grounding for that one in their private conversation at all. However, it did ring a bell in Durwin's mind. Considerable time previously, when Durwin and Canda had been good friends with her, or thought so, she had told the Lawtons of trouble with the minister of a previous church in which she was organist; he had among other things accused her of bad-mouthing him throughout the congregation; he was troubled by her popularity as organist, she had told the Lawtons at that time. Here now was a likewise scenario.

"Durwin looked across the table straight at her and asked politely, 'and you can sit there before me, looking straight at me, and say what you are saying?'

"She became jittery, 'I'm telling the truth,' she said with a quiver, 'I am a legal secretary, I am telling the truth.' Actually, there was no training for a legal secretary showing on the resume she had submitted to get the organists position."

Leo quipped again as he so often does, "She's implying that legal secretaries always tell the truth, but ministers of the church don't necessarily do so!"

"Something like that, I guess," said Collin, "another quirk of a warped and twisted mind.

"Durwin could sense that night that many key people on the board, who had previously supported him fully in his ministry and peace project, and had been friendly toward he and Canda, were now alligned with the organist. He also knew that if this matter exploded into a major problem, he had absolutey no recourse in the church at large. If he was free to do so, he could have handled the whole matter himself very effectively. However, he knew right well that whatever he did, it would be knocked down by the area church administration some of whom would surely be called in by local church officials, and whose custom it was to appease the lay people of the church in an attempt to halt the decline of membership. Actually, in the long run, it was having the reverse effect. It was a cause of the decline. Regardless, it wasn't Durwin's way.

"Furthermore, in the case of belittlers bringing down a minister who is no longer in the good graces of the church, either local or otherwise, members of the hierarchy at times conspire in a 'birds of a feather flocking together' sort of way to bring down their victim. Durwin knew this could happen to him now. He calmly left the meeting that night, and braced himself for what might happen. In time it came. In the meantime he carried on his ministry sincerely, energetically and peacefully as always.

"Let me tell you now," said Collin somberly, "how six people, some of them belittling power and control persons and others their followers, aligned themselves against Durwin in one of the most cruel deeds in Christendom since the Middle Ages. Let me describe these six characters and their hang-ups, and the axe they eventually ground to try to bring down, discredit and belittle Durwin in order to placate their own most warped and twisted thinking. Of course their end result would be to pacify the pied piper organist who had maneuvered much to usurp popularity away from Durwin and Canda, thinking in her most wayward mind that she had to do so in order to be popular herself.

"First, there was the singer, a pied piper associate by now. She was a dental assistant in secular life. Some months before the aforementioned trouble appeared on the horizon, it became time for Durwin to have a regular dental check-up and he began looking for a dentist in the area of this his second church. He previously had some very exceptional work done by a dentist in the area of his first church, a very good dentist indeed. That dentist had told Durwin that generally he had a healthy mouth. 'Your gums are good and your teeth are exceptionally hard and strong. You are of good hardy stock,' he told Durwin, 'if you had received present day kind of dental care back in your earlier years, you would have very few problems now.'

"'Times were different for me then,' said Durwin, as he expressed appreciation for the dentist's understanding way.

"For Durwin to continue with that dentist now from the area of his second church would mean a lot of long distance travel. So Durwin asked the singer about the dentist for whom she worked. She gladly recommended him as a good dentist, and furthermore a good Christian man, a member of such and such church of another denomination. Durwin was impressed and in time went to him for a general check-up.

"This dentist's office was located in a very well appointed strip mall on the edge of a well to do suburban area. The mall itself appeared well designed, tastefully decorated and impressive to the eye. It gave Durwin a sense of going to a trustworthy place. The entrance and waiting room made up the store front section. These were nicely furnished. Behind that lay several rooms; what appeared to Durwin when he got to see it all, more than was needful to keep one dentist going no matter how many technicians and assistants he had, and he had several. This dentist had all the latest in decoration, equipment, and the space to put it in.

"However, Durwin seldom saw any more than one other patient besides himself at any one time he was there. Furthermore, when a patient didn't turn up, the dentist would be near frantic and instruct his staff to get someone else in to fill the empty time. Call this one, or that one, or so and so, he would command. This happened on several of Durwin's appointments, until he got the impression that they were people the dentist was working on extensively and continually. Durwin also formed the opinion, almost from the beginning that in setting up his dream clinic, much too elaborate for the relatively small population of the area, he had over-extended himself, and was now having a difficult time keeping it going at sufficient capacity to meet his financial requirements on it. At that time though, Durwin had no reason to suspect shabby dental practices.

"On the first appointment there was the usual X-rays, examination, and cleaning, at which time Durwin told the dentist that he and his wife had dental insurance. He asked that if there was much work to be done, on both he, and his wife who would be coming to him later, could he keep it within the limits of their dental insurance benefits for that calendar year. If other work was needed, they could where possible wait and have it done in the next calendar year. The dentist responded by more or less murmuring, 'there are two or three fillings there that need attention. We'll see after that.'

"Durwin went for another appointment and had two of these fillings repaired. The third on the other side of his mouth had to wait for the next appointment. Between these appointments there was a special musical service at Durwin's church, which the dentist attended, having been invited by the singer. At this event, as well as conducting the service, Durwin preached a brief, five minute or so meditation of his usual high caliber.

"At his next dental appointment, the dentist curiously questioned Durwin about where he had studied theology, how long it took him to prepare a sermon for each Sunday, whether he prepared far ahead of time, and if he did a lot of reading. His whole attitude, as well as his questions, was one of strange curiousity. Of course Durwin wasn't able to answer him much, only a word here and there as the dentist worked on his teeth.

"The appointment lasted longer than usual. It wasn't until later when Durwin received a copy of the bill sent to the insurance company, that he realized the dentist had filled, not one, but three more teeth that day, and furthermore had him make another appointment for the following week. In the meantime, Canda had started with the same dentist and was having her teeth done.

"The dentist kept making further appointments for them both to keep coming back for more and more fillings, until they had gone nearly a thousand dollars over their insurance allowance for the year. They phoned the singer about it at her home. She brushed it off lightly and said the dentist would probable write it off seeing it is for a clergy. No such thing happened. The bill kept mounting up. By this time they were beginning to sense there was something radically wrong. They told the dentist themselves they could not have any more work done. His response was that Canda needed two more fillings and that would be it. Canda knew indeed that she had two cavities in need of filling. She could feel them with her tongue, and indeed it was these cavities that had prompted her to go to the dentist in the first place. She had been wondering when he would get around to fixing them. So she went to him again, and instead of repairing the two that needed it, he did fillings on three other teeth, not two, but three."

"He was playing a mind-game with her," remarked Brett somberly.

"Yes, he was," replied Collin, "and with Durwin as well, and ruining their teeth in doing so."

"Ruining their teeth?" questioned Donna Coyne.

"Yes, weakening them for the present, ruining them in the long run. It wasn't until the Lawtons moved out of Terraprima altogether and went to other dentists that they learned what this dentist had done. On a large portion of their teeth he had drilled away the silver fillings they had done in previous years, which had become hardened more and more over the years, and with a little touch up here and there would have lasted them a lifetime. Not only had he drilled them away but had made the drilled holes much larger than they were before, then filled them all with inferior plastic fillings. He did this work, and a lot of it at that, without asking for or being given permission. He just conned his way along until the Lawtons got wise to him.

"A friendly dentist to whom the Lawtons went much later told them that the plastic fillings, instead of hardening and becoming stronger as silver does, deteriorate over a relatively shorter period.

"Much later, another dentist told the Lawtons that the plastic filling material had, since that time, improved; also it was now used to color match one's own teeth. That no doubt is factual about plastic fillings. But the silver fillings the Lawtons previously had were in top condition, not giving trouble, and mostly positioned so that they did not show much. Had they been asked about their replacement they never would have had it done. An expense like that just for cosmetic reasons would not appeal to the Lawtons or their budget. Later on another dentist, mature and honest, affirmed that indeed silver fillings are much more sturdy and permanent than plastic fillings.

"Someday, Canda and Durwin may have to get these teeth all filled again. Next time, after more drilling, the cavities will be large indeed, and consequently their teeth will be weakened for life, if indeed they don't lose their teeth altogether.

"There were other wierd things about the Lawtons' encounter with this dentist. Both of them had their teeth cleaned by one of his leading assistants, other than the singer by the way. Previously they both had had their teeth cleaned at regular intervals so there was really no need for extreme measures to be taken at this time. However, these cleanings were like something they had never experienced before. It was as if the assistant was trying to clean their teeth away in too far past the gum line, at times by pushing the gums back beyond their normal position over the teeth, and, at other times it felt as if she was actually cutting the gum away a little in order to get at the tooth further in. They both came away from that event with considerable blood in their mouths from bleeding gums, and most of the tartar and discoloration still left on their teeth.

"Even though that was early in their associations with this dentist, they should have suspected something. But they had been so assured by the singer about this *Christian* active church member dentist, that for the longest time a suspicion never entered their minds. It was only much later, when living outside of Terraprima, that they were told by other dentists and doctors that their gums were very noticably receding. Previously to that they had always been told that they had healthy gums, and Durwin in particular, a very healthy mouth regardless of the fact that in his early years he had what would now be considered inadequate dental care. Most dentists, the older ones more surely were understanding of this.

"There was yet another strange twist or two in this experience. I will describe some of the work the dentist did on Durwin during all these filling sessions. Durwin's jaw teeth, on either side, were so strong and hard he could bite the hardest food, even hard candy without any problem of chipping or damage of any kind. There were only a couple of small silver fillings in them and they had been there for years without damage.

"Without even asking or notifying Durwin, the dentist drilled out a jaw tooth on one side and filled it with a plastic filling. On the other side, after creating a sense of urgency through innuendos to his assistant and remarks about how urgent it is we get this other tooth done today, he drilled out a jaw tooth on the other side and did a root canal on it. There had been no pain or inflamation or soreness, or sensitivity to hot or cold with this tooth. Nevertheless he did a root canal on it, and as Durwin was to find out from another dentist outside Terraprima, 'he shot something in there to fill it, I'm not sure what!.'

"So there was both sides of Durwin's mouth weakened as far as teeth go. But this sinister and greedy dentist didn't intend to stop there. Again, without consulting Durwin, the dentist made inferences to his assistant, 'It is now urgent that we get at the next phase now that the teeth, calling the jaw teeth by dental names, have been prepared. By this time, Durwin, very trusting person that he was, was getting wise to the way this dentist operated. He pulled his mouth away to get the dentist's fingers out of it. 'What is this next phase you are talking about?' he asked.

"The dentist immediately looked guilty, but quickly recovered his composure. With a brazen face on him, and as if it were the natural thing to be doing, he said, 'we have prepared your jaw teeth, and now we are going to prepare to fill in the gaps you have on either side of your lower jaw. We can now put a bridge on each side, anchoring them to these teeth we have prepared.'

"'How much will that cost?' asked Durwin.

"Instead of giving a total figure, which would have been quite large, the dentist gave the figures for each item in the process separately. These were much smaller figures, but Durwin added them up in his head on the way along. He was good at that kind of thing.

"'Just under four thousand dollars!' exclaimed Durwin.

"The dentist nodded his head.

"Durwin said, 'You didn't ask me if I wanted that, and I don't. So if you're finished with the teeth I already have, then that will be all for now. I am satisfied with the teeth I have, and besides, I can't afford any more.'

"'We can arrange credit for you,' he pushed further.

"'No thanks,' replied Durwin, 'I seldom do business on credit.'

"The dentist pulled a mocking face on himself as if Durwin were being outlandishly big in himself for protecting his self and his finances; a typical shakedown from a belittler and a con man. Durwin ignored it and left soon thereafter for the last time."

Brett shook his head in astonishment. "So he weakened Durwin's gums, then weakened his jaw teeth. Then he was going to anchor a bridge on to these weakened jaw teeth on each side at a cost of approximately four thousand dollars. When these weakened teeth later would give out and have to be pulled, it would have to be all replaced by a larger bridge or plates, at a cost of another four thousand or more, and on it would go over a period of years with Durwin paying it all out on credit with no doubt sizeable interest. Finally after it had cost him many thousands, Durwin would end up with full dentures."

"Right," agreed Collin, "and it would have placed him under financial stress for years to come. By the way, the very good dentist Durwin had in the location of his first church had spoken to Durwin about the option he could have of the bridge work, but told him he would be okay without it if he wished. So Durwin had been familiar with the matter before hand and therefore now felt assured in rejecting it.

"Also by now he was wise to the unethical tactics of this dentist. It would take some time, a move away from Terraprima, and appointments with other dentists before he would know the full extent of the damage done to his teeth and gums, and be able to piece the whole story together.

"It is ironic that the first dentist, that is the one in the area of Durwin's first church was a non-Christian, but he treated Durwin, a Christian minister, wonderfully well. The second dentist, near Durwin's second church was supposed at least to be a Christian, yet, he treated Durwin, a Christian minister, in a barbaric manner."

Owen spoke, "Collin, I'm beginning to see more clearly how they play a very sophisticated mind game in Terraprima. What I am wondering is, would that dentist have done such a thing to the Lawtons except that he somehow knew that Durwin was marked by the church for belittling and downgrading? If Durwin had proper acceptance and standing in the church and had many friends in it, my opinion is the dentist would not have dared to do such a thing to him."

"That is good observation," replied Collin, "and you are not paranoid in thinking that way. The dentist, a seasoned belittler and a crafty con man, upon getting to know Durwin, could easily have surmised that a person of Durwin's qualities being placed in an obscure out of the way church as he was, had no doubt been slated by the powers that be for downgrading and ruination. He could easily have been reassured of this on his visit to Durwin's church.

"Although Durwin hadn't become fully aware at that time that his second local church and the new supervisor were swinging against him, later reflection would establish this. So the dentist on his visit to the church, and more especially at the fellowship and refreshment hour that followed, could have easily gotten a nod toward Durwin and/or a shake of the head, a squint of the brow or a contemptuous push up of the lip, concerning Durwin, from a belittler in the congregation. Or, on the other hand this may all have been already accomplished through the singer and perhaps confirmed during the event at the church. However it was, it would give the belittler dentist a sense that he was safe in picking on the Lawtons. It is another example of the conspiracy of sorts."

"It really is a conspiracy of a sort, isn't it," commented Donna Coyne, "a conspiracy formulated by birds of a feather flocking together and carrying on in the same manner, playing the same game."

"Furthermore," added Collin, "in different places Durwin lived after that, he dealt with a variety of dentist, most of whom could detect from examination of his mouth that he had been mistreated. To some belittling dentists, this was an open opportunity to treat him likewise, and try to make plenty of money off him while doing it. Durwin was now a marked man among dentists, as he was in many fields. This added to the conspiracty of sorts. However, now being the wiser, through trial and error he was usually able to come up with an honest dentist wherever he was.

"Note, I said, through trial and error," added Collin. Let me tell you now of the experiences Durwin and Canda had with another Terraprima dentist, this time in a multi-staffed dental establishment.

"In time, after moving away from what I call Terraprima, Durwin shopped carefully around for another dentist for a regular check-up and cleaning of his teeth. He came across a dental establishment located in a building that had originally been built as a dwelling. Obviously it had been someone's lovely home at one time until commercialization of the area had taken place. Now it was a multi-staffed dental clinic, immaculately and tastefully kept. What attracted Durwin most of all was that inside on the walls there hung several tastefully chosen pictures with an appropiate Bible verse on a brass plate underneath each of them. Thought Durwin, people who profess their religion openly are usually sincere about the way they practice it. This may be the right place for us. He made an appointment for himself and then went home to tell Canda he had found a religiously oriented dental clinic that appears to be almost too good to be true. He felt almost sure now this was the place where he and Canda would get good dental care. It wasn't!"

The group members looked wide eyed. Gilda Emerson expressed the wonderment of the group when she asked, "What in the world could go wrong in such a place as you just described?"

Collin raised his brow and smiled pitifully, "Just let me tell you!"

"For heaven sake please do," replied Gilda curiously.

Collin went on with the story. "There were several dentists working in this clinic from which Durwin was assigned to a young woman who, it turned out, was originally from Terraprima. She led Durwin to a room and had him sit in the dental chair. She was a woman of very plain features including hair style and dress, perhaps not having come beyond her grade school years in the latter two. But she seemed, seemed at least, very nice in character, being very friendly towards Durwin, her personality bubbling all over him as though he were an old friend. Then she left the room saying she would return later after X-rays were taken.

"After she left Durwin reflected for a moment, *She's laying the friendliness on a bit thick. I hope it is sincere. Perhaps, being young and not long in the profession, she is a little over eager to please her clients.*

"Then another young woman came into the room. Her face immediately dropped into hostility as she sized Durwin up and down, 'I'm your dentist's assistant', she said in a cold, somewhat frightened manner.

"'Nice to meet you,' replied Durwin cheerfully, trying to loosen her up to put her at ease.

"She just went on arranging the dental equipment without further conversation. When she was ready, she took a whole assortment of X-rays, with the only comments being the verbal instructions necessary for the work being done.

"She doesn 't like me, Durwin thought to himself, *but she is only the assistant. The dentist may be okay.*

"When the dentist reappeared on the scene, she was overly friendly as before. Durwin figured that was better than not being friendly at all. The dentist, after some probing around in his mouth, informed Durwin that he had no cavities, but that he should have a crown placed on a previously treated tooth. Durwin agreed. In fact a previous dentist he had visited in the search for a reliable dentist, had told him the same. Work was begun on this tooth immediately, and at the next appointment, the crown was fitted in place. In doing this work, the young dentist showed she was very skillful and at ease with her dentistry. She did a marvelous job. She also talked very confidently and in a knowledgeable manner about her work.

"Before leaving that day, the dentist lastly informed Durwin that his teeth badly needed cleaning, and she would like for him to make another appointment to have it done as soon as possible. The appointment was made for Durwin to return the following week. He had expected all along that he would have his teeth cleaned, but was surprised by the urgency the dentist had placed upon it. He had gone only very little overtime since the last cleaning.

"At the next appointment the young dentist cleaned Durwin's teeth harshly. It seemed at times as though she was grinding them away. Durwin, now being more seasoned to Terraprima belittlers, began to have doubts, but he couldn't be sure yet. There were all those scripture plates on the walls. *Maybe, overall, this is a good place,* he thought.

"After that visit Durwin wasn't due to go back to the dentist for another six months. However, before much time had elapsed he felt some discomfort in one of his top front teeth. It was one of several teeth that years ago had been accidently damaged and on which he had had a very high caliber cosmetic bonding job done. Now he suddenly realized the bonding was much thinner in places, not only on the tooth in which he sensed a mild aching, but on two others as well. *Maybe the bonding is -wearing out after all those years,* he thought.

"So with the one tooth aching at times, he made another appointment and according to their custom he was assigned to the same dentist. Durwin told her in just what part of the tooth he was feeling the sensation. She probed around, checking it over, then said, 'it needs a small filling.' She then asked Durwin if he would need a needle for that. Durwin replied that he didn't know, but she could try without it to start. She began drilling near the gum line, on a different part of the tooth altogether than where Durwin was finding the foreign sensation. Durwin told her about this, and she replied emphatically that Durwin was wrong, the filling was needed right where she was putting it. She continued drilling until just to the point when Durwin was finding discomfort. Then she ceased drilling and quickly put a plastic filling in place.

"Over the following weeks Durwin experienced that this whole operation made no difference to the aching feeling in his tooth. He would later, again through trial and error, find out that the tooth had no cavity at all. The pain was from stress on the tooth caused by the continual poking, probing and hooking to clear it of food that very frequently was catching between it and the next tooth due to rough surfaces between them.

"In the meantime Canda had also been to this dentist, and had asked to have a particular tooth filled. The dentist froze the area with a needle. Then she put a new filling in an already repaired tooth nearby, leaving the cavity unfilled. Canda didn't notice what had been done until after the freezing had gone from her mouth. Some time after, with another dentist, she had to have a root canal procedure done on the tooth that should have been filled.

"Durwin observed that there were many genuinely nice people working at that dental clinic. The place, as far as Durwin could tell, was of high caliber. He met mainly well cultured people there. Generally the place seemed very good. He reasoned that the young dentist and her assistant, were not typical of the place as a whole. Somehow they slipped in there as part of the team. Durwin had observed that this young dentist could handle her dental equipment really well. She was not awkward, indeed she could be very capable when she wanted to be. Durwin is of the opinion that she didn't want to be capable when it came to his and Canda's teeth, except briefly at first to con them into having confidence in her. She was a belittler of the first degree, crafty and experienced at the game.

"As long as the Lawtons didn't catch on to her she would continue to do damage. When they began to show signs of catching on, she began the process of driving them away. She now showed a disinterest in them simply by her attitude and tone of voice, but also with the commonly used cover up and driving away tactic, 'I'm only young, and you never know what I might do.' It is a ploy often used as an alibi intended to cover belittlers against any suspicion that they have done their misdeeds intentionally to harm.

"In driving their victims away, belittlers feel in no way defeated. On the contrary, they are fulfilling another of their devious deeds. They love to get their victims on the run, especially after they see they can do no more damage that they can get away with, and can get no more money off them."

Collin interjected another aspect. "It may be debated whether this dentist was a belittler in the sense of the term we are using, or she was just a crafty person making more work and consequently more money for herself. She may have been the latter also, but by her tone of voice and actions which eventually showed through clearly, as they usually do, Durwin was convinced she was mainly a belittler, out to harm people she perceived to be 'big shots' who are a cut above her.

"The dentist's employer would not likely know much, if anything, about the game. This young dentist could have done excellent work on many patients and establish a satisfactory reputation for herself. The few people of caliber that came her way she could mutilate as much as possible before they dropped away. Most of her patients would speak well of her. Furthermore, there is no precedent in society for exposing the tactics of such people. The owner of the clinic may not have had any idea of such a concept as envious, hateful belittlers, Terraprima type. It has not been brought into the open. Durwin, had he complained, would likely have been brushed aside as a hard to please crank. Or again, if by chance her superior is just as crafty, the old 'she's only young and inexperienced' trick would come into play, and Durwin may be labeled *chicken* for letting a young woman upset him."

Donna exclaimed, "How much hatred is there in such envious people that they would mutlate a part of a human body?"

"Plenty," said Collin. "It's a way of life for them. Whether it's your car or your body, it doesn't matter to them. They are envious of you and hate you and will try to bring you down when the opportunity arises.

"But let's look at what this young dentist could have been. She was plain in appearance, but even if she was downright homely, she could have easily compensated for it with a beautiful character and personality, for which by the way, she showed potential by her phoney friendliness. But in her envy and craftiness she also showed she had never developed a truthful and trustworthy character and personality. Had she done so, and also with being very adept at her dental work when she wanted to be, she could have been an all around top notch dentist. As it is she will remain on the lower levels, hating and belittling those she deems to be above her, including many of them who might have gladly given her the most expensive business."

Brett remarked, "And persons like that dentist could breeze through dental or medical school without obstruction, getting top honors in their studies because among other things, they were no imagined threat to anyone in the school, or in college before that."

"Right Brett," responded Collin, "and whether this dentist is a belittler or a crafty person out to make more money, your remark is one of the main points I wish to make in telling this story. The second is this: if you were to make that remark to the powers that be, especially to psychiatrists, they would say you are envious of her because you didn't make the grade through medical school. They would say similar of Durwin Lawton, that he was envious of the dentist, and that through projection he was seeing her as envious of him."

"I know," said Brett, "but that would be another gross injustice. I seldom stop to think about it, but sometimes I do experience disappointment, but not envy, hatred or bitterness. I wouldn't give them the satisfaction of letting those traits become part of me and ruin my character and my life."

"Well done," remarked Collin, as the other group members expressed similar sincere compliments.

Collin questioned Brett curiously, "Have you ever experienced serious depression because medical school didn't materialize for you?"

"No, not at all," replied Brett, "I never allowed time for that. When one door closed I went quickly on to the next door that would open. That is a part of my nature."

"Good," responded Collin, "I asked that because the psychiatrists of Terraprima who also happen to be belittlers, would try very hard to pin that one on you, as well as the projection bit."

Leo remarked, "What I see in all this is that the church denomination in which Durwin ministered in Terraprima, practices widespread belittling. Therefore, in effect, that church supports the kind of behavior these wayward dentists were getting on with, and that's absolutely criminal."

Collin responded, "It certainly does give the church there a lot to think about, doesn't it Leo?"

"More than I'd want to have on my conscience," replied Leo.

Collin added, "My technical knowledge of dentistry is limited, but I think I have told these experiences adequately to make the point. There are other stories of belittling dentists I could tell you, but they all play pretty much the same games. So I will get back to the main thrust of the story."

He then continued, "Seasoned belittlers in occupations other than dentistry have their ways of detecting the belittled also. After Durwin was hit with a large reduction in remuneration as he went to his second church, he had to, for sound financial reasons, keep his car longer than he usually would. This gave some garages and their mechanics the thought that if such a person as this is driving a car that old, he must be a big shot on the way down, so they push him down a little further by doing faulty or needless repairs and charging a lot for it. However, with care and searching around, and sometimes like a fugitive on the run, Durwin, with great patience, was able to take care of himself on this matter of car repairs. There are a lot of good garage owners out there, as well as opportunistic belittlers.

"Durwin got taken occasionally, as I have already told you, but on the whole he made out well. I tell this now just to point out how people like us can become marked persons at the mercy of belittlers. At the same time I wish to say that the tactics of belittler repair garages and mechanics should not be confused with poor workmanship and shabby business practices of those who just do not have good ability in the field. It should not even be confused with those who do unnecessary repairs just to make more sales for commission or other profit. These are all differently motivated phenomenon. Sometimes you may get a combination of two or more of them, but usually belittlers do their unnecessary and/or inferior work, simply to put you down. They charge plenty for it, because belittlers love your money. They get as much of a power trip out of taking your money, as they do in damaging your car and your person. You can usually tell they are belittlers by their personal negative attitude towards you."

"I understand what you're saying," said Donna. "My father and I have not been familar with the term belittler in this regard until our use of it in this group. However my father is very careful not to hire people in his car dealership who have a chip on their shoulder against well-to-do people, or big shots, as belittlers often refer to them."

"By doing so, your father is protecting his business from failure," assured Collin, "and the point I am making in all of this is that Durwin was now pegged by numerous belittlers as game to be put down. It was open season on him. The seasoned belittlers could detect this and push him down all the more, taking as much of his money as they can in the meantime. So Durwin always had to be careful."

"And the church in Terraprima, in principle, supports that kind of behavior!" remarked Leo, aghast.

"They do in principle," said Collin, "and they practice similar themselves."

Gilda perked up in her chair, "So in the case of the earlier dentist you told of in detail, here you have Durwin getting wise to the dentist, and he still has the singer/dental assistant in his church. How did he handle that?"

"Good question," replied Collin. "as I told you before, Durwin knew that if there was trouble in the local church, he would take the blame for it and somehow be put down all the more by the church heirarchy. He said nothing more about the trouble with the dentist to the singer or anyone else in the church. He went on with his ministry as usual, and as I indicated earlier, he didn't yet know the full extent of the dental damages done to him and to his wife Canda. Also, as I said earlier, they would learn that through trial and error with future dentists.

"The singer stayed on in the choir. Occasionally she attempted a solo, but could no longer sing well before Durwin, her voice noticeably breaking down to a quiver at times and her eyes dropping as she tried to sing some deeply religious numbers. This person will come into the story again later in a startling way. But before that, I must tell you about the other five characters, then bring all six that I mentioned earlier, together near the end of the Lawtons' experience in the second church.

"The second character I wish to bring before you now is the austere person to whom I referred earlier. From here on I will refer to her as the power person. You may remember how I described her as previously causing friction in the church, and siding with other difficult people, and how under Durwin's friendship she got over that and became a pleasant person to work with. In time she offered herself to do various jobs of work for the church. Durwin continued to treat her well and she behaved cooperatively—until the pied piper power and control organist's influence began to go through the congregation. Then she began to revert back and show symptoms of the old power person again. It would take considerable time for me to describe adequately, power or power and control people, their symptoms and behavior. I will define it more for you later. Suffice it to say for now they have a strong bent toward dominating and controlling persons and events in order to prove themselves to themselves—sometimes to prove themselves superior, and often using belittling to do so.

"This power person I am speaking of became a good friend of the organist. As the organist asserted herself more and more, so the power person reverted more and more to her old self. Now, she not only wanted credit for what she was doing, but was taking credit for some of the things Durwin was doing. For example, Durwin composed and had her type a letter concerning a project of the church. She typed it with very poor lay-out. In fact, there was no layout at all, just straightforward, all in one paragraph without even indentation or spacing or blocking. Durwin let it go for that time. At a meeting later on she spoke of this letter she had done for such and such a project as if it was her idea, compostion and all.

"Much later, when Durwin had another letter to be done, it was much longer and also much more important that it be precise and very well done as it would go far and wide in its distribution. Durwin had done such letters in previous churches, and one such letter early in his ministry at this second Terraprima church. Now he was doing another. He wanted it to be a first rate letter, so he had Canda do it. She was very much more experienced in this type of work and did a professional job on it. Word got back to Durwin that there was a big stir in some circles of the congregation about it. It seems the 'right' people couldn't take credit for it—a childish thing, yet causing a big stir in power circles.

"Then, this power person became nasty toward Canda as they sang in the choir together. Canda was a high soprano and known for years to be able to go two notes higher than most people. Many choirs in which she had sung gladly utilized this, having sopranos stand next to her so she could help them carry the singing. The power person was a soprano also, but when Canda would strike a note or two higher than her, she would now contemptously place her hand over her ear and frown. As time went by she and others made uncomfortableness for Canda in the choir. However, Canda had been singing in a church choir since before her kindergarten year, and was not about to be driven out now by the envy and ignorance of a belittling power person.

"This power person now flip-flopped at times between being friendly toward Durwin today, cold toward him tomorrow; approving of his work at times, and unreasonably critical of it at other times. Eventually, being good friends now with most people in the church, and taking up more and more with the organist, she turned away from him and eventually turned on him. As I said with the singer previously, so with this power person, I will tell you later how she comes into the picture again in a dramatic sort of way."

Owen commented, "It seems to me this power person was easily able to revert back to her old ways, and also align with the organist, because from your description of events, the organist was a power person too."

"Yes indeed," agreed Collin. "so when it appeared the organist was becoming the more popular one, the power person reverted back and aligned with her; looking after number one, as the saying goes."

"Desert one leader for another when it is expedient for self; to heck with the church and what they are doing to it," remarked Leo. "Such is the character of some people."

"We come now to the third person, whom I will refer to as the unstable person," Collin continued. "By her own admission she was pathetically abused during her growing up years, and now as a young to middle age woman, was still searching to find her true self by going to support groups, often more than one at a time. Durwin and Canda bent over backwards to help with her needs in their Bible Study group. By her own admission it was indeed helpful to her. At first Durwin and

Canda hugged her as they did the other women as each Bible study meeting started. But Durwin quickly cooled it all around when he learned more about her unfortunate past. He knew that transference could cause serious problems.

"However, this woman, almost always arriving late for the Bible study sessions, had what could be called a near ritual. She went around the whole group and hugged everyone. It was a nice thing to do, Durwin thought. Certainly, in order not to offend, Durwin responded caringly. The woman had a need to be loved, and don't we all. But Durwin was careful with her at the meetings, and even moreso elsewhere. He and Canda got along well with her and her family.

"In time there came a mild difference of opinion on a matter that to the woman and her family was a personal matter, but for Durwin it could cause ill feelings on the ecumenical scene at which Durwin always worked so ernestly to facilitate. Durwin and Canda visited the woman and her family in their home and took care of the item in an effective way. It was all over and all well, that is until at a later date when the tide had turned against Durwin it would rise again as a reason to put him down. I ask you to also keep this woman, together with the others, in mind for later in the story."

"I think I've guessed what it is that's coming later in the story," said Leo, in a more subdued manner than usual for him, "but please let us hear about the other characters before you tell us."

"Okay, that would be better," agreed Collin, as he went on with the story.

"The fourth woman I will call the unsuccessful person. Although she did have some success in her life it had not been continuous, as you will see. Durwin's early observations were that this young woman was in church mainly because her relatives were there. She was a family oriented person. Her activity in the church had been minimal. Durwin activated her from one position to another in church activity until she began to take personal initative in things, making decisions and being generally useful. After some time, a relative of hers thanked Durwin very appreciatively for his attention to this person saying, 'It looked to us at times as though she might become disinterested in the church and leave it, but now, thanks to you she is very involved and interested. You have kept her in the church for us.'

"At one particular time, this person devised, organized, and headed up a very worthwhile project. Upon its completion, Durwin, in the company of others, hugged her with proper decorum. It was the only time he ever hugged this woman apart from special occasions such as Christmas or Easter when he gave every woman a mild hug together with a greeting of the season, at the church door as they departed from worship.

"In her younger years, this woman had worked in a far away city, making a real good career with an excellent future. She left it to come back home and be with family; a valid reason in many cases. Back home, she took an inferior job to which she had to commute considerable distance. Meanwhile, she was always hoping that some day she would be able to go to another large city and reclaim her lost career, not realizing she could have a similar job quite near home although in a much smaller city and corporation. But big cities were dangerous now, so she was understandably hesitant about going to them.

"In time this woman's present inferior job was phased out. It was a time of recession and most types of jobs were hard to find. She was at home doing nothing, bored, and as someone told Durwin, she was practically 'going up the wall.' Durwin had two contacts in work similar to what this woman had in the large city of her past. One was a considerable but reasonable commuting distance away. The other was quite near home, and to which Canda could introduce her, because Canda herself was employed with the corporation.

"Durwin asked Canda to invite the woman to lunch in the area of her work place, which she did. Here was contact with a business quite near home, similar, though smaller, to the one the woman had left behind in a large city. There was even another one a little further beyond that, and another beyond that again, all within reasonable distance, and all, at times, looking for people with experience similar to what this woman had. She could see first hand what she had previously overlooked. A week later, Canda, by phone, invited her to lunch again. She turned it down coldly, and remained cold toward Canda thereafter. Durwin phoned her one day and offered to put her in touch with the other contact he had in similar business elsewhere. She informed him she was getting on to another job and wouldn't be needing it.

"As time went on, it became obvious that with this woman, and her many relatives in the church, there developed a festering feeling of animosity toward the Lawtons. The Lawtons could only assume from all later attitudes and innuendos that it was because Canda had a good position where this unsuccessful woman could have all along had the career of her heart's desire. She could have had a choice, either close to home or not far away, according as she could have chosen if she had seen the opportunity there. But she hadn't. Now that the career was open to her again, instead of grasping it, she harbored her undiscipled pride, envy and hatred and turned herself and her family and friends from the Lawtons. Envy, the most warped and twisted of human emotions, took proirity. This woman too, will greatly affect the Lawtons' lives as I shall tell you later."

Collin took up number five on the list. "This next person, I will describe as the lady-like woman turned story twister, accomplice, dubious leader, in order to be on the side of the newly formed clique of the church. For convenience sake, I will refer to this woman as the dubious lady.

"When Durwin first came as minister of this church, this lady was his most ardent and foremost supporter in his total ministry, including his D. Min. peace project. She was appalled at the friction and open quarreling that had existed in this local church in the years before Durwin's arrival and often openly expressed her disgust of it. She was delighted, simply overjoyed with Durwin's plans for a peace project, and when it got going, supported it with her influence, and her full involvement with readily volunteered time and work.

"With one exception, Durwin never hugged this woman except at the church door on special occasions, as I have mentioned before, when he either very lightly hugged and/or kissed on the cheek, all the women of the congregation. The exception was when Durwin and Canda had an open house at their residence and dozens of members attended. This was an interesting event that illustrates how well things were going with Durwin's congregation, this lady included. It was when Durwin's ministry was at its peak there. At this reception there was food, fellowship, and laughter—a truly joyful time. People came and left as they wished. As a group of people were leaving, and Canda was seeing them to the door, they were each hugging her with warmth and appreciation. Durwin was busy nearby, passing food around. He happened to look as the lady, later the dubious lady, hugged Canda. In fun, he called out, 'hey, have you got a hug for me too?' The people sitting around laughed. 'Of course,' said the lady, as she stepped back into the focus of everyone present, and gave Durwin a warm hug to the enjoyment of everyone present. It was all taken well and in fun at that time. Please keep this lady in the back of your mind for now."

"It is obvious now, what is coming later," observed Owen, "but I would suggest you continue on, and tell us the climax in your own good time."

"What characters!" exclaimed Leo.

"What total lack of character," said Brett, as if in correction.

With very little pause Collin continued, "There was yet another noteworthy lady of sorts. When Durwin first took up duties in this second church, he noticed that she and her husband attended church occasionally, but were not active at all in the congregation. Soon it became noticeable they were attending more often. Late one afternoon, when he figured the whole family was at home, Durwin visited this family. The husband had not yet arrived, but the woman and the children were there. The woman very openly discussed with Durwin their church relationships. She and her husband had in the past on occasion attended a few church administration meetings, but quickly dropped out again because of the almost constant quarrelling that took place there. While continuing to attend worship only occasionally, they otherwise remained on the periphery in their church life. She told Durwin how they were appalled at the continuous anger and quarrelling that existed; the participants shaking the fist at one another and all but coming to blows at church meetings. "After Durwin's peace project had taken hold and done its work successfully, this couple attended church more and more. The husband was a very busy person in other areas of his life. But in time Durwin activated this capable woman in more and more of the church activities. It affected her positively and she began to use her own initiative and skills in several areas of the church program. She seemed to take on a new awarness of her abilities in this regard, so I will refer to this lady as the awakened person; newly awakened to the value of the gifts and graces with which she could serve the church. Her husband, being very active in community and business work, had no more time to spare, except to attend worship much more often. Durwin and Canda became friends with this family, was invited to their home on some very special family occasions, and enjoyed their association with them in church and community matters.

"In time, Durwin started a planned program whereby lay people would participate more and more in church worship services, reading scripture and other parts of the service. This was after, unknowingly to Durwin, his acceptance there had now passed its peak in favor of the pied piper organist. Durwin asked the church board to have an extra microphone installed in order to have this lay participation from the individual choir members with minimum of movement and disruption in worship services. The installation didn't come, not until some months later when the organist asked for it for her purposes. Then it was readily purchased and installed.

"In the meantime, the awakened person, not in the choir, had already been introduced to participation in the church worship. She did her part well. Not only was it appreciated by the congregation, but it was doing something for the woman; inspiring her and awakening her all the more in enthusiasm for the church. It was a good all around thing, so Durwin utilized it to the full.

"Don't tell me this woman was to turn on him too!" remarked Owen.

"Yes," Collin simply replied.

The others shook their heads in near disbelief.

"There you have the six characters," added Collin after a momentary pause. "Next week I will tell you what they did to Durwin. It will complete my story of the Lawtons. For now it is near our usual adjournment time, Dr. Eldren. Should I terminate for the evening?"

Dr. Eldren agreed.

The group members showed a strong eagerness to hear the remainder of the story the following week. Meanwhile, they with the exception of Brett, decided to have refreshments at the Corner Coffee Shop before going home.

Brett, as he sometimes did, went directly home to prepare with his wife the next day's work for the family business.

CHAPTER XI

The support group met the following week to hear the completion of the story of the Lawtons in Terraprima. The group members were beginning to wonder already where their project would go from here. But first the life stories were to be completed this evening.

The meeting came to order, and Collin said, "I won't keep you waiting in suspense; let's move on with it immediately and see what happened to Durwin and Canda.

"Not long after the Lawtons tried to help the unsuccessful person to a career of her hearts desire, strange things began to happen among Durwin's parishioners. Some people were becoming outright cold toward Durwin and Canda. Others simply remained aloof from them as they had not done before. The Lawtons could tell there was something in the air. After between one and two months of this, an officer of the local church, called a routine meeting of the board without even notifying, let alone consulting with Durwin. The Lawton's knew then that something was radically wrong.

"In the meantime, the Lawtons, only a small number of years away from retirement now, had been searching for retirement property in one of two areas of the country they had in mind. The one area was about five hours driving distance, and on seveal occasions they had left on a Friday evening when Canda came off work, travelled to the area, looked at properties next day, then arriving back home Saturday night for church services on Sunday.

"Another prospective area they had in mind for retirement was a much longer distance away, so they took a remaining two weeks vacation due them to look at property in that area. When they returned from that two weeks away, their world was shaken severely, very severely.

"The morning after their return, Durwin sat at his desk putting things in motion for a day's work. The telephone rang. It was the supervisor whom Durwin had tried so hard and long for two years now to have come for a visit and to talk. He hadn't come, nor was he coming this time. In a nonchalant voice and uncaring manner, he informed

Durwin that he had been accused in his parish of sexual harassment, and that the whole matter would have to go through a process. The first step of the process would be to meet with the supervisor, and the C.E.O. to have the accusations read to him.

"'Who is the person accusing me?' asked Durwin.

"'There is more than one, there are two of them,' came the reply from the supervisor.

"'Will you tell me who they are?' asked Durwin.

"'We will do that when you meet with us,' came the reply, and a time of meeting at the C.E.O's office was then arranged, to which Durwin and Canda would travel together a few days later.

"At this meeting, Durwin was to learn that there were not only two, but six women bringing accusations against him. From Durwin's observations he surmised that the supervisor told him of only two women, not to shield him any, but because the supervisor himself was sheepish and guilty about it. His further involvement in the case later indicated to Durwin that he was also a whimp, a coward.

"Before long, the Lawton's also learned from supporters, that it had been talked around Durwin's parish and among the residents of the area, that Durwin was to be investigated, for approximately two months before Durwin had been informed of it by the telephone call. This explains all the estrangement towards the Lawtons, and the meeting without notifying him, that I mentioned earlier in this part of the story. It was common gossip around town long before Durwin had been informed."

"Is it not true that his denomination is known as a champion of justice?" asked Gilda in disgust.

"Oh yes," replied Collin, but justice takes on some weird twists and turns when it is subject to envy—the most weird and twisted of human emotions.

"Canda took a day off work to go with Durwin to meet with the supervisor and the C.E.O. There the accusations of each of the six women were read. The Lawtons were astounded at the sinister contrivances in the accusations.

"In actuality Durwin was a friendly, easy going, caring and affectionate person. The complaints now made against were no mild accusations. They made Durwin out to be not just a michevious rascal of some sort as sometimes people are, but a monster of criminal proportions. In the actions of the accusers we see the power of envy to warp and twist human minds into hateful, harmful, potentially devastating actions. This motivation I wish to continue to focus on in the story, so I will omit the details of the accusations, lest sex overshadow the major issues being explored by this group.

"In essence it was a scheme born out of pricked, undisciplined pride, envy, and hatred over Canda's good job, now joining forces with the power and control organist's cause in her popularity contest with both Durwin and Canda. No matter how these accusations were handled, if they were to stick, the Lawtons would be marked for life and become third rate or lower people.

"The accusers had their own way figured out as to how the matter should be handled. They were going to be *nice* about it. They asked not for Durwin's dismissal or anything like that, but that he receive psychiatric treatment for his supposed problem. How nice and *Christian* of them, especially when the accusations weren't anywhere near the truth! This contrived mode of handling it was their pseudo-psychological skills coming into play in competition with Durwin's natural analytical ability in the field of human behavior generally. Now that their envy and hatred towards him had been stirred they had to outdo him on that one too.

"Furthermore, Durwin says the accusations against him were constructed so as to show him breaking some of the church's most stringet rules on conduct with regard to counseling - the ministry Durwin had chosen to follow. He is of the opinion the accusers would not have the knowledge of church rules sufficiently to do this themselves. It appeared they had help from within the wider church area structure to do so.

"However, before I tell you about the process and stress the Lawtons eventually had to go through, I think I should tell you about another bombshell Durwin received. It was a letter arriving the next morning after the phone call about the accusations. We should explore this first because most of the inquiry process concerning the accusations came months later."

Collin continued, "The second morning after their return from vacation and after receiving the phone call about the accusations, a letter arrived in the mail with another shock; a letter from the dean of the seminary, informing Durwin that his Doctor of Ministry paper was not at all satisfactory, that his time had run out, he was finished with the seminary, and there could be no appeal. The letter had a few 'soapy' parts in it, such as sorrow and concern over Durwin's failure. The remainder of it, using fantastically high brow language, was an assessment of Durwin's paper. This assessment appeared to Durwin to be designed to have the effect of them vaunting themselves haughtily above Durwin; perhaps an additional device to belittle and bring him down. In contrast, Durwin had previously been steered away from using such highly formal language in his paper, all by innuendo of course, but by the dean who was now using that kind of language in his letter.

"Durwin made a protest on the time factor by telephone and was met with a scathing rebuke because of 'what you have written,' said so contemptously, one would think Durwin had done somthing terribly wrong. There was no 'soapiness' or sorrow in the phone conversation; just harsh, cold, and scathing, all the way through, in which, among other things, Durwin was told he already had had an extension of time, and could not have another."

Albin spoke up in his sometimes excited way, "Collin, I may be wrong but I see a connection here again between the seminary and the church denomination. After both of them being down on him for a long time, now they both come down hard on him within a day of each other. I make a connection between the two. Is this birds of a feather acting together as you have mentioned at other times?"

Collin replied, "You could be right or you could be wrong, Albin. My opinion is it is quite normal for you to have such a thought because such things do happen in the world of reality. Durwin is of the opinion that there is plenty of circumstantial evidence of a conspiracy type of connections between many of Durwin's various belittling antagonists. If there was enough common knowledge about the matter throughout society, and if it was ever taken up legally in an efficient way, I think it could be proven. Either that or there would be a lot of perjury cases. As it is we cannot say for sure, Albin, so we have to put it on the back burner as the saying goes—to the back of our minds. You cannot make a firm decision on it unless and until there is concrete evidence one way or another. So I suggest that after pondering such thoughts you learn to put them aside to await further tangible evidence."

Albin replied, "To borrow Dr. Eldren's words, your suggestion is well taken."

"Actually, Durwin had had no extension of time," Collin said as he continued with the story. "He had read all the extra books suggested to him by the mentor, and written his whole paper in less than four months. Another two weeks at most, to add more personal crituque to the chapter in which he had not had time to do so, and a minimum of time after that, just a day or two perhaps to correct errors in composition, would have completed the paper. During the less than four months of writing there were delays, not on Durwin's part, but, for example, at the end of April, Durwin wrote them a letter stating that he hadn't heard from them concerning chapters he had sent to them in early March. So you see the delay wasn't on Durwin's part.

"One specific reason they gave for not allowing an extension of time was that he had taken so much time getting his formal outline done and approved. Actually, the major portion of the delay in getting his outline completed was caused by the dean setting him on a search through more books looking for the meaning of analysis and analyze, as I mentioned to you before. To review again, an analytical mind has always been one of Durwin's major characteristics, according to the honestly discerning minds who know him. However, the seminary powers that be wanted to destroy that too. They set him looking for methods of analysis in books that had little or nothing in them on the topic. They never offered to tell him where in those books; just another ploy to set him reading and to wear him down. Finally, when Durwin caught on and simply brought the dictionary meaning before them, they glossed the whole matter over and accepted Durwin's dictionary application. That factor, together with two or three other minor matters, on which they also left Durwin to guess his way out on his own, delayed the approval of the formal outline by about three months."

Owen Winslow remarked, “I get the impression they didn’t teach, help or guide him in any way; only criticize mostly without correction, and let him find his own way out of it on his own if he could, and apparently he did each time.”

“Right,” replied Collin, “there was no teaching, no real mentorship, only a vague rejection of what was done, but absolutely no direction at all of how to make it better. Durwin was alone as far as constructive help with the paper was concerned. Worse still, with them he was up against a wall of blocking by seasoned and crafty belittlers. They had him on a treadmill that would wear him out, so they thought, but it didn’t.

“Both the dean and the mentor wrote final letters to Durwin rejecting his paper as unsatisfactory. Their criticisms revealed still more of the trickery of hardened, seasoned belittlers. They pounced on some of Durwin’s better skills and charactersitics, making them out to be faulty, even deceitful. Let me tell you of some of them.

“Durwin had well over one hundred quotations in his paper of as many pages, all numbered and noted with full credit given; an average of approximately one per page. That is on par with some of the best of books. Regardless, Durwin was accused of using the ideas of others without giving acknowledgement. If Durwin had done so it was quite by coincidence that any idea or ideas he had presented had been previously written by someone else. The mentor or dean could have quite easily brought these to Durwin’s attention, stating what they were. For Durwin to find them himself could lead to a life-long and endless search. Think how that would wear him out if he was foolish enough to be conned into it. Actually, Durwin had once previously brought to their attention how an idea of his had been used by a staff member of the seminary.

“You may recall that further back, Durwin told one professor that objective thinking had to be used with regard to the unemployed, and she later replied it couldn’t be done. Now they accused Durwin of too much subjective thinking.

“Another criticism implied that Durwin did not put enough of his own original thinking into the paper; still another one implied that he did not utilize the scholars enough. One implication was that he was quoting too much, another that he wasn't quoting enough.

"One seemingly favorable yet absurd and inaccurate comment was that Durwin had followed his outline satisfactorily. Actually, Durwin had been lured far, far away from his original outline, so much so that even if he hadn't previously given up the idea of publishing a little book from the contents of his paper, he would most certainly give it up now. As I said before, Durwin made no claim to being a scholastic writer, and had not the faintest notion of ever becoming one. He knew he was good at a narrative type of writing, and had previously been published with short articles and sermons and had always been asked for more.

"Durwin was told there was no depth to his paper. No one had ever said that about Durwin's writing before. Comparing it with the papers of other students of the seminary, to which Durwin had some access, it fared at least as well, at least. Actually he did a little later show his paper to a scholar more renowned than any of this bogus seminary's faculty. This scholar did not have time to read the whole paper, but he did read a considerable part of it. He was so favorably impressed that he found it difficult to put it down and get on to his next appointment.

"Durwin knew he had good things in his paper. He would challenge, anytime, any number of fair minded professors in the field to read it and see for themselves. Making allowance for the unfinished parts that would need only a little more time, he knew it was a good paper.

"The essence of what Durwin had in his paper was an analysis of the causes of so much quarreling, dissention, and abuse of ministers in many congregations, and how it was caused mainly, not by issues, but by power and control people. He also offered sound well thought out ways to counteract this and bring peace to congregations so they could get on with the rightful mission of the church. It was an honorable and much needed dissertation."

Leo Aidan, in a disgusted manner added, "They turned his paper down, but I'll bet your bottom dollar they used the information in it for themselves and their own work."

"You may be right," agreed Collin. "At one point they accused Durwin of copying some other person's work. If that was so they should have told him who else had similar work. Then he could have used it in his paper and given credit for it. But no such information was given. However, sooner or later, some of Durwin's ideas will appear on the horizon, under someone else's name, or, under no name except the wider church grapevine. It is not impossible to scab other peoples ideas, even if they are copyrighted."

"Mafia type gangsters!" quipped Leo.

Collin continued, "Early criticism, implied only of course, was that Durwin's language was too scholarly. Durwin then decided to use his own level of narrative type language that had always brought good results for him. There were no criticisms of this all the way through the writing of his paper. But after, the letters of criticism that came were written in very formal scholarly language indeed. Perhaps that is one of the things they think gives depth to a writing."

"Quite often all it is is scholastic snobbery," said Owen further.

"Recall also for a moment how it was generally acknowledged that Durwin had an exceptionally analytical mind. But the dean set him on a wild and lengthy search for the meaning of the word as if Durwin didn't even know what it meant to be analytical."

"This could be both confusing and demeaning, if a person would let it be so," remarked Owen.

"To make matters worse," Collin added, "the parishoners who had worked with Durwin and the project for his paper, and who had told Durwin of all the feuding of the past in this church, now denied there had been any such problems in that church, even though Durwin had most of their reports of it on paper."

"Sounds like one big mind-game to me," said Owen further, "and if anyone was willing to let it, it certainly would confound, confuse and wear a person out, greatly discrediting him/her on the way."

Leo added, "Either it is that, or they are the most disorganized and disconnected bunch of scholastic clowns and idiots ever to establish themselves as professors and teachers."

"Decide for yourselves," said Collin, "I know in my mind which it is, and I am quite willing to make my stand on it. No more hiding from paranoia accusations by me.

"I believe they never intended, even from the beginning to approve of Durwin's paper. It revealed too much of themselves, and it revealed a problem in the mainline church that they didn't want to acknowledge; that some mainline congregations are not fit for human employment. In these congregations, the proud, egotistical power and control people, belittlers, seek to reduce a good minister to a mindless puppet on a string. It is dehumanizing, and depersonalizing; totally unhealthy spiritually, and accounts for many distorted and defensive characters in the ministry. Durwin's paper offered a well thought out solution for this. Readers may agree with him less than one hundred percent. Nevertheless, he made a logical case for his own viewpoint, and that should have been sufficient for the approval of the paper. What we see instead is a suppression of knowlege that takes us back beyond the Middle Ages."

Albin seemed bursting to speak. Suddenly he broke into the conversation, "Collin, no doubt about it, the seminary was playing a mind-game with Durwin. But so was the area church. Then again, news of accusations against Durwin, and news of the rejection of his paper came at approximately the same time. I cannot help but think there is a connection there. Did they all think they had him cornered now, and here was the time to jump on him, to reject his paper and discredit him in the church all at once? Perhaps there was some informal communication between the two on the matter." After a brief pause, and before Collin could speak, he continued again, "then back further in the story, when Durwin was attending the counseling school, soon after he discussed his pastorate problems with the class instructor, things started to go badly for him there, and—"

Collin interrupted, and affectionately and patiently replied, "Albin, Albin, be careful. It is possible that you are right. On the other hand there is insufficient evidence to establish it for certain. Due to that lack of evidence we have to regard it as an unsolved mystery so to speak. I cautioned you earlier, it's okay to toss around such an idea temporarily. Remember, however, that belittlers would see you branded a hopeless paranoid if they could, rather than admit to such a connection which really would mean a conspiracy. And there are many psychiatrists out there waiting to treat you for it. Don't ever let them do that to you Albin."

"Okay," responded Albin, "I won't allow myself to be possessed by such thoughts. I'm learning to put them aside after thinking them through."

Collin added, "But about the mind-game, there was plenty enough evidence to establish that is what it was. Whether the connections were there is difficult to prove. There is circumstantial evidence.

"Durwin also was convinced by now that it was a mind-game meant to be destructive of ideas, character, credibility and personhood, but they had greatly underestimated the stamina, resilience and resourcefulness of this not perfect, but genuinely Christian person."

Leo, getting legalistic, asked, "Supposing Durwin had been able to take the matter up with some higher authority, what do you think would have happened?"

"My guess is they would have covered themselves well," replied Collin. "In one of the final letters from the seminary there was mention for the first time that there were readers (plural). There had been no mention of readers before. But now, if the faculty could be found at fault, the blame could go down the line to some obscure readers. At first it appeared the mentor was the stooge. I'd guess he did his work on Durwin so effectively for them that they would cover for him as well, and as I said, place the blame on the obscure readers."

"No different, in principle, than the way the mafia operates," responded Leo briskly.

Said Collin, "Regardless of what might have happened if Durwin had protested by more authoritative means, he did not protest further, because he would place no value on a degree from such a place. Several times during the process he had thought this way not only when he announced near the end of the class year that he would not proceed to do a paper, but after he changed his mind and proceeded with the paper. There were times during that process when he felt a degree from this seminary would be no credit to him. However, once he decided to do the paper, he kept on with it mostly out of curiosity as to what they were trying to do with him, even though during the period there was at times some thought that they might be on the level.

"There was also one time when Durwin almost abruptly discontinued his connection with them. It was an incident when Durwin received an invitation to attend a convocation of the seminary, to be held in an outstanding church of the big city. He wondered why the invitation, and again, together with Canda, went mostly out of curiosity. He was the only person of his class to be there. Whether or not the others had received an invitation he has no way of knowing. One of the higher officers of the seminary preached a sermon that night. In the course of his preaching he hit hard at some of Durwin's beliefs and convictions that in various ways had been revealed by him throughout his association there.

"For example, you may remember, in his required statement of personal beliefs and practices Durwin had submitted with his transcripts for entrance into the seminary, he had written such things as he was a little right of center in both his theological and political motivations. This was for the purpose of revealing that he was a person of moderation in all things. Over and against this, you may remember, the dean later had declared himself to the class to be a Marxist. Now in his sermon this preacher, in a most animated sort of way said, 'In this seminary we are neither left or right or center, but only Biblical scholars. Our standards are the highest and we expect high scholarship from our students."

"Ah-h-h-," said Leo, "that was aimed at Durwin for sure. Looks to me like they are running scared now, and covering themselves."

"Yes, I agree," said Collin. "They were running scared, and were now indeed covering themselves. I am of the opinion Durwin was invited to that service for that purpose, so they could cover themselves. Whether the dean's former admission of being a Marxist was really true about himself, or had been a deceitful ruse to con Durwin into going that way and getting himself into grave trouble in a capitalist country, we do not know. Either way I think the sermon that night, if one could call it that, was a cover-up.

Gilda remarked, "I see the incident also as a breach of trust and confidentiality. Durwin had obviously opened his innermost self to these people in conjunction with his entrance requirements into the seminary. Now he gets it slapped up to him in a disguised but public manner. These people, ethically, are not trustworthy. They are completely lacking in proper decorum. It is a gross misuse of private information."

"Furthermore," continued Collin, "in the course of his studies Durwin had revealed how his own sermons were preached more for their content than for a vivacious and active pulpit display. The preacher this night did just the opposite in a very extra animated way. I understand his preaching style was usually animated, but on this night he overdid it and it was ludicrous to say the least. Many people were obviously shocked and embarrassed by such an overdone display of pulpit behavior. Following the service Durwin and Canda talked to one another briefly before leaving the pew.

"Said Durwin to Canda, 'I have never seen a renowned Christian pulpit so degraded.'

"'Me neither," added Canda, astounded.

"'I don't think I want a degree from this seminary, I don't think I want to be connected with it at all,' said Durwin.

"'I know just how you feel,' said Canda.

"'Perhaps we had better think of it some more though and not make a quick decision,' said Durwin with a second thought.

"Canda agreed, and as they proceeded to leave the sanctuary in line with other people they passed by the preacher. The preacher, who had often seen Durwin around the seminary, behaved as though he didn't know Durwin. 'We've never met,' he said.

"'Oh I've been around for a while now,' said Durwin.

"'Nice to see you again,' the preacher muttered awkwardly." Collin added, "The whole display was a type of cover-up frequently used by belittlers. Why else was Durwin invited to the event. Remember, the church professor from Terraprima used it on me in Lower Secundaterra after he shunned and omitted me at the preaching seminar he had conducted." Collin commented further, "It could always be debatable whether the whole happening was coincidental, or, whether it was purposely aimed at Durwin. However, my previous experience with belittlers' tactics strongly indicates they wanted to cover themselves on the previous Marxist admission of one of the staff, and at the same time make Durwin feel that according to them, his preaching style was inferior. Durwin still knew in his mind that his own style of preaching was best for him, and it had always brought good response from fair minded people and sincere Christians to whom he had preached.

"Durwin and Canda later decided that since the end of the process was near, Durwin would stay in and finish his paper, more out of curiosity as to what they were about, than to have a degree from such a place."

Owen raised a question, "The difference in styles of preaching and in theology, brings a matter to my mind. Was part of the problem that there being such a difference between their theology and political leaning and Durwin's that they could not accept his work anyway?"

Collin replied, "They could use that as an excuse for putting him down. Really though, broad minded people in educational circles should be able to accept the views of other people, even when different from their own. When a logical case is made for those views, credit should be given for it whether it coincides with their views and opinions or not. But over and above that if the seminary faculty were not willing to accept views different from their own, they should have told Durwin early in the process, perhaps even at application time, and saved him from the expense and work of a year of study and then writing a paper they had no intention of approving because it was of a different theology and/or philosophy of life than their own. The people at this seminary were not broad minded and mature enough for either of these positions of thought.

"As time passed, Durwin, time and again realized he was in the wrong school. He was led on, however, somewhat by the implication from them that the seminary was changing its theology. When he saw this was vague, he remained in mostly out of curiosity as to how they would treat him and how the whole thing would end. Well now you know how they treated him, and that it ended with him getting nowhere with them.

"But, it was more than a difference in theology. It was the strange behavior of belittlers in their desire to destroy an exceptional person who could see through them. Something similar happened to another student in another supposedly Christian school.

"This student had to do a paper for graduation purposes. He was by faculty assigned a smooth operating reader. The student wrote the paper and sent it to the reader. The reader returned it with instructions to do such and such to it for improvement. The student did so and sent the paper to the reader again, thinking that since he had done all he was asked to do, his paper would be approved. But no, the reader very nicely, smoothly and authoritatively returned the paper again, asking that some other such and such be done. The student followed directions and again sent the paper in. Once again the paper was returned by the reader for further adjustments, and on and on this went to six times. All the while, the reader was collecting a fee for each reading. The student had to get on with his life, so the paper never did get approved.

"My opinion is," added Collin, "that neither a crafty reader alone, nor a stupid reader alone could get away with this in a school that has any degree of both efficiency and honesty down through the ranks and in management. My opinion is, this reader was the up front man, the stooge, to send this trusting, unsuspecting young student down the drain. He didn't go down the drain but his life and that of his family was greatly affected by it. Because of the reader's tactics this student's later income was drastically cut until he found an honorable way around it. And this with enormous student loans to repay; loans that had paid his tuition in this very expensive school. In addition, the student had a family of small children."

Owen exclaimed in disgust, "and I suppose that reader claimed to be a Christian!"

"Oh yes, and working for a *well run* Christian school," quipped Collin ironically.

"Or a naive school, whichever," added Gilda.

"And the reader would have no regard for a person with a family of small children!" remarked Leo.

"Not the least," responded Collin.

Leo bristled, "As I have said before, even most hardened criminals in prisons turn on fellow criminals who have harmed children. These hardened belittlers are no different in principle, even worse; near psychopathic or sociopathic, if you ask me."

"You may be right," agreed Collin.

Collin added, "In Terraprima fallen, a favorite tactic of belittlers, that of having a young or different type or supposedly inexperienced person, plague the life out of you, is also applied in a unique way in academic life.

"A belittling faculty member chooses, for an exceptional and fine student, a mentor or reader as the case may be, who has, either in fact or faked by innuendo, a whole different perspective on theology, politics, society, and practically every aspect of life. The faculty chosen reader is also an experienced con-artist, a confidence person. He seeks to exalt himself above his victim and at the same time make the victim feel inferior and lacking. Then he smoothly promotes himself as the victims good friend, trying to help the poor fellow. The con-artist reader makes wayward suggestion after suggestion, gradually leading the student writer farther and farther away from his own opinions and what he would himself write. Eventually the paper is not anything like the student writer intended. So if someone else were to then read the paper, a second party or more, a case could easily be established to favor turning it down.

"That reader also rejects every personal opinion on any matter in the fine students paper. This eventually, over a long period of time, discourages the student from expressing any personal views on the subject at hand. Then they also put him down for lack of personal viewpoint. Eventually it may turn the unsuspecting student from trying any more. Then he is branded as a person who never finishes anything, a quitter, a dropout, and lacking in tenacity.

"If the deceit of their game was ever revealed, it could be all blamed on an inexperienced poorly prepared, and probably obscure reader. Or, they might say, well that was the reader's opinion, and he believes his opinion or viewpoint is right."

Brett remarked, "How self-centered could such a reader be, to allow only his own personal viewpoint!"

"It certainly wouldn't be a God-centered, Christian attitude," asserted Owen. "If the students viewpoints were well supported in his paper, whether they match those of the reader or not, they should indeed be acceptable."

Leo added in disgust, "I would say it is only one of two things: it is either ignorance and naivety of the foremost order, or it is the vicious, destructive, belittling mind-game meant to destroy."

"Referring again to Durwin's paper in particular," said Collin, "there had been very little comment on the paper throughout the process; mainly a few errors in composition, and a very occasional remark about something needing more elaboration; and a thumbs down on Durwin's use of the viewpoint of a world renowned scholar not listed among those they had recommended.

"However, their insincerity and the presence of a mind-game became more evident when Durwin, because of the time factor of two days they suddenly placed upon him, had to send his whole paper in as it was, and at once, without any personal viewpoint on just one section of it. When he did so, he would in time learn, they very noticably jumped on it and turned him down for, among other things, not having sufficient personal viewpoint. As I mentioned before, he could have remedied this omission in a matter of two weeks. But they would not give him time.

Collin paused briefly, and then added, "So that you members of this group won't at some time in the future be misused by it, I will tell you now of another misuse of students and their papers. This is carried on, not by belittlers in paricular, but by unscruplous professors looking after their own ends. Professors, in their writings often in a general way give students credit for ideas. That may be okay as far as it goes. But when a professor deliberately sets a paper for the purpose of extracting ideas from the student for use in the professor's publication; or, worse still, when a professor deliberately sets a series of papers for students, and then takes the students responses to these assignments, sets them in an appropiate order, edits them, and turns them into a book for publication, then that to me is abuse of rights and morals and decency. I have heard rumors of such things happening. It is planned robbery. Many students are wise to this, so in instances where they can choose their own topic for writing, they sometimes write on a most mediocre or less subject for even a doctoral paper. This is degrading to the profession and its quality."

Changing the emphasis of the story, Collin then said, "Let us now pick up the matter of accusations against Durwin.

"Within a week of the surprising, shocking phone call informing him of the accusations of sexual harassment in his church, Durwin, accompanied by Canda drove to the office of the C.E.O. Durwin was interviewed while Canda waited in another room. The C.E.O. in his now familar cold and callous attitude toward Durwin, remarked, "we won't be judgemental towards you concerning this.

"Durwin thought to himself, without speaking aloud, *I should hope not. Even if the accusations were true, which they are not, it is not any worse and probably not as damaging, humanly speaking, as what you people have done and tried to do to me over the past several years.* But he knew from experience, he would be speaking on callous and denying ears.

"The supervisor read the accusations, and Durwin was shocked at the vicious falsehoods they contained. He strongly and immediately protested. The C.E.O. remained callous, as always, toward Durwin. The supervisor shrunk at Durwin's protests.

"The supervisor had been belittling Durwin for two years, and no doubt he had thought this was to be his grand finale with him. Durwin showed him differently, and he literally shrank in his clothes. Near the end of the interview, the C.E.O. had Canda come into the office.

"'You should hear what these people are saying about me,' Durwin said to Canda, then sternly to the supervisor, 'read the accusations to her so she will know what we are up against. We work together.'

"The supervisor read one of the accusations with shaking hands and crackling voice.

"'Read another,' commanded Durwin.

"The supervisor shook all the more as he read another. Then out of pity for him that he might fall apart or have a heart attack, Durwin said, 'that will be enough to give my wife a first hand idea of what is going on.'

"Durwin was then informed of the process of inquiry he would have to go through. The interview ended with some perfunctory parting courtesies.

"Altogether, Durwin came away from the meeting feeling a little, just a little, on top of things. He felt he had made a dent in their armor and put them on the defensive for their action. At first, their attitude had appeared to be that Durwin had committed grave misbehavior, but they would still be nice to him, patting themselves on the back for doing so.

Towards the end of the interview, Durwin could detect some doubt in their minds as to the validity of the accusations, and whether this really would be the final belittling of Durwin by the supervisor to bring him down to where they wanted him. Belittling had been openly done by this supervisor over the past two or so years. The C.E.O. would be mostly exempted and protected from this by virtue of his office and the way he used it to cover himself. Each time Durwin had appealed to this C.E.O. he had been brushed aside and the problem handed on to a subordinate who showed little genuine interest in it. That was part of the game also. The C.E.O. time and again turned his head aside and let it all happen to Durwin. Durwin had no choice but to give up on the C.E.O., and eventually came to look upon him as not worth regarding to be worthy of his office or any other Christian ministry.

"Utilizing an illustration synonymous with a story he once read of an eastern caravan, Durwin told me how he figured this C.E.O.: "He saw him to be like the driver-leader of a wagon train in the early days of the American west. This wagon train leader had a reputation for getting his wagon train as a whole, through and on time to its destination in the west. He made a reputation for himself as being a very efficient wagon train leader. He took great care to ensure the train got through. However, he took little or no thought about the individuals who dropped by the wayside on the way. There was no particular care or pause for them at all. The wagon must go through, and the leaders reputation must be kept intact so that he could be regarded as a top-notch leader.

"That is the way Durwin saw this C.E.O., and I agree," said Collin. "But such a C.E.O. is so remote from Christian theology and behavior, which says God cares as much for the one as he cares for the whole. This is borne out in Jesus' parable of the Lost Sheep, the Prodigal Son, and other Biblical passages. This C.E.O. was in error by far when over the years he had ignored Durwin's plight and brushed him aside. Along the way, so arduous for Durwin, the C.E.O. had at times revealed his true colors, and they were not in Durwin's favor."

Leo came in with his now familar style of quip, "The C.E.O. hiding behind the virtue of his office, eh, and letting the lesser guys do the dirty work! That's the way I see it, and that to me spells gangsterism; no different in principle than the Mafia. Let the little, or more obscure guy do the dirty work. Then in case something falls through, the little guy can take the rap, and the higher office and the overall reputation of the organization, in this case the church, is protected."

Owen added, "Many organizations, including churches have a tier of executives, passing responsibility down the line. When utilized for good purposes and in good faith, I would say it is a good thing. If indeed something does go wrong, often the credibility of the total organization is protected. I see nothing wrong with that. When the same system is used with improper decorum for buck-passing and for evil purposes, then I agree with Leo's estimation of it."

"You have made your point well," commented Collin, "and now let's get on with the inquiry process Durwin had to go through.

"In approximately a week Durwin was called to meet with a committee of the wider church for an initial inquiry. The accusations were again read, and Durwin began making his defence. One member of the committee, a brash young man, appeared by his actions to want to be the champion of the committee. He was in appearance a good looking person in a brash sort of way; not what would be called fine looking to Durwin's generation, but, smartly agressive, and as I said brash. This brashness in his manner was reflected in his countenance. It was made known to Durwin early in the meeting by one of the more dubous members, that this young man, who stood out in a much different way than did Durwin himself, was minister of one of the larger churches in the area. Whether this was meant to intimidate Durwin one can only guess or surmise. Regardless, Durwin was not impressed by the young man and his actions and the encounter in no way intimidated him.

"This encounter with the brash young man became rough at one point. In his brashness and agressiveness he came on strongly, saying that he did not have much time for this meeting, so lets get on with it. Then he turned on Durwin savagely. He was to be the shake-down man to get a quick confession and have it all over with in a few minutes. 'How do you think you stand with the church now, after what you have done?' he said, harshly and loudly.

"Remaining undisturbed, Durwin quite calmly said to him, 'If the church will pay for it, I am quite willing to take polygraph tests, lie detector tests that is, on this whole matter.'

"The brash young man's face drooped and paled visibly.

"Durwin then quietly but firmly turned to the amiable chairperson of the committee, and himself taking leadership of the chaotic situation caused by the brash young man, Durwin made a suggestion. He proposed that the accusations of each of the accusers be read one at a time and that he in turn respond to each one singly. This suggestion was followed and a constructive meeting ensued, despite the occasional complaints of the brash young man concerning the time factor."

"Imagine," remarked Gilda, "that person being in such a hurry, when the meeting was so important to Durwin!"

"It was probably the most important meeting of his life," added Donna.

"Was the brash young man a belittler particularly set up to do the shake-down?" asked Albin.

Collin replied, "As I have said before, sometimes belittlers do set up a young, inexperienced or insignificant person for such a task so that if it falls through they can cover up by saying, 'but he is just a young person.' Whether he set himself up or was set up, it seemed from his interaction with some others on the committee, he was on the inside track of the church hierarchy. However, Durwin saw him for what he was that day, very tactfully put him in his place, and never saw him again after that."

Brett inquired, "I'm curious about one point. Durwin offered to take polygraph tests if the church would pay for it. Why did he insist that the church pay for it?"

"A good question," answered Collin readily. "At the hands of the church of Terraprima, Durwin had taken a severe financial as well as personal and psychological beating. The Lawtons had some financial resources, but these had all been gained during their years of hard work, careful saving and investment in Secundaterra and Lower Secundaterra. These resources were set aside for a secure and pleasant retirement. Durwin was not about to easily let the savage belittlers of this denomination of Terraprima fallen, practice another of their favorite tactics and bleed away their hard earned retirement money, all but a little of it earned and saved outside of Terraprima."

"Good for him," remarked Leo.

"I wish to add," said Collin, "the Lawtons would later find better circumstances in another part of the country, outside the Terraprima area, and improve on their retirement resources there, again through hard work and careful management. This enabled them to stay in the country in retirement as well. They loved living there and, regardless of the numerous wayward ones, they knew that by far the majority of the people there were friendly and nice.

He then continued, "There was such a contrast between the accusations and Durwin's defense, that the committee ordered a full inquiry into the whole matter. This full inquiry would be later carried on by another committee.'

"In the meantime, Durwin never did receive copies of the various accusations brought against him. After he quite successfully refuted them and offered in addition to take polygraph tests, and also to meet the accusers face to face with the committee, which the accusers refused, the matter took a different twist. Now the heirarchy took the original accusations out of circulation and they never surfaced again. In their place came a general and at times vague summary outline of the ways Durwin supposedly may have broken church rules and conduct. This was typical of the negative treatment of Durwin by the heirarchy over the years. Anything that Durwin got on top of or did well with usually disappeared. Thankfully, most of the later inquiry committee would treat him better.

"Had the problem been brought to a head and properly inquired into back when it became gossip in the community, it could have been all over with before summer. There was no indication of why it was delayed. Now when it was ready for inquiry, many people of the inquiry committee were away on vacation. The process had to wait till early fall.

"In the meantime, Durwin still had to work under the supervision of the person responsible for bringing the accusations against him. It was somewhat like having the same lawyer working for both sides in a case.

I will relate to you some of the difficulties this caused, and some of the bungling that came from it.

"There was absolutely no amicability, no friendliness from this supervisor. In an effort to establish how he stood and what was expected of him during the long summer of waiting for the inquiry, Durwin asked the supervisor some questions to clarify his present position. He asked of him, 'Am I expected to attend church area meetings as usual?'

"'Yes, you are,' growled the supervisor, in a tone that would indicate he thought Durwin was trying to back out of it.

"Durwin asked again, 'am I expected to continue as usual, my ministry to the congregation, according to my way of ministry?'

"'Yes,' he growled again, as though Durwin had to be prodded to perform his ministry well and fully.

"To Durwin that was simply his mandate for the coming months. To the warped mind of the belittling supervisor, it was he, the great strong man, whipping wayward Durwin into line.

"Again Durwin asked, "There are a group of ministers I have regularly met with ecumenically over the years for fellowship and Bible study. They wish to write letters of support on my behalf. Will I send the letters to you?'

"'No,' the supervisor growled again, 'such letters won't count. They will be of no use.'

"Durwin's response to all this was that he went into action very positively. On his first Sunday of worship after the initial inquiry, he walked up the aisle to the pulpit to set up his papers for the service. To his suprise the organist and the singer-dental assistant were there in a nearby area beside the organ and out of sight of the few of the congregation already gathered. As he came in sight of them, they jeered at him mockingly and in a very pronounced manner. Then momentarily they left the area until the prelude to the service was about to begin. As they were leaving and passing by Durwin, the singer reached out, patted Durwin on the arm and jeered some more. Durwin didn't let it upset him. He conducted his usual good worship service. On future Sundays, however, Canda very carefully went with him wherever he had to go within the church building until the service began, and then again after the service.

"Durwin also called a meeting of the local church board, imformed them that he had been instructed to carry on his ministry as usual, and that meant church meetings as well. He told them firmly that he was to be informed and consulted about all local church meetings; no more local church meetings behind his back, as they had been having.

"With regard to the letters of reference offered from other clergy of the area, Durwin accepted them anyway, and sent them to the supervisor. Later information was that he did nothing about them or with them. Some of the attitudes from him and some others were to the effect that Durwin had not any right to even defend himself. However, before Durwin sent those letters to the supervisor, he made several photo copies of them all. Later he submitted copies to the inquiry committee who informed him they hadn't heard of them before. There the letters were accepted and considered seriously. Durwin had efficiently taken over the leadership of his church again; more importantly also the ordering of his own life.

"His leadership of the local church did not last. As had happened at times before, so it would be now, Durwin would have the rug pulled from under him by area church officials. At another wider church meeting, Durwin was asked how the accusers were treating him at church. In an effort to show them the mockery and phoneyness of a report that the accusers were crying and sobbing as they reported on Durwin's supposed wayward treatment of them, Durwin reported that some of them were jeering at him in mockery and laughter.

"Shortly after that, Durwin was called in by the supervisor and another church official and told that his ministry to that congregation would be suspended until further notice. Durwin never found out if there was a connection between his report of jeering and mockery, and, the suspension. Nevertheless, it was done; the rug had been pulled from under Durwin's feet once again. This was nothing new for him in this church area. As it stood now, Durwin was cut off and isolated from all the congregation, friends and enemies alike, as his main means of rapport with them had been taken away. Further degrading incidents were yet to come.

"Durwin asked these two officials if it meant he stay on in the minister's residence or move out. They told him the supervisor would call a meeting of the local church board to arrange for him to stay in the residence and to have the local church continue to pay his salary. That was all a disheartening blow to Durwin. He had taken over leadership of the church very bravely; now they were taking him out of it. Not only that, but now his accusers and their supporters would be asked to pay his salary and keep him on in the residence. There was another blow yet to come.

"The supervisor informed Durwin that when the meeting with the local church board was arranged, he would come and Durwin was to attend with him. Durwin agreed to do so. On the evening of the meeting, the supervisor called at the minister's residence, and from there, he and Durwin went together to the church. On the way, the supervisor growled at Durwin, 'now you have to do the asking this evening. This is for you to do. You ask them if you can stay on in the residence, and also ask that your salary be paid, both until the matter is resolved. Durwin was still speechless when they arrived at the meeting. Here he was being sent begging to his accusers and their supporters. As he saw them, he quickly decided he would show no weakness before them in this dispicable task that had just been laid upon him. Also, he knew there were some silent supporters present, whom he would not let down with a display of weakness or defeatism.

"After opening the meeting, the chairperson, looking at the supervisor, asked what was the business of the evening. He remained silent, very silent, for considerable time, not looking at anyone, not even at Durwin whom he expected to respond with the business of the evening.

"Durwin, in his usual calm manner, spoke up confidently. 'The powers that be of the wider church, have decided that I should cease ministering in this church until further notice.' Some of the hostile faces brightened as Durwin paused. 'Furthermore,' he said, 'they ask that I be allowed to stay on in the residence for the present time.' The brightness was replaced by scowls on many faces. 'And further still,' continued Durwin, 'they ask that this local church continue to pay my salary as long as I am here.'

"The scowls deepened immensely, and hateful glares went towards the supervisor. He shrank in his clothes again, and began to quiver and fidget nervously. Durwin paused to give him time to speak. Not a word came. One of the board members, a respected person of influence, looked at the treasurer and shook his head. Durwin noticed it, but the supervisor was lost in a daze. The treasurer looked toward Durwin,'what if the money doesn't come in?'

"Durwin paused again to let the supervisor speak, but he did not. Durwin had no choice but to take the initiative as he had so many times before. Calling the treasurer by name, he said, 'well, if this request is not approved, I guess I'll be out in the street soon.' A shock came over the whole group. The supervisor sat still like a bump on a log. Many eyes turned to the respected and influential person who had previously shaken his head. 'Let's take a vote on it,' he said, in a relenting manner. So a vote was taken and passed in favor of the requests.

"I wish to point our here," added Collin, emphatically, "that I referred to a 'respected person of influence'. You should understand that this is quite different from a power and control freak; as different as chaulk and cheese. A respected person of influence is respected for his/her good character and motivation. He has the best interests of the church or community, or whatever, in mind and his actions are motivated by that. He becomes known and respected for it by the majority of better thinking people.

"On the other hand, the power and control people are those who would like to be up where the respected person of influence is but they don't possess the character and wherewithall to be there. So instead of doing what is in the best interests of the church for example, they do what, in their own warped and twisted minds, they think will make them look good. They come up with often cockeyed ideas, or they quarrel to get their own way, or they belittle to put others down so they can feel on top. They are self-centered people. Their world must revolve around them. They are motivated by their own self-centerd interests. These people don't usually come across to us as being powerful, but in their own minds they feel up there with the people of true influence and persuasion when they dominate a meeting through their own obnoxious behavior I just described.

"Getting on with the story, Durwin and the supervisor returned to the residence. In a brief conversation there, without being asked, the supervisor informed Durwin that he could have a lawyer to represent him if he wished.

"'Would the church pay for it?' asked Durwin, in the interests of not letting this bogus wider church bleed away his retirement money.

"'I don't know about that,' he replied vaguely.

"Durwin for a few days after thought about the issue of having a lawyer or not. He decided he had better get one lest he be taken advantage of in some unruly way. Some friends put him in contact with a very large and highly regarded law firm with experts in every field. Taking exception to his own rule, Durwin retained the services of a lawyer at his own expense. In an interview, the lawyer asked Durwin if it was okay if he write the wider church officials informing them that he was representing him. Durwin gave his okay. About two weeks and approximately a thousand dollars later, Durwin received a phone call from his lawyer who informed him he had received a letter from a church official stating that by church rule, Durwin wasn't allowed to be represented by a lawyer in the church investigation. He could utilize a lawyer for consultation only."

"That supervisor was a very inept clown!" wasn't he, remarked Leo. "I say that with apology to people who play the role of a clown for entertainment purposes."

"He should never have been in the positon he was in," agreed Collin, "but he got there because of academic qualifications, and he did later go on to even higher office in the church. It is noteworthy that nobody from the church told Durwin directly he couldn't have a lawyer. It was his lawyer who informed him. Nobody in the church bothered to call Durwin to tell him.

"That raises another noteworthy point," continued Collin, "For all practical purposes, Durwin was cut off, not only from the church hierarchy as he had been for the major part of his ministry in Terraprima, now he was stuck, actually stuck in the minister's residence, but cut off from contact with the congregation; actually living in isolation, but surrounded by enemies, and by silent supporters who could not show their support.

"The supply minister who traveled in from elsewhere to replace Durwin in the pulpit, came by the residence occasionally for information or to use church records. He took a very negative, cold, haughty and judgmental attitude toward Durwin, and at times appeared to be carrying on an investigation of his own. He was obviously biased toward the accusers to whom he was now ministering, and now that Durwin was isolated from the congregation he was even questioning Durwin's continuing contact with the other clergy of the area.

"Furthermore, Durwin was told by the supervisor that he was not to talk to any members of the congregation; have no contact with them at all. The tactic of isolating the victim is one of the belittlers' most deadly weapons. In isolation the victim cannot make his side of the story known at all. This gives the belittlers the upper hand with their side of the story.

"The Lawtons kept contact with their friends outside the denomination. Contact and interaction with people and the surrounding world is necessary to a healthy life. Some would have them cut off altogether, but the Lawtons wouldn't let it be so.

"There is a noteworthy incident that shows how Durwin kept active while continuing his devotion to duty during this period. Towards late summer, after Durwin had long been cut off from the congregation, a well-meaning parishoner with concern and sympathy for another parishoner who had been very ill and in serious condition in hospital for an extended period, approached Durwin. He asked that, since this woman was continually struggling between the brink of death and life, Durwin visit her as usual so she would not know and be upset by the disturbance in the local church. What this requesting parishoner did not know was that Durwin had already visited her seventeen times since the disturbance; visited her in the hospital twenty miles away; that's forty miles a trip. He had indeed said nothing to her about the disturbance. He assured the requesting parishoner that he would do the visiting.

"Durwin did things like that solely out of concern for people. For example, there was nothing to be gained for either himself or the church by his visitation of this person. She was a woman living in very modest yet well managed circumstances with a near meager income. Some people, at times, encourage a minister's visitation because it may bring financial gain to the church. That wasn't Durwin's criteria for visitation. He visited solely in the interests of the spiritual needs of God's people whom he served in God's name. As for any personal gain from such visitation, in all his years of ministry he had never expected such a thing.

"After about three months, with vacations over and the beginning of another church year, the main inquiry got underway. The inquiry committee was made up of an assortment of men and women with an assortment of suitablity criteria for the job. The chairperson, a very efficient, unbiased and street wise, or, social wise type of person was obviously very interested in doing a fair and credible job. A second person also was unbiased and socially wise. What I mean by socially wise, is that they have a knowledge and understanding of the average people out in the street in the usual avenues of life, and in a wise sort of way. These inquiry committee members would give Durwin a fair and rational inquiry.

"A third person, also would try his best to be fair and open minded. He wasn't at all socially wise; naive in some ways, I guess I would kindly say. Yet he would leave no stone unturned to see justice done. Durwin felt assured of fair treatment from him.

"A fourth person was very biased against Durwin. Her husband had practiced belittling on Durwin at every opportunity for some time. Now it was her turn. As Durwin would present his defense, she would try to cut it down and trivalize it in favor of the accusers even when it was very obvious that she was wrong. Much later in the hearings, almost too late, she came to herself, as did the prodigal son in Jesus' story, and changed her attitude.

"A fifth person, sentimental in nature, could not understand how Durwin could be so forward as to defend himself against women, some of whom had come to the inquiry with sorrow and crying. It seems she had never heard of crocodile tears. Durwin had seen such tears not so long ago at a church meeting, and also there had been the jeering and mockery from beside the pulpit that morning as I mentioned previously, which indicates that these tears were indeed crocodile tears.

"There was a sixth person on the inquiry who was from another country and a different culture, a culture in which belittlers openly and publicly carry on brazen belittling and feel justified in doing so. He would ask irrelevant questions such as how many brothers and sisters Durwin had, and how he got along with them and with other people. His questions were loaded for Durwin to bring out accusations of other people against him, or, as we would say, he was trying to lead Durwin into the paranoia trap. Durwin handled him well.

The remainder of the people on the inquiry board had very little to say, so did not reveal any qualities significant to the occasion, but of course they had a vote.

"The chairman of the inquiry committee did his best to facilitate a speedy hearing. He was sympathetic to the fact that months had passed before it was possible to get the whole inquiry committee together. In his desire to speed up the process so as to relieve the participants of more waiting, he unintentionally made things very difficult for Durwin in another way.

"For example, one evening the committee set a meeting with the accusers for six o'clock, figuring to be through with them by seven-thirty and then meet with Durwin. It didn't work out that way. It took more than three hours to deal with the accusers. The result was it was getting late when Durwin, after sitting and waiting for about two tiring hours, was called in before the committee, and it was nearly midnight before they were through. Under such stress it was tiring indeed.

"Durwin had previously offered to come before the inquiry committee at the same time as the accusers, meeting them face to face, but each and every accuser refused to do so, he was told. So the accused and accusers had to come before the inquiry committee separately, making it a prolonged and more stressful ordeal than necessary.

"After several meetings, a very thorough inquiry was completed, and the accusations against Durwin were dropped by the church. Once again there was no communication with the Lawtons. Others in the community and elsewhere heard of the outcome before they did. Anyone with any human understanding would know what an anxious time it must have been for them, yet the right party to do so never did contact them. They had to phone the wrong party to hear the results of the exhaustive inquiry.

"From my ample knowledge of the kind of person Durwin Lawton was, and what he accomplished even with such tremendous odds against him, I am convinced he could have had a flourishing ministry in the church at Terraprima had he been genuinely accepted by the area clergy and administration. He had more than enough capability and confidence to fulfill an outstanding ministry of any size they could offer him, even though he had no ambition for anything but a challenging pastorate that would appreciate his ministry.

"But persons like the one whose story I am just finishing relating to you are not supposed to survive in a properly functioning manner in the part of the nation to which he went. But this one did survive and do well considering the circumstances. His is a story of gross mental abuse and mental cruelity, coming mostly from the church. Had Durwin become a derelict in the streets, the church would have occasionally given him a free meal together with many other homeless people. They are quite good at that too.

"But as I said, under the circumstances Durwin still did exceptionally well, being the exceptional person that he was, and considering what such a person has to put up with in Terraprima.

"However, Durwin was of age to take early retirement, which he did after the inquiry ended. He decided upon retirement not altogether because of the accusations, as that was only but one symptom of the total sickness that was so prevalent in this denomination in Terraprima and which sought to destroy people like the Lawtons. In addition he just could not bring himself to minister any further under a hierarchy that was heading in wrong directions, trying hard to please and appease all the wrong people. The bias of the church there was in favor of belittlers and other inferior ones so that their wayward, undisciplined feelings wouldn't be hurt by the mere presence of the better quality people who were sooner or later turned off and often away.

"In many other aspects also, the church was doing very few of the right things. It was all like an exercise in futility, with emphasis on things of little consequence in the forefront and absolutely no emphasis at all on Christian character. Christian character was in very short supply in this denomination of the church of Terraprima. No wonder the area church was in decline.

"As Durwin prepared for retirement, the supervisor continued the mind-game playing. Now he played the part of the poor chap who didn't know any better—couldn't think of any other way to handle the crisis. There was no indication at all of him meeting with the group of supervisors and the C.E.O. as a whole, as they are meant to operate. Just this crafty one acting alone, so it seemed, and now to cover himself, acting the clown who didn't know better—a frequently used cover-up by belittlers. This behavior affirmed Durwin in his decision to retire.

"The Lawtons moved away from Terraprima to another state of the country. There were belittlers there to be sure, as there are everywhere. But there they are not in control or dominating the society, not yet anyway. The Lawtons bought a lovely home and settled down in it. Then Durwin began to look around, for a part time ministry. He felt he must in some way be true to his calling to a ministry of some sort. Also a paid part time ministry at this point would help the Lawtons in their transition to retirement. There were other employment opportunities open to Durwin, with far more remuneration, but he chose to stay with ministry if possible.

"I caution the group members here. Don't think for a minute that Durwin's problems were over now that he was retired. Belittlers have no respect for age. They keep up their tactics to the end.

"Durwin joined a Chaplain's group of volunteers at a city hospital near where he lived in retirement. Perhaps there would be opportunity there to put into service his training in Pastoral Care and Certified Pastoral Education (CPE), and it might eventually lead to what he was looking for.

"One of the meetings went like this: one minister of the group had recently returned from a trip to the Holy Lands. He told about some of his experiences over there. Durwin found it very interesting, and questioned in a complementary manner, 'it is safe to go over there again now then I guess, is it?'

"The minister flew into a defensive near panic, 'it's as safe there as it is in the big city in Terraprima, isn't it?' he blurted out defensively.

"'Well, I guess so, if you say so,' replied Durwin as nicely as possible, 'I don't know and I was just inquiring.' Obviously that minister's character had become warped over the years. His instant reaction was symptomatic of the character damages done to numerous protestant ministers by faulty relationships between pastor and certain types of laity in the congregation's structure, which makes some churches unfit for human employment. The details of that is another topic on which, in itself, a considerable size book could be written.

"Regardless of Durwin's tactful handling of the matter, there was a familar grunt of contempt from another minister, obviously a belittler, and as it turned out, from Terraprima, who then asked abruptly where Durwin had come from originally. Durwin told him where he was born, pronouncing it the way they do in that place. The minister snapped a correction angrily, making a big issue out of it, and pronouncing it as they do in some other areas, which by the way was different again than the way they pronounce it in some other areas of Terraprima. Durwin didn't answer. It wasn't worthwhile, he reasoned to himself. Then the minister, still in a very snappy manner came out with his pronounciation of it again, as though looking for a quarrel in which he could win over Durwin whom he wanted to bully in order to keep himself feeling superior. Durwin shrugged his shoulders and smiled, giving the minister no opportunity to play his silly immature game.

"Then the guest speaker of the morning arrived. He was a well educated, very interesting and informative man. Following his excellent presentation, nobody commented or spoke for what seemed the longest time. Then Durwin having some knowledge related to the speakers topic, carried on a conversation with him for some time. The guest obviously enjoyed it, and then left the meeting after receiving thanks from the person responsible for bringing him to speak.

"As the others stood up to leave there was the usual lingering for a minute or two, with handshaking and good-byes. Another minister, who had earlier said he was from Terraprima, when confronted by Durwin to say good-bye, turned away with a contemptous grunt, typical of his kind in the area from which he came. Durwin had seen him in action elsewhere, before this meeting. He appeared to be acting as the masterful type from Terraprima; the superior, father-like figure setting himself up as the champion of those around him, and now in this instance protecting them from this new smart-alec, Durwin, who was, as he seemed to see it, on the scene threatening their sense of superiority.

Durwin didn't quarrel with him, as he knew most of the others would take the belittler's side. As Durwin left, one of the sensible ministers present was trying to talk some sense into the grunter from Terraprima. Durwin knew from experience it would not work, at least not for long. He left and never went back to the group again. He wasn't looking for more trouble to unnecessarily take on.

"There wouldn't have been a place in that hospital for Durwin to exercise his ministry in a part time paid position, but under friendly Christian circumstances it could well have been a stepping stone leading to connections that would help him find similar work. However, Durwin had no desire, in semi-retirement to fight his way up the ladder through quarrel oriented ministers of warped and twisted mind.

"He eventually took a part time position in a little church that could not afford a full time pastor, and served in it for several years. Having retired previous to this he would not of course earn pension credits with the church. The end result would be that he would work for that denomination both in Terraprima and in his state of semi-retirement for nearly twenty years and get approximately two hundred dollars a month pension for it all told. His original pension potential had been much reduced when, as you may remember he had taken a drastic cut in salary in Terraprima previously, which in turn drastically affected his pension. Then his early retirement to protect himself from destruction and to get out from ministering under useless conditions, reduced his pension more.

"Durwin and Canda both would work well beyond their long-time planned ages of retirement. Through industrious effort and with careful planning they would now build up their own retirement fund to replace the very large portion of pension that was spoiled on them through the abusive treatment they received from the church in Terraprima.

"The important thing for Durwin was that he was answering his call to ministry. This is not to minimize the value of the salary coming in from this semi-retirement ministry. Canda continued to work in industry as well, and together they would do as they had done for many, many years before, make further provision for a secure retirement. Now they would build up new private retirement funds to keep them secure when they both would be too old to work. This wouldn't be easy to do, with so many belittlers and other hawks out to put them down and/or shake them down for their money. But they managed well.

"I mentioned the importance to Durwin of answering his call to ministry," continued Collin. "My own opinion is, that if a person who has recived an authentic call to a particular ministry is blocked and barred by belittlers in the church from pursuing it, then I would say it is quite in order for him to abandon that ministry. He can then pursue a personal ministry of one or more various sorts while earning a good living in secular life. Of course if he did that, those who blocked him would be quick to jump on him and say or infer that he faltered on his call to ministry, or, his call couldn't have been authentic in the first place; anything to discredit him as far as ministry goes.

"Actually," said Collin, giving his own opinion again, "considering the hard life they were always forced by belittlers to live, it would have been better for the Lawtons, health-wise, had they been able to completely retire at the earliest age possible in order to spare themselves from the continuous stress so that they could live to an elderly age. The Lawtons had planned for such a suitable retirement for years and then do a free lance ministry of their own, but the church in Terraprima messed it up on them badly. So here we see the Lawtons now making up for it when they should be retired and taking life easier.

"Someone once remarked to Durwin, 'You're a minister, you can always go into a church home when you are old.'

"Durwin knew he could never do that in Terraprima and stay healthy, for there he would for sure spend his final days standing practically alone even though living among others. And he would have to continuously be defending himself at close quarters, against belittling ministers, being shunned and ignored by them and being left out of things for the most part. Durwin has said that if ever he was going into a home it would be a secular place or at least a place where by far the majority of people were lay-people, of the right mind set, and not dominated by belittlers. He could always get along with people of good character quite well, even though there would surely be some belittlers there. So now past the usual age of retirement, he and Canda are still preparing, quite successfully for financial security in their older years, if indeed they live that long.

"My concern," commented Collin "is how long can they go like this and not get worn out and die young. I have seen it happen before. We often hear the saying, 'the good die young." I predict that Durwin Lawton, and perhaps Canda too, may not live to see what is now considered to be older years, because of their life time of mental and physical brutality caused by the wayward tactics of envious belittlers."

Leo fumed, "Like I said before, I say again, they are bloody murderers, even moreso in Terraprima than in Secundaterra."

Collin gave a pained type of smile, "I correct you again, Leo, they are bloodless murderers; bloodless and by slow and prolonged torture, and they get away with it. But let's keep our cool for tonight. That is the end of the story of Durwin and Canda Lawton. We can discuss it more rationally and objectively when we are refreshed at next weeks meeting. Meanwhile I would suggest we make arrangement with Dr. Eldren for that next session."

Turning to Dr. Eldren in courtesy, Collin said, "Dr. Eldren, this finishes my telling of experiences. Before we depart for the evening, I would like to discuss our format for the meeting next week."

"We certainly should do that," replied Dr. Eldren, "what do you have in mind, Collin?"

Collin replied, "Now that we have heard these life experiences in the area of our concern, I would like next week for us to offer some views on the concerns of people like us, and to do so in your presence so as to hear your professional perspective on it. Would you find that to be in order at this time?"

"I certainly would," replied Dr. Eldren. "It will bring out more information of the motivations you see behind it all, the 'whys and wherefores' as you people have appropiately named it. I look forward to our discussions and pondering of all that has happened to you people.

"However," said Dr. Eldren, "on Monday morning I am being admitted to hospital for tests. I have been having gall bladder attacks for some time now, a few years in fact, and recently the attacks have become more frequent and more painful. I have delayed these tests until your stories are finished, but I cannot delay any longer. The tests will be over a period of two days, in which case I possibly could be here next

Wednesday. Should I need surgery though, and it is likely I will, it will be two or three weeks before I return.

"It is my wish that this group keep on meeting in the meantime in order to keep up the open relationship we have here, and to discuss your whys and wherefores and concerns. When I come back we will review, and then see what we can do together. Meanwhile I feel it is important that you keep the discussions going and not let the group falter. We do have something here, I am sure. I will ask Owen to be the co-ordinator of the group in my absence, and will inform the Student Health Department I have done so. Please go ahead and explore your views and concerns together. Your conclusions will be of value when I return. In the meantime have a nice week or weeks till I am with you again."

Well wishes were expressed to Dr. Eldren by the group members as they all departed the room, Dr. Eldren to another appointment, the group members to the Corner Coffee Shop.

CHAPTER XII

Wednesday evening had come around again. The support group was gathering, and members were wondering about Dr. Eldren's condition since although usually on time he was not present now. Nobody in the room thus far had heard any news. Owen Winslow, usually early, had not yet arrived. There was speculation among the group that Dr. Eldren must have had the operation.

Owen rushed into the room about ten minutes late. Looking tense and flustered, he plumped down in a chair in a moment of dejected silence. The group members looked to him for news. After a pause, Owen seemed to find words, "There's bad news," he said. "I heard earlier in the week that Dr. Eldren had an operation, and I assumed it was a routine gall bladder operation. Now I've just come from the Health Services Department where they told me Dr. Eldren had an operation supposedly for gall bladder, but they found his liver and other body parts badly affected with terminal cancer. We're losing Dr. Eldren!"

Sadness settled in on the group as they heard further from Owen how that Dr. Eldren had had an emergency operation on the weekend and the terminal malignancy was discovered. A mixture of grief, sympathy, and appreciation for his concern and help, was expressed, and plans made to pass on the groups expression of caring to his family.

When the members were able to bring themselves around to it, they began to discuss the future of the group. Owen spoke up with determination. "Dr. Eldren expressed the desire that this group continue if he wasn't here tonight, and I think we should abide by his wishes. As he said, we have something going here, and it's worth keeping going. The Health Services Department has us in mind, and will have another psychiatrist overseeing us next week; a young man who has been counseling individuals for some time here at the university. They would have had him here tonight except he had a previous commitment, but as much as we will miss Dr. Eldren he will be our man in the future. His name is Dr. Pitt. The health department feels it is important to keep up these services without interruption."

Collin Seldon looked uncomfortable. Stress had visibly come upon him. "Do you know this new psychiatrist at all, Owen," he asked very soberly.

"No, not at all," replied Owen.

"Has anyone here ever met him," inquired Collin.

"No," came the collective reply.

"Then we could possibly be in trouble," said Collin.

There was silence. Collin elaborated, "In this group we have been discussing what most likely will be to the new psychiatrist a whole new exploration of human behavior. Even if he is the right type of open personality as was Dr. Eldren, there is still the fact that he hasn't been in on our discussions over the months. It may turn out to be a mystery to him, and heaven knows what opinions he will form of us. If he is not the right type, and he may even be a belittler himself, then we had better beware."

"What do you suggest?" asked Owen.

Collin replied, "First I would suggest that Albin Anders not be present next week. Albin, I suggest you wait down in the library with Vita until you hear from us. You are the younger and more tender of us. I would prefer you not meet this man yet for the same reason Vita avoids psychiatrists."

"I see what you mean," said Albin, "and I agree. Next Wednesday I will read in the library beside your wife until we hear from you."

Collin spoke again. "The remainder of you pick your choice. Come if you wish, or stay away."

"Are you coming, Collin," asked Brett Culver.

"Yes," replied Collin, "I'll give him a try."

The others all agreed to do so as well. Then everyone seemed at loose ends for a moment, until Gilda Emerson spoke up, "In our first semester sessions we all told our life stories to the extent that it applies to the concerns of this group. We have learned much along the way. What we really need now is some professional recognition of the problem that will enable us to better cope.

"This second semester however," she continued, "we have heard the story of a similar, yet more extreme problem in life in Terraprima; more extreme, more crafty, more severe. It having some differences and unfamiliarities to our own experiences, Collin, could you this evening just review the whole entity as it is in Terraprima. We need to become more familiar with it here, since it is, I believe, creeping into our society as well in an equally complex manner."

"Okay," replied Collin, "you're familiar with the Lawtons' basic story. Tonight I can review and analyze the numerous character flaws and activities of belittlers. It will help you, both here in the Secundaterras, and in Terraprima if you ever go there. Better understanding will be the first step to better coping. I assume then you wish to go ahead with a full meeting tonight as previously planned when Dr. Eldren was present."

All agreed to proceed with the meeting. So after the group members had time to be reconciled to the loss of Dr. Eldren, Collin led them into a session of intense review and analysis of the Terraprima concept of belittling.

He began, "The area of life I am about to analyze and explore with you, to my knowledge, has never been formally researched by psychology. I only wish it had. However, the knowledge I have of this area is not derived through projection—through the process of attributing one's own feelings and attitudes to others. Nor is it arrived at through transference, the transference of attitudes and tactics of one person towards you, to another person later on. Rather it is learned through years of experience with these people I call belittlers, and through objective observation of them, one after another, over and over again, down through a period of many years.

"I have tried to doubt myself many times on the conclusions I have drawn from this extensive observation, but time and again the same results continue turning up to reaffirm my knowledge of the matter. I may not be one hundred percent correct in my analysis of the problems and the people involved, but, if effective research was done in this area, I do not think I would be far off base at all. Incidentally, in a psychology class some years ago, I did try in discussion to bring up the matter of obnoxious people upsetting nice people. The professor, an expert in his subject of psychology, brushed my discussion aside with the remark, 'Oh, these people just have to grow up, thats all. They cause trouble all right but they never grew up.'

"Obviously he was aware of some difficult people out there, but his knowledge of their behavior was hazy to say the least. Psychology has taught us all the pitfalls of childhood, and what our parents did or did not do for us. All our adult troubles are blamed on our childhood experiences. While childhood experiences are important, yet considering there is no such thing as perfect parenting, we can surmise that with the factor of genetics as well, an awful lot of people are going to have some areas of their emotional make-up that are weaker than others.

"These areas would, in many cases, probably well withstand the usual stresses of life without major or often even minor emotional problems. But when the wrath of the belittlers is brought to bear on us fine people almost continuously, then our weakest area, as with the weakest link in a chain, is very susceptable to breaking. It seems to me then, the cause of such a breakdown as I have just mentioned is to be found, not in childhood, but in adulthood, often in young adulthood. Adult behavior has by comparison had very little research done on it.

"Despite all the research done and knowledge available on childhood and adolsecent development, still there has been a drastic increase in mental illness in our time. It is all blamed on weaknesses that developed in childhood. In many cases that may be true. But I say the vast increase in illness is due to extreme pressures brought to bear on people in their adult life, particularly but not always, in its earlier years, and often as in our cases, continuing throughout life. No matter how strong or weak a childhood has been, these pressures of adulthood may find a soft spot in which to do their work. There is no allowance made for this in diagnosis or therapy.

"So now, to express my observations of adult behavior as it affects you and I, let me begin by saying that belittlers are basically people who cannot look up to others with respect. They always have to be looking down in condescension, for that is their usual mind-set. This mind set is established when the person has taken on an outwardly superior attitude towards other people, while on the inside, often unconsciously, he feels inferior to many, and especially to people like us.

"Undisciplined, hollow pride, envy, hatred and hostility are common characteristics of a belittler. One, two, three or all four of these traits are usually very predominant in active belittlers, and to lesser degrees in the more passive belittlers. Other characteristics, such as self-centeredness, deceitfulness, and maligning gossipiness are often present also, although most of the maligning is done by hint and innuendo.

"The belittlers mind works like this: as long as there is nobody around who pricks his pride and shakes his ourward superiority which covers his inward insecurity, he is okay. He can be very friendly, nice, and helpful to persons on whom he can look down and feel that person is inferior to him. Please note, I am using the masculine gender 'he and his' for simplicity of expression, but what I say also applies to the feminie gender. There are equally numerous women belittlers. To continue, the big problem for the belittler is when someone appears on the scene who just by his presence and/or performance unintentionally shakes that hollow undisciplined outward pride that makes the belittler feel superior. Then the belittler feels his supposed superiority is threatened.

"But now, you may say, some nice people, persons other than belittlers, feel threatened when their security is shaken. To that I agree. This is where envy makes the belittler different. The belittler is not only shaken by the person whom he *perceives,* note that word perceives, to be superior to him, but is also envious of him. Then again there are two ways to be envious, and I remind you again how the Biblical Scholar, William Barclay in his 'The Daily Study Bible' describes envy. As we have discussed before:

'There is a good and a bad envy. There is the envy which reveals to a person his own weakness and inadequacy, and which makes him eager to copy and to rise to some great example. And there is the envy which is essentially a grudging thing. It looks at a fine person, and is not so much moved to aspire to that fineness, as to resent that the other person is fine. It is the most warped and twisted of human emotions.'" (William Barclay, The Daily Study Bible, The Letter To The Romans, P.28, The Saint Andrew Press, Edinburgh, 1966).

"This latter type of envy is characteristic of belittlers. They take on a vehement hatred for the person of whom they are envious, and seek either consciously or unconsciously to ruin, even destroy that fine person; the person in which they often see so much of what they themselves would like to be, but which their pride will not let them admit, even to themselves, that it is there.

"The writer of Interpreters Bible, the Letter to the Romans says, 'Envy is grieved at the success or happiness of others and is 'glad when they go wrong' and 'continually cuts away what is best in those around us and in our dealings with them.' (The Interpreter's Bible, Volume IX, P.402, Abingdon Press, 1954).

"The Interpreter's Bible comments on Paul's list of virtures and vices, including envy, under the caption, 'The Harvest of the Godless Mind,' (Ibid), leaving the impression that such vices are practiced only by people who leave God entirely out of their lives. I would hasten to add that all of the vices listed are practiced by many church members and clergy enormously so in Terraprima. Envy, to my mind, tops the list in its frequency and the amount of damage and destruction done by it to people who are innocent of any provocation to bring it on.

"The belittler's make-up will in no way allow him to look up to and respect a fine person. Neither will his mind-set allow him to admit that this person who shakes his pride really is a fine person. So he has to prove to himself, and he hopes, to others around him, that this person is not really the fine person he appears to be. The belittler searches diligently and constantly for faults and weaknesses in the fine person in order to bring him down and keep him down to where the belittler feels he can perceive the fine person to be inferior to the himself. Thus you can see why I use the term 'belittler' for such obnoxious people.

"The belittler thinks in a different way altogether in the area of human relations. Take for example the person whose face drooped so noticable as he walked away, when Durwin showed him a better way to cut off a tree limb. His reaction was negative. A normal reaction would have been an appreciative smile, and something to the effect of, 'hey, thats great, thanks, I've never had much experience at this.

"Take another example. When Durwin told of the literary wit of the actor who was able to present a spectacular two hour monologue of many parts of several writings of Shakespeare and other classical writers, another person's face drooped into noticable sadness without comment. A normal reaction would be in effect, 'wow', isn't it great for someone to be able to do something like that!' Belittlers are saddened by the higher attainments of others. The remainder of us are gladdened for them because of their splendid achievements, even though those achievements may be greater than our own.

"Usually, belittlers are perturbed first and foremost over a fine persons appearance. This can take on a strange twist. A fine person usually likes to keep self neat and tidy because we feel better that way. It is a characteristic of our fineness. Belittlers see this and say or insinuate that we are doing so just to look good for vanity sake. That accusation is often a projection of one of their own characteristics, that of wanting to attract the attention of others in practically everything they are and do.

"Again, a belittler may be an expert doing well in his own field, but will still belittle a fine person for doing well in his own field, whether the latter field be considered greater or lesser in worth or stature. The belittler simply does not want a fine person to have anything, and will indeed spoil everything possible on him.

"There are also belittlers, not doing as well as they might in any field. I once lived across the street from a person who although he had potential, had never bothered to do anything much with his life. He worked at unskilled jobs. As always I performed my ministry to the very best of my ability, and it was effective. Also Vita and I took very good care of our personal lives, possessions and private business. The person across the street resented us for all of this. His friends supported him and behaved unfriendly toward us. Their absurd attitude was as though I was wrong for being a fine and effective minister and person, and thereby making this other person feel badly. They belittled us heavily for it.

"You can see what kind of world we would have if belittlers were to get the upper hand everywhere. In places now where they are domineering, that area is a deteriorating place in which to live, as was much of Terraprima at the time of the Lawtons' story. Belittlers, when acting as a group of friends together, seek to whittle a fine person down to the lowest common denominator and below. They must, in their minds, get you down below every one of them.

"In the Lawtons' experience in the church of Terraprima, the belittlers tactics in their 'conspiracy of sorts' as I have called it, when a person is a marked man or woman by numerous belittlers all acting in similar manner, went like this: they ignore everything good you do and pretend they never saw it or heard of it. They treat you always as though you were doing nothing of significance. In truth they watch, and pout over, and talk about to one another everything you do. It is of great significance in their envious eyes, so much so that it stirs their hatred and hostility and incites them all the more to destroy you. Yet, as I said, outwardly they treat you as though you are doing nothing worthwhile at all. If you do manage to make some of your work visible to them, they trivialize it and imply it is of no value in their sight, or, you are just doing it or saying it to show off.

"Another tactic they use to wear you down is that they will often tell you or insinuate what they think you are doing wrong, but they will never tell you a right way to do it. They love to make you guess. Once you start guessing, they keep you guessing by continuing to tell you, or insinuate only, that you are wrong, again and again and again. If you ever can corner them on it, their response will be, 'well that's my opinion, or, oh, I didn't know; some such vague answer as that. This one is a favorite game of con artist professors.

"Furthermore, anything you do well, belittlers may if they are in a positon to do so, try to cut it out of the program in which you have done it, so that you will never have another opportunity to do well in it again.

"Another favorite game of theirs is that they try to lead or nudge you into stupid ways, often planting an idea in your head or having someone else do it for them, verbally at first, and then trying to push and pressure you into it non-verbally by hint and innuendo. They try to nudge you to do stupid things to upset your church or personal projects or plans, or, lead you into a ridiculously heavy work load to wear you down and/or make you quit. If you fall for it, then you get ridiculed for it by their accomplices, and perhaps appear unsuccessful to your friends and others.

"If you rebuke the belittlers for it, they play dumb, implying that they didn't know better themselves. If you complain to belittler authorities about it you will likely be told you are just not strong enough to take the rough and tumble of life, or you are over sensative. Branding you as over-sensative is one of their major weapons. It is used extensively by belittlers in all walks of life, including in psychology and psychiatry, professions by the way which hold the door wide open for such wayward behavior. Belittlers, some of them vicious, can play their destructive mind-games and do their devious deeds on you at will, and be openly supported by psychology that they have done little or nothing to you, except perhaps made a minor mistake, but you the victim being supposedly an over-sensative person, are over reacting to it.

"Pin the belittlers down on something drastic they have done to you, and they will simply give a whole different story than yours. They are of the foremost of blatent liars when it comes to covering up. And, of course, it is always convenient for them not to be able to remember. At times, being too immature to perceive the truth even in their own minds, they rationalize and come up with skeptical stories about what they did and why, always making it look like they meant it to be something good for their victim.

"Concerning Durwin's ministry in the church of Terraprima, the belittlers, time and again implied and insinuated that his ministry was not good, he wasn't doing much work, or what he was doing was insignificant. Durwin soon learned their reaction to his telling them and others about the better side of his ministry. They would quickly say or imply that he was boasting and bragging, or, believe it or not, that he was being too proud, and therefore deserving of being put down.

"It is noteworthy that many of the subtle tactics of belittlers are listed as violent abuses in the descriptions of domestic violence: glaring looks and gestures, putting a person down, making a person feel bad about oneself, making a person think he or she is crazy or no good, playing mind-games, humiliating a person, making a person feel guilty. These are all practiced in domestic violence cases, and are also used in the process of belittling, both within and outside the church of Terraprima. They are a part and parcel of violent abuses inflicted by abusive people in domestic violence cases to gain power and control over their victims; and in cases of belittling fine people, to render them feeling inferior and ineffective and to wear them out. In many ways the tactics of belittlers of people like us are no different than those used in domestic violence.

"In all of this the belittlers are trying to ruin your career by making you quit in exasperation, drive you away in fear, drive you berserk, wear you down and out; any or all of these things to somehow, any way that is possible, discredit you. It is nothing short of savage gangsterism in which persons are destroyed. Durwin Lawton went through several years of this ordeal before he fully realized what the belittlers of Terraprima, mainly in the church, were trying to do to him, and how they operated.

"To re-emphasize a point we covered earlier, a large percentage of average people may occasionally have some little trouble with belittlers. Often it is only minor, and is not life altering to any significant extent. I have know some good persons to be beset by a belittler harshly only once or twice in a lifetime, brought on by some localized curcumstance such as envy over a promotion or some newly acquired good fortune. Even these people, only occasionally beset, will tell you how hard it was for them, and that it nearly wrecked their nerves. Imagine then how difficult it is for fine and high caliber people who haven't yet found a pleasant niche in life and who are continuously harassed. Personally, I have never known a time in my adult life, and few in my younger years, when someone wasn't trying hard to bring me down or do me in.

"I remind you again that William Barclay, in his Commentary on 'The letter to the Romans,' writing on Paul's exhortation to live at peace with all people comments:

'Paul knew very well that it is easier for some to live at peace than it is for others. He knew that one person can be compelled to control as much temper in an hour as another person in a lifetime.' (Barclay, William,. The Daily Study (Bible, The Letter To The Romans. P.184. The Saint Andrew (Press, Edinburgh, 1966.).

"By saying this Barclay is indicating that one person can have as much trouble in any one hour or day of his life as another person may have in a lifetime. People who are unaware of this, including many psychiatrists and therapists, are therefore unsympathetic to fine, high caliber people, putting them down all the more by saying that everyone has such troubles and those troubles are a regular part of life. Often, as I said, they regard people like you and I as being too sensative, or we do not cope well, or we lose our temper too quickly. To have it suggested that we have such weaknesses only weakens us all the more if we are willing to listen to them. Actually it is the belittlers who are too sensative. That is why they turn on us when we unintentionally deflate their faulty undisciplined pride.

"Only fine people, well charactered, and of high caliber, usually have extensive trouble of the kind we are referring to with belittlers; so extensive that it is indeed life altering, and can be damaging to mental health, especially to younger adult persons who are not yet much experienced with it.

"As I referred to earlier, a chain is no stronger than its weakest link. So it is with people when the belittlers bring unreasonable stress to bear on the young adult or an older adult too if the stress is brutal enough. It may find his weakest spot and break him. A person may have an emotional area weakened by childhood, but it may never have given him trouble in adulthood were it not for the abnormal pressure and continual torment of the belittlers. Everyone has a weakness or weaknesses. The average person may go through life without those weaknesses causing him any problems. The fine person, under the continuous antagonism of belittlers, may very well have some sort of a nervous breakdown. He may then be wrecked all the more by being told, and perhaps made to believe, he is a weakling of some sort.

"One meaning of pride is 'a proper sense of personal dignity and worth!'(Funk & Wagnells Inc., Standard Desk Dictionary P.524. New York 1975). Another meaning is 'an undue sense of one's own superiority'. (Ibid). You and I take on the first meaning in our personalities, developing a proper sense of our worth, realizing our shortcomings as well as our capabilities, and realizing there are other people who can do better than we in some things, perhaps in everything we can do.

"The belittler, in his personality takes on an undue sense of his worth, making no room in his world for people who may be superior to him in performance of certain tasks, or in appearance, or in the ability to acquire worthwhile possessions or whatever. When a fine person with the greater ability to do those things comes along the person who is proud according to the second meaning takes to belittling in order to rid himself of the person he perceives to be threatening him.

"Because of my continuous trouble with people who are proud in the wrong sense, I personally, never use the word pride or proud in the sense of feeling good about myself or others. Rather, I prefer to say, 'I am pleased and/or happy with myself for what I have done, or, I am pleased and/or happy about my family, congregation or whatever. Since it can be such a loaded word, I prefer to leave the word 'proud' to the realm of the concieted and haughty. I often wish for a better word to be commonly used for personal dignity and worth, or a different word for an undue sense of one's own superiority, one or the other.

"The belittler also confuses pride and confidence; confidence meaning self-assurance. They see us with self assurance, and through their projection they see us as putting on airs which they will condemn in us but which is so much a part of themselves at times. This, in their own minds, give them leverage to discredit our character and belittle us all the more. All through my younger years I had continually to refrain from showing too much confidence in myself so as not to be picked on all the more by belittlers.

"Again the difference between the proud person and the confident person is that the proud person has an overall air of superiority set in his closed mind which must not be shaken. The confident person feels competent in the spheres of his familiarity, while retaining an open mind to the fact that there is still something to learn from others in their spheres. He recognizes there are other areas of life of which he may know very little, but of which others may know a great deal. His mind is continually open to this fact and to these people, accepting it as a part of the course of life. Consequently he is not threatened, nor does he lose his confidence when he is outdone or outshone. He accepts this as a normal part of life.

"Incidentally, that is another characteristic the belittler cannot understand about the belittled. When the belitter engages in rivalry, as he sometimes does when he feels he will safely win, he goes all out and outdoes you in something. Then he cannot understand why you are not devastated by it, and how you can even smile at it and compliment him on his success. To lose in that kind of competition would upset the undisciplined pride of the belittler and shake his world. All it means to we confident people is that just as we can do some things a little better than some other people, so some other people can do some things a little better than we can, or sometimes a great deal better and it makes no difference.

"Proud, envious belittlers are usually self-centered people as well. To give you a simplified illustration of their thinking: if he doesn't like apples and you do, he sees it as you having something wrong with you because you like apples. A complaint about a self centered belittler is often taken by them as a complaint about the whole church or the whole country. A belittler can be so proud and sure that his way is the whole church's or country's way, that if you don't fit in with him, he thinks you don't fit in at all. He looks to see you change and become subserviant to him in all his power and glory. When you don't, he rejects you as a misfit. He doesn't realize that it is he who is the odd-ball.

"Pride and humility are also frequently misunderstood by belittlers. One meaning of humble is 'free from pride or vanity.' (Funk & Wagnalls Standard Desk Dictionary, P313, Funk & Wagnalls, Inc., New York, 1975). Another meaning is 'lowly in station or condition. (Ibid). The proud are categorized by belittlers as the rich and the well to do. The humble, in their book, is usually the poor and perhaps the average. I have met many rich, and many well to do people in very high positions of influence in government, business, science, education, and all fields, who are by nature very genuinely humble in character, and with sincere concern for those less gifted and less prosperous than themselves. I have also met many of them who are very arrogantly proud, haughty and conceited. But also, I have met many poor and many average people who are likewise humble, and many who are arrogantly proud and conceited. The difference is not in the economic or social status, but in the character and personality of the inner person.

"It is popular among belittlers, and some others, to bash the rich. To accomodate this envious habit, the rich are mostly all placed in one category. Regardless of character they are looked upon as the 'dirty rich'. But oh how many of these belittlers wish and strive to be in their shoes! Since they often don't have what it takes to get there, they turn on them all the more in envy and hatred. Incidentally, when a poor person does acquire considerable money, he is then looked upon by his belittler friends as just that; not a rich person, but still one of them, a poor person but with a lot of money.

"Many belittlers will get the idea that you are as you are, a fine person, because either you are rich or you came from a rich family and was especially privileged. They have no idea of your thrift, wise spending and smart living, as opposed to their stinginess or squandering and meager or extravagant life-style. So they treat you with the same contempt they have for the rich, because you have been practical and attained a good standard of living that they could well have afforded if they knew how to use their money and their lives properly.

"I have now told you how belittlers basically behave, and given you a picture of them in their 'worst state,' so to speak. Between this worst state and the state of the belittlers that are passive only, we have many varying degrees of belittling, some mild, some extreme, many in between, all grossly harmful to society.

"In this analysis and in all our story telling, I think we in this group can feel assured that we have not overstated our case. On the contrary, if anything, we have understated it. Belittling is a vicious, severely damaging evil in society.

"As in every area of life, however, there are no hard and fast patterns. Belittlers do though, I have come to believe, have many qualities of character in common, the foremost of which is, their undisciplined pride requires them to defend their outward sense of superiority. So when they come into interaction with a person like one of us, they see us as wrong for hurting their pride, even though we do it just by being what we are and being in their presence. We see them as wrong for hurting us with their abnormal disposition of hostility, toward us. Both sides see themselves as right, hence it is sometimes dubbed, by the more naive elements of psychology as a personality conflict, and its analysis in psychological circles goes no further than that.

"As I told you in the first semester, for daring to discuss this entity with a psychiatrist who knew all about childhood but nothing about adult life out in the market place, I was labeled paranoid and started on the downward road to disability. As you already know, I did manage, with some difficulty, to get off that track. Following that initial experience with psychiatry, I had, in my younger adult life, some breakdowns, or more accurately, periods of complete emotional exhaustion as, to my relief, they were later diagnosed. These were the result of working hard, sometimes extra hard, under the extreme stress of a sequence of severe adult experiences brought on by belittlers, many of them vicious in their imagined injured pride and envy fed hatred. It isn't that I was weak. It was that because of the kind of person I was, I had to endure far more stress than the average person does in life. No human can stand such bombardment day after day, year after year, without it doing harm to his mental and physical well being, and his career.

"This activity of belittlers is also, both inside and outside of psychological circles, at times labled as just plain ignorance, and no more thought given to it than that. Very definitely, however, belittlers may be found in abundance in all walks of life. It is not a matter of the poor against the well-to-do, or the uneducated against the educated. Neither is it the uncultured against the cultured or the irreligious against the religious. Doctors, lawyers, preachers, teachers, office clerks, store clerks, factory workers, mechanics, laborers, you name the occupation, and they all have their share of belittlers among them. It is not merely ignorance. It is a major personality problem throughout society.

"How major is it? First of all, it can begin in the home and affect a person's home life. The finer the child, the more he is discriminated against by a belittling mother, father, sister, or brother. It may be a passive and negative attitude only, without verbal or physical putting down. Even at that the child may grow up feeling inferior or unwanted, or with a sense of being discriminated against.

"Still, the child would have a good chance of surviving that if he were given a reasonable opportunity in school. But give him a belittling teacher or two, and some belittling classmates with a similar attitude and the opportunity to discourage him in school work; also make him feel inferior to the other students, and the groundwork is layed for a child with a serious problem. Hence, some of the finest and best all around children are stymied early in life, while other children less gifted in character, are free to go on.

"Yet even such a stymied child, perhaps by the Grace of God, and/or the love of some true friends, may overcome even that. He may somehow get through school and even university, all the while pushing against the belittlers. But seldom, if ever, will he realize his full potential because of having to work against such odds. Society therefore is robbed of a fine person at full potential, and the fine person is robbed of his right to develop his potential fully. Many people, such as Brett, are turned away from their chosen professions, leaving some of them perhaps with a lifetime sense of loss or injustice.

"Many industry and commerce establishments are drastically affected because they are either unaware of or unable to cope with belittlers within their organization. They fail to see that belittlers drive away some of their better employees, as they did in the case of Donna and her first year supervisor, as we discussed last semester.

"Then there are many business establishments whose management oddly enough, supports belittlers, and cannot stand to have a fine, smart person of genuine integrity around. Such businesses never take the leadership in their field. They remain second rate, and often, sooner or later fold, usually not knowing where they went wrong.

"Government also is affected by belittlers, perhaps moreso than industry. Since many people have made their career in government for its security and benefits, they sometimes come to resent people who have taken the risk of less security but more money in the private sector. This establishes in the civil service a battery of belittlers which have to be dealt with by others both within and without the offices of government. Belittlers, as you can see are a serious problem in all areas of life."

Collin contined with his summaries and analyses. "You no doubt have noticed from our story telling that the problem with belittlers in that part of our neighboring country I call Terraprima is much more severe than in the other two places of interest to us. There in Terraprima, some aspects of the mind-game of belittling stand out more to the objective observer. Concerning Durwin Lawton's experiences in the church of that land, it seems there were many simple Biblical lessons that both clergy and lay people had either never learned, or never paid any attention to. Paul the Apostle states some of them quite simply and clearly. Take for example, 'Having gifts that differ,' (Romans 12:6, R.S.V.) It is so obvious that it should be taken by everyone as a fact of life. It is not taken so by belittlers in their dealings with fine people.

"The worst in this regard are belittlers in the academic field both inside the church and outside it. They miss another simple and obvious lesson in the writings of the Apostle Paul. 'To one is given through the Spirit the utterance of wisdom, and to another the utterance of knowledge according to the same Spirit (I Corinthians 12:8, R.S.V.) Paul separates these gifts of wisdom and knowledge as two distinct gifts.

"Take now the academic belittler. Perhaps he had done very well, maybe even exceptionally well in his university studies. He is an expert at absorbing and imparting knowledge. But what if, because of his wayward character make up and/or his own natural inclination, he has attained very little wisdom or creativity. Woe betide then the wise, fine, well charactered student or employee who comes under his tuteledge or employ. Whether the student or employee has better or lesser academic standing makes no difference. If he has been endowed with wisdom or creativity he can expect to be treated badly by the belittler.

"You may recall from our previous discussions of professors, some are experts in absorbing and imparting knowledge. When they need an answer or a quotation, if its in a book they can come up with it, most likely far better than you and I. But if it's something that requires original thought or creativity, they are lacking. Some people are very accepting and humble about this. But not belittlers. Of the proud and envious academic belittlers, people like us had better beware. They guard their undisciplined academic pride, and they envy the wisdom and creativity of others. A few people are blessed with both knowledge and wisdom and/or creativity and are humble about it. These are rare gems indeed; very lovely people, and an excellent asset to humanity.

"To make another contrast which may affect knowledge and wisdom, a person may not be a good auditory learner, which means he does not get maximum benefit from a lecture, as would other people. He does not readily absorb auditory knowledge anywhere near one hundred percent. But he is a good visual learner, and in the visual process, he is able to take the time to see more deeply into things, analyzing them on the way. This should be regarded as a gift of a different sort. While it may short change the person on the absorbtion of knowledge, it gives the gift of deeper insight. Many academics detecting this become envious and belittling. While the visual learner may respect them for their high degree of absorbtion and sometimes higher grades, they, if they are envious belittlers, cannot respect the visual learner for his high degree of insight, even though he may have lesser grades in his academic record. So for the academic who cannot properly and maturely handle his pride on this, envy may set in, accompanied by hostility and belittling.

"Another cause that triggered the belittling of Durwin and Canda Lawton in Terraprima was the fact that they were not only fine people, but they were fine people from Lower Secundaterra. Had the Lawtons not been such fine smart people it wouldn't have mattered where they were from. But no way were proud belittling Terraprimans going to have people from such a place as Lower Secundaterra show them anything. So they had to, in essence, destroy them.

"Normal people would have reasoned that it was quite a phenomonen for two people to come from that little far away place, and catch on and do so well in Terraprima, including the big city and all. The majority of people did. The abnormal people of hollow, undisciplined pride and of emptiness of anything sound in life turned against them with belittling to attempt to surpress, oppress and destroy them.

"It is ironic, when the Vatican needed someone to fill the high position of Secretary of State, they once chose someone from Lower Secundaterra. Again, when the Pope wished to take a tour in North America, the Vatican placed a person from Lower Secundaterra in charge of the planning of it. Scholars and creative people from Lower Secundaterra, once they have had a chance to adjust elsewhere, have become Principals and Presidents and high standing professors of colleges and universities, and have rated highly in all fields of life. When hopefuls come from there to Terraprima, if they have anything new or different on the ball at all, they are oppressed, driven away or destroyed. Even though Durwin Lawton had no further ambition than to adjust well and have a pleasant and viable pastorate, he was squashed mercilessly because he was exceptional in some ways. When a fine, exceptional person comes to this protestant denomination of the part of America I call Terraprima, they do him in, or try to at least. No wonder this mainline protestant Church is in decline.

Then he continued, "If they deem you to be a cut above them, without saying anything outright, but with much insinuation and innuendo they will try at every imaginable opportunity to vaunt themselves above you. They want you to feel they are superior to you. At the same time they work even harder on you to make you feel inferior to them. Again they can do this without ever saying anything outright. They negatively imply, infer and insinuate; with much innuendo they treat you as though you have something wrong with you and try to make you believe it. By using this method they put down your finest points of character and your most able gifts and talents, implying that in their opinion they do not see much merit in them.

"They will treat you with pity, but very scantily at that, and as if they are doing you a great favor by giving you that much. They imply that they think you are not much of anything, but that they feel sorry for you, and so will help you out as best they can, considering you are not much to go on in the first place. You go to them for help and they will shake hands with you, even hug you, then offer in a pitying manner some paltry help that actually is no help at all, but only something to dampen your spirit and send you further down."

Leo Aidan interrupted with a quip in keeping with his character, "they betray you with a kiss!" (See the Gospel according to Luke 22:47, 48).

The other group members couldn't find it conducive to laugh at that one. They seriously nodded in agreement.

"That's about what it amounts to," agreed Collin, and continued, "they use such tactics as greeting you with a grin or a cheesey smile that can be taken as being friendly or offered in mockery. The only way you can distinguish between the two is to wait, sometimes for a long time, to figure whether it is followed up by positive or negative actions towards you. For example if a supervisor is negative in his actions towards you over a period of time, you will pretty well know his grin was an attempt to make you feel uncomfortable, and perhaps to make you cower before him.

"If they can, by all this implication, make you believe that you are inferior, or, if they think you are believing it, then down, down, down they will push you, all the while with a phoney smile of pity for you on their faces. I call it the 'pitying for no reason game'. If somehow you outwardly prove them wrong and show them up, they can make the whole of the implications disappear, and they will, in a manner of surprise imply, or even state that nobody said a word about you, that it's all a mistake on your part, you are imagining things. If you trip them up in some concrete manner, say by having a witness or witnesses to some wrong they said or did, they will blatantly say it isn't so. Truth or lies, good or bad, right or wrong, doesn't matter to belittlers; only what appears to make them look good or appears to put them in the right.

"If it turns out to be a case where they can't by innuendo or lies make it disappear, they smoooth it all over either by spoken words or implication that they didn't know the difference, they misunderstood, and thought they were doing the right thing. If you know this to be phoney and don't offer forgiveness, then they hold you up as having an unforgiving spirit and holding on to grievances.

"Their cover-up doesn't end there. They sometimes get through, wherever possible, to any supporting friends you have. Using innuendo again they unsuspectingly imply to your supporters that you have a lot of misunderstandings, or are oversensative, as I have mentioned before. One of the favorites of the church belittlers is that ministry is more stressful than most other occupations, and you are just not strong enough to stand up to it.

"Another of the many tactics of belittlers is that they try to confound you so that they can make you out to be 'nuts' as they call it in the vernacular. This devious trickery is used by belittlers in many walks of life, but more effectively by academic belittlers. They tried it on Durwin Lawton when he did his Doctor of Ministry paper. They don't have the ability themselves to think deeply about a subject; only to learn about it from other peoples writings. It would drive them 'bugs' as they call it, to even try to think deeply. So they figure it should do the same to people like us. Therefore, they try in every way possible to lead us into deep thinking, meanwhile confounding us all the way, to wear us down and drive us 'bugs' or 'nuts', which is what would happen to them under much less confounding circumstances. When it doesn't happen to us they get all the more perplexed and angry with us, sometimes openly revealing their true attitude toward us in their mixture of whimsical remarks and angry attitude.

"When Durwin wrote his paper, and before he got fully wise to them, they led him every way possible with more and more books to read, and therefore more and more material to analyze in his paper. When he was part way through the paper, and realized what they were up to, he took up the challenge, covered all the material and wrote a good paper. They turned it down, with many different and conflicting outlandish reasons, altogether a disgrace for a supposedly Christian seminary. Durwin didn't get his degree, but his person, his character, and his theology remained courageously intact.

"Still another of their devious mind-games is that they will get someone, usually a young person of no obvious consequence to plant an idea in your head, verbally, and quietly on the side. Then the others by inference, implication and pressure try to push you in that direction; usually not a direction suitable for you or your career.

"Another one is they will get some seemingly insignificant young person or persons often a young woman to plague the life out of you by fouling up everything you do, or having them pretend they don't think you and your work are very good; putting it down by innuendo and even verbally at every quarter. Among other tactics, they interrupt your conversations by butting in and/or drowning you out and taking over the conversation. The only way out of it for you is to quarrel with them, which is what they would like and then blatantly blame you for it, or, you just have to forfeit what you wanted to say. Its okay for these young persons to play naive and come out in the open with their tactics. If you complain about such persons you will be trivialized and scoffed at for letting young inexperienced people like that especially a woman, bother you. If these supposedly young inexperienced people break you or drive you away, then you are marked as being oversensative to these insignigicant people. They make you out to be a real chicken. Once you have been branded this way, your credibility is in real trouble.

"Incidently, as I indicated before, even belittlers in organizations that see themselves as champions of equality for women, still use the young woman mind-game to belittle people. To complain that *a young woman* was causing you trouble would really get you branded as over-sensative, as if the age or gender of the person bugging you would make any difference.

"While all this is going on, officials who are belittlers, stand on the sidelines watching the game with these supposedly insignificant people to see which way it goes. If you win the game they stand back in silence, waiting for another chance at you. If you lose the game, then they put you on record in as negative a manner as they openly dare according to all the circumstances.

"Once the belittlers have ear-marked you for belittling, it passes from one belittler to another, and with each of them finding his or her way of putting you down some more. It catches and spreads, so that in an environment or circumstance where belittlers are predominant, you have no choice but to get out or be put down, down, down by what amounts to unspoken slander. You can see what I mean when I call it a conspiracy of sorts."

Leo bristled again, "plunderers of human dignity, gangsters".

Owen remarked more seriously, "it is evil all right, sinister."

"The epitome of evil", added Gilda.

"It took Durwin several years to learn the dirty, evil game well enough to climb out from under it," said Collin.

"What makes me wonder," questioned Donna, "is, what about the young children of the belittled. Some of the belittled must have families; the children must suffer too."

"It makes no difference to the belittlers, not an iota," said Collin. "I've seen and heard of cases where the children were greatly affected, and other cases where they could have been perhaps severely damaged were it not for the ongoing perserverance and ingenuity of the belittled parents. Belittlers give no thought to such a consequence."

"That's disgusting," remarked Leo, "again I say that, with the exception of sex offenders and perhaps a few others, even the most hardened criminals would be abhorred at the thought of doing anything to harm a child; sounds worse than psychopathic to me."

"It is extreme and gross evil; a scourging evil of the most corrupt and vicious kind," added Owen.

"They give it no thought," responded Collin, "their concern is their undisciplined pride and our downfall. In addition, if you were to openly accuse them of picking on you out of envy, they, having by now put you down and built themselves and other envious belittlers up, would attempt to twist it all around. They would try, and very hard, to establish that you are envious of your belittlers. That is one of the things about it all that gives them the most satisfaction. We in this group are well aware that belittlers are such because they are envious of people like us. I emphasize again, another of their main wayward manipulations is that after they have vaunted themselves above us and put us down, or think they have, they try hard to make us behave enviously of them. They cannot understand why the things that made them envious of us, doesn't make us envious of them. The answer is we have different values than they, and envy is not a part of us at all. As Brett said earlier, there is pain, disappointment, and sometimes anger, but that is not anything like envy. Still they try ever so hard, try that is, to make us envious of them.

"They deal with the issue of over-sensitivity in much the same manner. They are the ones who are over-sensitive. Their silly pride is easily upset. Yet they try very hard to twist that around and make us out to be over-sensative. Verbally, and by innuendo they imply from the beginning of their onslaught that we are over-sensative. Then they set out to make it so by bugging the life out of us. I would say that if anyone of us allowed them to intensely bombard us with their devious deeds long enough it would eventually make us sensitive to it like it did with Brett's high school English teacher, as we discussed first semester. That would not be human weakness, just a characteristic of human nature. So that is what they set out to do using all their belitting tactics. Again, in effect, psychology supports them.

"Furthermore, that brings us to another twist, or clash; psychology's treatment of the whole matter with its absurd conception of paranoia. From my experiences psychology would say, in the first place, that for thinking, even objectively thinking of oneself as a fine person, we are having delusions of grandeur. Furthermore, for thinking the belittlers are against us purposely belittling us to put us down, psychology would say we are having delusions of persecution or we are paranoid. On top of that, psychology would say that because we accuse belittlers of being envious of us it really means that we are envious of them but we are projecting our feelings of envy onto them. Psychology has opened the flood gate to allow people like you and I to be mentally mutilated.

"From this you can easily see the hopelessness of persons like us going to a psychiatrist or therapist for help with our problem of being belittled, put down, discriminated against. If we were to allow ourselves to be lulled or persuaded to think of it as psychologists would have it, we would be drawn away from our world of reality, perhaps never to find it again. We would never again be able to cope with the world as it exists for people like us. We would be destroyed as persons and become degenerate."

Gilda questioned, "If belittling is so prevalent in the church even to the extent of being a conspiracy of sorts, how can it be reconciled to Christian character?"

"It cannot," Collin replied. "It never has been brought into the open to be examined and tested, but if it was, it could never be reconciled. Worse than that, I know of no other organization that plays this game, this conspiracy of sorts, more craftily, as the denomination of the church in Terraprima in which Durwin Lawton served.

"There are many causes of envy, within the church as well as outside it, in addition to academic pride. There is, for example, within the church two main categories of ministers which I will refer to for the purpose of identification as the converted minister and the career minister. Lay people of the congregations can also be divided that way, but I will in this discussion refer to the ministry only.

"There is a notable difference between the two. The one, the converted minister is a person who has experienced God intimately in his inner being, and thereby having received the Grace of God in his life, would not knowingly do anything to harm any of God's people. The career minister, on the other hand has learned of God from books, including the Bible, and from other modes of communication, and believes in God, but has never properly humbled himself before God in repentance, and received God's grace and the humble confidence it brings to replace wayward, undisciplined pride and self-sufficiency. These two facets of the Christian church produce a very different way of thinking and behaving, each from the other. I imagine the same two categories could exist in other enlightened religions as well, but I will restrict my discussion to Christianity. The truly converted minister is not as likely to become an envious belittler, unless he has not received enough proper nurture in his faith. In that case the shortcomings of his culture, including belittling, may still be predominant in his character.

For example, before his conversion he may have been a self-centered and envious person. If that part of his original culture is not now dealt with, overcome and removed from his character, he may continue with this self-centered outlook. Then he may expect that anyone who hasn't had a religious experience exactly as his own, is not truly a Christian. He may also become envious of any special gifts and graces that another converted Christian may have. Actually there are numerous varieties of religious experiences among people, and continuous experiences in each individual. Also, "there are varieties of gifts." (I Corinthians 12:4, NRSV). For a converted Christian to become envious of another Christian, or any other person, because of his experiences, or gifts, or for any reason, is an indication that the word has fallen on "poor soil."(see Matthew 13:1-9). Of course, poor soil can always be improved with additives and nurture.

Also there are some career ministers who are not belittlers; they are people of good character, given their point of view. On the other hand, though, many belittler Christian ministers come from the career type. Among their foremost envys is their envy of the converted Christian. They cannot accept that God would somehow visit the life of another person and not theirs. After all, they have given themselves to a career in God's church—and they are proud of it. If it is undisciplined pride, not grace, but undisciplined pride, one of their main methods of protecting it is belittling.

"The difference between the two, the converted and the career types, is exemplified in various translations of the Bible. For example: the R.S.V. and New R.S.V. translations say in the Gospel of Luke, 17:21, 'the kingdom of God is *in your midst,'* and, 'the kingdom of God *is among you,'* respectively; each with a foornote of *'within you.'* The *within* concept is secondary.

"On the other hand the original KJ.V. and also the New K.J.V. translates, 'the kingdom of God *is within you,* with a foornote of *'amongyou'* or *'in your midst,'* respectively. In these translations the *within* concept is primary.

"And so it is, many career types pay little or no attention to God within, and concentrate on God among, deriving their foremost satisfaction mainly, and sometimes totally, from what has been known as the social gospel. Converted ministers first and foremost, concentrate on God within, and their various forms of social action are secondary. Their motto could well be, 'the value of what I do will be according to what I am.' (Author unknown). Of course both are valid Christian characteristics. Indeed, the case has been well made numerous times that faith and works are both necessary to the Christian life. However, to the converted Christian, the within concept cannot be omitted and must be in first place.

"To give another vivid illustration of the difference between the two types, there is the hymn, 'All Praise To Our Redeeming Lord", by Charles Wesley, which calls us in one of its lines, 'to build each other up.' To the convert this means to be built up in faith and grace and the sound type of confidence that comes with it. He lives in such a way as to increase his faith and that of his neighbor. To the career person, 'to build each other up' means to build people up in pride. The career person lives in such a way as to increase and protect his pride and that of his alike friends who return the deed. Some of them take to belittling to protect this pride. Obviously then, it is a source of belittling in the church.

"Another of many differences between the convert and career minister may be observed. When a proud belittler does not have a son or daughter follow him into ministry, and there is a fine minister and family who does, there will often be prejudice shown. I have seen it happen too many times. Personally, I did my best to show my children the pitfalls of ministry in an effort to make them think twice, or more, about going into it. Of course, God himself has the final word and issues the sense of call.

"Belittlers generally like the Old Testament, often preferring it to the New Testament. They particularly adhere to the prophets' speaking out about the rich and the high and mighty and claim God is biased toward the poor, as they themselves usually are. They overlook the fact that many of God's called and chosen Old Testament people were wealthy indeed according to what constituted riches in their time. They overlook such unbiased verses of the Old Testament, such as Leviticus 19:15 (NRSV):

"You shall not render an unjust judgement; you shall not be partial to the poor or defer to the great; with justice you shall judge your neighbor."

They also overlook what the New Testament teachings can do about both rich and poor. Ironically, they overlook many passages of Old Testament Scripture such as Isaiah 3:5 and what happens to society when oppression, including the oppression from belittlers, continually brings down the better type of people. Isaiah 3:5 (R.S.V.) reads:

'And the people will oppress one another, evey man his fellow and every man his neighbor; the youth will be insolent to the elder, and the base fellow to the honorable.'

"The mature convert Christian treats others according as God's Grace directs him. He is nurtured into this by the spirit and teachings of the New Teatament, some of them very simple, such as Jesus' Golden Rule, 'So whatever you wish that [people] would do to you, do so to them;." (Matthew 7:12a. R.S.V.) To the career Christian turned belittler this is child's play. It doesn't get you anywhere, so he thinks. He treats others according to what is good for his own pride and position. Even in a routine conversation with some of them, one can often detect their biases, prejudices, wrath, and whimsicalness; say the wrong thing and their face may droop, or they will push up the lip, or pout, even go into a near tantrum of spite and whining, and walk away.

"The career ministers turned belittlers in the church are often ambitious for themselves and covet the higher positions and larger, or crucial and well-known congregations. They not only volunteer for them, but sometimes manipulate, maneuver and bow down to the powers that be to get these positions. Then after they get them they sometimes expect others to bow to them in order to be on the inside track with them. This gives them a sense of power and control which in turn pads their pride all the more.

"They belittle those of us who do not bow down, and will see to it that we never get a good position if they can at all prevent it. They don't understand why when we don't get to move ahead, we don't get down about it and pout, which is their way of behavior under such circumstances. The end result is, of course, the church often gets wrongly motivated people in higher and often crucial places, and the church, both at large and locally, gradually diminishes under them, even though it may show some temporary gains at times.

"Sometimes the church makes the mistake of placing a converted minister and a career minister in a church together, perhaps with the latter as senior pastor of the two. It seldom works well as envy may set in and cause hardship for the converted one. The career person usually prevails, in the short run at least, especially if he is a subtle and deceitful one, a manipulator and cover-up type of person, a mind-game player—all of which are unchristian to the truly converted.

"In actuality, belittlers are a phoney, childishly whimsical oversensative people. They live in such a wastefulness and lostness in their way of life! They cause such a waste of true talent all around them! They cause untold tensions and stresses in life. Just go to a conference of genuinely mature Christians and you can have a wonderfully good and pleasant time with relaxed people free from hangups. Go to a conference of career Christians, a substantial number of them belittlers, and the air will be filled with tension and political and social maneuvering of various sorts, all designed and employed by these misguided people for the purpose of trying to keep their childish, undiscipled pride intact.

"Many belittlers try to pick your brains, scab your ideas, and imitate your way of life. They may gain some knowledge from it, but they are still lacking in the Grace of God. The Grace of God cannot be cloned or counterfeited. They may try to imitate it by being smooth operators with cheesey smiles, and include familar religious platitudes in their activity, but it may be only an act. If it isn't genuine, their true character, with all its hangups, will eventually show through. As I said, the Grace of God cannot be cloned or counterfeited. It has to be the real thing.

"Further exploration of the concept of converted versus career ministers and lay people of the church could be extensive and take us outside the sphere of our concern in this group. Actually it would become another subject altogether, a theological one. I have used it sufficiently for now to bring us illustrations of another of the causes of belittling in the church, so we will leave it at that and talk a little more about belittlers generally.

"Belittlers know that we are solid, candid people of integrity, and not wheelers and dealers as they often are. It bothers them immensely. They continually try to find ways to make our integrity out to be questionable and thereby upset us about it. Our only defense is to not let them bother us on it no matter what. So when we don't get disturbed it baffles them, because they themselves get so easily upset. They don't understand the difference between us and them. We are people, not of undisciplined pride and the insecurity that often lurks behind it, but people of integrity and the much more solid confidence that goes with it.

"One of the most dehumanizing mind-games is one that I have mentioned before in which the belittler starts treating you as though you have something wrong with you, and tries to make you and perhaps your supporters believe it. Then he practically takes over your life, or tries to, making your decisions for you as though you weren't capable of making them yourself, and then by inference and innuendo he nudges you into following those decisions. If a victim wasn't wise to this, he would of course eventually deteriorate into having something wrong with him indeed. This in turn would seem to justify the belittlers tactic in the first place. Some higher up power and control church officials constantly plagued Durwin with this one. He kept them at bay as best he could.

"If knowledge of such games was more widely known in society, I feel sure the lawyers who become wise to it could take care of the matter legally for us. In one such case I know of a would-be victim who was fortunate enough to be able to take care of a similar matter by a sworn statement barring the brazen belittler from any authority over him, the intended victim. It worked but it is a rare case to date.

"Another case in which the law, if properly informed on the matter, could help us is when belittlers expect that I, for example, as a Christian minister, must be nice and friendly to them under all circumstances, no matter how they behave towards me. If I keep them at a distance and do not submit to their demands, either insinuated or spoken outright, they come on with their shake-downs such as, 'what you a Christian minister and not going to be friends with me!' It is an attempt at intimidation. Many ill-informed protestant ministers are naive to such opportunistic shake-downs and fall for it. Belittling ministers will turn a blind eye to it or openly support your assailant on it. Either way it is very poor theology and interpretation of scripture."

Collin added, "I have the desire to see lawyers take hold of this human problem we have been exploring. I would like very much to have justice for everyone oriented lawyers take up the matter, with litigation and all, and come up with ways to curb and bring to justice, belittlers in their destroying of character, personhood, and even life itself; their intentional infliction of emotional distress, meant to damage or destroy other people just to protect their own self-centered, undisciplined pride.

"Intentional infliction of emotional distress is already unlawful. However it is generally applied to spousal or child abuse. Lawyers need to know how it is continually practiced by belittlers in society. As was mentioned earlier, many of the psychological tactics used by belittlers on people like us are the same as those used in spousal abuse.

"The problem is of enormous magnitude and worsening. Children are learning it in and even before Middle School. High School students are masters at it. And people wonder why there are shootings in schools by students who at one time had the makings of nice, clean-cut, and at times, in some ways outstanding individuals. But there is little room for individuality. As time went by, they didn't fit into the common run of the mill mold, and were therefore singled out and treated negatively. In other words they were 'picked on.'

"It is noticeable that white Caucasians at the true top in almost any field are getting fewer and fewer, and it is mostly, not all, but mostly envious white belittlers who are causing it to be so. By true top I mean that which could be attained by exceptional people if they were unimpeded by belittlers, as opposed to the secondary top belittlers create for themselves and for people of lesser calibre by pushing others beneath them.

"In North America business and industry is coming more and more under foreign ownership or management. Why? Because in North America there is less and less opportunity for young, fine, smart would be entrepreneurs to make their way up through the belittler oppression to attain such positions. They are stymied on the way. The belittlers themselves do not have the ability to make it to the true top, and they prevent those who could develop such ability by blocking their way up through the education and employment ranks.

"Note another point: I mentioned earlier the belittlers may try to make your supporters believe you are in some way inferior. I previously gave examples of this in Durwins case, for example, the woman who found it hard to believe that the good special church service was of Durwin's making; another acquaintance who came to believe Durwin's great problem was he couldn't stand up to the rigors of ministry. "Belittlers have even been known to try to drive a wedge between husband and wife by downgrading, even trying to lead astray the husband, meanwhile being nice to the wife, or vice versa. If the spouse does not fall for it, then he/she is also belittled so as to go down with the main victim.

"One last but very notable mind-game often played by belittlers is that if and when you are moving away and/or breaking contact with them they will most always do some nice thing to you or offer a nice gesture. This is meant to smooth over all the past trickery and hopefully put doubt in your mind as to whether you have been taking them all wrong, that they are really nice people. This is hard to fall for after you have been grossly mistreated for any length of time."

Collin paused for a moment, causing a break in his review and analysis. He looked around at the other group members. "These are my insights into the way belittlers generally think and operate. A lot of them, especially in the church of Terraprima because the church supports it, practice their wayward craft quite openly because they mistakenly think that most people agree with them on it. Others practice it in ways that only those familiar with it can detect it. Durwin Lawton and his wife Canda with him went through all this and more during his several years of ministry in Terraprima, coming through it victoriously.

"Such are the ways of the belittlers of Terraprima, and it is increasing in the Secundaterras; people of undisciplined, hollow pride that issues in envy, hatred and hostility; the kind of pride that oppresses and tears down others in order to keep itself intact."

Collin paused again, stirred himself out of his presentation more completely, saying in a more relaxed tone, "Guess that will do it for now folks. I hope it will be of help to you all."

"Thank you Collin for sharing your insight with us. It will surely help each of us to understand and to cope not only if any of us ever move to Terraprima, but also in our present location if and when it spreads to here in such an extensive way," remarked Owen Winslow appreciatively.

"I wish I had such insight and help ten or fifteen years ago," added Brett Culver.

The remaining members expressed their appreciation for Collin's and each others's help and support.

Owen brought the meeting to an end, saying, "It is time to relax for the evening folks, anyone for the coffee shop?"

They all agreed to go.

However, as they gathered there the atmosphere was more subdued than on previous occasions. They were concerned for Dr. Eldren. They were also very anxious as to what might transpire with the new psychiatrist. Conversation came around to the latter, but they quickly decided that speculation about it was neither relaxing nor helpful.

Sooner than usual the members walked to the parking lot as a group, there dispersing to their respective cars for the drive home, all wondering what would be in store for them next Wednesday evening.

CHAPTER XIII

It was Wednesday evening meeting time once more. Collin and Vita Seldon approached Quilibet University, entered by the glass doors, walked up the half set of steps to the main floor, where they paused in front of the entranceway to the library.

"I will come to the library for you after the meeting," said Collin, "it may be sooner, it may be later. You know how it is, a new psychiatrist in charge and we don't know how it will work out."

"Be careful what you're getting into," cautioned Vita, as she had done many times before.

"Yes, I will be very careful," said Collin, "and as I mentioned before, Albin Anders will be with you in the library. He will meet you in the main reading room. Both of you remain there until I come or you hear from me. I want to be very careful what he is getting into also. See you later!"

"Good Luck," said Vita as she touched her husband softly on the arm and left for the library, as Collin headed for the elevator and room 405.

I wonder, I wonder, what are we in for this evening? pondered Collin to himself as he tensed up while the elevator took him to the fourth floor. *I had hoped, through Dr. Eldren, we would somehow make an impact on psychology and psychiatry concerning this almost unnoticed, and certainly unexplored area of life. But now with Dr Eldren's terminal illness, that is gone. With the new psychiatrist, even if he is compatible, it will take a long time to get through to him. It may mean doing the whole thing over again. That would be arduous indeed. Oh well,"* he finalized his thought of the moment as he approached the door of Room 405, *no point in making plans until we get to know the new psychiatrist.*

It was still several minutes before seven when Collin entered the room. The other group members had already arrived, except for Brett Culver, and of course, Albin Anders who would be with Vita at the library. The five sat down and began to discuss their feelings with one another.

"None of us have met the new psychiatrist yet," said Owen, and then with sincere concern for the outcome of the group, continued, "I think we have no choice but to trust him, whose name by the way is Dr. Pitt. I would suggest we level with him from the beginning about the uniqueness of this group and its problems, thereby helping him to help us."

Collin shook his head gently as Owen looked to him for response. "I am very dubious about it," replied Collin, "but I have nothing better to suggest. If our first minutes of introduction to him impress us favorably, then maybe we can begin at least to familiarize him with our trend of thought gently and gradually, remembering that it will be something new to him."

"I don't like it," added Gilda, "but it's that or lose the whole thing."

Donna and Leo agreed. They too would take their chances.

Just then, at one minute to seven, a man entered briskly through the open doorway of Room 405, closing the door behind him as he twisted suavely around on one foot to do so. Then strutting part way across the room to the center of the group, he whirled around again on his right foot, swinging the left foot around in front of him, planting it firmly on the floor then bringing the right foot up beside the left, all with near military precision.

"Good evening folks," he said, with an air of efficiency, "I am Dr. Pitt. I am to be your new group facilitator. I'm sorry to hear of Dr. Eldren's serious illness, but now that I have been appointed to take his place, I am sure we can continue with this group satisfactorily."

Dr. Pitt was a tall young slender man with a small size thin, rather flat looking face, as though somehow it had been just a little squashed by some great pressure brought to bear between the top of his head and bottom of his chin. His complexion had a rough hewn, uncared for looking appearance that did nothing to help overshadow the fact that he was not naturally outstanding in profile. As if in contradiction to this fact, his slightly curly coal black hair was styled, and in quantity on top, sides and back, making it both too long and too bulky for the size of his face. It was combed immaculately and looked like it was held in place with hair spray or some other product commonly used by many for the purpose of tidiness. On a full and round face, such a hair style would be in good taste. On Dr. Pitt the total effect was a mismatch with his small facial features.

He wore a good quality salt and pepper suit of a mixture of various brown and beige colors which didn't become him. His movement with near military percision combined with his speaking in overbearing tones gave, outwardly at least, the impression of having an air of overconfidence and unrealistic authority. It was as if this was his biggest career assignment to date and he was on a high over it.

Dr. Pitt stood out all right, as he obviously wanted to—but not as a fine person. Altogether, any knowledgeable observer of people would get the impression from outward appearance for sure, that Dr. Pitt was very proud and visibly vaunting himself before the group. It remained to be seen how his total personality would stack up against the humility and openness of the group members, and what conflict it would bring to them if they were to get deeply involved with him. Outward appearances, however, usually reflect the character of the person.

Looking around and spotting an empty chair, Dr. Pitt pulled it into the circumference of the circle, sat down and continued talking as though to a group of young subordinates.

"Would you introduce yourselves to me please, just briefly for now; your name and your occupation, and any little information you may wish to add. We will get to know each other better as time goes on."

Collin was very uneasy about this new man. *I think we should be as brief as possible,* he thought to himself. *The less this psychiatrist knows about us the better. At least, thats my feeling so far, so I'll try to set the pattern for this round.* Then aloud politely, "I'm Collin Seldon, and I'm a clergyman."

Dr. Pitt looked for more, but Collin remained silent, avoiding the doctors eyes with their non-verbal request for more information, and turning to Leo Aidan next to him, motioning to him to speak.

Leo caught the idea, "I am Leo Aidan, office worker and part time student," he said and turned immediately to Donna.

"I am Donna Coyne, a secretary and part time student," said Donna, then immediately passing on to Gilda.

"I am Gilda Emerson, student," said Gilda, looking in turn to Owen.

"I am Owen Winslow, teacher and student," said Owen, after the pattern of the others.

Dr. Pitt spoke up again as an adult would to children, "That's a little more brief than I had intended, but it will do for now. As I said, we will get to know each other in time. Now I have been told by the University Health Services Department that you are a group of people who seem to have trouble with some of your professors. Is that correct?"

The group members looked at one another in a near petrified manner. Then, just in time, and as if to the rescue, the room door opened, and in walked Brett Culver, catching the attention of all, including Dr. Pitt. This brought temporary relief to the group from a question they were reluctant to try to answer in a nut-shell if at all to this man.

"Sorry to be late again," said Brett as he closed the door and came to sit among the members, "but you know how it is with me."

"In future," said Dr. Pitt in his brisk assertive manner, you will have to be on time. Once the group meeting begins we cannot have interruptions."

"I'll try to do better, sir," said Brett.

"Good. I am Dr. Pitt, psychiatrist and overseer of this group, taking up Dr. Eldren's work, and what is your name, may I ask?"

"Brett Culver, sir," came the reply.

"And what is your occupation, Mr. Culver."

"I am in business for myself, Dr. Pitt," said Brett pausing for a moment, then speaking again as Dr. Pitt looked at him obviously expecting more information.

"I own a chain of service stations and car washes, and am at present getting into the manufacture of ignition parts," added Brett.

Oh-h," responded Dr. Pitt, becoming self conscious, and squeamish in his chair over such accopmlishments of another person, then asking hautily, "and what brings *you* to this university?" The manner in which he asked the question did nothing to camouflage his contemptuous emphasis on the word you.

"I am taking evening courses in business administration Dr. Pitt," replied Brett politely, by this time beginning to get some idea of what he and all the group were in for.

"And I suppose," continued Dr. Pitt, as if conducting a cross examination, "one of the reasons you have trouble with your professors is that you are late for classes frequently?"

Brett kept calm. "No sir,' he answered, "I find being a little late is a minor matter with most professors, especially for a first class of the evening. Many students come rushing in late or the last minute, often because they were late getting away from their place of employment."

"Tell me then, Brett," pressed the doctor futher, now a little more perturbed after being wrong with his assumptions, "just what in essence is your problem with professors?"

Brett took a deep breath, as if exasperated already with this man who had been appointed to lead the group.

Collin saw Brett's predicament and summed it up in his thoughts. *If Brett, or any of the other group members for that matter, get into deep contoversy with this psychiatrist, they may eventually have to break off their studies at this university, and that would be a great loss to them. If, however, I have to leave, its no loss to me, since I am taking the course in psychology more out of curiosity than anything else. So I can stick my neck out at no great risk.* Before Collin could speak, Brett, feeling pressured by Dr. Pitt began to speak again.

"Well sir," said Brett hesitatingly, "it isn't because we don't do well enough that we have problems with some professors, rather its because we do too well in some areas of our work and lives and some professors get upset with us as though they were threatened."

"Oh-h-h," drawled Dr. Pitt, sarcastically, "that sounds very strange to me; a professor, one who has two or three and possibly more degrees in his subject, being upset and threatened by a student who is just learning that subject. That sounds very strange indeed."

Brett appeared to be getting very uneasy. He had been caught unawares, and now he was in a jam. Dr. Pitt appeared to be victorious in his confrontational debut. It was more obvious than ever now that this group and Dr. Pitt would never click. Collin had by now a moment to think this through. He decided to bring out a point first, and then try to get the group off the hook.

"Dr. Pitt," Collin spoke up in a firm overbearing voice in order to draw the attention away from Brett, "you find Brett's statement concerning his problem with professors to be strange?"

"Yes, indeed I do," replied the doctor.

"Strange, like paranoia?" asked Collin inquiringly, and with softer and gentler tones to avert an argument.

"Well yes," answered the subdued Dr. Pitt. "Yes, since you have mentioned the diagnosis yourself, it does speak very much of paranoia to me, with some overestimation of oneself as a student, included."

Collin decided to press this point no further, but to smoothly change course. "It may sound like perhaps a little touch of delusions of grandeur, Dr. Pitt, but you see we have found the real problem with the members of this group after several months of discussion under the guidance of Dr. Eldren. There is one thing we all have in common," said Collin. The other group members sat in wide eyed apprehension thinking Collin was about to attempt to put the whole true story across to Dr. Pitt, even though by now they had all assumed it would be useless to do so.

"And this one thing we all have in common," Collin went right on without giving anyone else time to speak, "is that the group members are all what is loosely call strong personalities—a little stiff-necked you know. When we come in close contact with a professor who is equally strong minded and stiff-necked, we have what is generally termed a personality clash."

The group members gazed around at one another, relieved and pleased, but holding back their smiles as best they could. Dr. Pitt started to speak, but Collin kept on going with his alibi.

"We decided in the group that the best way for each of us to handled this predicament we find ourselves in at times is to avoid taking classes from professors with whom we may have this problem. This can be done by getting to meet and to know the professor of a particular course we may wish to take, before the course begins, or, inquire from fellow students who have already taken a course from him or her. This is not always possible. So if we do get registered in a class where we eventually find we are not compatable with the professor, there is another opportunity. At a university this size it is usually possible to take the same course from another professor, and there is a period with a deadline, in which a student may ask for a transfer."

Dr. Pitt again made an effort to speak, but Collin kept on talking without pause.

"Certainly, we group members could all go for individual psychotherapy as a means to improve our personalities, but as you know Dr. Pitt, that is a very long process. It is more often measured in years than in months, so that would not be practical for our immediate circumstances. It is therefore left to each individual member to decide for him or her self whether they will go for private therapy. So you see we had about concluded our process, and as you know the semester is mostly gone anyway, meaning that this particular group would have dispersed after this or the next meeting. At least that's the way many of us feel about it, having a sense of accomplishing our purpose. So it's hardly fair to you Dr. Pitt to get you involved for so short a period, when it would be of little further help to us. You could no doubt be using the time to organize another group with different needs for next semester."

Collin ceased talking, leaving time for Dr. Pitt to respond. From the subdued tones in which his response came, the potentially explosive situation had been defused, even though Dr. Pitt was not entirely satisfied.

"That explains things very well, Mr. Seldon, "he said appreciatively, but," he remarked curiously, "you don't strike me as a particularly stong personality, neither does Mr. Culver, however, I do not know either of you well, and first impressions are not always complete."

"In addition," remarked Collin, "I am getting older and mellowing somewhat, and besides, as you say, first appearances do not always reveal the person. However, if Brett was not a strong personality, I doubt if he could be so far ahead in business at so young an age."

Dr. Pitt shuffled in his chair again, bothered by Brett's success in business, a symptom sometimes displayed by some envious academics over the accomplishments of someone in another sphere of life. But then, as if it was bringing him relief, he said, "Well, if you people have fulfilled your needs insofar as this group is concerned, and have no futher need for it, I see no reason why it should not be dispersed. There are many students in the university coming from troubled homes and difficult childhoods who can benefit greatly from group therapy," he said as he continued regaining his composure and stance since he now dealt in an area with which he was familar and comfortable. "I will set about immediately making provision for such a group for next semester. I assume then it is agreed by all of you that this present group be dispersed?"

By this time Owen had slipped down low in his chair with his crossed legs entending way out in front of him as if in complete relief. The whole group was now in an air of relaxation.

"Agreed," came the unanimous reply from the members, signifying they had no further need for the group. Owen pulled himself straight up in his chair.

"Dr. Pitt," he said, "may I, on behalf of the group thank you for coming here this evening and for your interest in us. We appreciate your concern."

The other members joined in with expressions of thanks, and Dr. Pitt responded that he was always glad to be of help. Collin, unnoticed by Dr. Pitt looked at Owen, tossed his head slightly towards the door, then stood up in order to get the group moving out before further conversation ensued.

"I'm going for coffee," said Owen Winslow winking at the others, taking Gilda by the hand, suggesting she come too and leading her through the door.

"I'm going too," said Brett, "would you join me Leo and Donna?"

"Sure," they replied and followed him out.

Collin started toward the door, pausing to shake hands with Dr. Pitt on the way.

As they shook hands, Dr. Pitt brought on further discussion. "Mr. Seldon," he said, regaining his firmness, "I am still not so sure about your friend Brett Culver. I wonder does he have some notion that he is better academically than he really is, and when a professor comes down on him for not doing well he thinks its because he is doing well! Perhaps he really does have some grandiose ideas about himself, being in such big business and all."

Collin shook his head. "No, Dr. Pitt, I don't think that is exactly the case," said Collin, "you see, when you get two strong personalities with opposite viewpoints, each thinks he is right and the other is wrong. It is possible that if a prolonged debate takes place between them, either or both of them could get the idea, I suppose, that the other is down on him. However I don't see that as grandiose or paranoia—just strong personality."

"I see your point," admitted Dr. Pitt in submission again, "but maybe he does need further help with the problem you describe."

"You may be right, Dr. Pitt, I'm not sure," said Collin attempting to disarm him, "but as you know, he is a man with substantial financial means, and can afford a private therapist if he feels the need. I will discuss your comments with him and let him decide."

With that little bit of giving on Collin's part, Dr. Pitt regained his outward confidence and composure once more, continuing the fluctuation that is so often characteristic of such inwardly insecure people.

"And what about you, Mr. Seldon," he inquired again, "you have the same problems with professors and possibly with other people, that Mr. Culver has. I am not convinced that you do not have personality problems that need attention."

Collin looked at him to continue, but the doctor waited for Collin's response.

"Personality problems such as strong personality?" asked Collin.

Dr. Pitt replied, "m-m-m-m-, and more!"

"More!" said Collin, raising his eye brows, "like delusions of grandeur, and paranoia?"

"Perhaps," responded Dr. Pitt, obviously well trained in traditional abnormal psychology and automatically looking in it for a slot in which to place Collin and Brett, as he probably does with most or all of his acquaintances.

For a moment Collin debated whether his final response to this obnoxious man would be furious rejection or gentle disarming. He decided to try the latter first. Smiling gently and speaking softly, Collin said, "I too, Dr. Pitt, through my profession, have access to personal counselling and therapy of which I have already availed myself considerably. I will let them help me decide what my problems are, but I do get along very well with most people."

Dr. Pitt's drooping face revealed that his shallow confidence had waned again. Collin decided that was a good way to leave him, hoping it might possibly make him introspective enough to take a look at himself.

"You and I may or may not meet again, Dr. Pitt," said Collin, bringing the conversation to a close. "In the meantime good luck with your new group, good-bye, and God bless you."

At that point, Collin quickly made his final exit from Room 405, went via the elevator down to the main level, then into the library where his wife Vita, and Albin Anders were engrossed in reading.

"Come to the coffee shop with me," he motioned them hurriedly and urgently, the other group members will be there already. On the walk down I will give you an outline of what has happened."

As Collin, Vita and Albin entered the coffee shop they looked across to the corner where the large sheets of plate glass met overlooking the street intersection. The other group members were there and already had two square tables pulled together. As the three approached from across the shop there was, from the other group members waving of hands and shouts of "yea, yea, yea." Collin laughed as he sat down with the others.

Leo Aidan quipped, "Quite a story teller for a minister!"

"Not bad, not bad at all," came remarks from the others.

Replied Collin, "I just told it the way most people who do not understand it, really see it. Any other explanation would be confusing to them unless they had months of schooling in it as we did in our support group."

The group members seriously agreed.

"But what do we do from this point?" asked Albin Anders, now troubled at the thought of losing his group support.

"A good question Albin," replied Collin. "Let's talk about that now."

The other group members agreed to this, and again Collin took the lead.

"First let me say that technically speaking at least, we group members are all free to continue studying at this university, either full time, or, part time evenings as most of us presently are. What I mean is, and I will ask Owen to bear me out on this, Dr. Pitt may have whatever opinions of us he pleases. However he cannot interfere with us in any way unless we go to him for his services. Would you agree with that Owen?"

"Yes, definitely," replied Owen, both from the stand point of the protocol of the medical profession, and the rules and practices of the Student Health Services of this University."

"Fine," said Collin, "and even though you may meet Dr. Pitt in the hallways of the university sometimes, which may make you feel uncomfortable, it will do you no harm. It's in your favor that, with the exception of Brett and I, he may not even remember you since he had so little conversation with you and our meeting was so short. Albin he does not know at all, and that is good since he is still in his young and tender years. Brett and I he may well remember since we were in a vivid confrontation with him. As for myself, however, I have no plans to study here next year anyway, so there will be no problem for me, even if Dr. Pitt might be one to discuss such matters with the director of Student Health Services."

Brett spoke, revealing his circumstances. "For me," he said, "it is just a short time to exam time for the course I'm taking. Then I will be through for the forseeable future. It's not as though I'm studying for a degree. I may want to take further courses sometime, and I would prefer to take them here and likely I can, but if I have to go elsewhere, that is a sacrifice I will have to make. You know how it is with people like us Collin, we do the best we can where best we can, always ready to forfeit when it is necessary for peace and for survival."

"I know," answered Collin, "and do you feel you have a chance of a fair mark from your professor, Brett?"

"Yes, I think so," replied Brett, "this course I'm taking is techinical enough that I can command perhaps a B Grade, which will be okay. No matter how well I do, I don't think he would give me an A."

"That must bother you," remarked Owen.

"Well, yes some," said Brett, "but I'm reconciled to such things by now. Also it would be nice to continue to study for another degree, but with the increasing responsibilities of my growing business and the occasional hassle with belittlers in that area of life, I don't need more hassle with belittlers here. It would be too much and I would do justice to neither!"

"Too much indeed," replied Owen, "for anyone; every person has limitations."

"Will you write your exam, Collin?" asked Owen. "I notice how mute and low profile you have had to be in class. I don't know how you have been able to take it. Its been a little better for me, because Professor Yates knows I am on the staff here in addition to being an evening student. He is fearful of what connections I may have, but I know I bother him tremendously."

Collin replied, "Since you are qualified to be a staff member of the university, Professor Yates will have no choice but to give you a fair grade in your course, Owen. As for me, I think I could command him, by the quality of my paper, to give me a pass. Maybe he would do even a little better, but not much, I know from previous experiences, so no, Owen, I will not write the exam. I am never one to quit on something I really want, but as you know my reason for taking this course was that I was looking for something in particular. It turns out that this something was not in the course but in this support group. I've only continued the course this far so as to qualify me for membership in this group. As Brett said concerning his circumstances, it would be nice to continue and accomplish, but I don't need the extra hassle.

"But now, Owen, what about you?" asked Collin, "there is a good possibility that you have come through this unscathed. If it does flare up, with your diplomacy can you smooth things over in the Student Health Services Department?"

"Yes," said Owen, "I can emphasize the fact that I was in the group as its organizer and facilitator, moreso than for my own needs. Yes, I'm sure I can take care of the matter one way or another, if the need arises, but I doubt if it will come to anything much if at all." Owen continued, "I think the remainder of us are in the clear, thanks to you and Brett bearing the brunt for us. I plan to teach and study here for another year. Gilda will be graduated by then, and we plan to move south of the border, not to one of your Terraprima fallen states, but another nearby, make our life there, search for that happy niche that hopefully is out there for us, and at some as yet unset time, be married."

"Congratualtions and good luck," everyone chimed in cheerfully, "wonderful."

"And what about you, Donna," Collin asked.

Donna blushed a little, and smiled. "I think you had better ask Leo first," she said, "since it was his idea in the first place. I must say though, I didn't have much trouble agreeing with him."

"Okay Leo, let's have it," Collin said suspectingly.

Leo laughed and said, "Our story is similar to that of Owen and Gilda in many ways, although we are not so far along in our careers as they. We plan to continue evening studies here at Quilibet University for the present, and if circumstances warrant it in the future, change to full time study. When we feel our careers are advanced enough in the field we hope opens to each of us in the future, we will be married. Where we take it from there only time will tell."

"I'm happy for you both," said Collin sincerely, "I know you will be a great asset to each other."

The other members expressed joy and best wishes for them.

"And that brings us to Albin," said Collin caringly, as he smiled hopefully at him. "You do plan to continue studying here at Quilibet don't you Albin?"

"Yes, I hope to," said Albin with a shadow of doubt showing in his response.

Collin spoke up in reaffirming tones, seeking to reassure Albin. "Owen and Gilda," he said, "You will both be here for another year, and, Leo and Donna, you will likely be here as long as it takes Albin to graduate. I would like to suggest that the five of you keep in close touch, by telephone, by having lunch or evening snack here at the coffee shop, or by whatever means you may devise. Help one another to choose your courses and the professors you will take them from. Scout around as one semester nears completion, to decide on your professors for the next semester wherever possible. There may be occasions when you will have to forfeit a course and take another in its stead. Or, you may decide to stay in a class with a wayward professor and take a lower grade in order to get the subject.

"Furthermore, I would hope you will all keep in touch with me, Albin in particular, so that I can help you to better handle difficult situations. In addition to that, I will wish to know how and where you all make out in the future; and Brett won't be here at the university either, but let's all keep in touch, and meet occasionally."

It was agreed enthusiastically throughout the group to follow the plan of helping each other in the manner Collin had proposed. Noticeable relief came over Albin as he spoke, "Thanks Collin, and all the group. I know I can do it now that I have friends to give real practical help. Furthermore, knowing I have supportive friends, makes it possible for the brighter side of life rather than the darker side to dominate my mind. This makes me happier and more effective. I can study a whole lot better. I'm real glad we'll all be keeping contact with each other."

"We will Ablin, we will," assured Collin, and the others gave similar assurance to Albin.

Suddenly, with a mild burst of emotional interest, Leo turned toward Collin, "and what about you Collin? We all have plans to go places and do things from here. Tell us your plans for the future so we can help you also."

Collin replied, "I have no specific plans for the future, except to continue with my parish ministry to the best of my ability under the circumstances with which I have to live. All the while I will be looking forward to retirement at the earliest age I can afford to do so. I hope for an early retirement because, although I have no way of knowing for sure beforehand, I do not think I will be able in my older years to stand up to the extreme stress caused by belittlers to persons like us. With some precedents in mind, I have the feeling that I would die relatively young if I were to try to continue to full retirement age. Again, I repeat, you have heard the expression, 'the good die young!' Leo, it is generally true you know. Except that I still hope to beat it one way or another."

On hearing this, Leo's emotions swung to the opposite extreme, "I won't say it but you know how I feel," he said emphatically, his face red with anger. But then he controlled himself.

Collin responded, "I understand how it makes you feel Leo, but one thing you must learn and practice well if you are to get ahead in spite of them, is to keep calm, cool, collective and rational, under most circumstances at least. There is occasionally a time when nothing other than an angry blast at them works to shock them. Even at that, they will always try to turn it around on you, and blame the trouble on you. In the doing of it they gain the support of many of the people with the same bent of envy as they, together with many of the green ones who know nothing of the belittlers ways. And I'll repeat one more point, Leo," said Collin with a grin, "the belittlers are not bloody murderers." Then, more seriously; "they are very bloodless indeed in their relentless work of ruining and destroying lives to protect their own pride. Being bloodless, they are all the more difficult to expose."

"Basically, for me at my age now, Leo, life cannot be changed, at least not greatly," continued Collin, "so we have to accept it. There will be some further growth in my life ahead as there was for me with this group these past months, and there is always opportunity for further service. As for fulfillment, it is already taken care of with a conscience that tells me I did my best against very uneven odds. That's good enough, I say."

Leo nodded his head. There was silent approval.

"Time for us all to be going home," remarked Collin in a lively tone that took away the deep thoughts of the group members. "From now on we are no longer a support group, we are friends who help each other."

"That is right," responded Owen, "and I thank you Collin, and Gilda, Donna, Leo, Brett and Albin for responding to my call to come into this group in the first place. It didn't end the way we had hoped, but maybe someday we can make something out of it. Let's keep that in mind over the years too."

All agreed that as friends with problems in common they ought to keep contact with one another and hopefully sometime in the future do something more to help people such as themselves to a better life.

Handshakes and hugs brought an end to the gathering. They departed the coffee shop, scattered to various places in the parking lot, Owen and Gilda driving away together, Leo and Donna doing the same. Brett drove off alone, heading home to his wife. Collin and Vita walked young but maturing Albin to his car, and with words of encouragement and assurance bid him good night as he drove away.

"As I look at Albin Anders, with some differences in circumstances, I see so much of you in your younger years, Collin," said Vita as they once more drove toward the expressway.

"I see it myself," said Collin. "Our childhood, youth and family experiences were quite different, some of our adult experiences similar, but the damage done each of us was much the same. That is why I am so anxious to help him. The thought of someone so like myself having to live life as I have had to live it makes me sympathetic indeed. However, we will be able to help him a great deal now."

Vita continued, "But what about the many like yourself whom you have never met, Collin, and who have no help. How can you help them now that Dr. Eldren is not available?"

"I can write a book," replied Collin as he raised his brow towards Vita.

"Yes, sure you can," said Vita, "You can very well do that now. It is all so fresh and so recently reviewed in your mind. This would be a very opportune time to put it all on paper."

"I think so," replied Collin, "and I wonder about people who have been through all this, survived it, and come out successfully as we did. Would they come forward and speak out in support of my book when it is published? Psychology has already heard the muddled stories of the broken ones and attributed their problem to their own weakness. Psychologists go by the stories of the embittered, and interpret it as their own envy projected upon the belittlers. They go by the experiences of the broken, the sick, the brainwashed, and the degenerate, all of whom are already too far down to have a clear perspective of what happened to them. I just wonder, when I publish a book on the topic, will the successful, the overcomers, come forward and speak out on the matter?"

Vita replied, "I believe you will be surprised at how much support you will have."

"I must take the risk anyway," affirmed Collin. "At my age I have little to lose, except old age itself."

"I think it is fair to warn you, that you may also bring the wrath of some upon you," added Vita.

"Yes," replied Collin, "I expect it may even become a life-long debate over whose story is truth, mine or the numerous belittlers who have assailed me and others like me. I realize that probability, but it has to be done."

"I also fully expect the wrath of some belittlers who will insist that such things that I write never happened, that they could not happen in North America, that it is a fabrication of my mind, or projection, and that I am crazy. All this regardless of the fact that over the years I have volunteered for much psychological testing which continually came up with the result that I have nothing psychologically wrong with me, and am of sound character. Then there are belittlers who will say I have only written it because it is gnawing away at me and I want to get it off my chest. That will only be projection on their part. It gnaws at them when they see people like *us* living life victoriously. That is why they treat us the obnoxious way they do. "Again, the belittlers' stories are always different than those of their victims, except on very rare occasions when one of them may admit to his misdeeds. The belittlers of the Lawtons in Terraprima have by now, you may be sure, concocted their own defensive stories concerning what I would have to say about them in a book. They have their alibis in place to soothe their consciences. There will be much denial from them. I dare to say that some of them may even think they are fooling God.

Vita added, "I expect also that some of our acquaintances, especially in the church, will fall away from us. But our true friends will remain. And I would guess we will have some new friends and many supporters after your book is published."

"Right," said Collin, "and there will be the problem of getting past belittler editors and assistant editors who will side with our adversaries. In particular there are the would be writers who know all the technicalities of writing, but can come up with nothing creative to write about. They will invent ways to say my writing is stilted and therefore I am pompous. And that being so in their minds they will claim I deserve all the abuse that has been thrown at me over the years, as though the abusers were just trying to bring me down a notch or two. But we'll just go ahead with it, and however each cookie crumbles we will deal with them individually. We'll take it as it comes and cope with it under God's Grace and Guidance."

Continuing with optimism Collin said further, "I would hope that one of the foremost attainments of such a book would be to alert psychiatrists and lawyers to the phenomenon of belittling; that it is very real, severely damaging, frequently used and often subtle. People should not have to fear being negatively branded for life when they talk about their experiences of it to a psychiatrist, or to anyone for that matter. Also, especially when belittlers become desperate enough, or when they think they are winning over a victim and can get away with it, they often become very open with their mind-games and belittling. Lawyers could easily make a good case out of it if they understood the whole phenomenon, how it generally works and how it often breaks the law in many ways including by fraudulent practices.

Then he continued on a less happy yet determined note, "As I have said before to write a book on this subject and include the church in it, which I will have to do, is to break an old unwritten church rule that all criticism of the church should be done within, in order to protect the church's public image.

"The way I see it however, the church in Secundaterra, including Lower Secundaterra, has nothing to lose. In fact it has much to gain. The mind-game is not played in a big conspiracy sort of way in these places yet, although there are occasional instances of birds of a feather acting together. Here the belittling is done mostly by envious individuals to whom the remainder of the church needs to become more wise."

"In addition, the church of the Secundaterras has, from the top hierarchy down through the ranks, openly acknowledged the problem of harmful conflict in many of its local churches and are dealing with it constructively on their own, with their own devised means.

"Power and control people, as categorized in Durwin's Doctor of Ministry paper, play havoc with many local churches everywhere making these churches, in my opinion, unfit for human employment. These power and control people are often belittlers with at times a somewhat different agenda. But as I have said before the more extensive details of that make for another topic.

"The church in Terraprima, however, their pride being more important to them than their church, is reluctant to admit to serious problems in its pastorates, or to the presence of control freaks as they are sometimes referred to, - power and control belittlers in its ranks, although they are there aplenty from top to bottom. Durwin's efforts, through his paper, were therefore sabotaged. I am of the opinion that some key people could see themselves in what he had written. After my book is published, Durwin's efforts could then be put to good use instead of having it all shot down by envious Terraprimans within the church, only to likely rear its head through other writers twenty to fifty years later.

"Furthermore concerning the church in Terraprima, Durwin and Canda did everything possible to let the church belittlers, hierarchy and all, know that the Lawtons would not be led astray, put down, or driven away. The belittlers relented not a bit in their adverse behavior over the period of nearly a decade."

Collin continued, "As I have mentioned many times, Durwin, and I myself take no pleasure in talking about the church in this manner. Again, as I said, Durwin gave the belittlers of the church in Terraprima every opportunity to change their ways towards him. For example, like the time the C.E.O., because of Durwin's near presence, became unstrung and emotional before hundreds of people. Durwin turned away giving him a chance to regroup his faculties and pull himself together. Much later, the C.E.O., miscalculating an incident at the time, tried to unstring Durwin before a similar gathering. His attempt failed. However, that's the way they are. Give them a chance and they will take it at the time. But sooner or later they will turn on us for it. Kindness and goodwill towards them is taken by them as weakness, offering them another chance to get at us. We have no choice but to speak of them as they are. We can feel justified in going public with the story and having it published."

"I agree," responded Vita.

Collin continued his summation of possible scenarios: "Belittlers are so used to winning over their victims, one thing for sure many of them will try to imply is that I am writing out of despair, instead of victorious living amid all the obnoxiousness, and thereby try to brand me a whimp.

"Another problem that will surely arise will come from many academically well qualified psychiatrists and psychologists who will be miffed at such a book coming from someone they will see as a much less qualified person. From them we can expect plenty of criticism of my writing, and from the belittlers among them there will be criticism of me personally. They will most likely overlook the fact that back near the beginning of the twentieth century, reform of the whole mental health system was started, not by psychiatrists and psychologists, but by a victim of the system as it then was—by a patient."

Then as he had often done before, Collin solicited Vita's help. "You will help me with the project, I suppose, through your computer expertise and other gifts?" Collin asked of Vita.

"Yes, you know I will," came the firm reply.

Upon reaching the expressway, they drove happily away into the night together. This was nothing new to them. Travelling to various places by car, both short and very long distances, was one of their main hobbies. Now, however, a new avenue of service was opening up to them which would take up all their spare time for quite a while. They would travel again later.

THE END

About the Author

Cleon E. Spencer, in his early adult life, had a wide variety of experiences in commerce, industry and government, in which he was employed for several years, During that time, he and his wife lived in a variety of cities and towns, and traveled in various parts of North America. He later went into the ordained ministry of a mainline denomination. Over the years he got to know people of rural, suburban and urban settings.

Having lived in a fair number of places in eastern North America, and having traveled in most other areas of the two countries that make it up, he has had a wide variety of experiences with people. Because of the kind of person the author is, many of his adverse experiences in particular were unique to a person of his makeup, as also it was for his wife, and many of their acquaintances.

During his career he has come to know many other people who are exceptional in some ways and have had similar experiences as his own. It is on these unique experiences in the marketplace of society and in the church that the writings of this book are based.

The hope of the author is that the book will promote a type of personal character that will rise above the harmful maladies of culture written of herein.

The author and his wife Ada recently celebrated their fifty-fourth year of happy marriage.